VISUAL QUICKSTART GUIDE

Photoshop 2.5

FOR THE MACINTOSH

Elaine Weinmann
Peter Lourekas

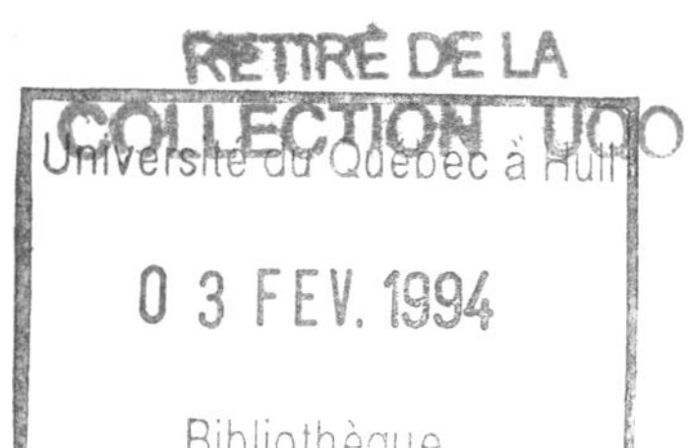

Visual QuickStart Guide

Photoshop 2.5 for the Macintosh

Elaine Weinmann and Peter Lourekas

Peachpit Press, Inc.
2414 Sixth Street
Berkeley, CA 94710
(510) 548-4393
(510) 548-5991 (fax)

Notice of Liability

The information in this book is distributed on an "As is" basis, without warranty. While every precaution has been taken in the preparation of this book, neither the authors nor Peachpit Press, Inc. shall have any liability to any person or entity with respect to any liability, loss, or damage caused or alleged to be caused directly or indirectly by the instructions contained in this book or by the computer software and hardware products described therein.

Trademarks

Throughout this book, trademarked names are used. Rather than put a trademark symbol in every occurrence of a trademarked name, we are using the names only in an editorial fashion and to the benefit of the trademark owner, with no intention of infringement of the trademark. Where those designations appear in this book, the designations have been printed with initial caps.

ISBN: 1-56609-053-9

0 9 8 7 6 5 4 3 2 1

Printed and bound in the United States.

TECHNIQUE CHANGES BUT ART REMAINS THE SAME.

— *Claude Monet*

Thank You.

Ted Nace, Peachpit Press publisher, for responding to innovations in computer technology with innovations in computer education.

Paula Baker, Roslyn Bullas, John Grimes, Keasley Jones, April Netzer, Cary Norsworthy, and the rest of the staff at Peachpit Press, for always being helpful and "on the ball."

John Stuart, New York City-based photographer and friend, for his photographs.

Nadine Markova, Mexico City-based photographer, for her photographs.

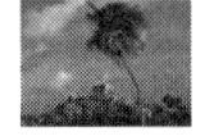

Johanna Gillman, New York City-based artist, friend, and desktop publisher, for introducing us to Nadine Markova through her photographs.

Paul Petroff, Great Neck, New York-based motion picture special effects designer, photographer, and traveler, for his photographs.

Cara Wood, New York City-based artist and friend, for her photographs, her assistance with the index, and her special tomato sauce.

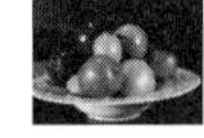

Leah Krivan, Raisa Grubshteyn, and ***Jin Kim,*** Parsons School of Design students, for their computer-generated artwork (Gallery).

Phil Allen, New York City-based artist and friend, for exploring another side of Photoshop (Gallery).

Stan Pinkwas, managing editor of Video Magazine and copy editor of this book, for his careful attention to detail.

Bob Schaffel, Executive Director of the Professional Prepress Alliance, for his comments on Chapters 3 and 19.

Howard Greenberg, Vice President of Axiom Design Systems, a New York City prepress service bureau, for his comments on Chapter 19.

DX (Digital Exchange), New York City prepress service bureau, for producing color separations for the Gallery.

Michael Callery, Faculty Coordinator of the New School Computer Instruction Center, for reading our manuscript and offering his comments.

Tad Crawford, attorney, author, and Allworth Press publisher, for contributing *Ten Key Copyright Questions and Answers.*

Adobe Systems, Inc. for designing terrific software, and, in particular, Jon Cohan, Matt Brown and the technical support staff who assisted us through the Beta testing and beyond.

And ***Teddy and Christ Lourekas,*** for introducing their son to art at an early age, and putting up with his art at a later age.

All other artwork was created by the authors or anonymous Greek photographers.

Table of Contents

THE BASICS 1

AN ASTOUNDING ARRAY of visual effects can be created using Photoshop, the digital image editing program from Adobe Systems. Photoshop has revolutionized the photography and prepress industries and has provided commercial and fine artists with an exciting new medium.

Using this book, you will learn Photoshop's fundamental techniques. You will learn how to scan pictures, adjust brightness and contrast, and create type. How to sharpen, blur, and smudge edges. How to mix, choose, and apply colors. How to paint, draw, collage, clone, apply filters, create blends and textures, adjust color, and print. You will also learn how to modify just a portion of a picture by creating a selection. You can open pictures in many different file formats or create a picture entirely within Photoshop.

In the *Visual QuickStart Guide* tradition, step-by-step instructions are abundantly illustrated with photographs and screen captures. Also included are numerous tips and recommendations. The first five chapters provide a comprehensive orientation for newcomers. The remaining chapters can be sampled in any order. Special terms are defined in a mini-glossary in this chapter and in Appendix A.

You can use Photoshop's wide array of commands to modify many different types of pictures. They can be applied at various intensities and can be combined in different sequences with other commands. The instructions in *Photoshop 2.5: Visual QuickStart Guide* will help you learn Photoshop's basic features, but you can also use them as a point of departure for developing your own formulas. Once you learn the basics, you'll be able to explore Photoshop's limitless picture editing possibilities!

PHOTOSHOP FEATURES USED TO PRODUCE "STONE": ADD NOISE, EMBOSS AND SPHERIZE FILTERS, LEVELS AND COMPOSITE CONTROLS DIALOG BOXES, AND SHARPEN/BLUR, DODGE/BURN AND PAINTBRUSH TOOLS. THE TYPE WAS IMPORTED FROM ADOBE ILLUSTRATOR USING THE PLACE COMMAND.

The Photoshop screen.

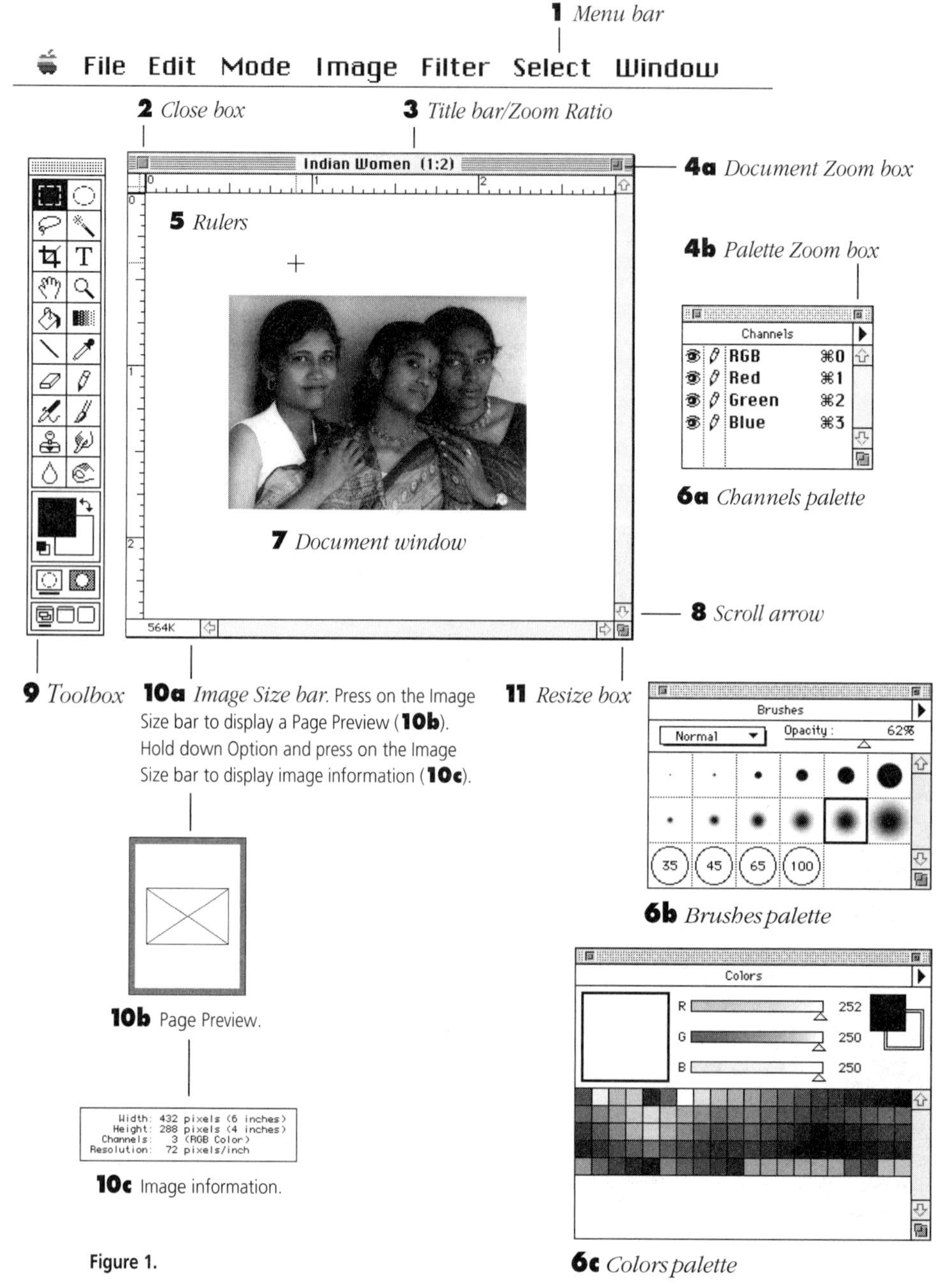

10b Page Preview.

10c Image information.

Figure 1.

Key to the Photoshop screen.

1 ***Menu bar***
Press any menu heading to access dialog boxes, pop-up menus, and commands.

2 ***Close box***
To close a picture or a palette, click its Close box.

3 ***Title bar/Zoom ratio***
Displays the picture's title, color mode, and display size ratio.

4a,b ***Zoom boxes***
Click a document window zoom box to enlarge the window or shrink it to its previous size. Click a palette zoom box to shrink the palette or restore it to its previous size.

5 ***Rulers***
Choose Show Rulers from the Window menu to display rulers. The position of the cursor is indicated by a mark on each ruler.
(See "To choose ruler units" on page 223)

6a,b,c ***Palettes***
Three of five moveable palettes that open from the Window menu. The other palettes are Info and Paths. Double-click a palette name to shrink the palette to a title bar.

(Appendix B lists keyboard shortcuts for opening palettes. See also the Restore Windows option in "General Preferences" on page 222)

7 ***Document window***
The picture display window.

8 ***Scroll arrow***
Click the down arrow to move the picture upward in the document window. Click the up arrow to move the picture downward.

9 ***Toolbox***
Click once on a tool to select it. Double-clicking most tools will open an Options dialog box for that tool. The Foreground and Background colors and screen preview modes can also be chosen from the Toolbox. Press Tab to hide the Toolbox and all open palettes. Press Tab again to show the Toolbox and all previously displayed palettes.

10a,b,c ***Image Size bar***
Displays the picture size in bytes. K equals 1,000 bytes, M equals 1 million bytes. Press and hold on the Image Size bar to display the Page Preview, which is a thumbnail of the picture relative to the paper size, including custom printing marks, if chosen. Hold down Option and press and hold on the Image Size bar to display information about the picture, including its dimensions, number of channels, mode, and resolution.

11 ***Resize box***
To resize a window or a palette, press and drag its resize box diagonally.

The Toolbox

The Toolbox contains 20 tools used for picture editing. Click once on a tool to select it. An Options dialog box opens for most tools when they are double-clicked. The painting and editing tools are customized using the Brushes and Colors palettes. Press and drag the top bar to move the Toolbox. Press Tab to hide or show the Toolbox. The Foreground and Background colors, Quick Mask mode, and screen modes are also accessed from the Toolbox.

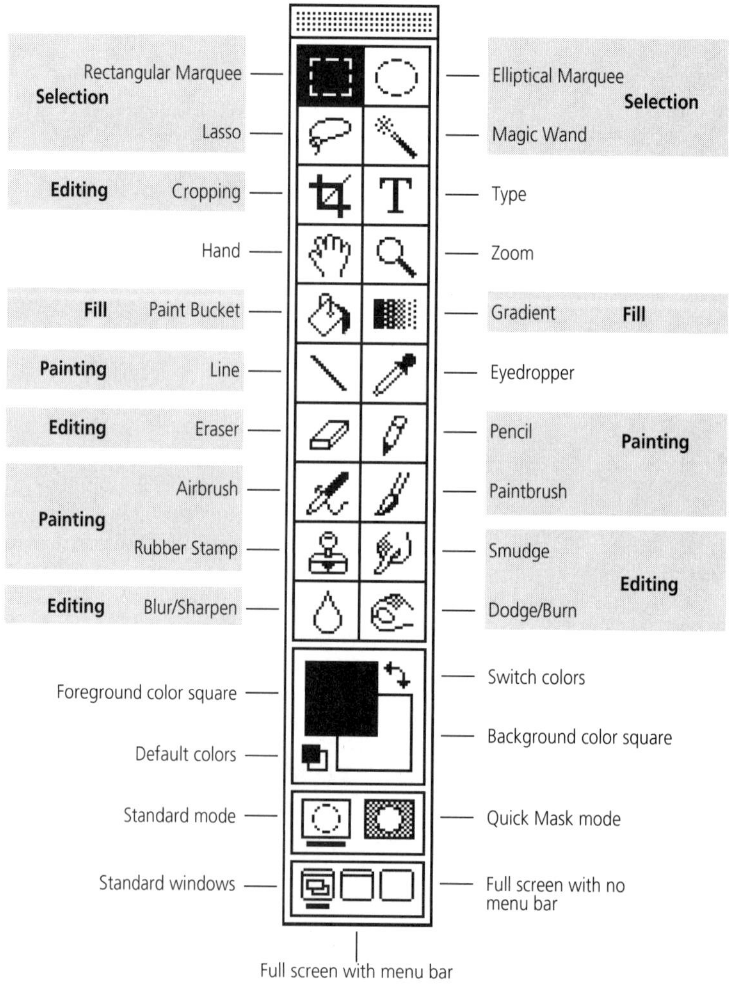

Figure 2. The **Toolbox**.

The Pen tool is accessed only via the Paths palette (see page 18).

Pointer icons.

The pointer matches the icon on the Toolbox when most tools are used. In addition, you will also see the pointer icons below. Press Caps Lock to turn all pointers into a crosshair for precise editing.

Arrow *Crosshair* *Scissors* *Gavel* *Cancel* *Eraser*

How to use the mouse

The mouse is used in three basic ways.

Click Press and release the mouse button quickly.

Use to: Choose a tool, brush tip, color, channel, or other palette option; choose a dialog box option; close a window or a palette; select an area with the Magic Wand tool; create a path handle; or accept, cancel, or deselect a selection or modification.

Double-click Press and release the mouse button twice in quick succession.

Use to: Launch Photoshop, open or place a file, open a tool options dialog box, or highlight an entry field.

Press and drag Press and hold down the mouse button, move the mouse on the mousepad, then release the mouse button. Press and drag when you read the instruction "drag" or "move."

Use to: Choose from a menu or a pop-up menu; create, resize, add to or subtract from a selection; draw a line; stroke with a painting or an editing tool; or move a selection, slider, dialog box, palette, or window.

Instruction Terms

Check/Uncheck

☒ ☐

Click a check box to turn an option on or off. An x in a box indicates the option is turned on.

(See "Dialog Boxes" on pages 13-14)

Choose

Highlight a menu or a pop-up menu entry, or pick a color or other palette or dialog box option.

(See "Menus" on page 8)

Enter

0	1.00	255

A highlighted field.

15	1.00	255

A new value entered.

Highlight an entry field (referred to as "field") in a dialog box and replace with a new number. Press Tab to highlight the next field in succession. Press Shift-Tab to highlight the previous field.

Move

Press and drag a triangle slider.

Press

Quickly press and release a key on the keyboard, usually as part of a keyboard shortcut.

(See "Keyboard Shortcuts" on page 19)

Select

Isolate an area of a picture using a selection tool so the area can be modified while the rest of the picture is protected.

(See Chapter 5: "Selections")

Mini-Glossary

Size The file storage size of a picture, measured in bytes, kilobytes, or megabytes.

Dimensions The width and height of a picture.

Selection An area of a picture that is isolated using the Rectangular Marquee, Elliptical Marquee, Lasso, or Magic Wand tool so it can be modified while the rest of the picture is protected. A moving marquee marks the boundary of a selection.

Floating Selection A selection that floats above, and can be altered without affecting, the underlying pixels. A floating selection is created when the Type tool is used, a selection is copied, or the Float or Paste command is executed.

Background Color The color applied when the Eraser tool is used or a selected area of underlying pixels is moved or deleted.

Foreground Color The color applied when a painting tool is used, type is created, or a Fill command is executed.

Picture The entire contents of a document window, including any border surrounding the image.

Image The picture itself, not including its border.

Pixels (Picture Elements) The dots used for displaying a bitmapped picture on a rectangular grid on a computer screen.

Underlying Pixels The pixels comprising the unmodified picture, on top of which a selection, path, pasted image or placed image can float. When a floating selection is deselected, it replaces the underlying pixels.

Brightness The lightness (luminance) of a color.

Hue The wavelength of light that gives a color its name, such as red or blue, irrespective of its brightness and saturation.

Saturation The purity of a color. The more gray a color contains, the lower its saturation.

See "Appendix A: Glossary" for other definitions.

Menus.

Each menu heading provides access to related commands for modifying pictures. The seven Photoshop menus are illustrated on the following pages.

To choose from a menu, press and drag downward through the menu or to the right and downward through the pop-up menu, then release the mouse when a desired entry is highlighted.

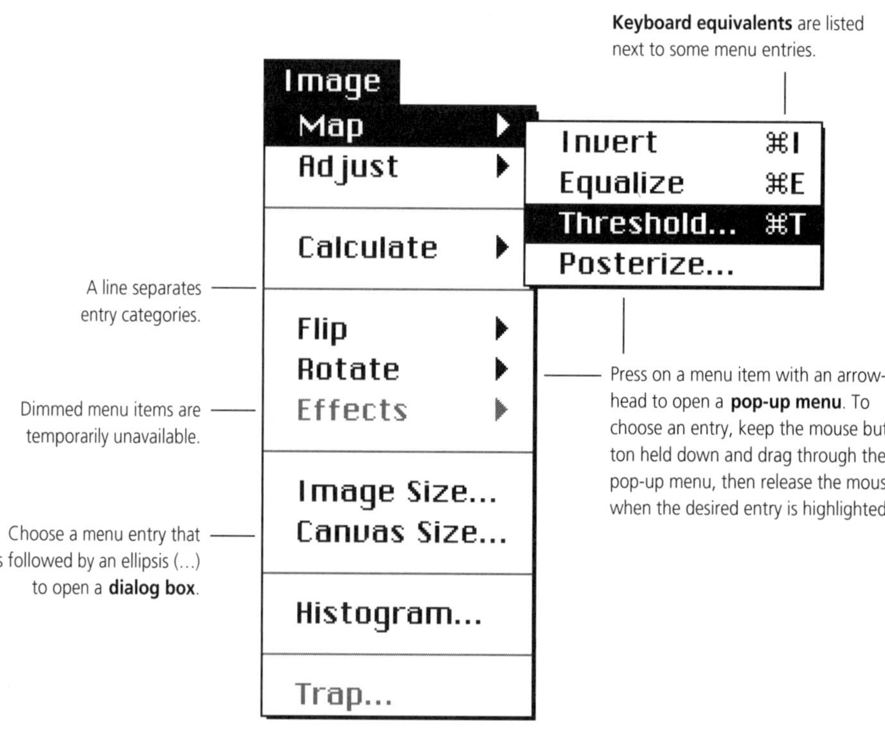

Figure 3. A Photoshop **menu**.

Note: *The term "pop-up menu" is used to describe what is also known as a "submenu."*

The File menu.

File menu commands are used to create, open, place, close, save, scan, export or print a picture, as well as set defaults and quit Photoshop.

The Edit menu.

Edit menu commands include Undo, which undoes the last modification made, the Clipboard commands Cut and Copy, and the Paste options. The Fill and Stroke commands, and Composite Controls, which affect how an image is pasted, are also executed via the Edit menu.

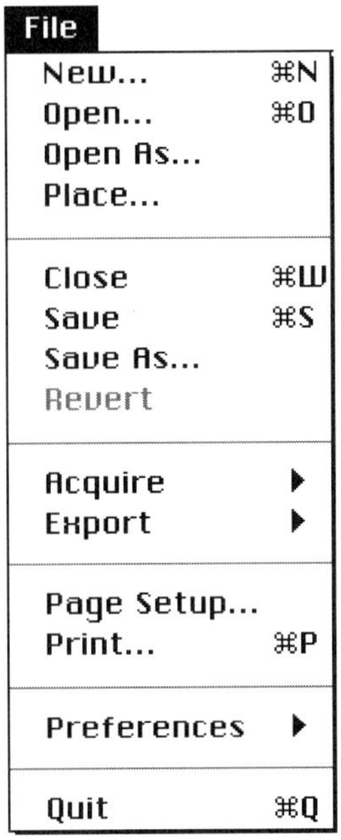

File
New... ⌘N
Open... ⌘O
Open As...
Place...
Close ⌘W
Save ⌘S
Save As...
Revert
Acquire ▶
Export ▶
Page Setup...
Print... ⌘P
Preferences ▶
Quit ⌘Q

Figure 4. The **File** menu.

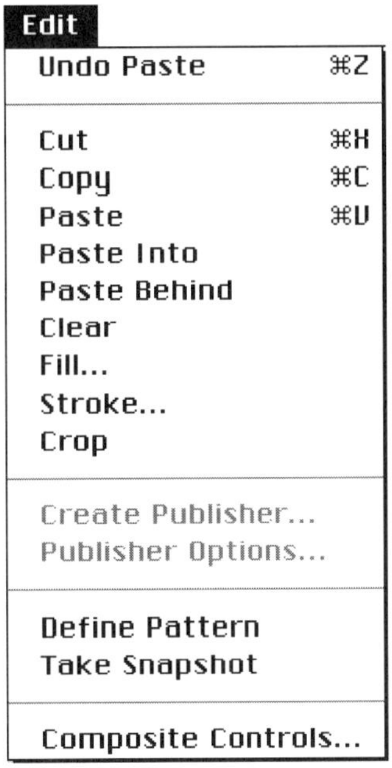

Edit
Undo Paste ⌘Z
Cut ⌘X
Copy ⌘C
Paste ⌘V
Paste Into
Paste Behind
Clear
Fill...
Stroke...
Crop
Create Publisher...
Publisher Options...
Define Pattern
Take Snapshot
Composite Controls...

Figure 5. The **Edit** menu.

The Mode menu.

A picture can be converted to any of eight black and white or color modes using the Mode menu.

The Image menu.

Commands under the Image menu are used to modify a picture's brightness, contrast, orientation, size, dimensions, and resolution. The Canvas Size dialog box is used to add a border to a picture.

Mode
- Bitmap
- Grayscale
- Duotone
- Indexed Color...
- ✓RGB Color
- CMYK Color
- Lab Color
- Multichannel
- Color Table...

Figure 6. The **Mode** menu.

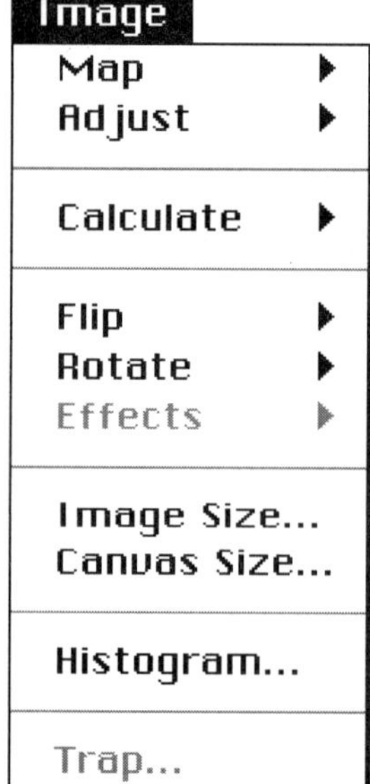

Figure 7. The **Image** menu.

The Filter menu.

Filters are organized in pop-up menu groups. Some filters are applied in one step by choosing the filter name. Other filters are applied via a dialog box.

Filter
Last Filter ⌘F
Blur ▶
Distort ▶
Gallery Effects Vol 1 ▶
Noise ▶
Sharpen ▶
Stylize ▶
Video ▶
Other ▶

Figure 8. The **Filter** menu.

The Select menu.

The "All" Select menu command selects an entire picture. The None command deselects all selections. Other Select menu commands enlarge, load, and save selections, and modify selection edges.

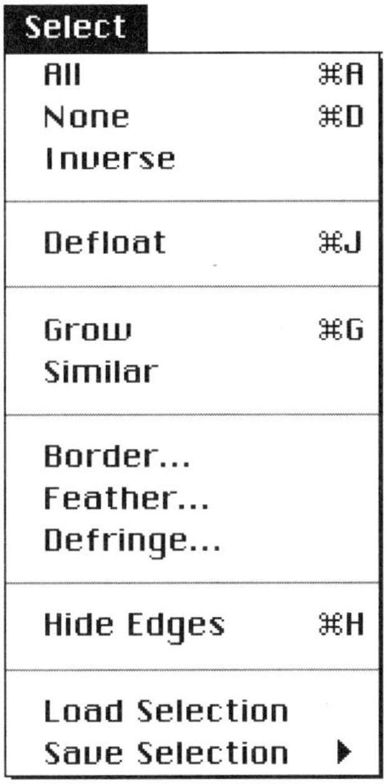

Select
All ⌘A
None ⌘D
Inverse
Defloat ⌘J
Grow ⌘G
Similar
Border...
Feather...
Defringe...
Hide Edges ⌘H
Load Selection
Save Selection ▶

Figure 9. The **Select** menu.

The Window menu.

Window menu commands control new window creation, display sizes, and the display of rulers and palettes. Open pictures are listed and can be activated using the Window menu.

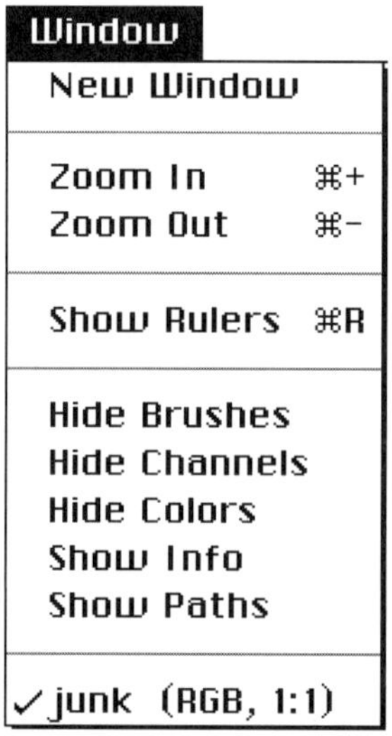

Window
New Window
Zoom In ⌘+
Zoom Out ⌘-
Show Rulers ⌘R
Hide Brushes
Hide Channels
Hide Colors
Show Info
Show Paths
✓junk (RGB, 1:1)

Figure 10. The **Window** menu.

Dialog boxes.

Dialog boxes are like fill-in forms with multiple choices. The various ways to indicate choices are shown in **Figures 11-13**.

To open a dialog box, use a keyboard shortcut, or select any menu item followed by an ellipsis (...).

Some modifications are made by entering numbers in entry fields. Press Tab to highlight the next field in a dialog box. Hold down Shift and press Tab to highlight the previous field.

Other modifications are made by moving sliders to the left or the right. Slider modifications preview in the picture while the dialog box is open.

Click OK or press Return to accept modifications and exit a dialog box.

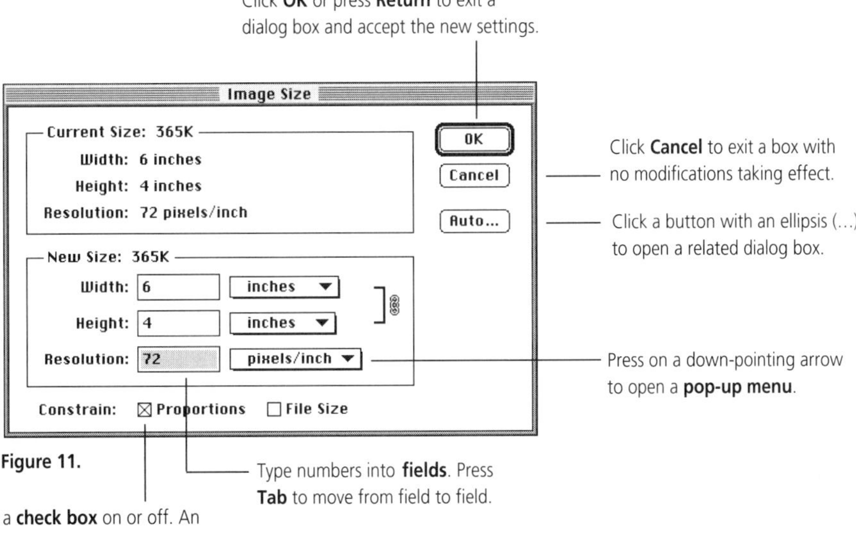

Figure 11.

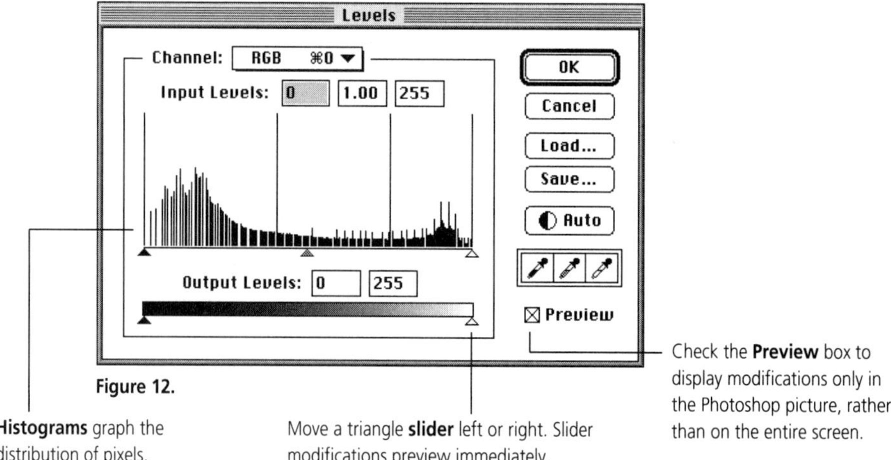

Figure 12.

Histograms graph the distribution of pixels.

Move a triangle **slider** left or right. Slider modifications preview immediately.

Check the **Preview** box to display modifications only in the Photoshop picture, rather than on the entire screen.

To move a dialog box, press and drag its **title bar**.

Brush Options

Diameter: 47 pixels

Hardness: 62 %

Spacing: 25 %

Angle: 0 °

Roundness: 100 %

OK

Cancel

Hold down **Option** and click **Reset** to undo changes made in a dialog box. The word **Reset** will appear in place of **Cancel**.

Preview box.

Figure 13.

The Colors palette.

The Colors palette is used for mixing and selecting colors to be applied with the painting, editing, and fill tools. Color models, chosen from the pop-up menu on the right side of the palette, affect which colors are available. Colors can also be appended, loaded and saved using the Colors palette.

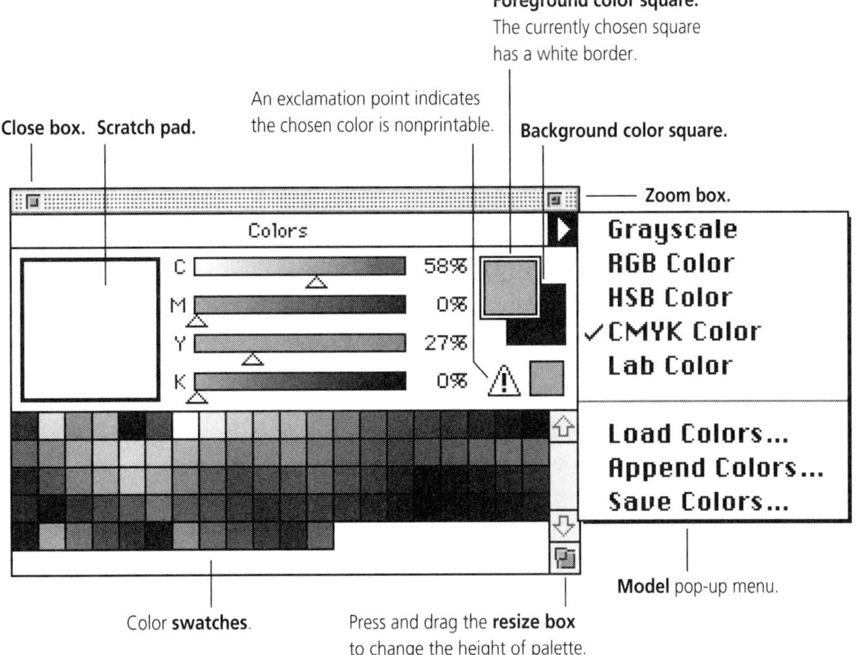

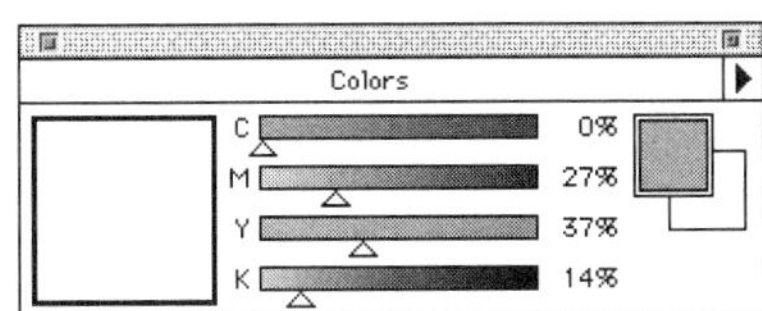

The Colors palette resized by clicking once on its Zoom box.

The Colors palette resized by double-clicking the palette name.

Figure 14. The **Colors** palette.

Colors Palette

The Brushes palette.

The Brushes palette is used for defining painting and editing tool attributes — tip size, edge, opacity, pressure, and mode. Each tool retains its own settings. You can choose commands to further customize, add, delete, save and load brushes using the pop-up menu on the right side of the palette.

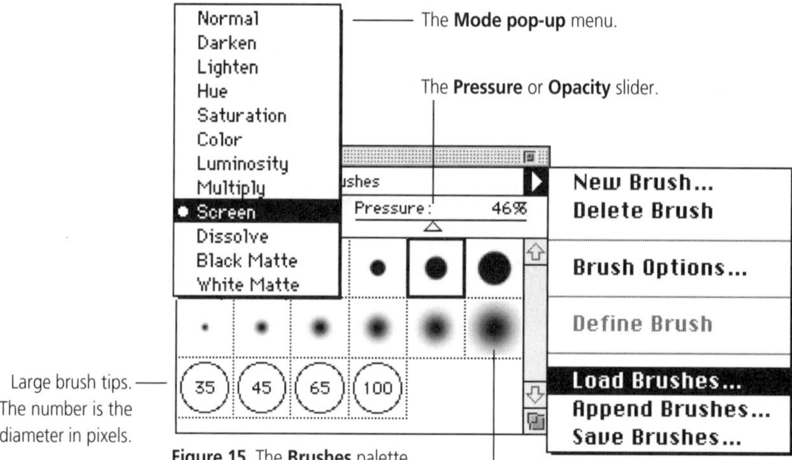

Figure 15. The **Brushes** palette.

The Channels palette.

The Channels palette is used to display one or more of the channels that make up a picture and any specially created alpha channels, which are used for saving selections.

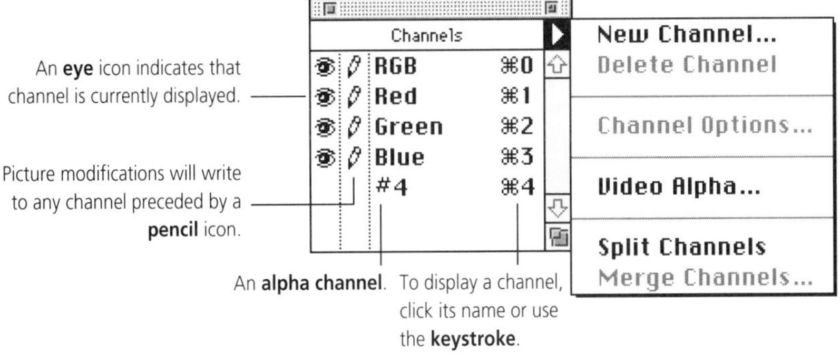

Figure 16. The **Channels** palette.

The Info palette.

The Info palette displays a color breakdown of the pixel under the pointer.

The Info palette also shows the position of the pointer on the picture, as in Figure 17, and may show dimensions and angle of rotation, depending on which tool is selected. To make these options available, choose Options from the pop-up menu on the right side of the palette, and check the Show Mouse Coordinates box. The unit of measure can also be chosen from the same dialog box.

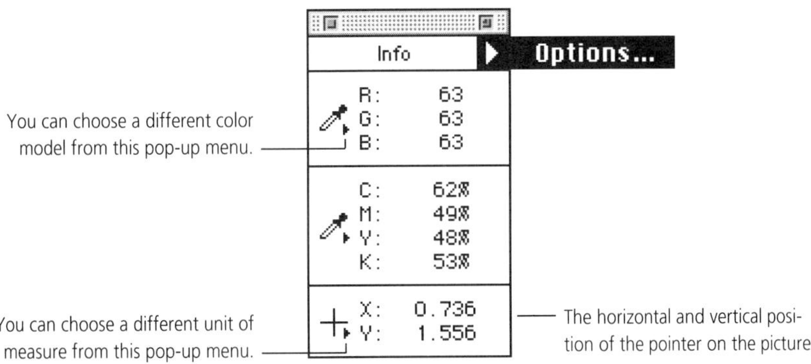

Figure 17. The **Info** palette.

The Paths palette.

The Pen tool creates curved and straight line segments connected by anchor points. Together they form a path. The Pen tool and its variations for modifying a path are selected from the Paths palette. A path can be saved and used as a selection, and can be stroked or filled.

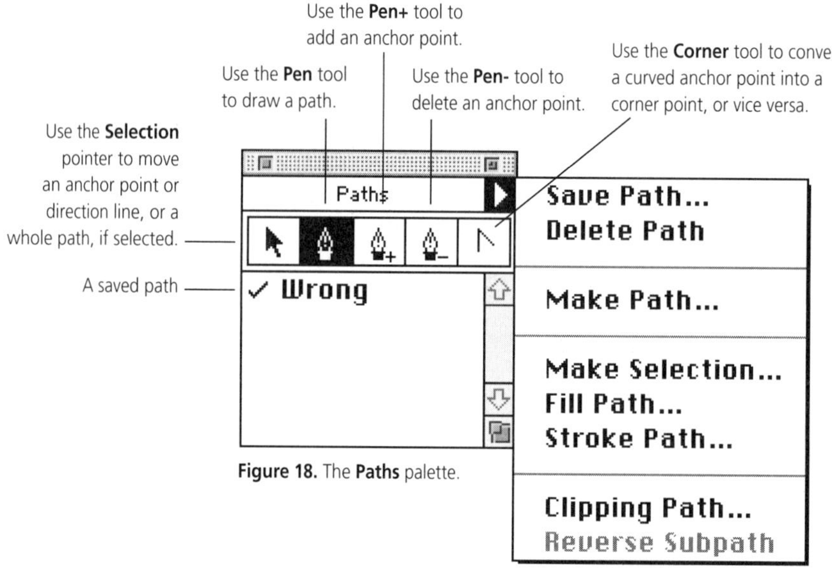

Figure 18. The **Paths** palette.

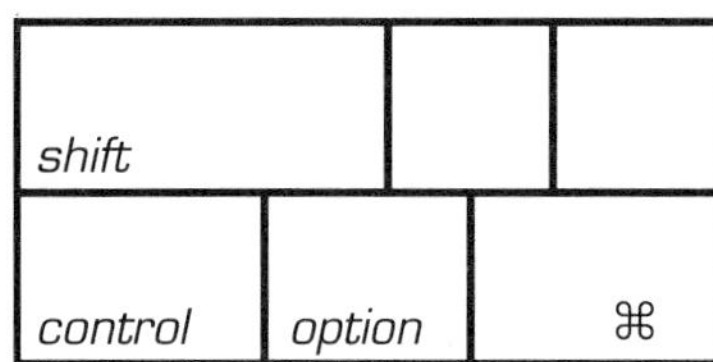

Figure 19. The **Shift, ⌘ (Command),** and **Option** keys are situated on the left and right side of the keyboard, and are used in keyboard shortcuts.

Keyboard shortcuts:

Some commands have keyboard equivalents. To perform a keyboard shortcut, hold down one or more keys, such as ⌘ and Shift, press and release a second key, then release the first key or combination of keys **(Figures 19-20)**.

(See Appendix B for a list of shortcuts)

To perform the Save command:

1. Hold down ⌘.
2. Press and release the "S" key.
3. Release ⌘.

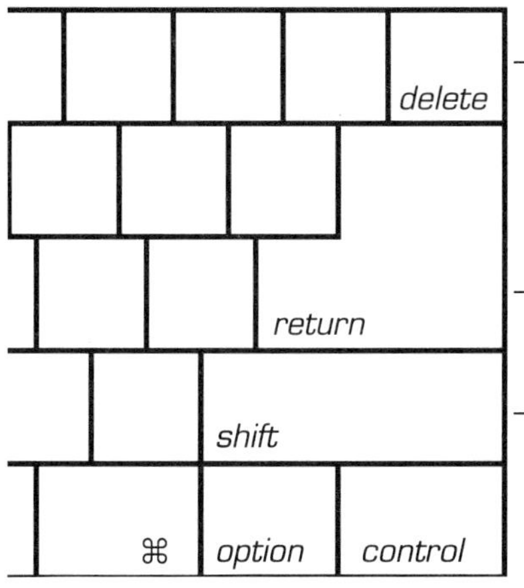

Press **Delete** to delete characters to the left of the cursor in a dialog box, or to fill a selection with the Background color.

Press **Return** to create a new line of text in the Type Tool dialog box, or to exit a dialog box.

Hold down **Shift** to constrain a line drawn with a painting tool to a horizontal or a vertical axis, to create a round or square selection, or to add to a selection.

Figure 20. The right side of the keyboard.

Keyboard Shortcuts

Other keys.

Press **Tab** to highlight the next field in a dialog box and to hide or show the Toolbox and palettes.

Press a **Function** key (F1-F12) to execute a command assigned to that key. To change the command assigned to a Function key, use the Function Keys dialog box, opened from the Preferences pop-up menu under the File menu.

Hardware.

Photoshop will run on a Mac SE or II with at least 2 megabytes of RAM (random access memory), System 6.04 or later, and a hard disk. It will run faster on a Mac IIci, IIvx, Quadra, or Centris with at least 8 megabytes of RAM and a large hard disk (200 megabytes or more). For optimal speed, we recommend a Quadra or Centris with 24 megabytes or more of RAM and a large, fast-access hard drive (200-300 megabytes/9-11 ms).

Photoshop requires a lot of RAM because it works with three copies of a picture: a copy to work on directly, a copy for the Undo command, and a copy for the Revert and From Saved commands.

To improve Photoshop's performance speed, the first step is to increase your RAM. An add-in accelerator board will also speed up processing operations by increasing the computer's clock rate. Accelerator boards come with 25, 33, 40, or 50 Megahertz clock rates. For a Mac II you can purchase a "Quadra-style" 040 processor card to improve processing speed.

Color monitors display 8-bit, 16-bit, or 24-bit color, depending on the video card. With an 8-bit card, 256 colors are available for on-screen color mixing. With a 24-bit card, 16.7 million colors are available. A 24-bit card provides optimal display, because every color can be represented exactly. Video performs best on a 16-bit display, which is an option with a 24-bit card. All Photoshop pictures are saved as 24-bit, regardless of the resolution of the monitor.

You may also want to purchase a removable storage device — such as a SyQuest or magnetic optical drive — to save files and transport files to and from a service bureau.

If you have the means to invest in a fast Macintosh with a large hard drive and adequate RAM, you will be able to work efficiently. A good monitor will help you to do accurate color work.

Disk storage.

Disk Type	Capacity
Double density (DD) floppy	800KB
High density (HD) floppy	1.4MB
Syquest removable	44MB *or* 88MB
Hard drive	80MB, 120MB, 1GB…

File size units.

Byte = 8 bits of digital information *(approx. one black or white pixel, or one character*

Kilobyte (KB) = 1,024 bytes

Megabyte (MB) = 1,024 kilobytes

Gigabyte (GB) = 1,024 megabytes

HOW PHOTOSHOP WORKS 2

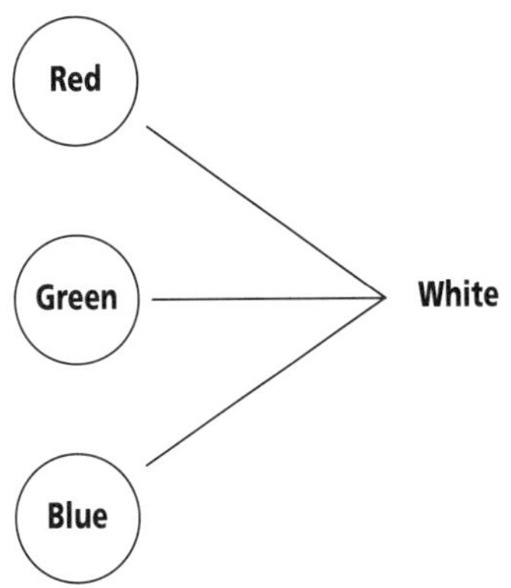

Figure 1. The additive primaries on a computer monitor.

THE FOLLOWING summarizes basic Photoshop concepts. You may want to refer back to this chapter occasionally, particularly the section on picture modes. Special terms are defined in the Mini-Glossary on page 7 and in the full Glossary in Appendix A.

Color

Red, Green, and Blue light are used to display a color picture on a monitor. When Red, Green and Blue (RGB) light (the additive primaries) in their purest form are combined, they produce white light **(Figure 1)**.

The three subtractive primary inks used in process printing are Cyan (C), Magenta (M), and Yellow (Y). When combined, they produce a dark, muddy color. To produce a rich black, printers usually mix Black (K) ink with Cyan, Magenta, and/or Yellow.

The display of color on a computer screen is highly variable and subject to ambient lighting and temperature conditions. Only a carefully calibrated monitor can display color accurately, but even very carefully calibrated screens can only simulate CMYK ink colors.

Many colors seen in nature cannot be printed, some colors that can be displayed on a screen cannot be printed, and some colors that can be printed can't be displayed on a screen. A warning indicator will appear on the Colors Palette and in the Color Picker if you choose a non-printable color.
(See Figure 4 on page 130)

Channels

Every Photoshop picture is a composite of one or more semi-transparent color "overlays" called channels. For example, a picture in RGB Color mode is composed of Red, Green and Blue channels. To illustrate, choose Show Channels from the Window menu, then click Red, Green, or Blue on the Channels palette to display only that channel **(Figure 2)**. Click RGB to restore the full channel display. *(Check the Color Channels in Color box in the General Preferences dialog box. See page 222)*

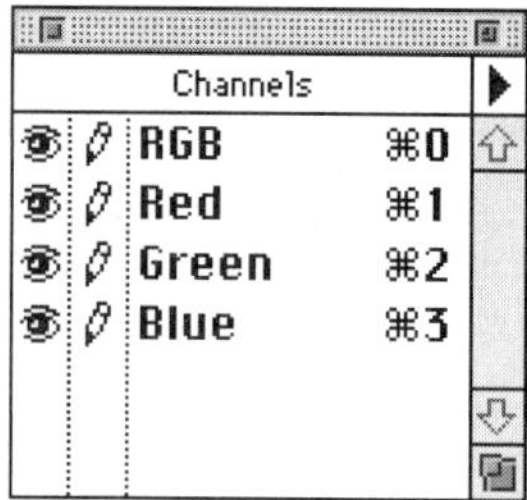

Figure 2. The **Channels** palette.

Modifications can be made to an individual channel, but normally modifications are made and displayed in the multichannel, composite image, and affect all a picture's channels at once.

The more channels a picture contains, the larger its file storage size. The storage size of a picture in RGB Color mode, composed of three channels (Red, Green, and Blue), will be three times larger than the same picture in Grayscale mode, which is composed of one channel. The same picture in CMYK Color mode will be composed of four channels (Cyan, Magenta, Yellow, and Black), and will be four times larger.

Pixels

The screen image in Photoshop is a bitmap, which is a geometric arrangement (mapping) of a layer of dots of different shades or colors on a rectangular grid. Each dot, called a pixel, represents a color or shade. By magnifying an area of a picture, you can edit pixels individually **(Figure 3)**. Every Photoshop picture is bitmapped, whether it originates from a scan, another application, or entirely within the application using painting and editing tools. (Don't confuse Bitmap mode, discussed in the next section, with the term "bitmapped.")

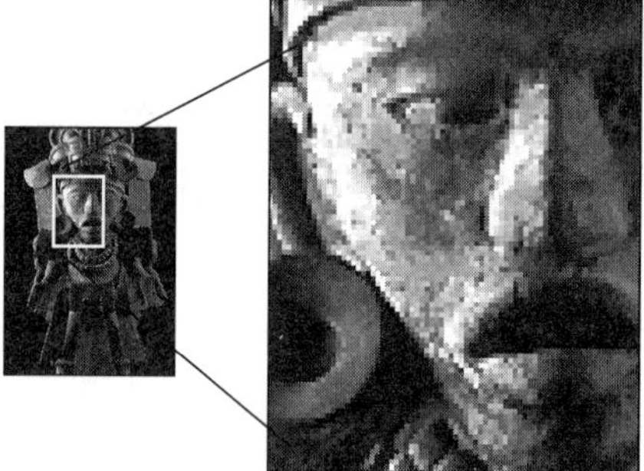

Figure 3. Close-up of a picture, showing individual pixels.

If you drag with a painting tool across an area of a picture, the new pixels replace the single layer of underlying pixels, regardless of the number of channels the picture is composed of. When modified, the exact attributes of the underlying pixels can be restored only by choosing Undo or Revert or by using the Rubber Stamp tool with its From Saved option.

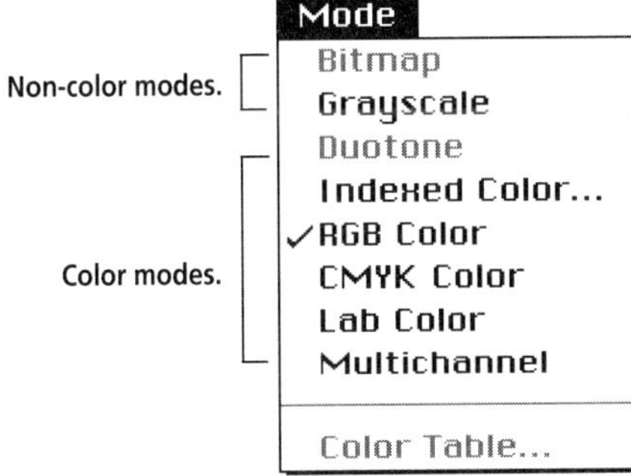

Figure 4. The **Mode** menu.

Picture modes

A picture can be converted to, displayed in, and edited in eight picture modes: Bitmap, Grayscale, Duotone, Indexed Color, RGB Color, CMYK Color, Lab Color and Multichannel. Modes are selected from the Mode menu **(Figure 4)**.

For example, a picture in RGB Color mode can be converted to CMYK Color mode, and vice versa. A novel effect can be created by converting an RGB Color picture to Grayscale mode, converting it back to RGB Color mode, then restoring parts of the color image.

If a picture is converted to a different picture mode, its colors may change. Some mode conversions cause noticeable changes; others cause subtle changes. Very dramatic changes may occur when a picture is converted from RGB Color mode to CMYK Color mode, because printable colors are substituted for rich, glowing RGB colors. Color accuracy may diminish if a picture is converted back and forth between RGB and CMYK modes too many times. You can use the Save As command to create a CMYK version of a picture and preserve the original RGB version.

Some output devices require you to save a picture in a particular picture mode. For example, a picture must be in CMYK Color mode to color separate it on an imagesetter. Commands and tool options in Photoshop also vary depending on the currently selected picture mode.

Here are brief descriptions of some commonly used picture modes.

In **Bitmap** mode, pixels are 100% black or 100% white only, and no editing tools, filters, or Adjust commands are available. The Invert command is available. A picture must be in Grayscale mode before it can be converted to Bitmap mode.

In **Grayscale** mode, pixels are black, white, or up to 255 shades of gray. A Grayscale picture can be colorized by first converting it to a color mode. If a picture is converted from a color mode to Grayscale mode and then saved, its hue information is deleted and cannot be restored. Its luminosity (light and dark) values remain intact.

A picture in **Indexed Color** mode has one channel and a color table containing a maximum of 256 colors or shades. To open a Photoshop picture in some painting or animation programs, it must first be converted to Indexed Color mode. You can also convert a picture to Indexed Color mode to create "arty" color effects.

RGB Color mode is the most versatile because it is the only mode in which all the tool options can be used. Some video and multimedia applications can import a Photoshop picture in RGB Color mode.

Photoshop is one of the few Macintosh programs in which pictures can be displayed and edited in **CMYK Color** mode. Convert a picture to CMYK Color mode to output it on a color printer or to color separate it (unless the output device is a PostScript Level 2 printer).

Lab Color is a three-channel mode. The channels represent lightness, the colors green-to-magenta, and the colors blue-to-yellow. Save a picture in Lab Color mode to print it on a PostScript Level 2 printer or to export it to another operating system.

(Duotone mode is discussed on page 220)

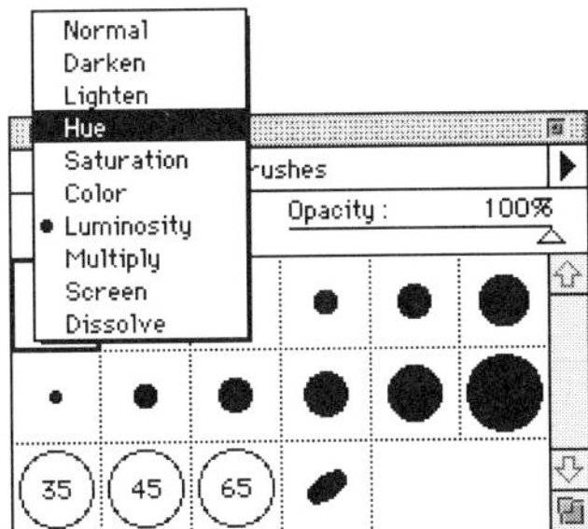

Figure 5. You can customize editing and painting tools by choosing a mode and other options from the **Brushes** palette.

Tools

For each editing and painting tool, you can choose from ten modes on the Brushes palette **(Figure 5)**. A tool's mode affects how its strokes modify pixels. For example, if you stroke with a painting tool with Normal mode chosen, pixels of any color under the stroke will be replaced with the stroke color. With Luminosity mode chosen, only luminosity values are modified. Try using a tool with different modes to see how its effects vary. With practice, you will learn which modes produce which effects.

(See page 147)

Other tool attributes — like opacity, hardness, and pressure — can also be specified using the Brushes palette. For example, you can make an Airbrush tool tip soft and transparent, or a Paintbrush stroke round and opaque. An illusion of semi-transparency can be created using a tool or Fill command with a light opacity. Most tools have an options dialog box, opened by double-clicking the tool, that you can use to further customize the tool.

Rectangular Marquee tool.

Lasso tool.

Elliptical Marquee tool.

Magic Wand tool.

Figure 6. Selection tools on the **Toolbox**.

Selections

When an area of a picture is selected, modifications — like filters, brush strokes, and fill commands — are limited to that area. The rest of the picture is protected. The selection tools (Rectangular Marquee, Elliptical Marquee, Lasso, and Magic Wand) are used to create differently shaped selections, from rectangular to irregular **(Figure 6)**. Some menu commands are only available when an area is selected.

When the Paste or Float command is chosen, or type is created, or a copy of a selection is moved, the selection floats above the underlying pixels. Once deselected, the floating selection replaces the underlying pixels.

A selection can be duplicated, moved within a picture, superimposed over another image to create a double exposure effect, or moved to another picture to create an electronic collage.

Masks

A selection can be saved to a special grayscale channel called an alpha channel. An alpha channel selection can be loaded onto a picture at any time and used like a stencil **(Figure 7)**. Alpha channels are accessed via the Channels palette.

Figure 7. An alpha channel selection.

Photoshop's new Quick Mask mode can be used to turn a selection into a translucent mask. Usually, the Quick Mask covers the protected areas of the picture with transparent color, leaving the unprotected area as a cutout. Painting tools can be used to modify the contours of the mask. When Quick Mask mode is turned off, the cutout area turns into a selection.

Modifications

Pictures are modified using tools, menu commands, palettes, and dialog boxes. Some modifications require only one step, but many involve multiple steps. In this book, the same command or feature may be used in different sequences to produce different results.

You can choose the Undo command from the Edit menu to undo the last modification. Or choose the Revert command from the File menu to restore the last saved version of a picture. And by using the Rubber Stamp tool with its From Saved option, you can drag across an area of a picture to restore part of the last saved version.

Modifications made using dialog boxes opened from the Adjust and Map pop-up menus under the Image menu preview immediately in the picture. Using this instant feedback, you can learn what settings to use to produce a particular effect.

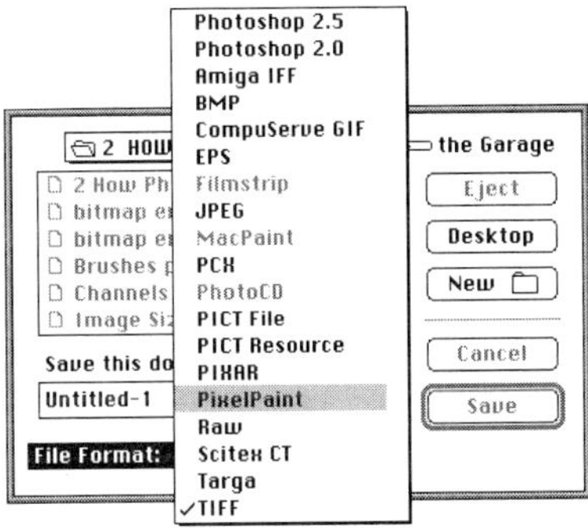

Figure 8. A picture can be converted to another **File Format** using the **Save As** command.

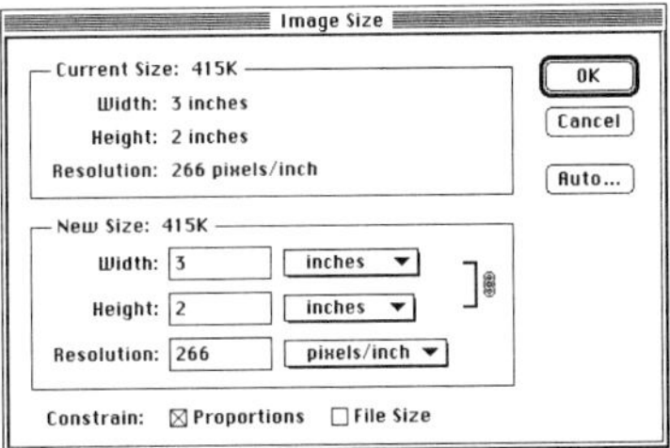

Figure 9. Using the **Image Size** dialog box, a picture's dimensions, resolution, and file storage size can be modified.

To speed up production, you can stop the screen from redrawing by performing another action, such as choosing a different tool or command.

File formats

A picture can be created, opened, edited, and saved in 19 different file formats **(Figure 8)**. Of these, you may use only a few, such as TIFF, PICT, EPS, and the native Photoshop file format. Because Photoshop accepts so many formats, images can be gathered from a wide variety of sources, such as scans, drawing applications, video captures, and other operating systems — and output from Photoshop on many types of printers. Using the Save As dialog box, you can generate a new version of a file and save it in a different format.

(See page 51)

Resolution

In most applications, a picture's resolution cannot exceed the monitor's 72-dots-per-inch resolution. In Photoshop, however, a picture's resolution is independent of the monitor's resolution, and can be customized for a particular output device, with or without modifying its file storage size **(Figure 9)**. It is best, though, to scan your picture at the resolution required for your final output device.

(See page 31)

STARTUP

IN THIS CHAPTER you will learn how to launch Photoshop, scan a picture, create a new document, open an existing document, change a picture's dimensions, resolution, and file storage size, crop, flip, rotate, or add a border to a picture, save a picture in a variety of file formats, close a picture, and quit Photoshop.

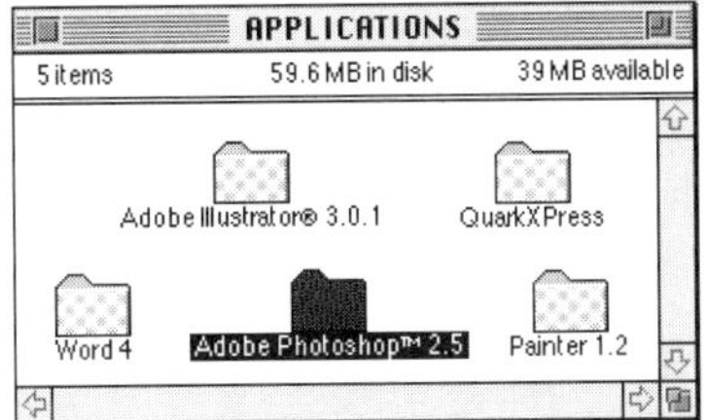

Figure 1. Double-click the **Adobe Photoshop folder**.

To launch Photoshop:

Double-click the Adobe Photoshop folder on the desktop **(Figure 1)**, then double-click the square Photoshop application icon **(Figure 2)**.

or

Double-click a Photoshop file icon **(Figure 3)**.

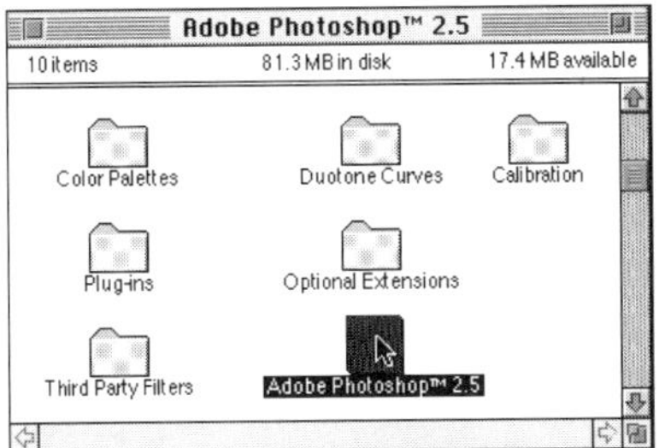

Figure 2. Double-click the **Adobe Photoshop application icon**.

✔ Tip

- If you are using System 7 or later, you can create an alias of the application icon so Photoshop can be launched from the Apple menu. Click the Photoshop application icon, choose Make Alias from the File menu, then move the alias to the Apple Menu Items folder in the System Folder.

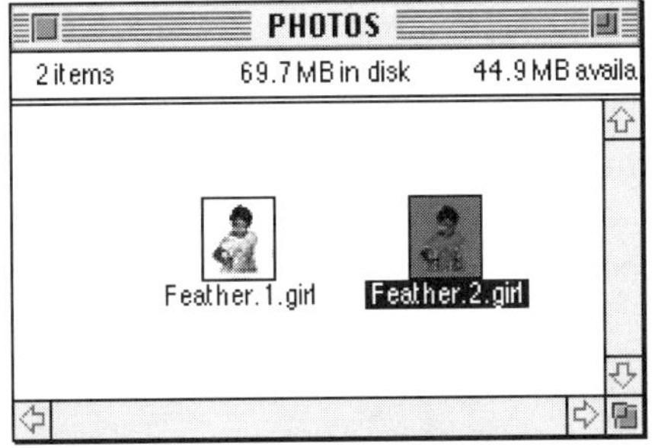

Figure 3. Or double-click a **Photoshop file icon**.

Where pictures come from.

Scans, video captures, and computer-generated artwork in most file formats can be opened and edited in Photoshop. Pictures can also be created entirely within the application.

Kodak Photo CD files can also be opened in Photoshop if you install the proper plug-in module and system extension. If your Macintosh doesn't have a built-in CD-ROM drive, you can purchase one separately. Be sure it's compatible with the Photo CD format. Each Photo CD disk can hold a hundred or more digitized photographs. You can purchase stock photographs on a CD, a service bureau can scan transparencies onto a CD, or film can be developed onto a CD.

Scanning

Using a scanning device and scanning software, a slide, flat artwork, or a photograph can be translated into numbers (digitized) so it can be read, displayed, edited, and printed by a computer. You can scan directly into Photoshop or use other scanning software and save the scan in a file format that Photoshop imports.

Scanners

The quality of a scan will partially depend on the type of scanner you use. If your print shop is going to use the original photograph for printing and the scan will only be used to indicate the picture's position or you are planning to dramatically transform the picture in Photoshop, you can use an inexpensive flat-bed scanner. If color accuracy is critical, scan a transparency on a slide scanner. Scan a picture that is going to be printed electronically on a high-resolution CCD scanner, such as a Scitex Smart-Scanner, or on a drum scanner. A high-quality scan can be obtained from a ser-

Scanning Tip

To produce a high-quality scan, start with a high-quality original. Some scanners compress gray values and increase contrast, so use a photograph with good tonal balance. Set the scanning parameters carefully, weighing such factors as your final output device and storage capacity. The most sophisticated retouching or correction techniques cannot make a lousy scan look good.

Service providers (commonly known as *service bureaus*), perform essential prepress operations, such as high-resolution scanning, imagesetting and color proof printing. They provide the link between your digital files and the printing press. Some print shops perform these services in-house.

vice bureau. Unfortunately, high-resolution scans usually have very large file sizes.

Scanner software

Scanning software usually offers most of the following options, although terms may vary. The quality and file storage size of a scan are partially defined by the mode, resolution, and scale you specify, and whether you crop the picture.

Preview: Place the art in the scanner, then click Preview or PreScan.

Scan mode: Select Black-and-White Line Art (no grays), Grayscale or Color. A picture scanned in Color will be approximately three times larger in file size than the same picture scanned Grayscale.

Resolution: Scan resolution is measured in pixels per inch (ppi). The higher the resolution, the better the scan, and the larger its file size. Choose the minimum resolution necessary to obtain the best possible printout from your final output device. Don't choose a higher resolution than required, because the picture will be larger in storage size than necessary. It will take longer to render on screen and print, and there will be no improvement in output quality.
(See Chapter 19: "Printing")

Before selecting a resolution, determine the resolution of the printer or imagesetter and the halftone screen frequency your offset printer intends to use. (The scan resolution is not the same as the resolution of the output device.)

As a rule, choose a resolution that is 1½ times the halftone screen frequency (lines per inch) of your final output device for a grayscale picture, and twice the halftone screen frequency for a color picture.
Use a high scanning resolution (600 ppi or higher) for line art.

For example, if your offset printer intends to use a 133-line screen frequency for black-and-white printing, choose a scanning resolution of 200.
(See "Tip" on page 41)

Cropping: If you intend to use only part of a picture, reposition the handles of the box in the preview area to reduce the scan area. Cropping will reduce the storage size of a scan.

Scale: To enlarge a picture's dimensions, choose a scale percentage larger than 100%. Enlarging a picture in Photoshop or any other software program may cause it to blur, because the program uses mathematical "guesswork" to fill in additional information. A picture's original information is recorded only at the time of scanning.
(See page 42)

Scan: Click Scan and choose a location in which to save the file.

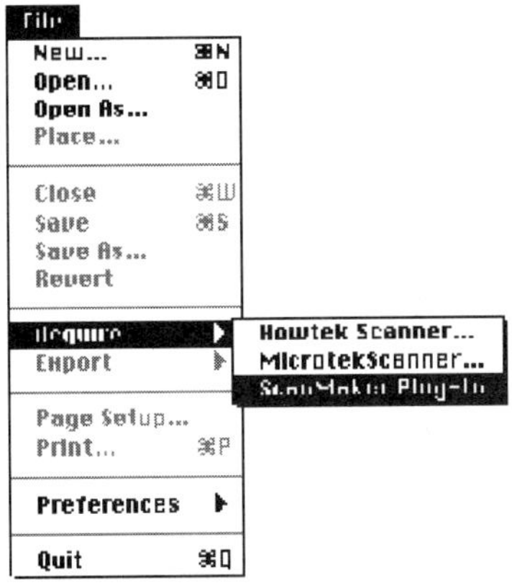

Figure 4. Choose the scanning module from the **Acquire** pop-up menu under the **File** menu.

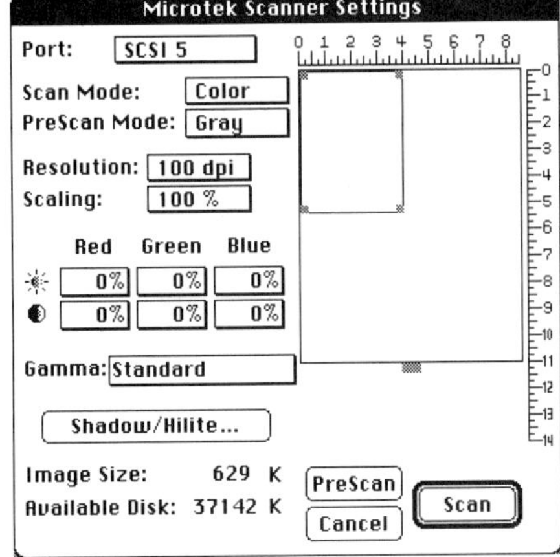

Figure 5. In the scanner dialog box, click **PreScan,** choose a **Mode, Resolution,** and **Scaling** percentage, crop the picture, if desired, then click **Scan**.

Note: To scan into Photoshop, the corresponding plug-in module for the scanner must be in the Photoshop Plug-ins folder. *(Consult the Photoshop documentation for more information about scanning modules)*

To scan into Photoshop:

1. Choose a scanning module from the Acquire pop-up menu under the File menu **(Figure 4)**.
2. Click PreScan.
3. Following the guidelines outlined above, choose a Mode **(Figure 5)**.
   and
   Choose a Resolution.

Steps 4 and 5 are optional.

4. Choose a different Scale percentage.
5. Crop the picture.
6. Click Scan. The scanned picture will appear in a new, untitled Photoshop window.
7. Save the picture.
   (See pages 48-49)

File storage sizes of scanned images.

Size (In inches)	PPI (Resoution)	Black/White 1-Bit	Grayscale 8-Bit	CMYK Color 24-Bit
2 x 3	150	17 K	132 K	528 K
	300	67 K	528 K	2.06 MB
4 x 5	150	56 K	440 K	1.72 MB
	300	221 K	1.72 MB	6.87 MB
8 x 10	150	220 K	1.72 MB	6.87 MB
	300	879 K	6.87 MB	27.50 MB

Potential gray levels at various output resolutions and screen frequencies.

Output Resolution (DPI)	Screen Frequency (LPI) 60	85	100	133	150
300	26	13			
600	101	51	37	21	
1270	256*	224	162	92	72
2540		256*	256*	256*	256*

Note: Ask your print shop what screen frequency (lpi) you will need to specify when imagesetting your file. Also ask your print shop or prepress provider what resolution (dpi) to use for imagesetting. Some imagesetters can achieve resolutions above 2540 dpi.

*At the present time, PostScript Level 1 and Level 2 printers produce a maximum of 256 gray levels.

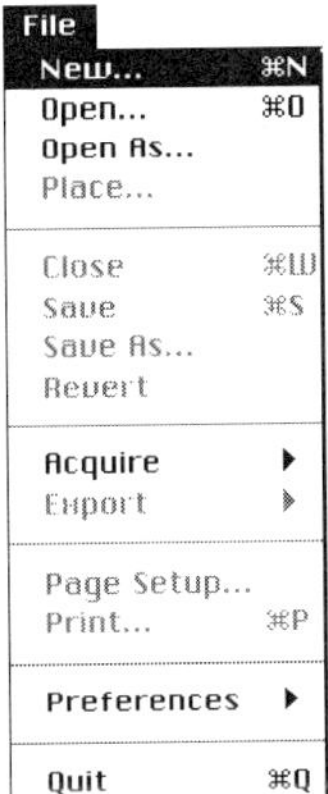

Figure 6. Choose **New** from the **File** menu.

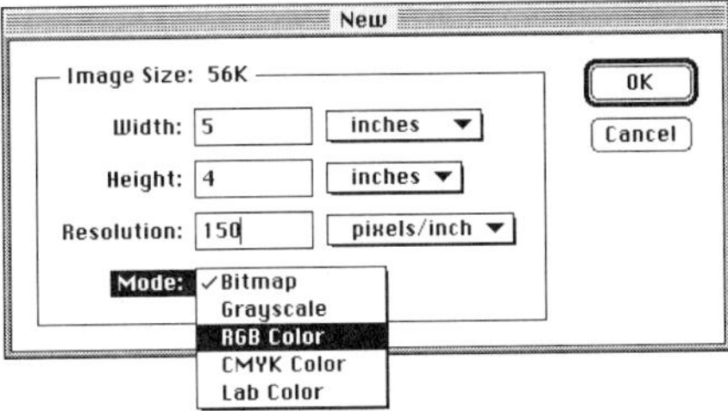

Figure 7. In the **New** dialog box, enter **Width, Height,** and **Resolution** values, and choose a **Mode**.

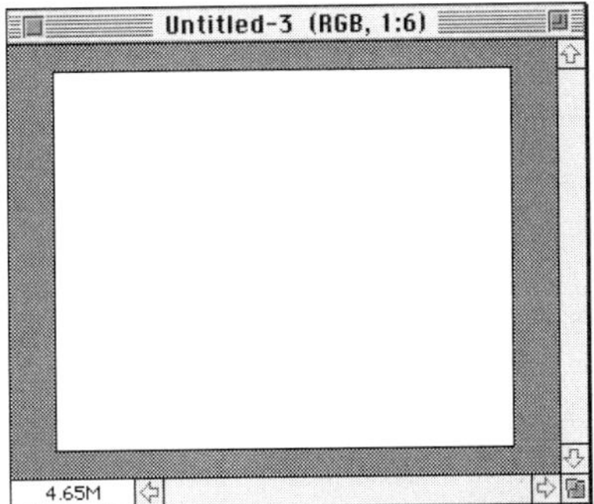

Figure 8. A new document window will appear.

To create a new document:

1. Choose New from the File menu **(Figure 6)**.
2. Choose a unit of measure from the pop-up menus next to the Width and Height fields **(Figure 7)**.
3. Enter numbers in the Width and Height fields.
4. Enter the resolution required for your final output device in the Resolution field.
   (See "Resolution" on page 31)
5. Choose a mode from the Mode pop-up menu. The picture can be converted to a different mode later.
   (See "Picture Modes" on page 23)
6. Click OK or press Return. A document window will appear **(Figure 8)**.

Note: Pictures in most file formats can be opened in Photoshop using the Open dialog box. If a prompt appears indicating the file cannot be opened, follow the instructions on the next page. To open an Adobe Illustrator file, follow the instructions on page 38 or 39.

To open a picture from within Photoshop:

1. Choose Open from the File menu **(Figure 9)**.
2. Locate and highlight a file name, then click Open.
   or
   Double-click a file name **(Figure 10)**.

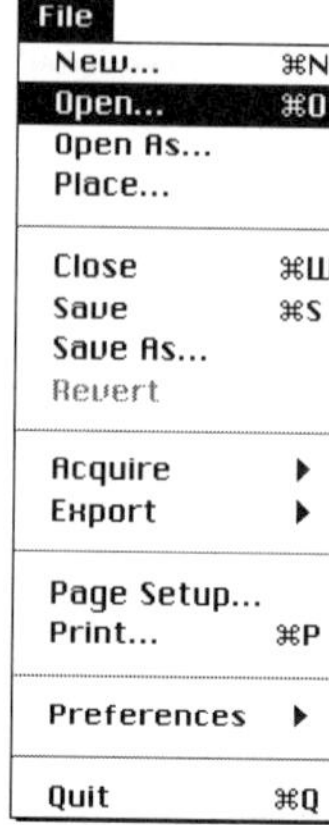

Figure 9. Choose **Open** from the **File** menu.

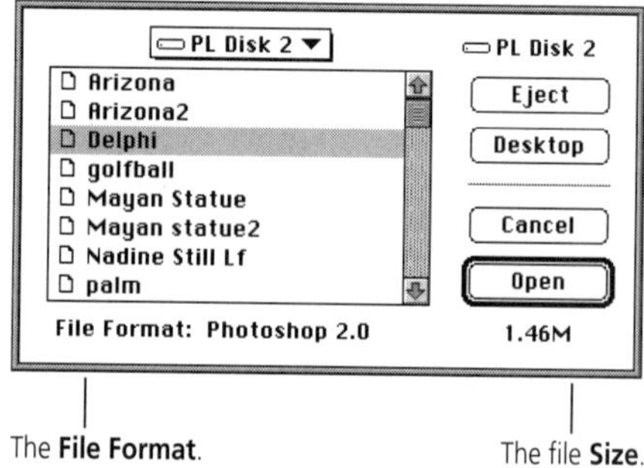

Figure 10. Double-click a file name in the **Open** dialog box.

To open a Photoshop picture from the Finder:

Double-click a Photoshop picture file icon in the Finder **(Figure 11)**. Photoshop will be launched if is not already open.

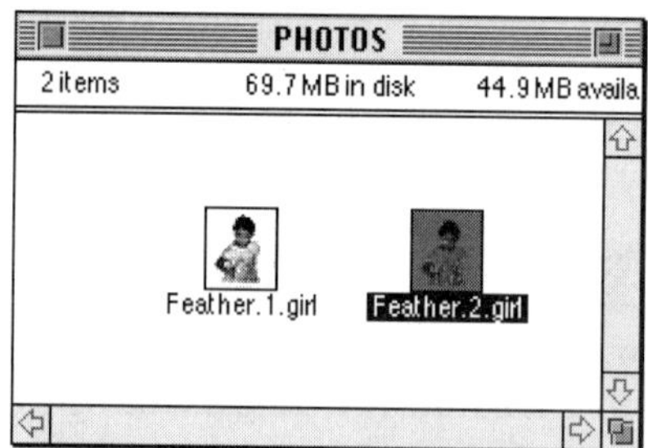

Figure 11. Or double-click a **Photoshop file icon**.

Open a Picture

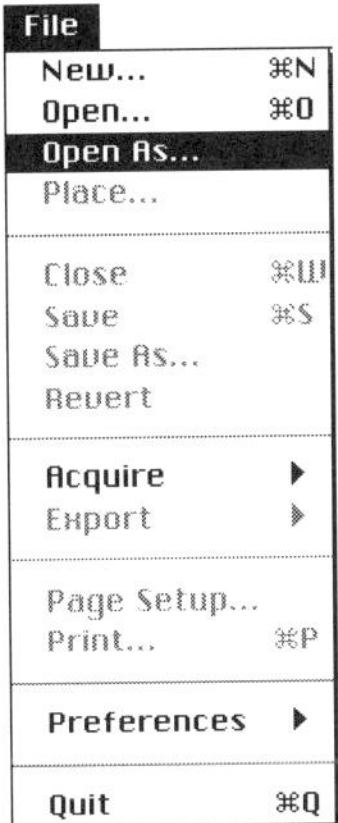

Figure 12. Choose **Open As** from the **File** menu.

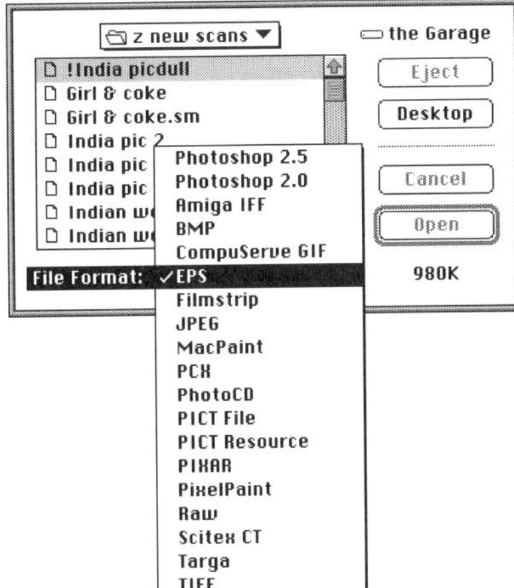

Figure 13. In the **Open As** dialog box, highlight the file to be opened, and choose a format from the **File Format** pop-up menu.

Use the Open As dialog box to convert and open a file that has been created on another platform or to help Photoshop identify its format if the program doesn't recognize it using the Open command. Once opened, a picture can be saved in any format Photoshop supports.

To open a picture using the Open As dialog box:

1. Choose Open As from the File menu **(Figure 12)**.
2. Locate and highlight the picture to be opened **(Figure 13)**.
3. Choose a format from the File Format pop-up menu. Do not leave the File Format as Raw.
4. Click Open.

✓ Tip

- If you open an EPS file, the EPS Rasterizer dialog box will open. Follow steps 3-8 on the next page.

Open a Picture

When an EPS file is opened or placed in Photoshop, it is converted from its native object-oriented format into Photoshop's pixel-based format. Follow these instructions to open an EPS file, such as an Adobe Illustrator graphic, as a new document. Follow the instructions on the next page to place an EPS file in an existing Photoshop file.

Note: An Adobe Illustrator file containing a pattern, stroked text, text used as a mask, or placed artwork cannot be opened in Photoshop.

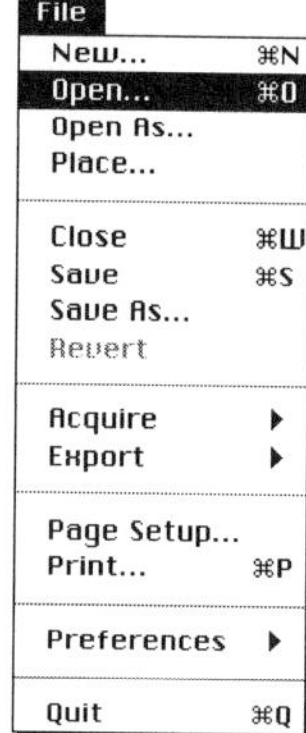

Figure 14. Choose **Open** from the **File** menu.

To open an EPS file as a new document:

1. Choose Open from the File menu **(Figure 14)**.
2. Locate and highlight an EPS picture to be opened, then click Open.
   or
   Double-click a file name.

Steps 3 and 4 are optional.

3. In the EPS Rasterizer dialog box, check the Constrain Proportions box to preserve the file's height and width ratio **(Figure 15)**.
4. Choose a unit of measure from the pop-up menus next to the Height and Width fields, and enter new dimensions.
5. Enter the resolution required for your final output device in the Resolution field.
   (See "Resolution" on page 31)
6. Choose a picture mode from the Mode pop-up menu.
   (See "Picture Modes" on page 23)
7. Check the Anti-aliased box for optimal rendering of the picture.
8. Click OK or press Return.

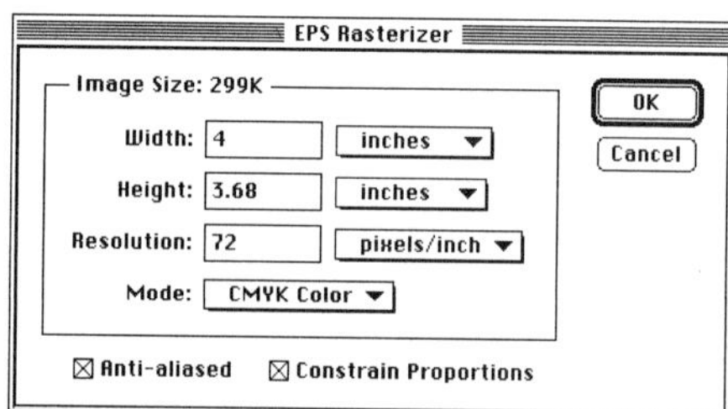

Figure 15. In the **EPS Rasterizer** dialog box, enter the required **Resolution,** choose a **Mode,** and check the **Anti-aliased** box.

Figure 16. Choose **Place** from the **File** menu.

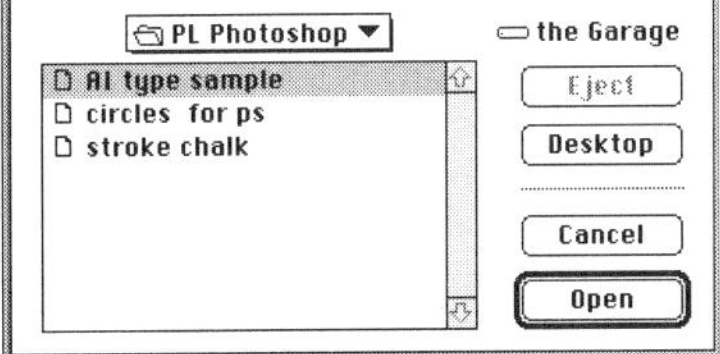

Figure 17. Highlight an EPS file, then click **Open**.

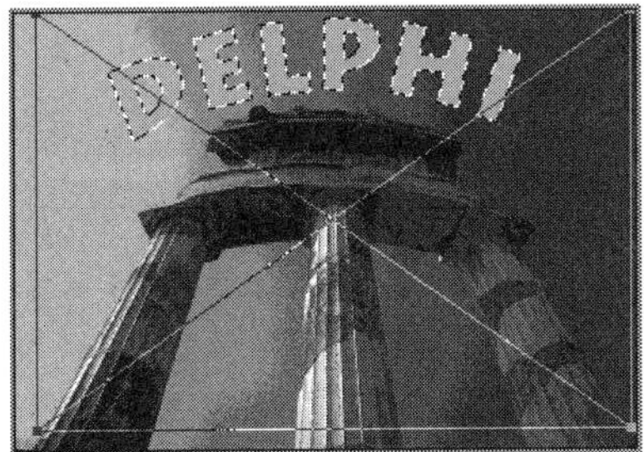

Figure 18. In this illustration, the word "Delphi" was created in Adobe Illustrator and placed in a Photoshop file.

(See "Note" on the previous page)

To place an Adobe Illustrator picture into an existing Photoshop file:

1. Open a Photoshop picture. *(See page 36)*
2. Choose Place from the File menu **(Figure 16)**.
3. Locate and highlight the EPS picture to be opened, then click Open. A box will appear. Pause to allow the image to draw inside it **(Figures 17-18)**.

Steps 4 and 5 are optional.

4. Drag a handle to resize the image.
5. To reposition the image, place the pointer over the "x" in the middle of the box and drag with the arrow pointer.
6. To accept the placed image, position the pointer over it and click with the gavel pointer icon. The image will become a floating selection.

✔ Tips

- For optimal rendering of a placed image, before choosing the Place command, check the Anti-aliased PostScript box in the General Preferences dialog box, opened from the Preferences pop-up menu under the Edit menu. The option you choose will be the default for future placed images.
- To remove a floating selection, position the pointer outside it, then click with the cancel pointer icon.

To modify a picture's dimensions:

1. Choose Image Size from the Image menu **(Figure 19)**.
2. To preserve the picture's width-to-height ratio, check the Proportions box. To modify the picture's width independently of its height, uncheck the Proportions box **(Figure 20)**.
3. *Optional:* To preserve the picture's resolution, uncheck the File Size box.
4. Choose a unit of measure from the pop-up menu next to the Width and Height fields.
5. Enter new numbers in the Width and/or Height fields. The Resolution will change if the File Size box is checked.
6. Click OK or press Return.

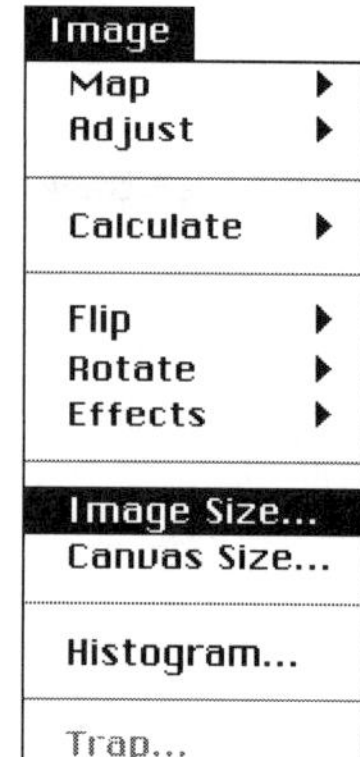

Figure 19. Choose **Image Size** from the **Image** menu.

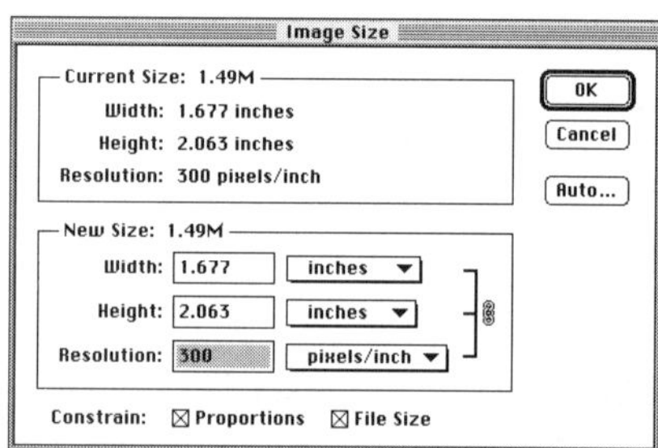

Figure 20. Enter numbers in the **Width** and/or **Height** fields in the **Image Size** dialog box.

✔ Tips

- If you modify a picture's dimensions with the File Size box unchecked, you will not be able to use the Rubber stamp tool with the From Saved option to restore a portion of it. Save a picture immediately after modifying its dimensions to establish a new From Saved reference. *(See page 172)*
- Changing a picture's dimensions in Photoshop may cause it to blur, so it is best to scan it at the desired size. If you must change a picture's dimensions in Photoshop, apply the Unsharp Mask filter afterward to resharpen. *(See page 42)*

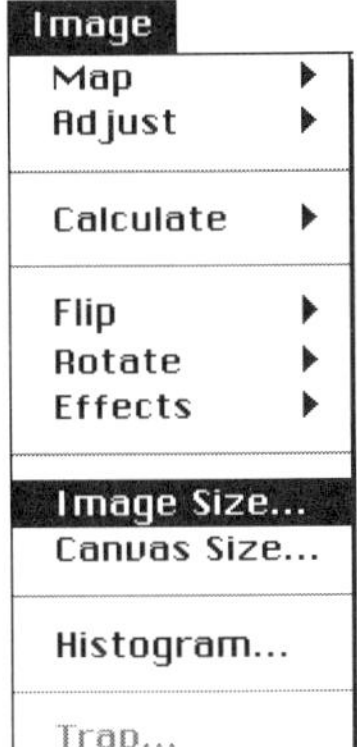

Figure 21. Choose **Image Size** from the **Image** menu.

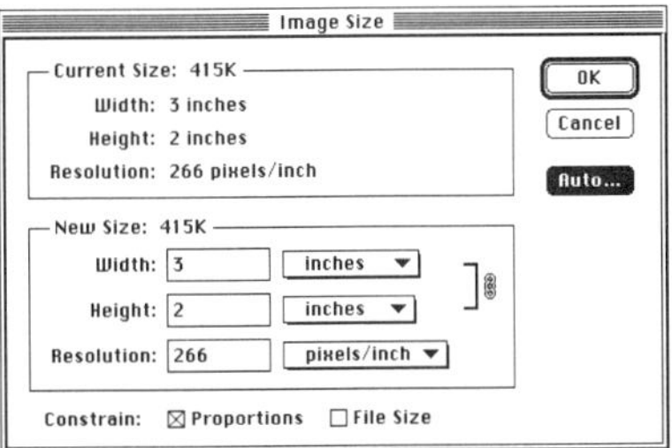

Figure 22. Enter a number in the **Resolution** field in the **Image Size** dialog box. Click **Auto** to have Photoshop calculate the resolution.

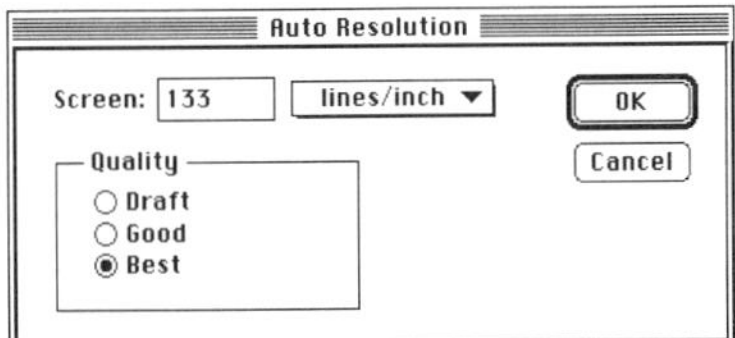

Figure 23. Click **Draft, Good,** or **Best** Quality in the **Auto Resolution** dialog box.

Note: When you increase a picture's resolution (resample up), pixels are added and the picture's file storage size increases, but sharpness diminishes. When you decrease resolution, information is deleted and cannot be retrieved once the picture is saved. Blurriness caused by resampling may only be evident when the picture is printed; it may not be discernible on screen. It is best to scan a picture at the proper resolution. Follow the instructions on the next page to resharpen a resampled picture.
(See "Resolution" on page 31)

To modify a picture's resolution:

1. Choose Image Size from the Image menu **(Figure 21)**.
2. *Optional:* To preserve the picture's dimensions (width and height), uncheck the File Size box **(Figure 22)**.
3. Enter a number in the Resolution field.
4. Click OK or press Return.

✓ Tip

- To calculate the proper resolution and file size for a scan, create a new RGB document and choose 72 ppi. Then open the Image Size dialog box, click Auto, and enter the resolution of your final output device, the lpi that your printer will use, click Draft (1x Screen frequency), Good (1½ x Screen frequency), or Best (2 x Screen frequency), and click OK **(Figures 22-23)**. Note the resolution and file size, and use those values when you scan your picture. You can also use the Auto Resolution dialog box to calculate the proper resolution for an existing Photoshop picture.

If you modify a picture's dimensions or resolution or convert it to CMYK Color mode, it may blur as a result of a process called interpolation. Despite its name, the Unsharp Mask filter has a sharpening effect.

You can choose from three interpolation methods in the General Preferences dialog box.
(See page 222)

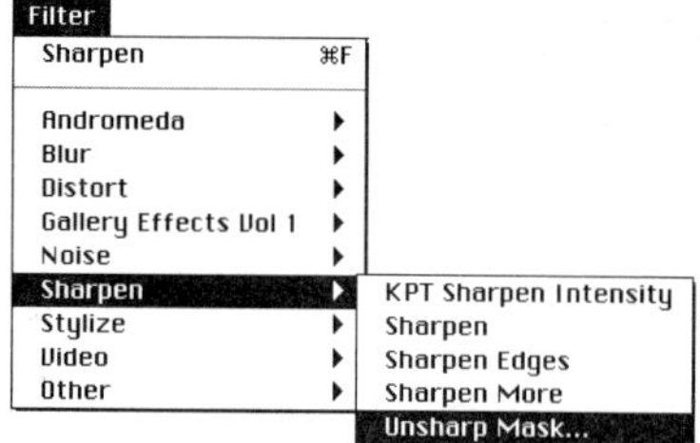

Figure 24. Choose **Unsharp Mask** from the **Sharpen** pop-up menu under the **Filter** menu.

To apply the Unsharp Mask filter:

1. Choose Unsharp Mask from the Sharpen pop-up menu under the Filter menu **(Figure 24)**.
2. Enter approximately 50 (the amount of sharpening) in the Amount field **(Figure 25)**. The picture will become pixelated if the Amount is too high. The minimum is 1 and the maximum is 500.
3. Leave the default Radius (the number of pixels surrounding high contrast edges that will be modified) at 1.0, or enter a number between 0.1 and 100.
4. Enter a number between 0 and 255 in the Threshold field or leave the default at 0. The Threshold is the minimum amount of contrast an area must have before it will be modified. At a Threshold of 0, the filter will be applied to the entire picture. At a high Threshold, the filter will be applied to high contrast areas only.
5. Click OK or press Return.

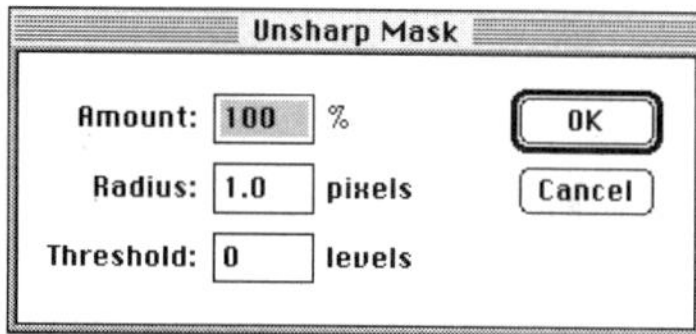

Figure 25. Enter a number in the **Amount, Radius,** and **Threshold** fields in the **Unsharp Mask** dialog box.

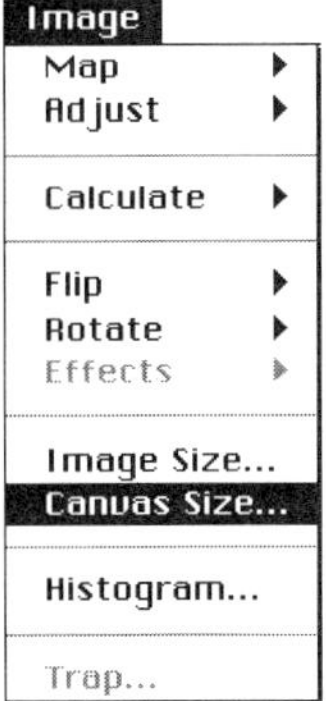

Figure 26. Choose **Canvas Size** from the **Image** menu.

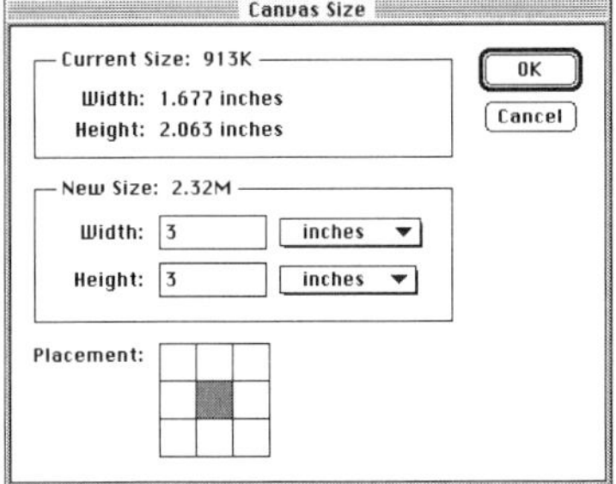

Figure 27. In the **Canvas Size** dialog box, enter numbers in the **Width** and/or **Height** fields.

To add a border to a picture:

1. Choose a Background color. *(See pages 130-132)*
2. Choose Canvas Size from the Image menu **(Figure 26)**.
3. *Optional:* Choose a different unit of measure from the pop-up menus.
4. Enter higher numbers in the Width and/or Height fields **(Figure 27)**. Changing the Width will not change the Height, and vice versa.
5. *Optional:* To reposition the image, click a Placement square. The gray square represents the image relative to the new border.
6. Click OK or press Return. The border will automatically fill with the Background color **(Figures 28-29)**.

Figure 28. The original picture.

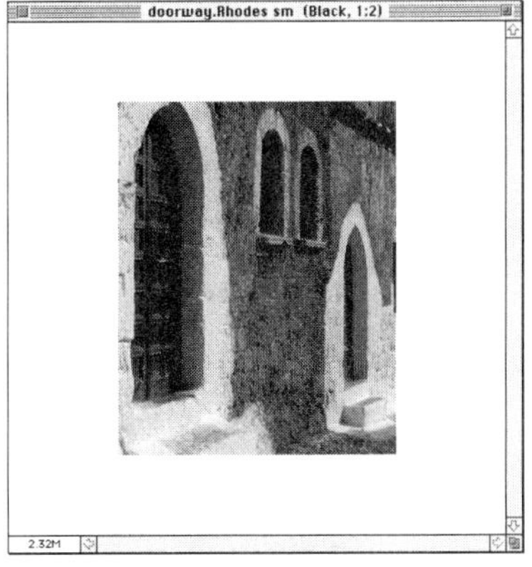

Figure 29. The same picture with a border.

To crop a picture:

1. Click the Cropping tool **(Figure 30)**.
2. Drag a marquee over the portion of the picture you wish to keep **(Figure 31)**.

Steps 3-5 are optional.

3. To resize the marquee, drag any handle with the arrow pointer **(Figure 33)**.
4. To reposition the marquee, hold down ⌘ and drag a handle **(Figure 34)**.
5. To rotate the marquee, hold down Option and drag a handle in a circular direction **(Figure 35)**.
6. Position the pointer inside the marquee, then click with the scissors pointer icon **(Figure 32)**. If you rotated the marquee, the rotated image will be squared off in the document window.

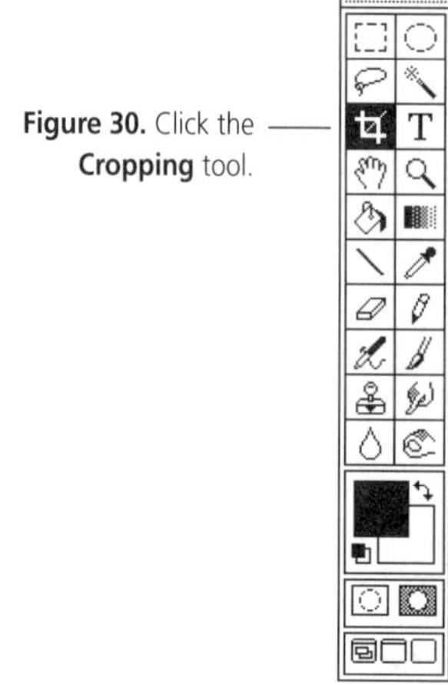

Figure 30. Click the **Cropping** tool.

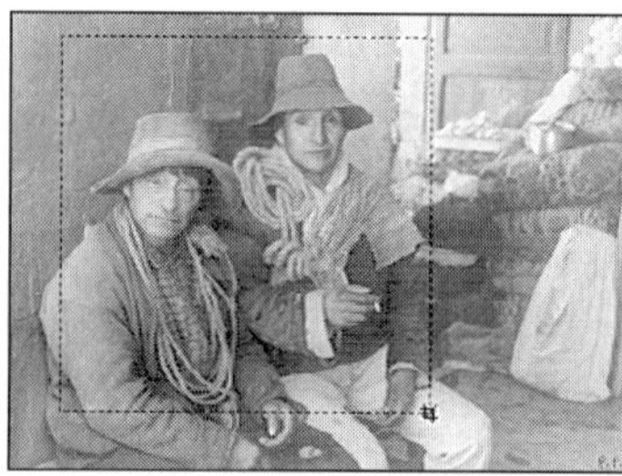

Figure 31. Drag a marquee over the portion of the picture you wish to keep, then click inside it.

✓ **Tips**

- To stop the cropping process before clicking with the scissors, click outside the marquee. To stop the cropping process after clicking with the scissors, click the cancel button in the Progress dialog box.
- To specify a height-to-width ratio and/or resolution for a cropped picture, double-click the Cropping tool and enter values in the Cropping Tool Options dialog box, then follow steps 2-6 above.
- As you drag the cropping tool, the dimensions of the crop marquee will be indicated in the W and H fields on the Info palette. (If the W and H fields are not displayed, choose Options from the Info palette pop-up menu and check the Show Mouse Coordinates box.)
- To resharpen a picture after cropping, apply the Unsharp Mask filter. *(See page 42)*

Figure 32. The cropped picture.

Figure 33. To resize a crop marquee, drag any corner handle. Hold down Shift while dragging to preserve the proportions of the marquee.

Figure 34. To reposition a crop marquee, hold down ⌘ and drag a corner handle.

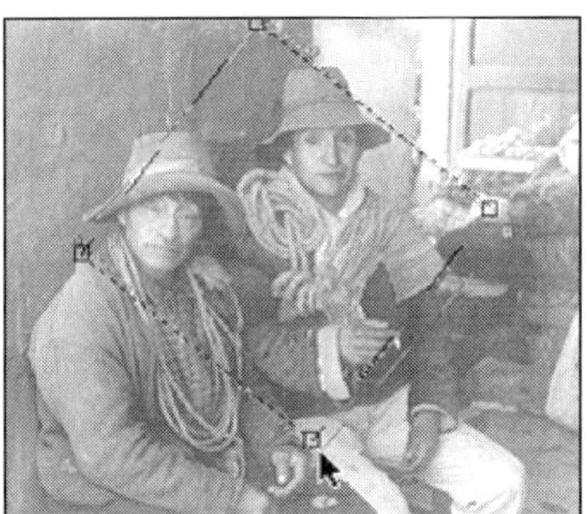

Figure 35. To rotate a crop marquee, hold down Option and drag a corner handle in a circular direction.

To flip a picture:

From the Flip pop-up menu under the Image menu, choose Horizontal to flip the picture left to right **(Figures 36-38)**.

or

Choose Vertical to flip the picture upside-down to produce a mirror image **(Figure 39)**.

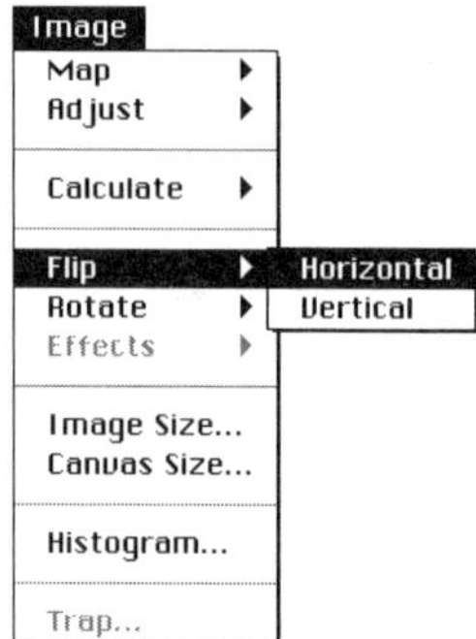

Figure 36. Choose **Horizontal** or **Vertical** from the **Flip** pop-up menu under the **Image** menu.

Figure 37. The original picture.

Figure 38. The picture flipped horizontally.

Figure 39. The picture flipped vertically.

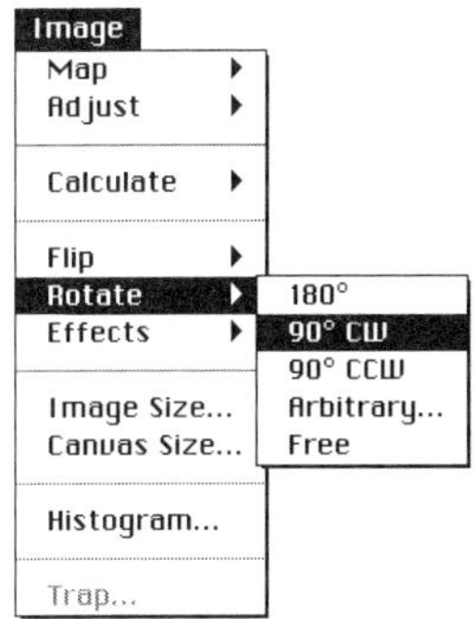

Figure 40. Choose **180°, 90°CW, 90°CCW,** or **Arbitrary** from the **Rotate** pop-up menu under the **Image** menu.

To rotate a picture a preset amount:

Choose 180°, 90° CW (clockwise), or 90° CCW (counterclockwise) from the Rotate pop-up menu under the Image Menu **(Figure 40)**.

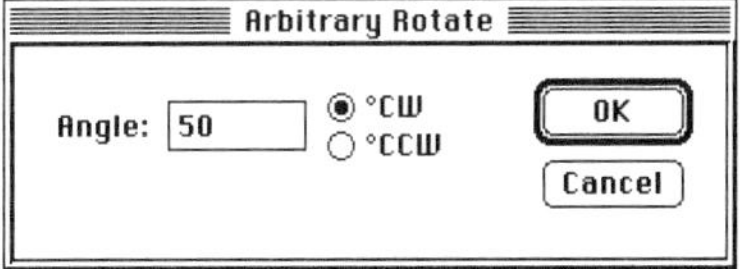

Figure 41. In the **Arbitrary Rotate** dialog box, enter a number in the **Angle** field, and click **°CW** or **°CCW**.

To rotate a picture by specifying a number:

1. Choose Arbitrary from the Rotate pop-up menu under the Image Menu **(Figure 41)**.
2. Enter a number between -359.9° and 359.9° in the Angle field.
3. Click °CW (clockwise) or °CCW (counterclockwise)
4. Click OK or press Return **(Figure 42)**.

Figure 42. After rotating a picture 180°. Compare with Figure 39 on the previous page.

Rotate a Picture

Special instructions for saving in the EPS, PICT, and TIFF file formats appear after the general instructions below. Other file formats are covered in the Photoshop User Guide.

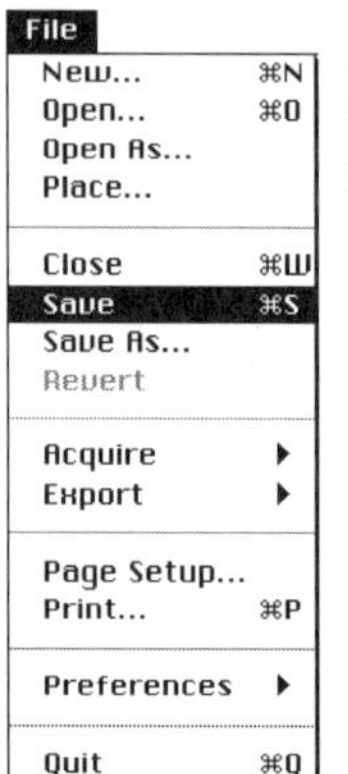

Figure 43. Choose **Save** from the **File** menu.

To save a new document:

1. Choose Save from the File menu **(Figure 43)**.
2. Enter a name in the "Save Current Document as" field.
3. Click Desktop **(Figure 44)**.
4. Highlight a drive, then click Open.
5. *Optional:* Highlight a folder in which to save the file, then click Open.
6. Choose a format from the File Format pop-up menu.
7. Click Save.

✔ **Tip**

■ Most programs will not import a picture in the Photoshop file format.

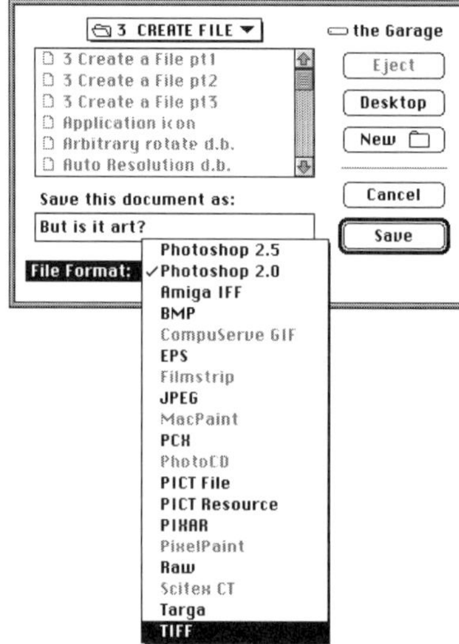

Figure 44. Enter a name in the **Save this Document as** field, choose a location in which to save the file, then click **Save**.

An EPS file can be imported into many drawing and page layout programs, such as **Adobe Illustrator** and **QuarkXPress**.

To save a picture as an EPS:

1. Follow steps 1-5 above.
2. Choose EPS from the File Formats pop-up menu.
3. Click Save.
4. Click 1-bit Macintosh for a grayscale preview; click 8-bit Macintosh for a color preview **(Figure 45)**.
5. Click Binary.
6. If the picture is in CMYK Color mode, leave the DCS option off unless your prepress service bureau has instructed you otherwise.
7. Click OK or press Return.

Binary Encoded files are smaller and process more quickly than **ASCII** files. However, some applications and some PostScript "clone" printers cannot handle Binary files.

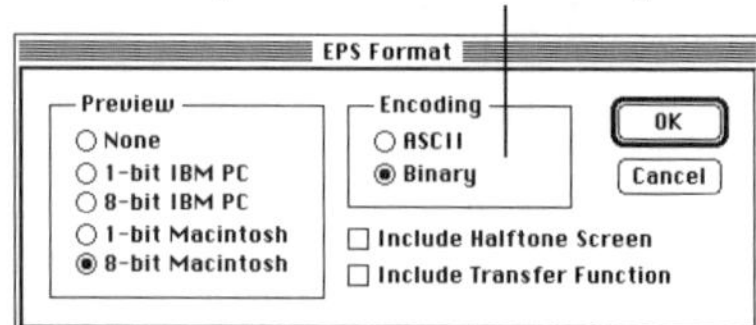

Figure 45. Click **1-bit Macintosh** or **8-bit Macintosh** in the **EPS Format** dialog box.

Save a New Document, Save as an EPS

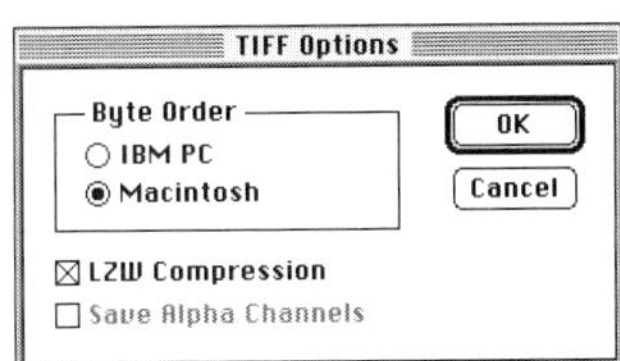

Figure 46. Click **Macintosh** in the **TIFF Options** dialog box.

A TIFF file can be imported by **QuarkXPress**. A CMYK TIFF can be color separated from QuarkXPress.

To save a picture as a TIFF:

1. Follow steps 1-5 on the previous page.
2. Choose TIFF from the File Formats pop-up menu.
3. Click Save.
4. Click Macintosh **(Figure 46)**.
5. *Optional:* Check the LZW Compression box to reduce the file size. No picture data will be lost.
   (See page 212)
6. Click OK or press Return.

A PICT file can be opened as a template in **Adobe Illustrator**. A PICT file can also be opened in most **multimedia animation** applications.

Note: PICT compression options are available only if the QuickTime extension is installed in the System Folder.

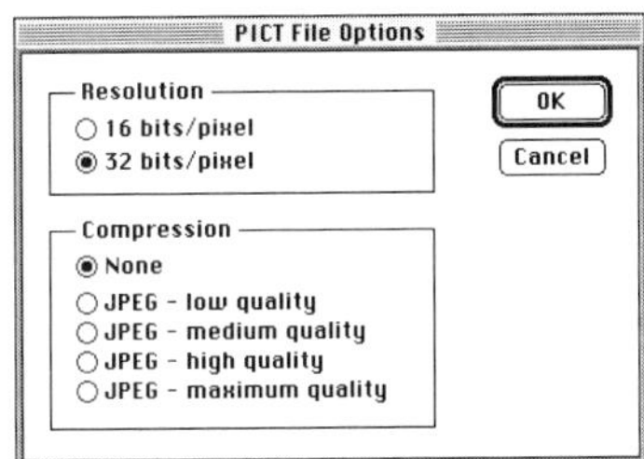

Figure 47. Click a **Resolution** in the **PICT File Options** dialog box.

To save a picture as a PICT:

1. Follow steps 1-5 on the previous page in "To save a new document."
2. Choose PICT File from the File Formats pop-up menu.
3. Click Save.
4. Click 16 bits/pixel or 32 bits/pixel **(Figure 47)**. For a picture in mode, check 2, 4, or 8 bits/pixel **(Figure 48)**.
5. Read page 212 before choosing any Compression setting other than None.
6. Click OK or press Return.

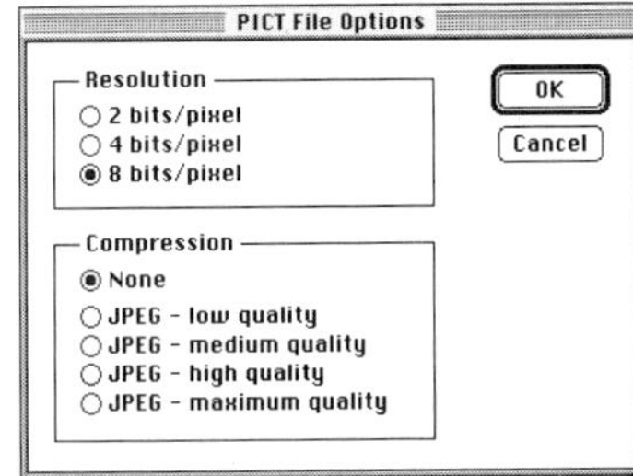

Figure 48. The PICT File Options dialog box for a Grayscale mode picture.

✔ Tip

■ A picture in CMYK Color mode cannot be saved in the PICT file format.

The prior version of a file is overwritten when the Save command is chosen.

To save an existing file:

Choose Save from the File menu **(Figure 49)**.
or
Hold down ⌘ and press "S".

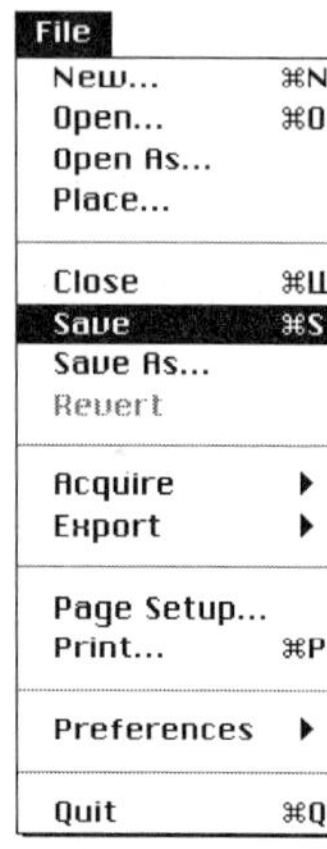

Figure 49. Choose **Save** from the **File** menu.

To revert to the last saved version:

1. Choose Revert from the File menu **(Figure 50)**.
2. Click Revert when the prompt appears **(Figure 51)**.

✔ **Tip**

- To revert only a portion of a picture, use the Rubber stamp tool with its From Saved option.
  (See page 172)

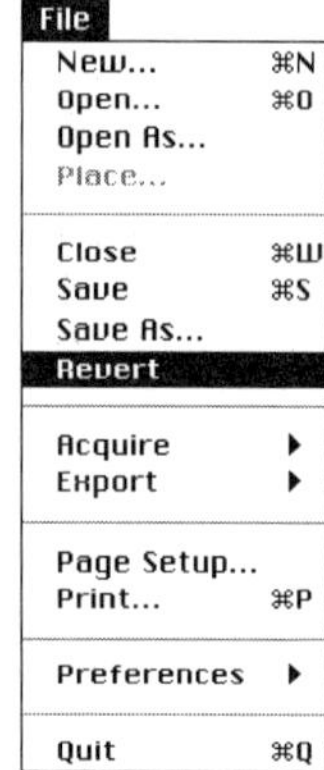

Figure 50. Choose **Revert** from the **File** menu.

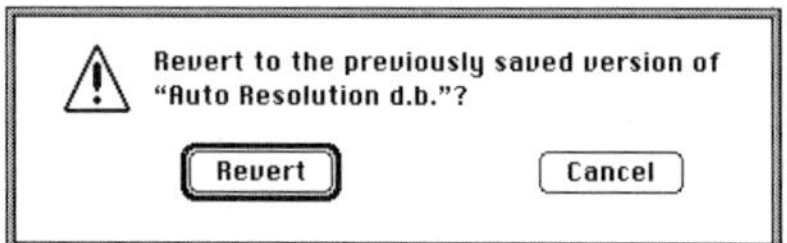

Figure 51. Click **Revert** when this warning prompt appears.

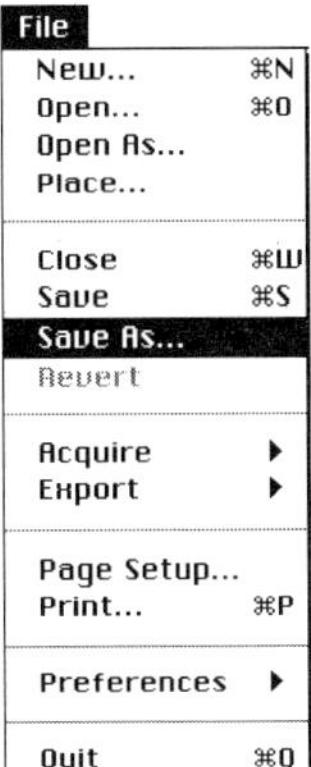

Figure 52. Choose **Save As** from the **File** menu.

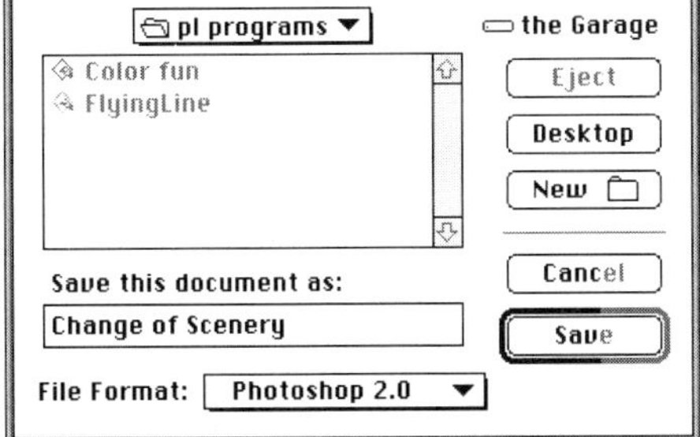

Figure 53. In the **Save As** dialog box, modify the name in the **Save this document as** field, choose a **File Format**, and choose a location in which to save the new version.

You can use the Save As dialog box to save a picture in a different file format so it can be exported to another Macintosh application or other operating system. You can use Save As to create a new version of a file and save the new version in a different picture mode. For example, you can save a version of a picture in CMYK Color mode to color separate it, while retaining the original RGB Color version. You can also spawn design variations from a file using Save As.

To save a new version of a file:

1. Open a file.
2. Choose Save As from the File menu **(Figure 52)**.
3. Enter a new name in the "Save this document as" field **(Figure 53)**.
   or
   Modify the existing name.
4. Choose a location in which to save the new version.
5. *Optional:* Choose a different File Format.
6. Click Save. For an EPS file, follow instructions on page 48. For a TIFF or PICT file, follow instructions on page 49. Consult the Photoshop manual for other formats. The new version will remain open; the original file will close automatically.

✔ Tips

- If you do not alter the name of the file and you click Save, a warning prompt will appear. Click Replace to save over the original file or click Cancel to return to the Save As dialog box.
- Your picture may need to be in a particular mode for some File Formats to be available.

  (JPEG is discussed on page 212)
  (See "Picture Modes" on page 23)

Save a New Version of a File

To close a picture:

Click the Close box in the upper left corner of the document window **(Figure 54)**.

or

Choose Close from the File menu **(Figure 55)**.

✔ Tip

- If you attempt to close a picture and it was modified since it was last saved, a warning prompt will appear. You can choose to close the file without saving, save the file, or cancel the Close operation **(Figure 56)**.

Figure 54. Click the **Close** box.

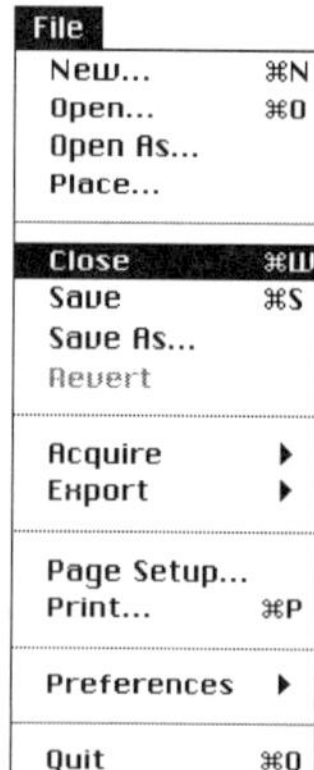

Figure 55. Choose **Close** from the **File** menu.

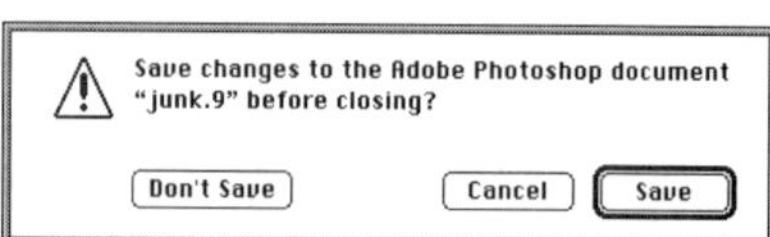

Figure 56. If you chose **Close** and the file has been modified since it was last saved, this prompt will appear.

Figure 57. Choose **Quit** from the **File** menu.

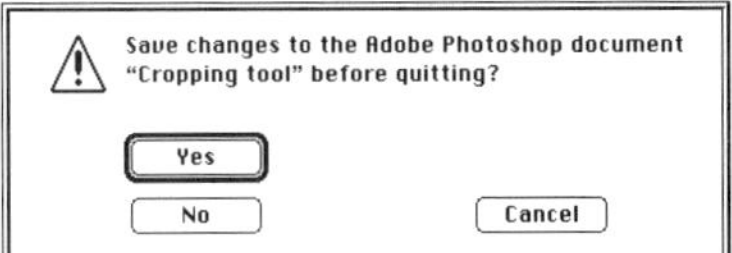

Figure 58. If you chose **Quit** and changes have been made to an open file since it was saved, this prompt will appear.

To quit Photoshop:

Choose Quit from the File menu **(Figure 57)**.

or

Hold down ⌘ and press "Q".

✔ Tip

- If you Quit Photoshop, all open Photoshop files will close. If changes have been made to an open file since it was saved, a prompt will appear. You will have the option to save the file before quitting or cancel the quit operation **(Figure 58)**.

GETTING AROUND

THIS CHAPTER covers how to change display sizes, how to display a picture in two windows simultaneously, how to switch screen display modes, and how to move a picture within its window.

The display ratio.

Untitled-2 (RGB, 1:2)

971K

Figure 1.

You can display an entire picture within its window, or magnify a detail of a picture to modify individual pixels. The display size is indicated as a ratio in the title bar **(Figure 1)**. The display size can range from a minimum of 1:16 (reduced 16 times) to a maximum of 16:1 (enlarged 16 times). The display size of a picture does not affect its printout size.

Window
New Window
Zoom In ⌘+
Zoom Out ⌘-
Show Rulers ⌘R
Hide Brushes
Hide Channels
Hide Colors
Show Info
Show Paths
✓junk (RGB, 1:1)

Figure 2. Choose **Zoom In** or **Zoom Out** from the **Window** menu.

To modify the display size via the Window menu:

Choose Zoom In from the Window menu (or hold down ⌘ and press "+") to magnify the picture **(Figure 2)**.

or

Choose Zoom Out from the Window menu (or hold down ⌘ and press "–") to reduce the display size.

To modify the display size via the Zoom tool:

1. Click the Zoom tool **(Figure 3)**.
2. Click on the picture or drag a marquee across an area to magnify that area **(Figure 4)**.
   or
   Hold down Option and click to reduce the display size **(Figure 5)**.

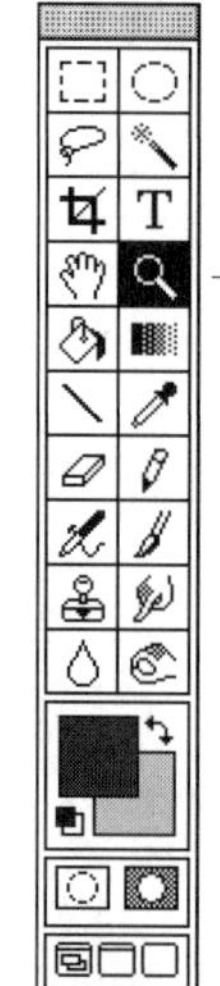

Figure 3. Click the **Zoom** tool.

✔ Tips

- Double-click the Zoom tool to display a picture in 1:1 view.
- A picture's display size equals its actual size only when the display ratio is 1:1 and the picture resolution and monitor resolution are 72 ppi.
- To magnify the display size when another tool is selected or a dialog box with a Preview option is open, hold down ⌘ and Space bar and click. To reduce the display size, hold down Option and Space bar and click.

Figure 4. Click on the picture to enlarge the display size. Note the plus sign in the magnifying glass pointer.

Figure 5. Hold down **Option** and click on the picture to reduce the display size. Note the minus sign in the magnifying glass pointer.

Window
New Window
Zoom In ⌘+
Zoom Out ⌘-
Show Rulers ⌘R
Hide Brushes
Hide Channels
Hide Colors
Show Info
Show Paths
✓junk (RGB, 1:1)

Figure 6. Choose **New Window** from the **Window** menu.

In Photoshop, up to seven pictures can be open at a time. You can open the same picture in two windows simultaneously: one in a large display size, such as 4:1, to edit a detail and the other in a smaller display size, such as 1:1, to view the whole image.

To display a picture in two windows:

1. Open a picture.
2. Choose New Window from the Window menu **(Figures 6-7)**. The same picture will appear in a second window.
3. *Optional:* Reposition either window by dragging its title bar, or resize either window by dragging its resize box.

Figure 7. A picture displayed in two windows simultaneously: one in a large display size for editing, the other in a smaller display size for previewing.

To change the screen display mode:

Click the left display mode icon on the Toolbox to display the picture, menu bar, scroll bars on the document window, and Finder (Desktop) **(Figure 8)**.

or

Click the center icon to display the picture and menu bar, but no scroll bars or Finder. The area around the picture will be gray **(Figure 9)**.

or

Click the right icon to display the picture, but no menu bar, scroll bars, or Finder. The area around the picture will be black.

✔ Tips

- Press Tab to hide the Toolbox and any open palettes; press Tab again to display the Toolbox and previously open palettes.
- Use the Hand tool to move the picture in its window when the scroll bars are hidden and the picture is magnified **(Figure 10)**. Hold down the Space bar to turn the currently selected tool temporarily into the Hand tool.

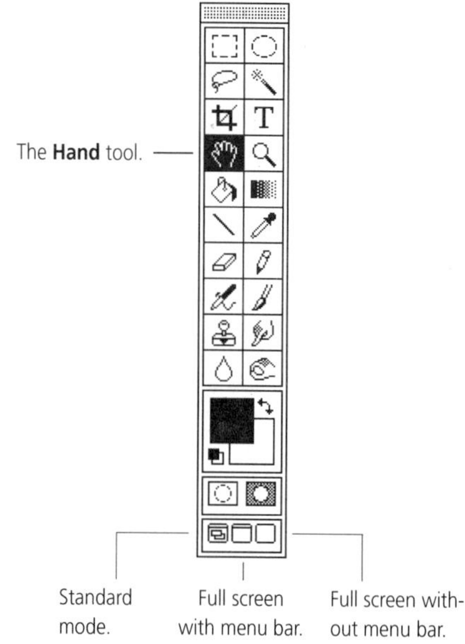

Figure 8. Display modes.

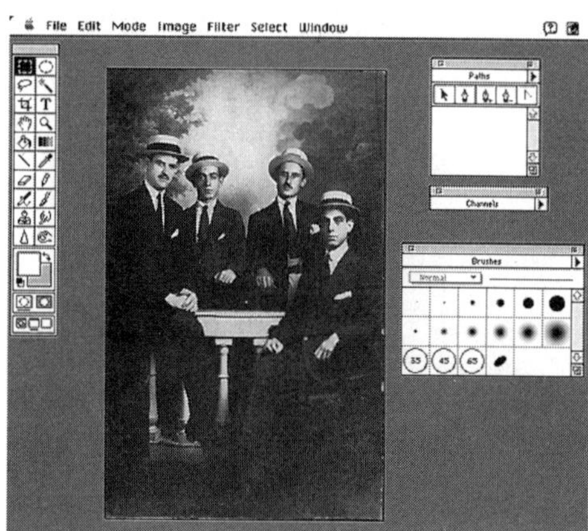

Figure 9. Full screen with menu bar mode.

Note: If the scroll bars are not active, the entire picture is displayed, and there is no need to move it.

To move a picture in its window:

Click the up or down scroll arrow **(Figure 10)**.

or

Move a scroll box to move the picture more quickly.

or

Click the Hand tool, then drag the picture.

✔ Tips

- Double-click the Hand tool to fit the picture in the largest document window your monitor accommodates.
- Hold down Space bar to turn the currently selected tool temporarily into the Hand tool.

Figure 10.

SELECTIONS 5

Tip.

Make all your modifications to a selection before deselecting it, because it is very difficult to precisely reselect an area.

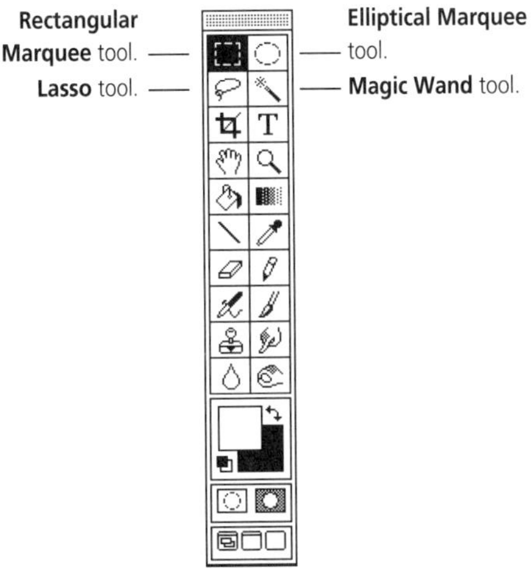

Figure 1.

YOU CAN USE Photoshop's selection tools — Rectangular Marquee, Elliptical Marquee, Lasso and Magic Wand — to isolate an area of a picture **(Figure 1)**. When a command or effect, such as a filter, is applied to a selection, only the selection is affected. The rest of the picture is protected. A selection is defined by a moving marquee. Some Image menu commands are available only when an area is selected.

The creation of selections is covered in this chapter, including using the Rectangular Marquee tool to create rectangular selections, the Elliptical Marquee tool to create elliptical selections, the Lasso tool to create irregular or polygonal selections, and the Magic Wand tool to select areas of shade or color. Other topics include creating a frame selection, and deselecting a selection.

The selections covered in this chapter are non-floating — they contain the underlying pixels. The creation of floating selections is covered in other chapters.

Selection modifications are covered in Chapter 6, path selections in Chapter 7, and masks in Chapter 8.

Select
All ⌘A
None ⌘D
Inverse
Defloat ⌘J
Grow ⌘G
Similar
Border...
Feather...
Defringe...
Hide Edges ⌘H
Load Selection
Save Selection

Figure 2. Choose **All** from the **Select** menu.

To select an entire picture:

Choose All from the Select Menu or hold down ⌘ and press "A" **(Figure 2)**. A marquee will surround the picture.

To create a rectangular selection:

1. Click the Rectangular Marquee tool **(Figure 3)**.
2. Drag diagonally across an area of the picture. A marquee will appear **(Figure 4)**.

✔ Tips

- As you drag the mouse, the dimensions of the selection will be indicated in the W and H fields on the Info palette. (If the W and H fields are not displayed, choose Options from the Info palette pop-up menu and check the Show Mouse Coordinates box.)
- To specify the width-to-height ratio or dimensions of a selection before you drag the mouse, double-click the Rectangular Marquee tool, click Constrained Aspect Ratio or Fixed Size, enter width and height values, then click OK. If you clicked Constrained Aspect Ratio, drag across an area of the picture. If you clicked Fixed Size, click on the picture.

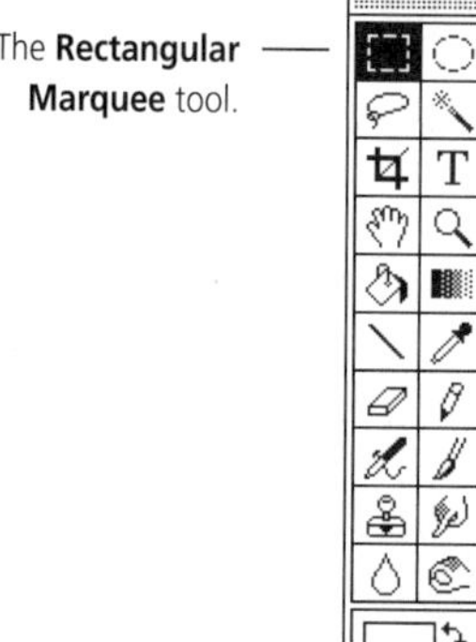

Figure 3.

Figure 4. Drag diagonally to create a rectangular selection.

To create an elliptical selection:

1. Click the Elliptical Marquee tool **(Figure 3)**.
2. Drag diagonally across an area of the picture. A marquee will appear **(Figure 5)**.

✔ Tips

- To create a square or a circular selection, start dragging with the Rectangular Marquee or Elliptical Marquee tool, then hold down Shift and continue to drag. Release the mouse, then release Shift.
- To drag from the center of a selection, hold down Option and drag. Release the mouse, then release Option.

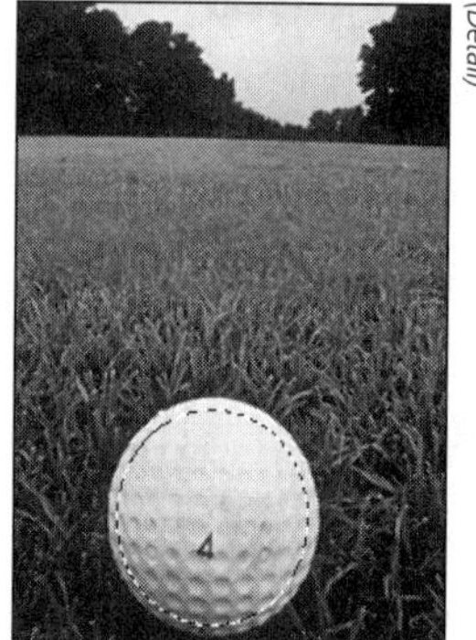

(Detail)

Figure 5. Drag diagonally to create an elliptical selection.

Figure 6. Click the **Lasso** tool.

To create an irregular selection:

1. Click the Lasso tool **(Figure 6)**.
2. Drag around an area of a picture. When you release the mouse, the open ends of the selection will join automatically **(Figure 7)**.

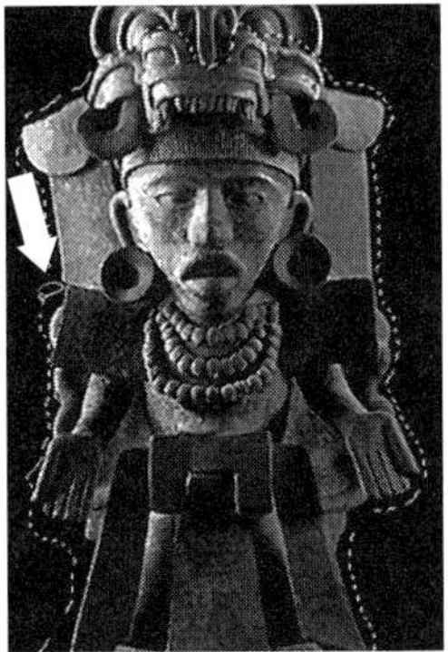

Figure 7. Drag around the area to be selected.

To create a polygon selection:

1. Click the Lasso tool **(Figure 6)**.
2. To create straight sides, hold down Option and click to create points. The open ends of the selection will join automatically when Option is released **(Figure 8)**.

✓ **Tip**

- To create a curved segment while drawing a polygon selection, press and drag while continuing to hold down Option. Release the mouse before clicking again to create the next straight side.

Figure 8. Hold down **Option** and click to create points.

When you click on a pixel with the Magic Wand tool, a selection is created that includes adjacent pixels of a similar shade or color.

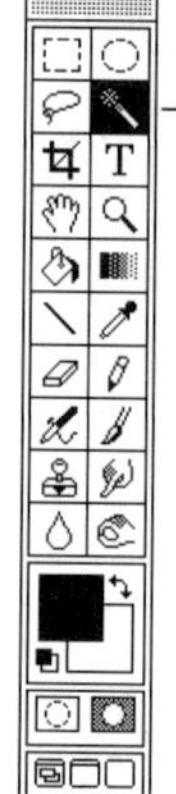

Figure 9. Click once on the **Magic Wand** tool to select it. Double-click the Magic Wand tool to set its Tolerance range.

To select an area by color:

1. Click the Magic Wand tool **(Figure 9)**.
2. Click on a shade or color in the picture **(Figure 12-13)**.

Steps 3-5 are optional.

3. To enlarge the selection, choose Grow from the Select menu one or more times **(Figure 10)**.
   or
   Hold down ⌘ and press "G."
4. To select other, non-contiguous, areas of similar color or shade, choose Similar from the Select menu.
5. To specify a different Tolerance range, double-click the Magic Wand tool, then modify the number in the Tolerance field **(Figure 11)**.
   (See "Tolerance" on the following page)

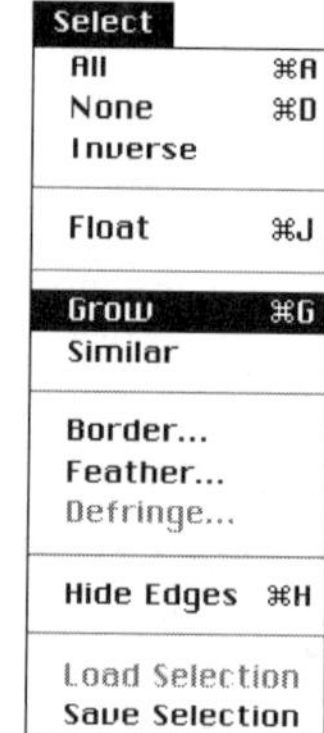

Figure 10. Choose **Grow** or **Similar** from the **Select** menu.

✔ Tips

- Choose Undo from the Edit menu to undo the last Grow command or selection.
- To add to a selection with the Magic Wand tool, hold down Shift and click outside the selection. To subtract, hold down ⌘ and click inside the selection. You can also use another selection tool, like the Lasso, to reshape a selection.
  (See page 75)

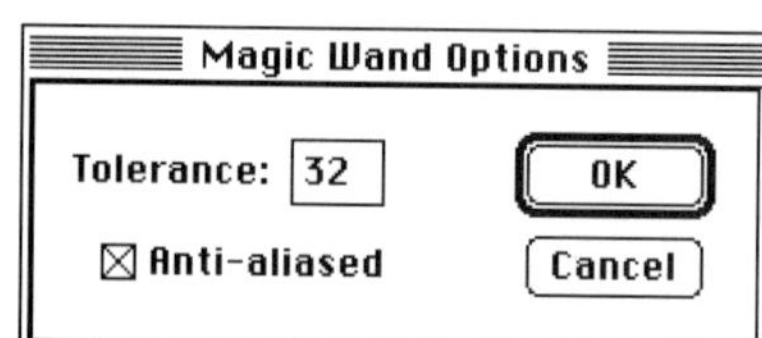

Figure 11. Enter a number between 0 and 255 in the **Tolerance** field in the **Magic Wand Options** dialog box.

Tolerance.

To increase or decrease the range of shades or colors the Magic Wand tool selects, double-click the Magic Wand tool and enter a number between 0 and 255 in the Tolerance field **(Figure 11)**.

For example, with a Tolerance of 32, the Magic Wand will select within a range of 16 shades below and 16 shades above the shade on which it is clicked. Enter 1 to select one color or shade.

To gradually narrow the range of shades or colors selected with the Magic Wand tool, modify the Tolerance value between clicks.

Figure 12. A Magic Wand selection using a Tolerance of 16.

Figure 13. A Magic Wand selection using a Tolerance of 40.

To create a frame selection:

1. Click the Rectangular Marquee tool.
2. Press and drag to create a selection **(Figure 14)**.
3. Hold down ⌘ and drag to create a smaller selection inside the first selection **(Figure 15)**.

✓ **Tip**

- You can also create a frame selection using the Elliptical Marquee tool.

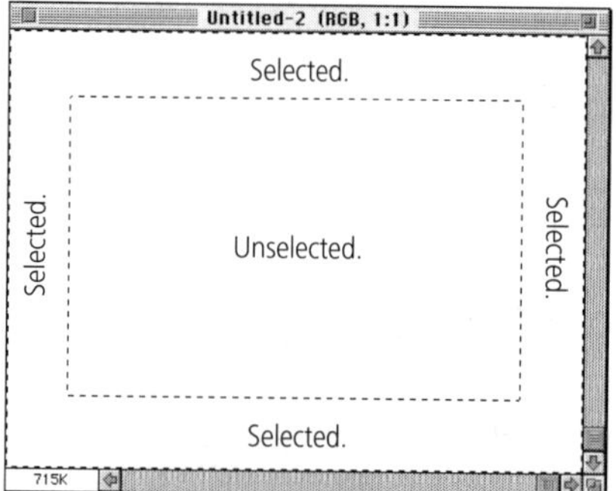

Figure 14. A frame selection created with the Rectangular Marquee tool.

Figure 15. A blend was applied to a frame selection to produce this illustration. *(See page 159)*

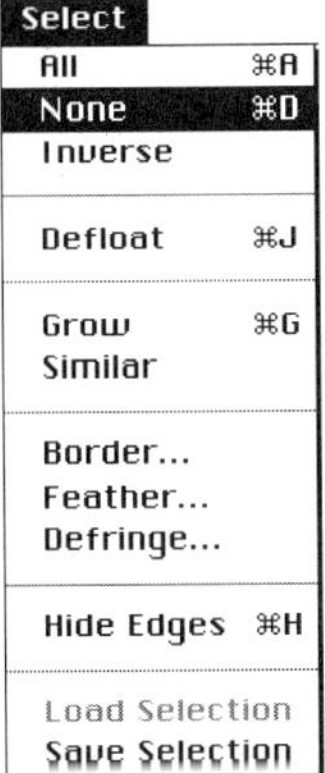

Figure 16. Choose **None** from the **Select** menu.

To deselect a selection:

With any tool selected, choose None from the Select Menu, or hold down ⌘ and press "D" **(Figure 16)**.

or

Click **outside** the selection with the Rectangular Marquee, Elliptical Marquee, or Lasso tool **(Figure 17)**.

or

Click **inside** the selection with the Magic Wand tool. If you click outside the selection with the Magic Wand, you will create an additional selection.

✔ Tip

- Deselect only when you have finished modifying a selection, because it will be difficult to reselect the same area of pixels. If you unintentionally deselect, choose Undo from the Edit Menu immediately.

(See also page 71)

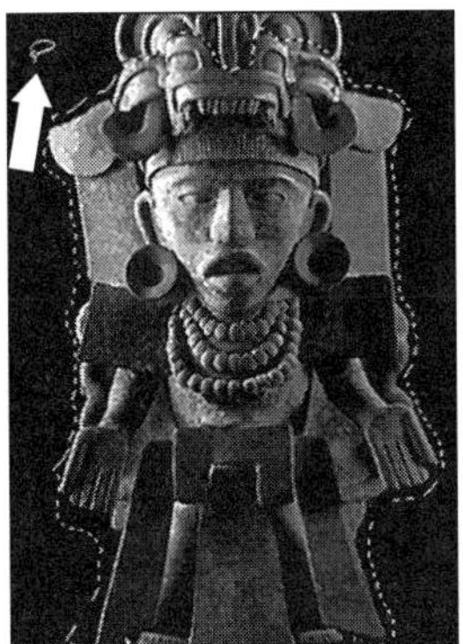

Figure 17. Click **outside** a selection to deselect it with the Rectangular Marquee, Elliptical Marquee, or Lasso tool. Click **inside** a selection to deselect it with the Magic Wand tool.

MODIFY SELECTIONS 6

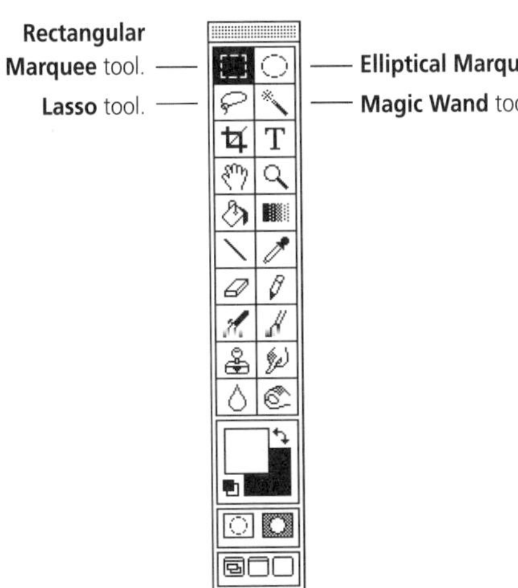

Figure 1.

IN THIS CHAPTER you will learn to move, copy, flip, rotate, resize, add to, subtract from, feather, and defringe a selection. You will also learn to move and hide a selection marquee and create a vignette. Read Chapter 5 first if you are not familiar with how the selection tools work. Masks are covered in Chapter 7, and path selections in Chapter 8.

Figure 2. A marquee being moved.

To move a selection marquee:

1. Click the Rectangular Marquee, Elliptical Marquee, Lasso, or Magic Wand tool **(Figure 1)**.
2. Position the pointer over a selection, then hold down ⌘ and Option and drag. Only the marquee will move, not the contents of the selection **(Figure 2)**.

✓ Tip

- To determine the exact position of a marquee, position the pointer over one of its edges and note the X and Y coordinates on the Info palette. (If the X/Y coordinates are not displayed on the palette, choose Options from the palette pop-up menu and check the Show Mouse Coordinates box.)

To move a selection:

1. Click the Rectangular Marquee, Elliptical Marquee, Lasso, or Magic Wand tool **(Figure 1)**.
2. Position the pointer over a selection, then drag. Both the selection marquee and its contents will move. The exposed area will fill with the Background color **(Figures 3-4)**.

✔ Tips

- Choose a Background color before moving a selection.
  (See pages 130-132)
- Press any arrow key to move the selection in 1-pixel increments.

(See also page 78)

Figure 3. Drag a selection.

Figure 4. The selection in a new position.

To hide a selection marquee:

Choose Hide Edges from the Select menu **(Figure 5)**. The selection will remain active.

✔ Tips

- To display the selection marquee again, choose Show Edges from the Select menu.
- To verify that a selection is still active, press on the Select menu. Most commands will be available if a selection is active.

Figure 5. Choose **Hide Edges** from the **Select** menu.

Figure 6. Hold down Option and drag a selection.

Figure 7. A copy of the selection is moved.

Select
All ⌘A
None ⌘D
Inverse
Float ⌘J
Grow ⌘G
Similar
Border...
Feather...
Defringe...
Hide Edges ⌘H
Load Selection
Save Selection

Figure 8. Choose **Float** from the **Select** menu.

When you copy a selection, the copy becomes a floating selection and the original selection is unchanged. When the floating selection is deselected, it replaces the underlying pixels.

To copy a selection:

1. Click the Rectangular Marquee, Elliptical Marquee, Lasso, or Magic Wand tool **(Figure 1)**.
2. Position the pointer over a selection, then hold down Option and drag. A copy of the selection will move **(Figures 6-7)**.
   or
   Choose Float from the Select menu (or hold down ⌘ and press "J"), position the pointer over the selection, then drag **(Figure 8)**.

✔ Tips

- Select Defloat from the Select menu to replace the underlying pixels with the selection, which will remain active.
- To delete the selection copy, choose Clear from the Edit Menu.
- Use the Composite Controls dialog box, opened from the Edit menu, to make a floating selection translucent. *(See pages 179-180)*

To flip a selection:

Choose Horizontal from the Flip pop-up menu under the Image menu to flip a selection left to right **(Figures 9-11)**.
or
Choose Vertical to flip a selection upside-down, creating a mirror image.

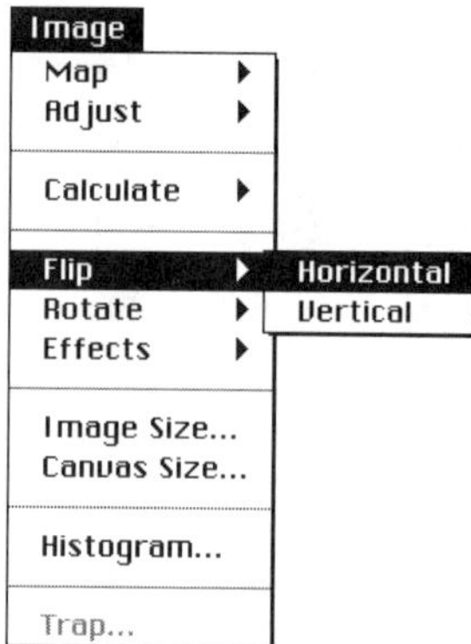

Figure 9. Choose **Horizontal** or **Vertical** from the **Flip** pop-up menu under the **Image** menu.

Figure 10. The original picture with an area selected.

Figure 11. The selection flipped horizontally.

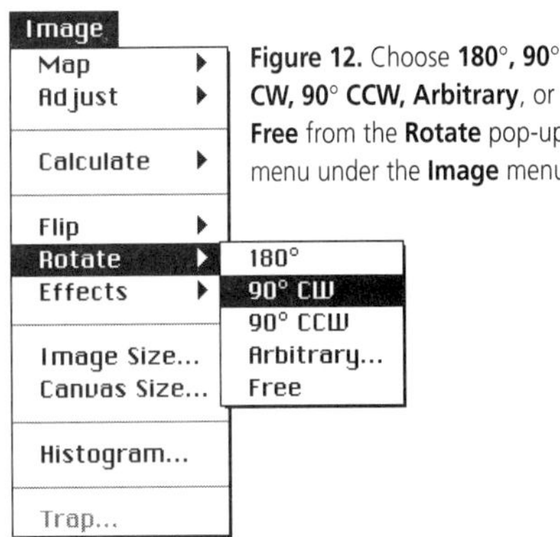

Figure 12. Choose **180°, 90° CW, 90° CCW, Arbitrary,** or **Free** from the **Rotate** pop-up menu under the **Image** menu.

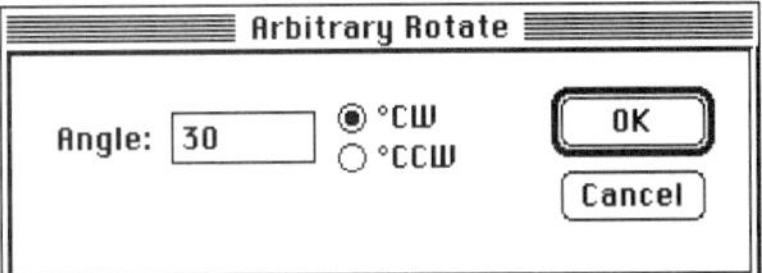

Figure 13. Enter a number in the **Angle** field and click °**CW** or °**CCW** in the **Arbitrary Rotate** dialog box.

Figure 14. A floating selection rotated 30°.

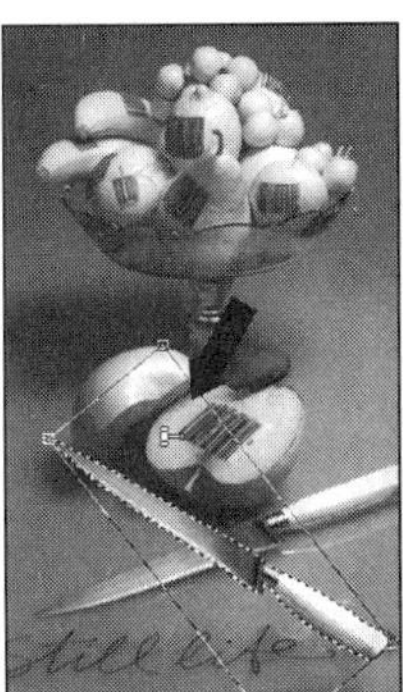

Figure 15. Drag a corner box, then click on the selection to accept the new angle.

To rotate a selection a preset amount:

Choose (180°, 90° CW (clockwise), or 90° CCW (counterclockwise) from the Rotate pop-up menu under the Image Menu **(Figure 12)**.

To rotate a selection by specifying a number:

1. Choose Arbitrary from the Rotate pop-up menu under the Image Menu **(Figure 12)**.
2. Enter a number between -359.9° and 359.9° in the Angle field **(Figure 13)**.
3. Click °CW (clockwise) or °CCW (counterclockwise).
4. Click OK or press Return **(Figure 14)**.

To free rotate a selection:

1. Choose Free from the Rotate pop-up menu under the Image Menu **(Figure 9)**. Corner handles will appear.
2. Drag a handle in a circular direction with the arrow pointer **(Figure 15)**.
3. To accept the new rotation angle, click on the selection with the gavel pointer icon.

✓ Tip

- To restore the original angle, click outside the selection with the cancel pointer icon. The selection will remain active.

To resize a selection:

1. Choose Scale from the Effects pop-up menu under the Image Menu. Corner handles will appear **(Figure 16)**.
2. Position the pointer over a corner handle and drag with the arrow pointer **(Figure 17)**.
3. Position the cursor over the selection and click with the gavel pointer icon **(Figure 18)**.

✓ Tips

- Hold down Shift while dragging a corner handle to preserve the height and width ratio of the selection.
- To restore the selection's original size, position the pointer outside it and click with the cancel pointer icon. The selection will remain active.
- Choose a Background color from the picture before scaling a selection, so any exposed area will be filled with a matching color.
(See page 131)

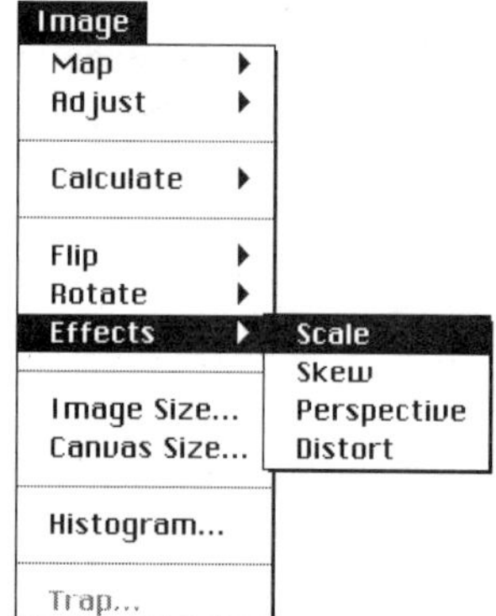

Figure 16. Choose **Scale** from the **Effects** pop-up menu under the **Image** menu.

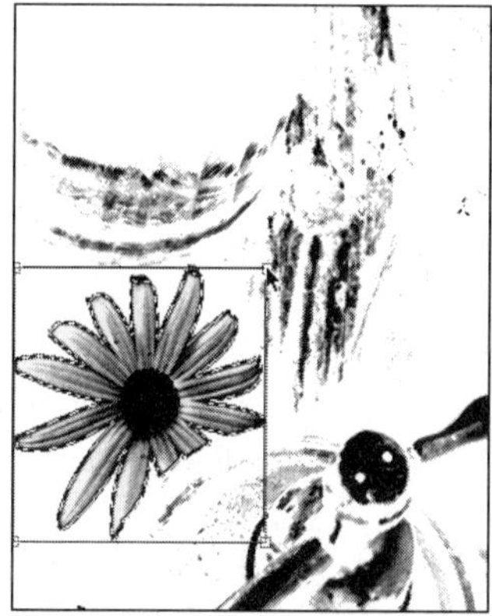

Figure 17. Drag a corner handle.

Figure 18. Click on the selection with the gavel icon.

Figure 19. Hold down Shift and drag with the Rectangular Marquee or Elliptical Marquee tool to define an additional selection area.

To add to a selection:

Click the Rectangular Marquee or Elliptical Marquee tool, then hold down Shift and drag to define an additional selection area **(Figure 19)**.
or
Click the Lasso tool. Position the cursor over the selection, hold down Shift and drag to define an additional selection area.
or
Click the Magic Wand tool, then hold down Shift and click on any unselected area.

 **Tip**

- If the additional selection overlaps the original selection, it will become part of the new larger selection. If the addition does not overlap the original selection, a second, separate selection will be created.

Figure 20. Hold down ⌘ and drag with the Lasso tool around an area to be subtracted.

To subtract from a selection:

Click the Rectangular Marquee or Elliptical Marquee tool, then hold down ⌘ and drag over the area to be subtracted.
or
Click the Lasso tool, hold down ⌘ and drag around the area to be subtracted **(Figure 20)**.
or
Click the Magic Wand tool, then hold down ⌘ and click on the area of shade or color to be subtracted.

Apply the Feather command to fade the edge of a selection a specified number of pixels inward and outward from the marquee. For example, a Feather Radius of 5 will create a faded area 10 pixels wide.

Note: The feather will not appear until the selection is modified with a painting tool, copied, pasted, moved, or filled, or a filter or Image menu command is applied to it.

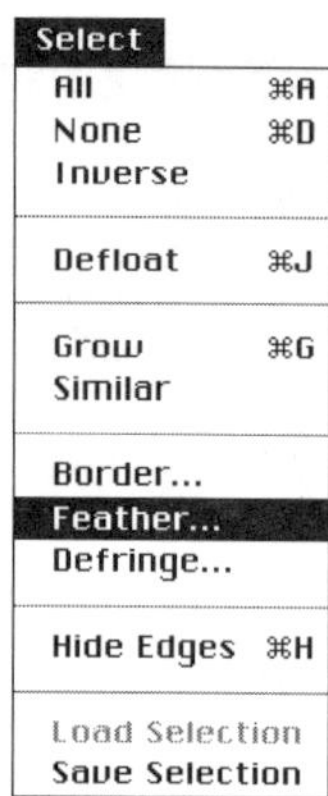

Figure 21. Choose **Feather** from the **Select** menu.

To feather a selection:

1. Choose Feather from the Select menu **(Figure 21)**.
2. Enter a number between 1 and 64 in the Feather Radius field **(Figure 22)**.
3. Click OK or press Return **(Figures 23-25)**.

✔ Tip

- To specify a Feather Radius for a selection before it is created, double-click the Rectangular Marquee, Elliptical Marquee, or Lasso tool and enter a number in the Feather Radius field **(Figure 23)**.

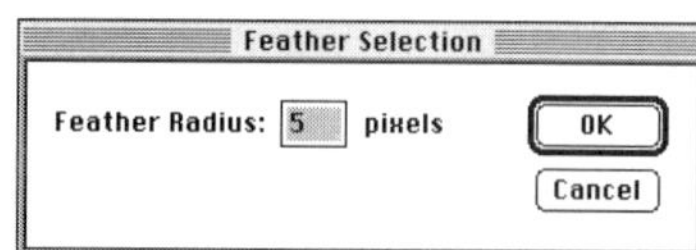

Figure 22. Enter a number between 1 and 64 in the **Feather Radius** field in the **Feather Selection** dialog box.

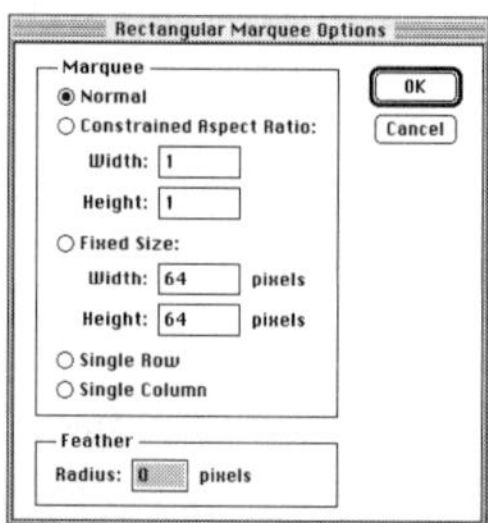

Figure 23. Double-click the **Rectangular Marquee** or **Elliptical Marquee tool**, then enter a number in the **Radius** field.

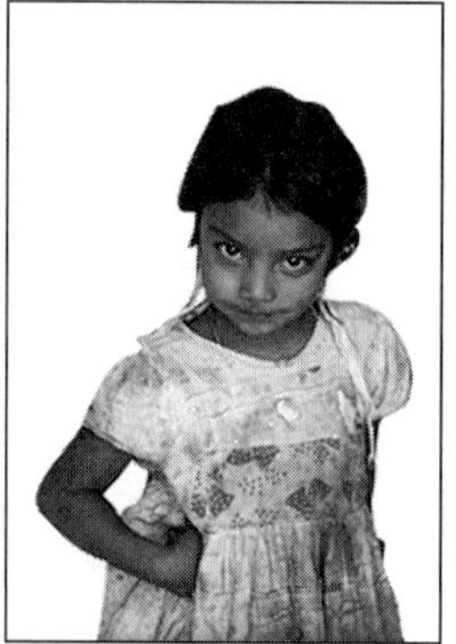

Figure 24. A selection copy with a Feather Radius of 0.

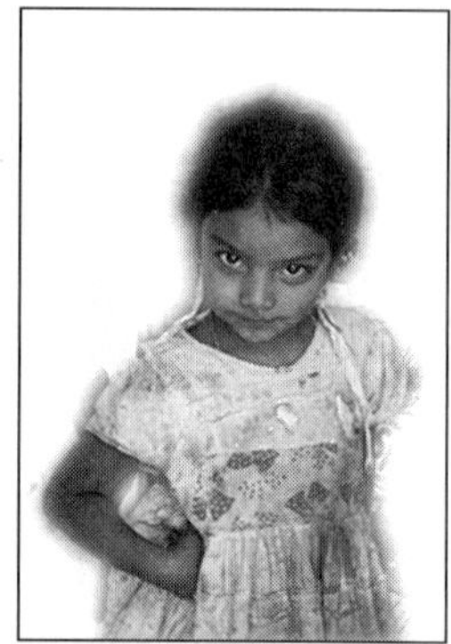

Figure 25. The same selection copy with a Feather Radius of 5 pixels.

Feather a Selection

Figure 26. An elliptical area of this picture was selected.

To vignette a picture:

1. Choose white as the Background color.
   (See pages 130-132)
2. Click the Rectangular Marquee or Elliptical Marquee tool and select an area of a picture **(Figure 26)**.
3. Choose Feather from the Select menu **(Figure 21)**.
4. Enter 15 or 20 in the Feather Radius field **(Figure 22)**.
5. Click OK or press Return.
6. Choose Inverse from the Select menu.
7. Press Delete **(Figures 27-28)**.

Figure 27. Auntie Alias, Uncle Fill and other relatives.

Figure 28. Another vignette.

Use the Defringe command to blend pixels on the edge of a moved or pasted selection with pixel colors from just inside the edge to eliminate a noticeable "seam." You can specify a width in pixels for the Defringe area.

To defringe a selection:

1. With the selection still floating, choose Defringe from the Select menu **(Figure 29)**.
2. Enter a number in the Width field. Try 1, 2 or 3 first **(Figure 30)**. The edge of the selection may lose definition if you specify too high a Width.
3. *Optional:* Reposition the selection.
   and/or
   Apply any Image or Filter menu command.
4. Choose None from the Select menu **(Figures 31-32)**.

Select
All ⌘A
None ⌘D
Inverse
Defloat ⌘J
Grow ⌘G
Similar
Border...
Feather...
Defringe...
Hide Edges ⌘H
Load Selection
Save Selection

Figure 29. Choose **Defringe** from the **Select** menu.

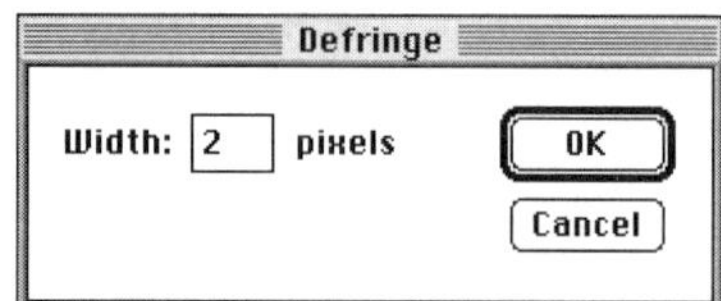

Figure 30. Enter 1, 2, or 3 in the **Width** field in the **Defringe** dialog box.

Figure 31. A pasted image before choosing the Defringe command. Note the white edge around the hat and the boy's head.

Figure 32. After applying the Defringe command.

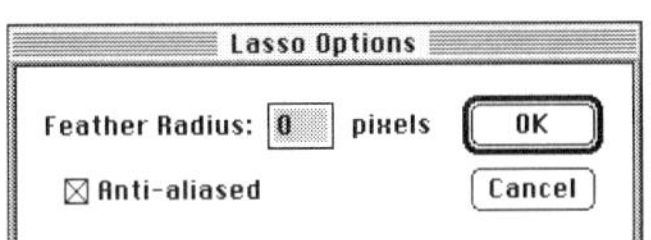

Figure 33. Double-click the **Lasso** or **Magic Wand** tool, then check the **Anti-aliased** box.

To turn on Anti-aliasing:

To turn on the Anti-aliased command for the Lasso or Magic Wand tool, double-click either tool and check the Anti-aliased box in the Options dialog box. The jagged edges of a selection made with either tool will be softened **(Figure 33)**.

Select
All ⌘A
None ⌘D
Inverse
Defloat ⌘J
Grow ⌘G
Similar
Border...
Feather...
Defringe...
Hide Edges ⌘H
Load Selection
Save Selection

Figure 34. Choose **Inverse** from the **Select** menu.

To switch the selected and unselected areas:

Choose Inverse from in the Select menu **(Figures 34-36)**.

✓ Tip

- Choose Inverse again to switch back.

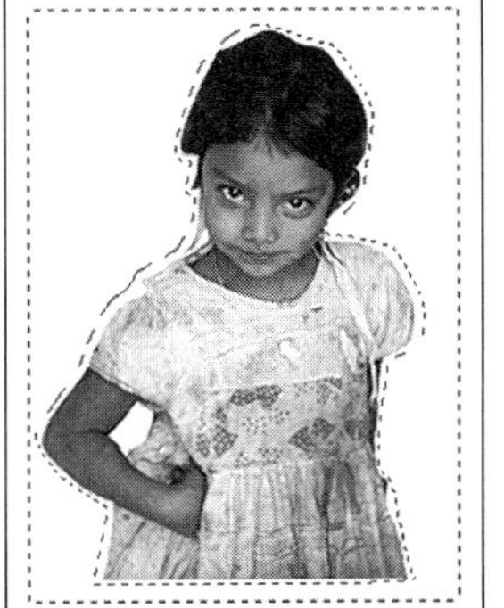

Figure 35. The background is selected using the Magic Wand tool.

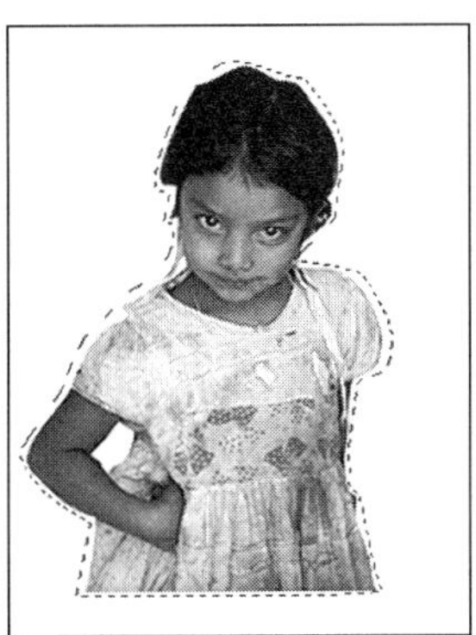

Figure 36. The Inverse command is chosen, and the girl is selected.

MASKS

Show Channels.

The Channels palette is used throughout this chapter. Choose Show Channels from the Window menu to display it **(Figure 1)**.

Window
New Window
Zoom In ⌘+
Zoom Out ⌘−
Show Rulers ⌘R
Hide Brushes
Show Channels
Hide Colors
Show Info
Hide Paths
✓Untitled-1 (CMYK, 1:1)

Figure 1. Choose **Show Channels** from the **Window** menu.

THIS CHAPTER covers two selection variations: alpha channels and Quick Mask mode.

You can save a selection to a specially created grayscale channel, called an **alpha channel**, and load the selection onto the picture at any time. For example, a selection with an irregular shape that would be difficult to reselect could be saved to an alpha channel. The instructions for creating shadow type on pages 118-121 include saving type to an alpha channel.

More than one alpha channel can be created in a document, but each channel increases the picture's storage size by approximately 25%. Alpha channels are accessed via the Channels palette **(Figure 2)**.

(See "Tip" on page 90 to convert an alpha channel to a path to reduce the storage size of a file)

Using Photoshop's **Quick Mask** mode, the selected or unselected areas of a picture can be covered with a semi-transparent colored mask, which can then be modified using any editing or painting tool. Unlike an alpha channel, a Quick Mask cannot be saved, but the new selection can be saved when you return to Standard (non-Quick Mask) mode.

Note: If you are unfamiliar with Photoshop's basic selection tools, read Chapters 5 and 6 before reading this chapter.

Picture modifications will write to any channel preceded by a **pencil** icon.

The **eye** icon indicates the channel is displayed.

Alpha channels.

Channels
RGB ⌘0
Red ⌘1
Green ⌘2
Blue ⌘3
#4 ⌘4
#5 ⌘5

Figure 2. The **Channels** palette.

To save a selection to a channel:

1. Select an area of a picture **(Figure 3)**. *(See pages 62-65)*
2. If no alpha channels have been created for the document, choose Save Selection from the Select menu. A new channel number will appear on the Channels palette **(Figures 4-5)**.
   or
   If an alpha channel has already been created for the document, choose New from the Save Selection pop-up menu under the Select menu.

✔ Tips

- You can save an alpha channel with a picture only in the Photoshop, TIFF or PICT (RGB) file formats. A warning prompt may appear if you attempt to save the picture in any other format **(Figure 6)**.
- If you save a floating selection to a channel, it will replace the underlying pixels in the picture.

Figure 3. Select an area of a picture.

Figure 4. Choose **Save Selection** from the **Select** menu (or choose New from the Save Selection pop-up menu).

Select
All ⌘A
None ⌘D
Inverse
Float ⌘J
Grow ⌘G
Similar
Border...
Feather...
Defringe...
Hide Edges ⌘H
Load Selection
Save Selection

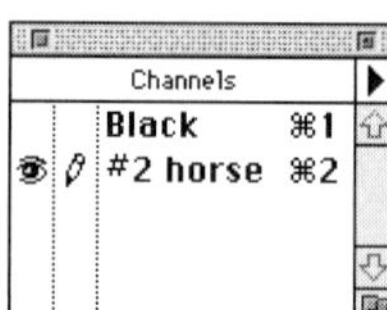

Figure 5. The new channel is listed on the **Channels** palette.

Figure 6. This warning prompt will appear if you attempt to save a picture as an alpha channel in other than the Photoshop, TIFF or PICT (RGB) formats.

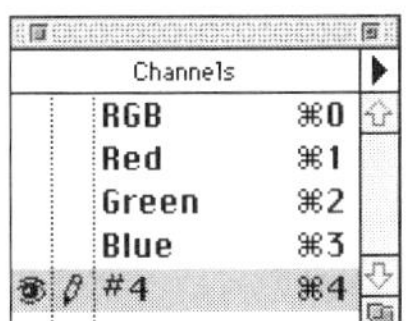

Figure 7 Click an alpha channel number on the **Channels** palette.

Figure 8. An alpha channel: the selected area is white, the protected area is black.

An alpha channel can be displayed without loading it onto the document as a selection.

To display a channel selection:

1. Click an alpha channel name on the Channels palette. The selected area will be white, the protected area black **(Figures 7-8)**.
2. To restore the normal picture display, click the top channel in the palette.

✔ Tips

- If the selection has a Feather radius, the faded area will be gray and will be partially affected by modifications.
- The mask can be modified with any editing or painting tool using black, gray, or white "paint."

Select
All ⌘A
None ⌘D
Inverse
Float ⌘J
Grow ⌘G
Similar
Border...
Feather...
Defringe...
Hide Edges ⌘H
Load Selection
Save Selection

Figure 9. Choose **Load Selection** from the **Select** menu.

To load a channel selection onto the picture:

1. If the composite picture is not displayed, click the top channel on the Channels palette.
2. Choose Load Selection from the Select menu **(Figure 9)**.
   or
   If there is more than one alpha channel, choose from the Load Selection pop-up menu under the Select menu.

✔ Tips

- If the Load Selection command is gray, there are no alpha channels.
- Any selected area of the picture will be deselected when you choose Load Selection.
- Choose Inverse from the Select menu to switch the selected and unselected areas.

You can superimpose an alpha channel selection as a colored mask over a picture, then reshape the mask.

To reshape a mask:

1. Make sure there is no selection on the picture.
2. Click an alpha channel name on the Channels palette. An eye icon will appear next to it **(Figure 10)**.
3. Click in the leftmost column at the top of the palette. An eye icon will appear. There should be only one pencil icon: next to the alpha channel name **(Figure 11)**.
4. Click the Pencil or Paintbrush tool on the Toolbox.
5. On the Brushes palette, choose a 100% Opacity.
   and
   Choose Normal mode.
6. Click the Default colors icon on the Toolbox to restore the Foreground color to black and the Background color to white **(Figure 12)**.
7. To enlarge the masked (protected) area, stroke on the cutout with black as the Foreground color **(Figure 13)**.
   or
   To enlarge the unmasked area, click the Switch colors icon on the Toolbox to make the Foreground color white, and stroke on the mask **(Figure 14)**.

✔ Tip

- Use a painting tool with an opacity setting of less than 100% to create a partial mask.

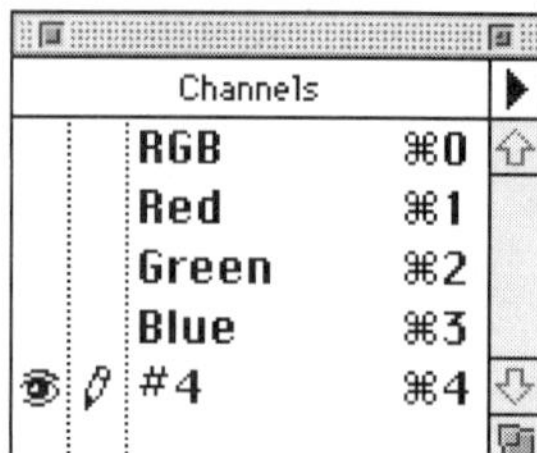

Figure 10. Click the alpha channel name on the **Channels** palette.

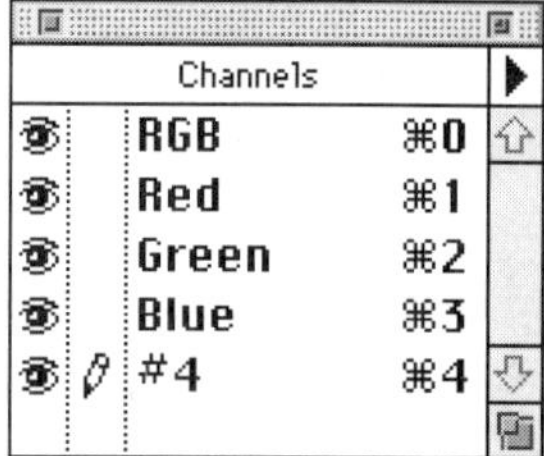

Figure 11. Click in the leftmost column at the top of the palette. Make sure the Pencil icon only appears next to the alpha channel name.

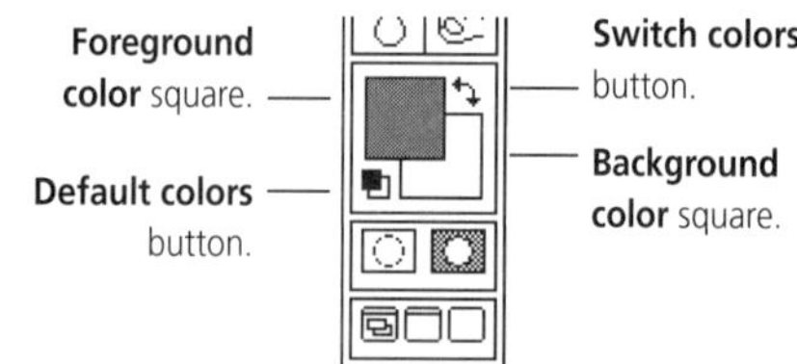

Figure 12. The **Toolbox**.

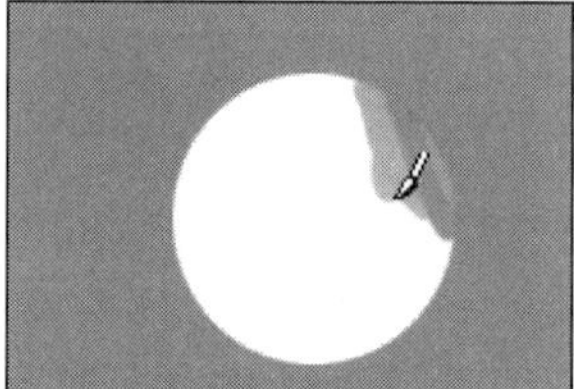

Figure 13. Enlarge the masked area by stroking on the cutout with black as the Foreground color.

Figure 14. Enlarge the unmasked area by stroking on the mask with white as the Foreground color.

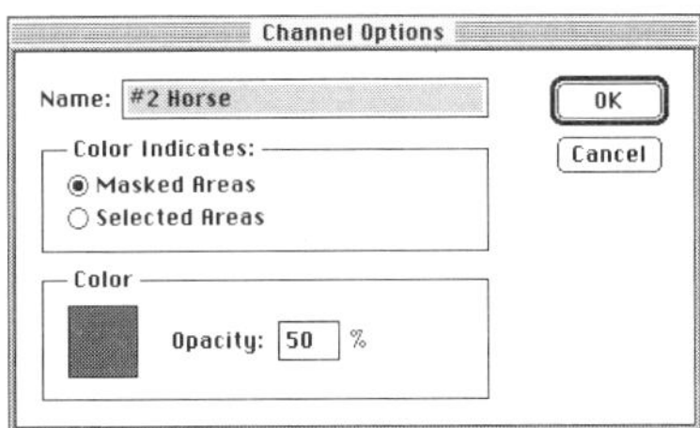

Figure 15. In the **Channel Options** dialog box, enter a new name in the **Name** field.

Figure 16. The horse is selected.

Figure 17. The horse is still selected, but it is now black instead of white.

To rename a channel:

1. Double-click a channel name on the Channels palette.
   or
   Click a channel name, then choose Channel Options from the pop-up menu on the right side of the palette.
2. Enter a new name in the Name field **(Figure 15)**.
3. Click OK or press Return.

✔ Tip

- Normally, the selected areas of an alpha channel are white and the protected areas are black or colored. To reverse these colors without changing which area is selected, double-click an alpha channel name on the Channels palette, then click Selected Areas **(Figures 16-17)**.

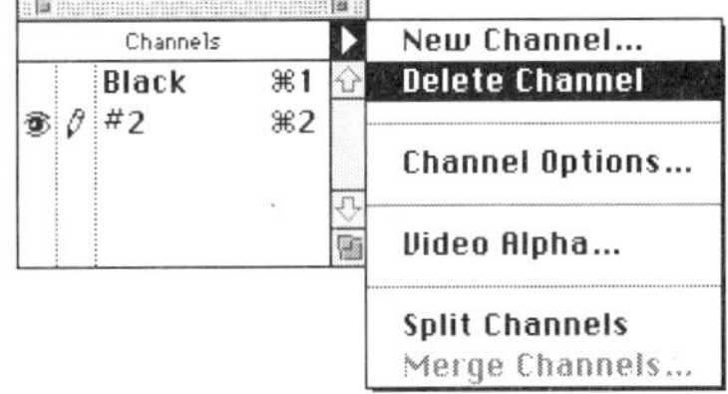

Figure 18. Click the name of the channel to be deleted, then choose **Delete Channel**.

To delete a channel:

1. Click a channel name on the Channels palette.
2. Choose Delete Channel from the pop-up menu on the right side of the palette **(Figure 18)**

If you choose Quick Mask mode when an area of a picture is selected, a semi-transparent tinted mask will cover the unselected areas and the selected areas will be revealed in a cutout. The cutout or mask can be modified with the Pencil or Paintbrush tool. Unlike an alpha channel, a Quick Mask cannot be saved in Quick Mask mode.

Figure 19. An area of a picture is selected.

To create a Quick Mask:

1. Select an area of a picture **(Figure 19)**.
   (See pages 62-65)
2. Click the Quick Mask icon. A mask will cover part of the picture **(Figures 20-21)**.
3. Click the Pencil or Paintbrush tool.
4. On the Brushes palette, click a tip.
   and
   Move the Opacity slider to 100%.
   and
   Choose Normal from the Mode pop-up menu.
5. Click the Default Colors button on the Toolbox **(Figure 20)**.
6. Stroke on the cutout to enlarge the masked (protected) area.
   or
   Click the Switch Colors button on the Toolbox to make the Foreground color white, then stroke on the mask to enlarge the cutout (unmasked area).
7. Click the Standard mode icon to turn off Quick Mask **(Figure 20)**. The selection will still be active.
8. Modify the picture. Only the unmasked area will be affected.
9. *Optional:* Save the selection to an alpha channel to preserve it for later use.
   (See page 82)

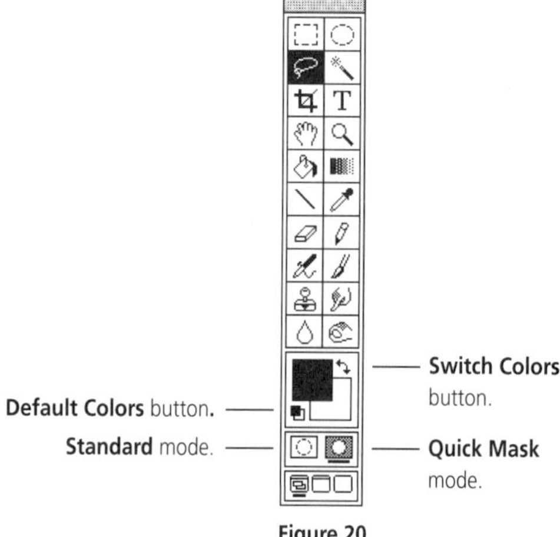

Figure 20.

Figure 21. The unselected area is covered with a mask.

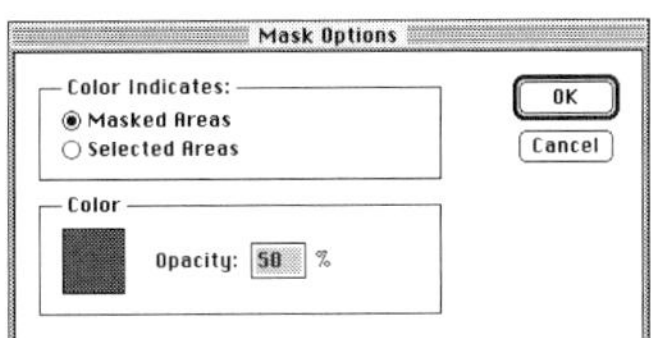

Figure 22. In the **Mask Options** dialog box, choose whether **Color Indicates Masked Areas** or **Selected Areas**, or click the **Color** square to choose a mask color.

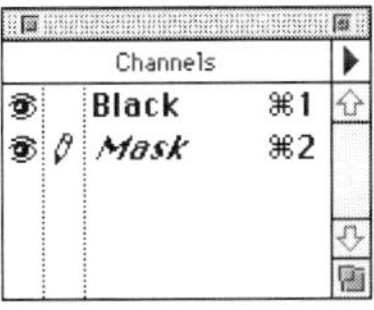

Figure 23. "Mask" appears on the **Channels** palette. To open the Mask Options dialog box, double-click "Mask," or double-click the Quick Mask icon on the Toolbox.

✔ Tips

- To create a selection by hand, click the Pencil or Paintbrush tool, double-click the Quick Mask icon, click Selected Areas, then stroke on the picture. Use a soft-edged brush to produce a soft-edged mask.
- To cover the Selected Areas with a mask instead of the protected areas, double-click the Quick Mask icon on the Toolbox, then click Selected Areas **(Figure 22)**. To quickly switch the mask Color between the selected and masked areas, hold down Option and click the Quick Mask icon on the Toolbox.

  In the Mask Options dialog box, you can also click the Color box and choose a new mask color or modify the Opacity of the mask.
- When you click the Quick Mask icon, the Foreground color defaults to black and the Background color to white. The previous Foreground and Background colors are not restored when you return to Standard mode. To preserve a color, add it to the Colors palette before clicking the Quick Mask icon.
  (See page 133)
- "Mask" will be listed on the Channels palette while Quick Mask mode is on **(Figure 23)**.
- If you modify a Quick Mask using a tool with a low opacity, that area will be partially affected by modifications. If you then choose Standard mode, the area will remain partially protected, but will not be bordered by a selection marquee.

PATHS 8

Show Paths.

The Paths palette is used throughout this chapter. Choose Show Paths from the Window menu to display it **(Figure 1)**.

Window
New Window
Zoom In ⌘+
Zoom Out ⌘-
Show Rulers ⌘R
Hide Brushes
Hide Channels
Hide Colors
Show Info
Show Paths
✓Untitled-2 (RGB, 1:1)

Figure 1. Choose **Show Paths** from the **Window** menu.

LIKE THE Pen tool in Adobe Illustrator, the Pen tool in Photoshop is used to create outline shapes, called paths, consisting of anchor points connected by curved or straight line segments. A path can be reshaped by adding, deleting, or moving its anchor points. A curved line segment can also be reshaped by adjusting its Bezier direction lines.

The Pen tool and its variations are chosen from, and paths are displayed, using the Paths palette **(Figure 2)**. There is no Pen tool in the Toolbox.

A path can be saved, converted into a selection, or exported to and used as a path in Adobe Illustrator. You can also convert a selection into a path.

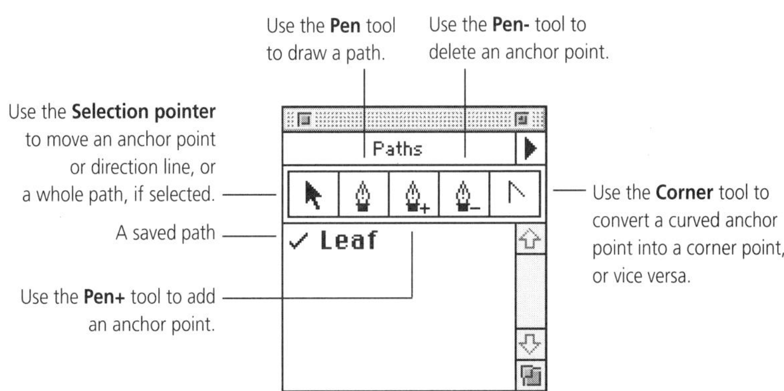

Figure 2. The **Paths** palette.

To convert a selection into a path:

1. Select an area of a picture **(Figure 3)**. *(See pages 62-65)*
2. Choose Make Path from the pop-up menu on the right side of the Paths palette **(Figure 4)**.
3. Enter 3, 4, or 5 in the Tolerance field. The minimum is 0.5; the maximum is 10. At a low Tolerance value, many anchor points will be created and the path will conform precisely to the selection marquee. At a high Tolerance value, fewer anchor points will be created so the path will be smoother, but it will conform less precisely to the selection **(Figure 5)**.
4. Click OK or press Return **(Figure 6)**.

✔ **Tip**

- When a path is saved with a picture, the storage size of the picture does not increase, unlike when an alpha channel is saved with a picture. To save storage space, you can convert an alpha channel into a selection and then into a path, save the path, delete the alpha channel, then save the picture. Later on you can convert the path back into a selection and save the selection to a new alpha channel.

  Follow the instructions on page 83 to load an alpha channel selection. Follow steps 2-4 on this page and the steps on page 93 to save the path. Then click the alpha channel name on the Channels palette, choose Delete Channel from the pop-up menu on the right side of the palette, and save the picture. Follow the instructions on page 94 later if you need to convert the path back into a selection.

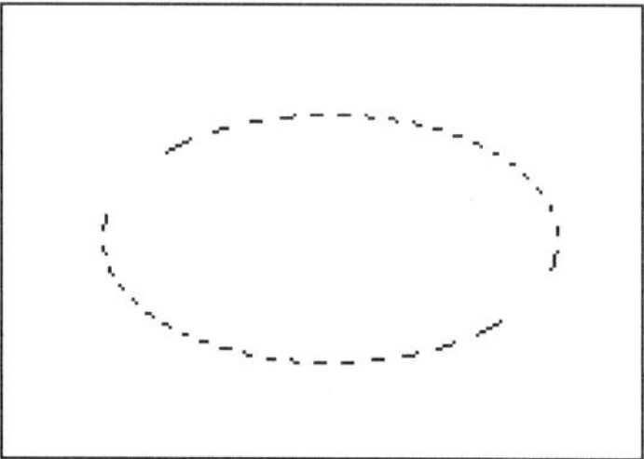

Figure 3. Select an area of a picture.

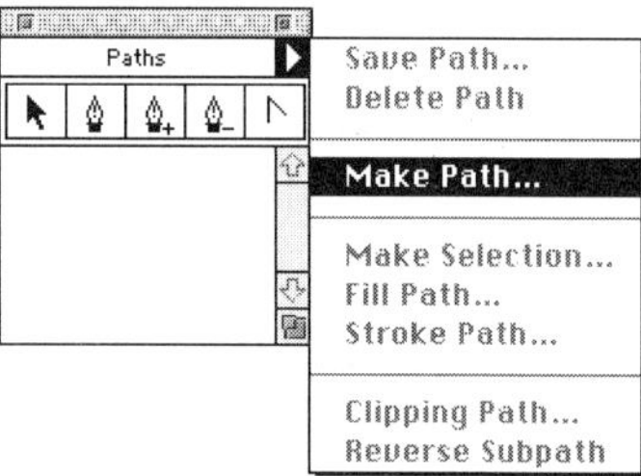

Figure 4. Choose **Make Path** from the **Paths** palette.

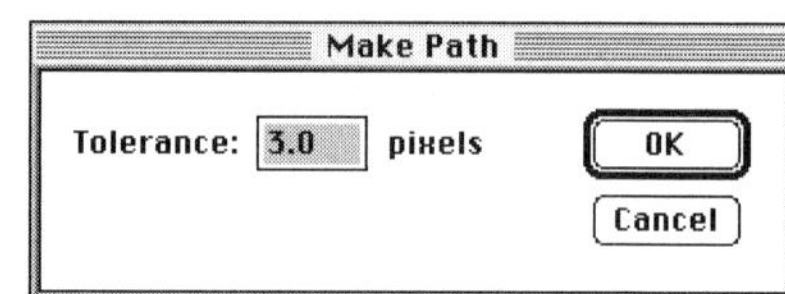

Figure 5. Enter a number in the **Tolerance** field in the **Make Path** dialog box.

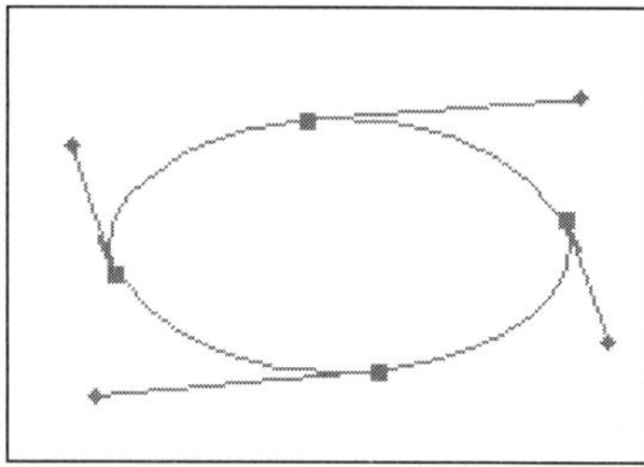

Figure 6. A selection converted into a path.

Double-click the **Pen** tool on the Paths palette.

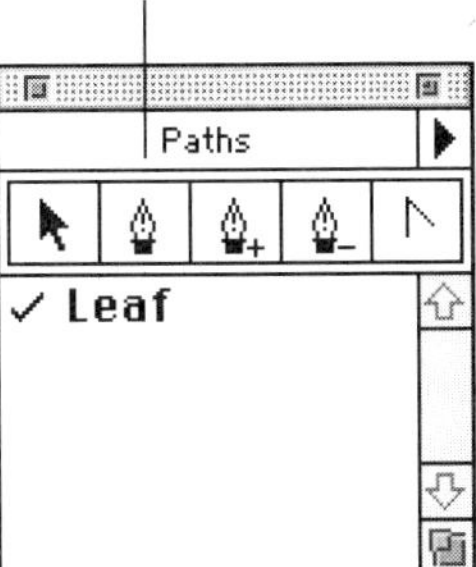

Figure 7.

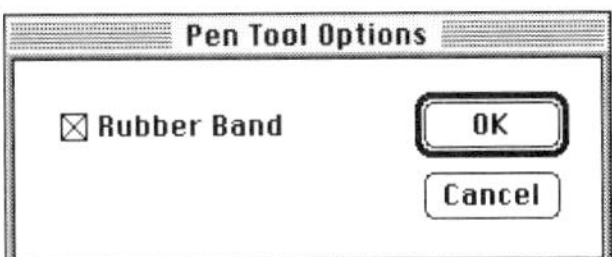

Figure 8. Check the **Rubber Band** box in the **Pen Tool Options** dialog box.

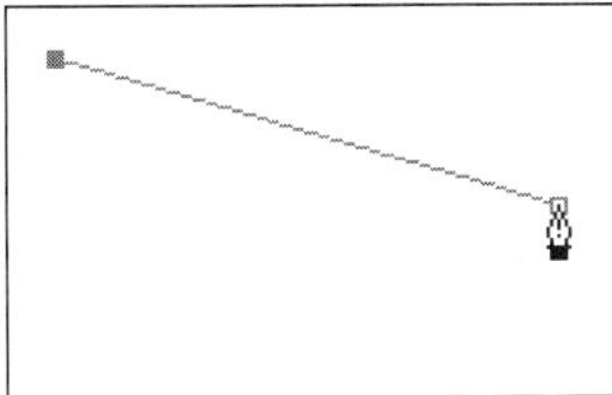

Figure 9. Click to create straight sides.

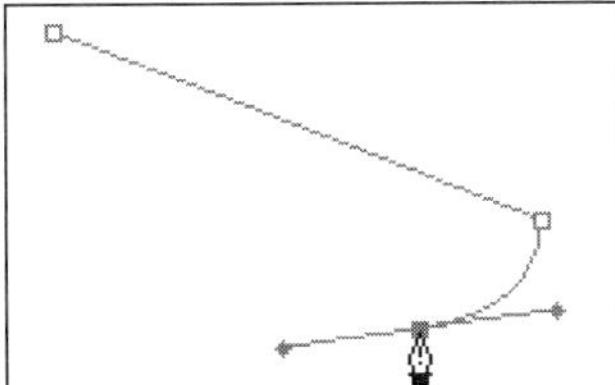

Figure 10. Press and drag to create a curved segment.

Click with the Pen tool to create anchor points connected by straight line segments. Press and drag with the Pen tool to create anchor points connected by curved line segments (Bezier curves).

To create a path using the Pen tool:

1. Double-click the Pen tool on the Paths palette **(Figure 7)**.
2. Check the Rubber Band box to preview the line segments as you draw **(Figure 8)**.
3. Click OK or press Return.
4. Click, move the mouse, then click again to create a straight segment.
   or
   Press and drag to create a curved segment, then release the mouse. Direction lines will appear **(Figures 9-13)**.
5. Repeat step 3 as many times as necessary to complete the shape.
6. To leave the path open, click the Selection pointer on the Paths palette or choose a different Tool from the Toolbox.
   or
   To close the path, click on the starting point (a small circle will appear next to the pen pointer icon).

✔ Tips

- Hold down Shift while clicking to constrain a straight line segment to the nearest 45° angle.
- Press Delete to erase the last anchor point created. Press Delete twice to delete the entire path.
- To use the Pen tool at its optimal speed, make sure the Direct Bits plug-in module is installed in the Plug-ins folder in the Photoshop folder.

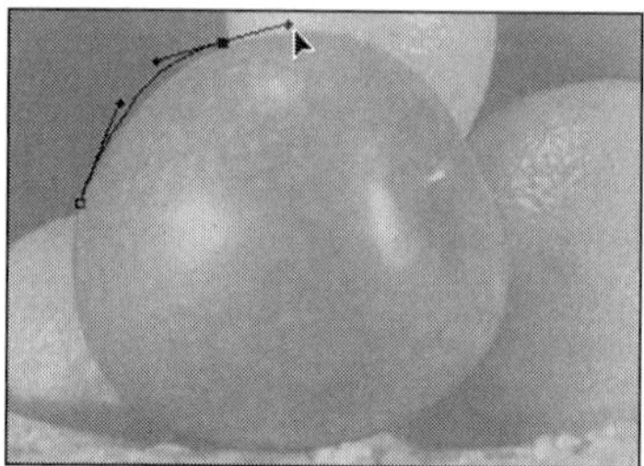

Figure 11. Press and drag to create curved segments around a shape.

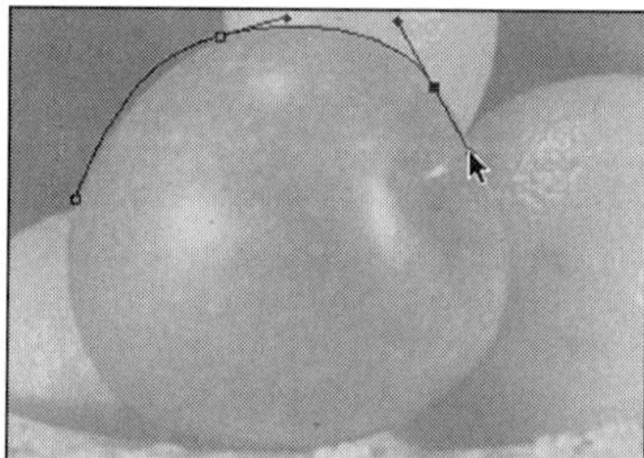

Figure 12. A third anchor point is created.

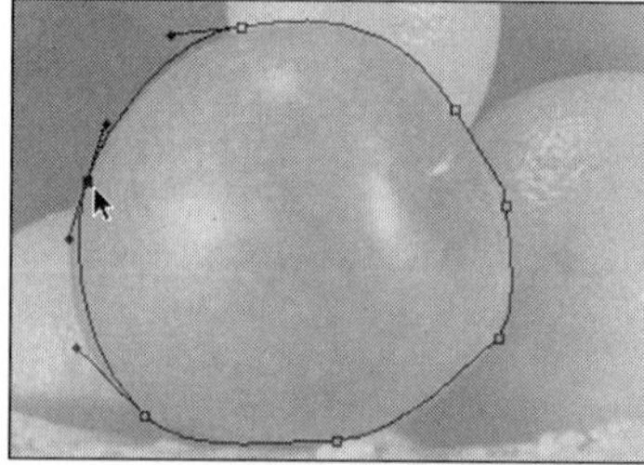

Figure 13. The completed path.

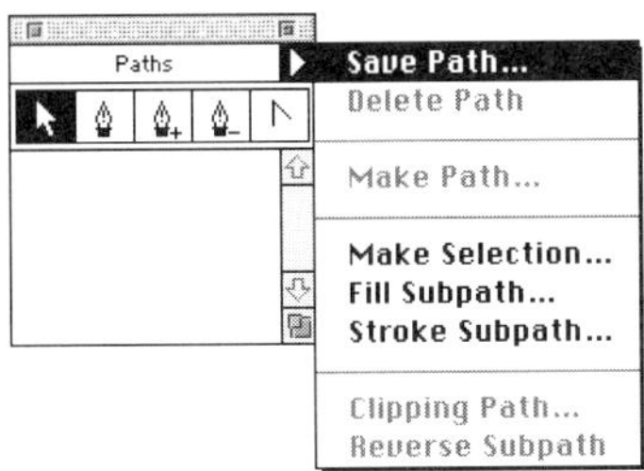

Figure 14. Choose **Save Path** from the Paths palette.

To save a path:

1. Choose Save Path from the pop-up menu on the right side of the Paths palette **(Figure 14)**.
2. Enter a name **(Figure 15)**.
3. Click OK or press Return. The path name will appear on the palette **(Figure 16)**.

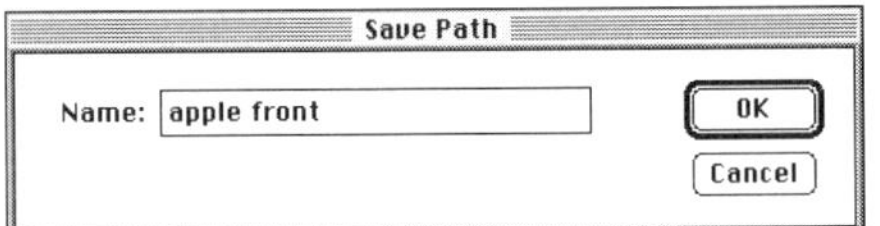

Figure 15. Enter a **Name** in the **Save Path** dialog box. All currently displayed paths will be saved under one name.

To display a path:

Click a path name on the Paths palette **(Figure 16)**.

To hide a path:

Click on the white area on the Paths palette below the path name.

To select a path:

1. Click a path name on the Paths palette **(Figure 16)**.
2. Click the Selection pointer.
3. Click on the path.

✓ **Tip**

- To select all the anchor points on a path, hold down Option and click on the path. An entire path can be moved when all its points are selected.

To deselect a path:

1. Click the Selection pointer.
2. Click outside the path.

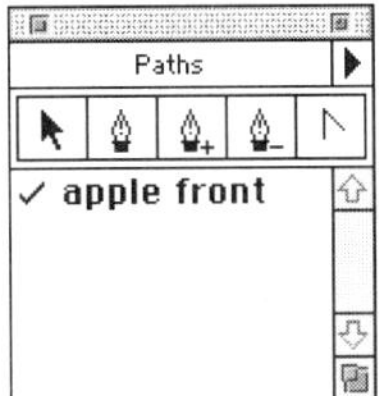

Figure 16. To display a saved path, click its name on the Paths palette.

To delete a path:

1. On the Paths palette, click the path to be deleted. A check mark will appear next to it **(Figure 17)**.
2. Choose Delete Path from the pop-up menu on the right side of the palette.

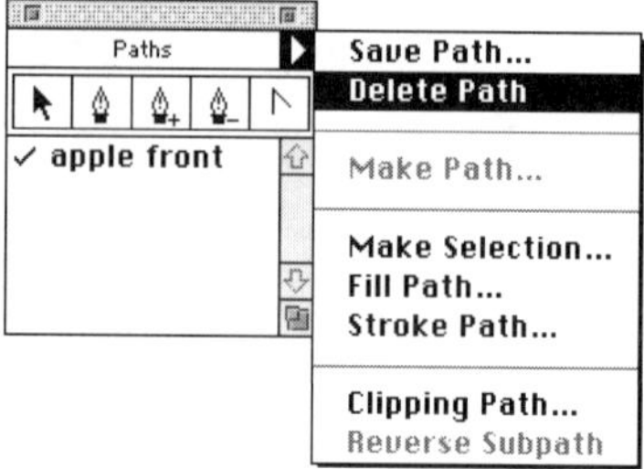

Figure 17. Click a path name, then choose **Delete Path** from the pop-up menu.

To convert a path into a selection:

1. Create a new path or display a saved path.
2. Choose Make Selection from the pop-up menu on the right side of the palette **(Figure 18)**.
3. *Optional:* To feather the selection, enter a number in the Feather Radius field **(Figure 19)**. Enter a low number to soften the edge slightly.
4. Click OK or press Return. The selection will appear on top of the path.

✔ **Tip**

- To move the selection, click any selection tool, then hold down ⌘ and Option and drag the selection.

(See also "Feather a selection" on page 76)

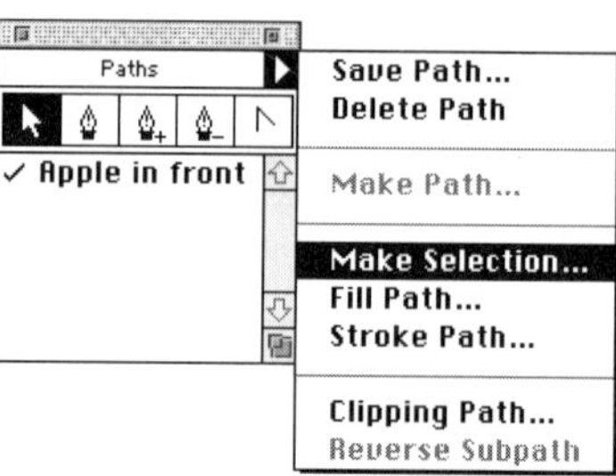

Figure 18. Choose **Make Selection** from the **Paths** palette.

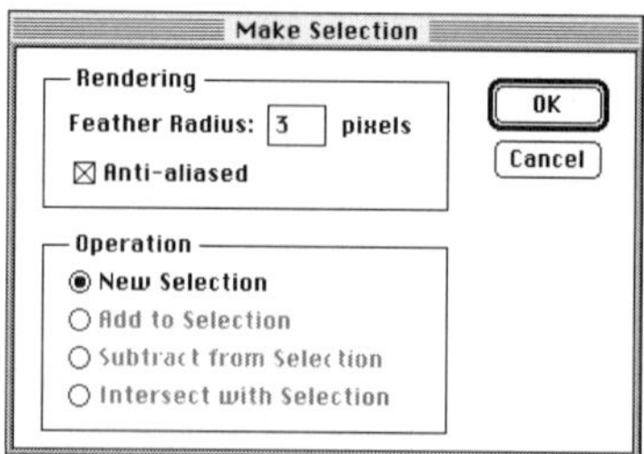

Figure 19. To feather the edge of the selection, enter a number in the **Feather Radius** field in the **Make Selection** dialog box.

Figure 20. Click a path name, then click the **Selection** pointer.

You can drag, add, or delete an anchor point to reshape a path. To modify the shape of a curved line segment, move a direction line toward or away from its anchor point or rotate it around its anchor point.

To reshape a path:

1. *Optional:* To reshape a saved path, click a path name on the Paths palette **(Figure 20)**.
2. Click the Selection pointer on the Paths palette.
3. Click on the path to select it.
4. Drag an anchor point **(Figure 21)**.
   and/or
   Drag or rotate a direction line **(Figure 22)**.
5. Click outside the path to deselect it.
   or
   Click a different tool on the Toolbox.

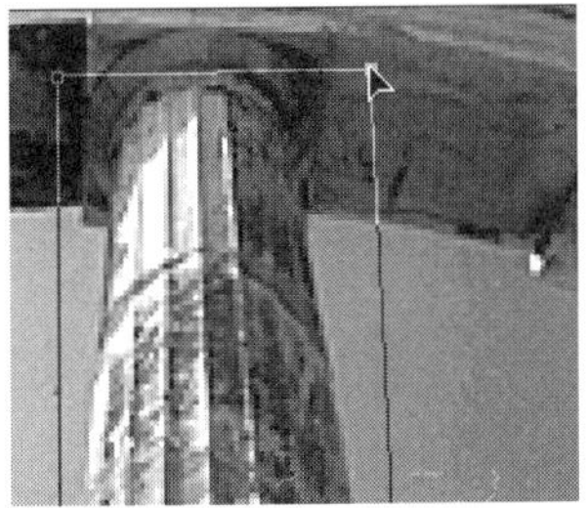

Figure 21. Drag an anchor point.

✔ Tips

- To add an anchor point to a path, click the Pen+ tool, then click on a line segment.
- To delete an anchor point from a path, click the Pen– tool, then click on the anchor point.
- Use the Corner tool to rotate half of a direction line independently. Once the Corner tool has been used on part of a direction line, you can use the Selection pointer to move the other part.
- To convert a curved point into a corner point, click the Corner tool, then click the anchor point (deselect the Corner tool by clicking another tool). To convert a corner point into a curved point, click the Corner tool, then drag the anchor point.
- Once a path has been saved, it is resaved automatically each time it is modified.

Figure 22. Pull or rotate a direction line of a curved anchor point.

Use the Stroke Path command to apply color to the edge of a path.

To stroke a path:

1. Create a new path or display an existing path.
2. Click the Pencil, Paintbrush, Airbrush, Rubber Stamp, Sharpen/Blur, Dodge/Burn, or Smudge tool.
3. If the Brushes palette is not displayed, choose Show Brushes from the Window menu.
4. On the Brushes palette, click a tip **(Figure 23)**.
   and
   Choose a mode.
   (See page 147)
   and
   Move the Opacity (or Pressure) slider.
5. Choose a Foreground color.
   (See pages 130-132)
6. Choose Stroke Path from the pop-up menu on the right side of the Paths palette **(Figure 24)**. The path will be stroked with the tool you chose and its current attributes **(Figure 25)**.

✓ Tip

- If you do not have a painting or editing tool highlighted when you choose Stroke Path from the Paths palette, the Stroke Path dialog box will open. The current attributes for each tool will apply **(Figure 26)**.

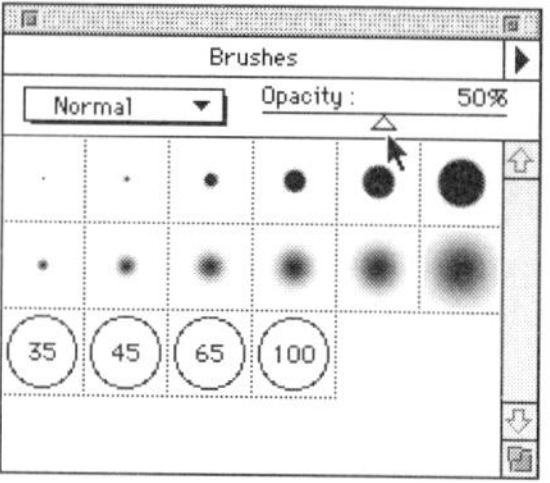

Figure 23. On the **Brushes** palette, choose a Mode, Opacity (or Pressure) and soft-edged or hard-edged tip.

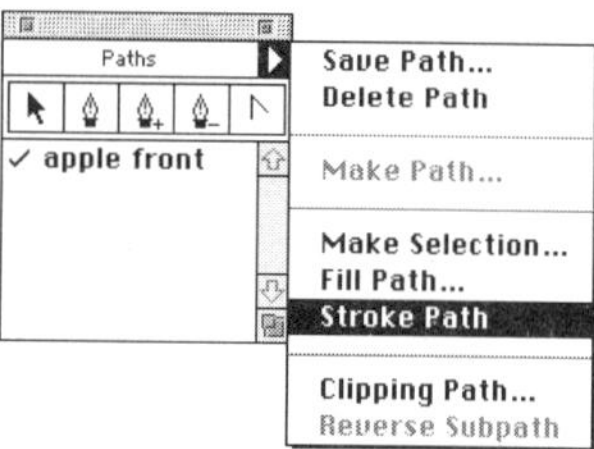

Figure 24. Choose **Fill Path** or **Stroke Path** from the pop-up menu on the **Paths** palette.

Figure 25. This glowing line was created by creating a path, clicking the Paintbrush tool, moving the Opacity slider to 30%, and choosing Stroke Path from the Paths palette.

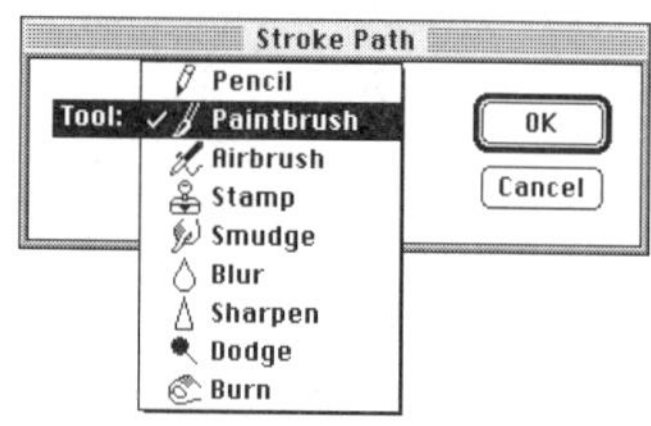

Figure 26. Choose from the **Tool** pop-up menu in the **Stroke Path** dialog box.

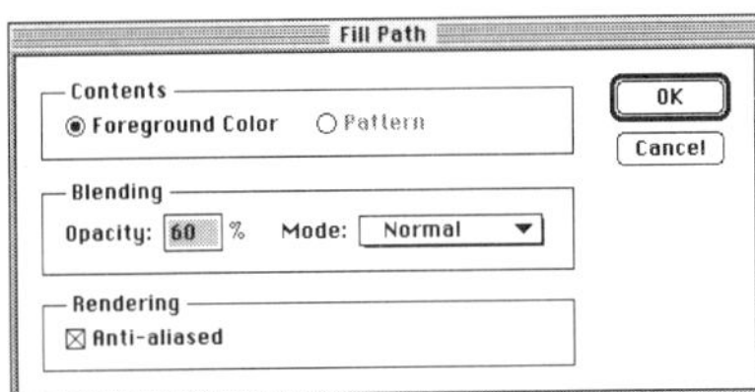

Figure 27. In the **Fill Path** dialog box, enter an **Opacity** and choose a **Mode**.

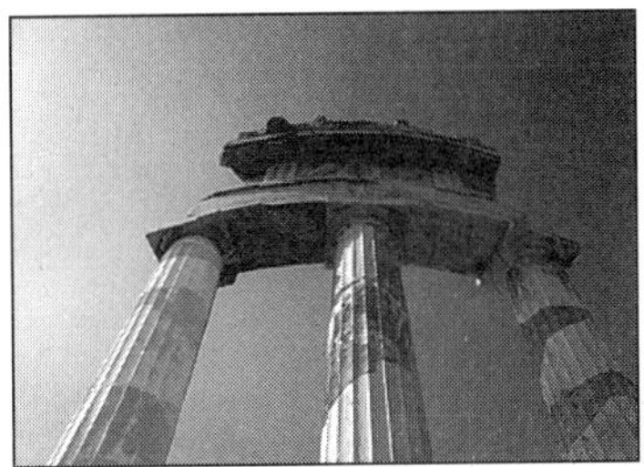

Figure 28. The left column was filled with white at an Opacity of 40%.

Use the Fill Path command to fill a path with the Foreground color.

To fill a path:

1. Create a new path or display an existing path.
2. Choose a Foreground color. *(See pages 130-132)*
3. Choose Fill Path from the pop-up menu on the right side of the palette **(Figure 24)**.
4. Enter an Opacity **(Figure 27)**.
   and
   Choose a Mode.
5. Click OK or Press Return **(Figure 28)**.

✓ **Tip**

- You can stroke or fill an open or closed path.

Fill a Path

A path created in Photoshop can be exported to Adobe Illustrator and used as a path in that program. For example, you can create a path in Photoshop, add type to it in Illustrator, then place it back in the Photoshop document **(Figure 31)**. *(See "Place an Adobe Illustrator picture" on page 39)*

To export a path to Adobe Illustrator:

1. Create a path or click a path name on the Paths palette.
2. Choose Paths to Illustrator from the Export pop-up menu under the File menu **(Figure 29)**.
3. *Optional:* Modify the name in the "Export paths to file" field.
4. Choose a location in which to save the path file **(Figure 30)**.
5. Click Save.

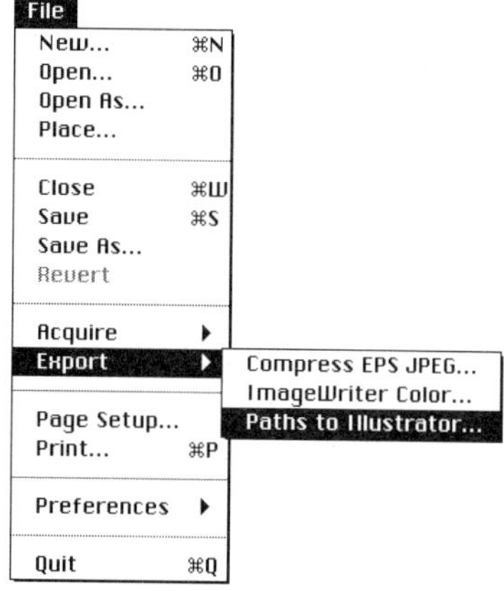

Figure 29. Choose **Paths to Illustrator** from the **Export** pop-up menu under the **File** menu.

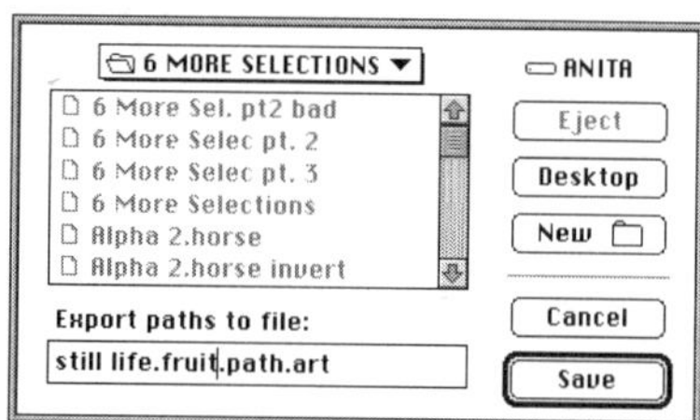

Figure 30. Choose a location in which to save the path, then click **Save**.

Figure 31. To create this illustration, a path was exported to Adobe Illustrator, where type was added to it. The type was then added to the Photoshop picture using the Place command.

LIGHTS & DARKS

The Preview check box.

Dialog boxes opened from the Map and Adjust pop-up menus (Image menu) have a Preview box. Changes affect the entire screen with the Preview box unchecked. Changes preview only in the picture or in a selection with the Preview box checked. CMYK color displays more acccurately with Preview on.

To reset a dialog box.

To undo changes made in a dialog box, hold down Option and click the Reset button.

THIS CHAPTER covers the adjustment of light and dark values using dialog boxes opened from the Map and Adjust pop-up menus under the Image menu, and using the Dodge/Burn tool.

You can make one-step modifications by choosing any command from the **Map** pop-up menu under the Image menu. For example, you can Invert a picture to make it look like a film negative, Posterize it to decrease the number of shades, or change all the pixels to black and white to make it high contrast.

You can precisely adjust lightness or contrast in a picture's highlights, midtones, or shadows using dialog boxes opened from the **Adjust** pop-up menu under the Image menu. All the Adjust dialog boxes are available for a picture in a color mode. Only the Levels, Curves, Brightness/Contrast, and Variations dialog boxes are available for a picture in Grayscale mode.

Finally, a large or small area of a picture can be darkened or lightened by dragging over it with the **Dodge/Burn** tool.

All the commands discussed in this chapter can be applied to a color picture, but try applying them to a grayscale picture first to learn how they work.

(See "Appendix A: Glossary," for definitions of *Contrast, Film negative, Grayscale, Highlights, Histogram, Invert, Lightness, Luminosity, Midtones, Posterize, and Shadows*)

Choose the Invert command to make a picture look like a film negative. Each pixel will be replaced with its opposite brightness and color value.

To invert a picture's lights and darks:

Choose Invert from the Map pop-up menu under the Image menu **(Figures 1-3)**.

or

Hold down ⌘ and press "I."

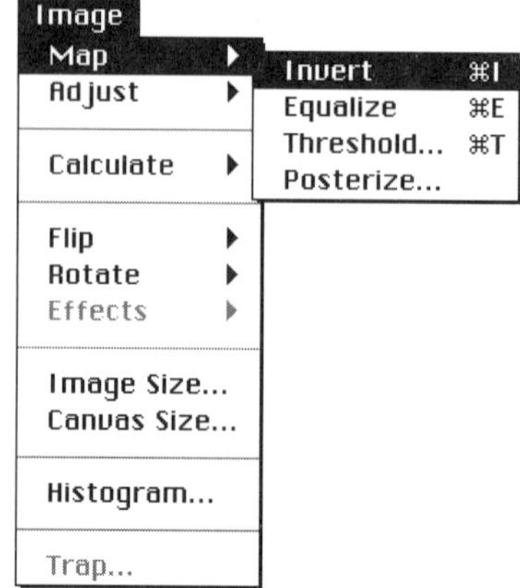

Figure 1. Choose **Invert** from the **Map** pop-up menu under the **Image** menu.

Figure 2. The original picture.

Figure 3. After choosing the Invert command.

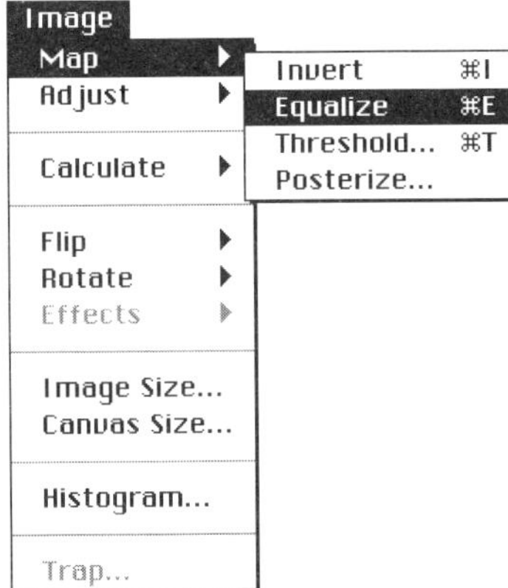

Figure **4.** Choose **Equalize** from the **Map** pop-up menu under the **Image** menu.

Use the Equalize command to redistribute a picture's light and dark values. It may improve a picture that lacks contrast or is too dark.

To equalize a picture's lights and darks:

Choose Equalize from the Map pop-up menu under the Image menu **(Figures 4-6)**.

or

Hold down ⌘ and press "E".

 **Tip**

- To limit the Equalize effect to a portion of a picture, select an area, then click Select Area Only in the Equalize dialog box. To equalize a picture based on the values within the selected area, click Entire Image Based on Area.

Figure 5. The original picture.

Figure 6. After choosing the Equalize command.

Use the Threshold dialog box to make a picture high contrast by converting color or gray pixels into only black and white pixels.

To make a picture high contrast:

1. Choose Threshold from the Map pop-up menu under the Image menu **(Figure 7)**.
   or
   Hold down ⌘ and press "T".
2. Move the slider to the right to increase the number of black pixels **(Figure 8)**.
   or
   Move the slider to the left to increase the number of white pixels.
   or
   Enter a number between 1 and 255 in the Threshold Level field. Shades above this number will become white, shades below become black.
3. Click OK or press Return **(Figure 9-10)**.

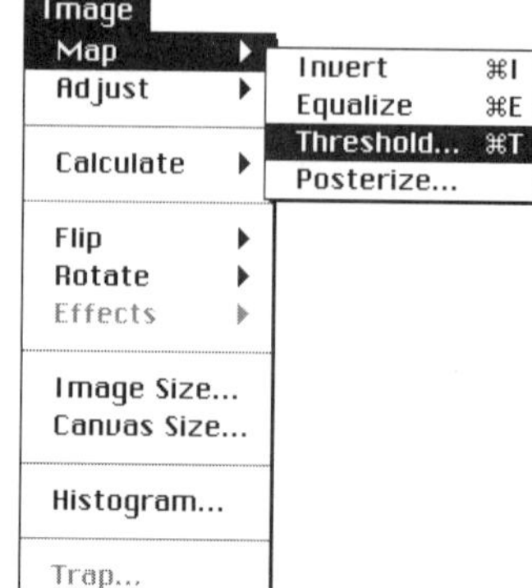

Figure 7. Choose **Threshold** from the **Map** pop-up menu under the **Image** menu.

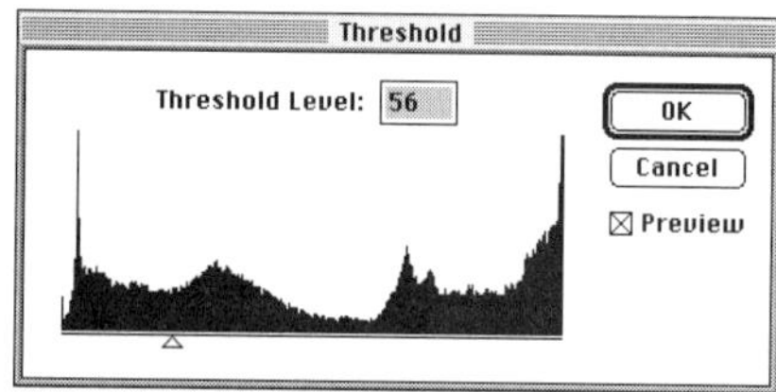

Figure 8. In the **Threshold** dialog box, enter a number in the **Threshold Level** field or move the slider.

Figure 9. The original picture.

Figure 10. After choosing the Threshold command.

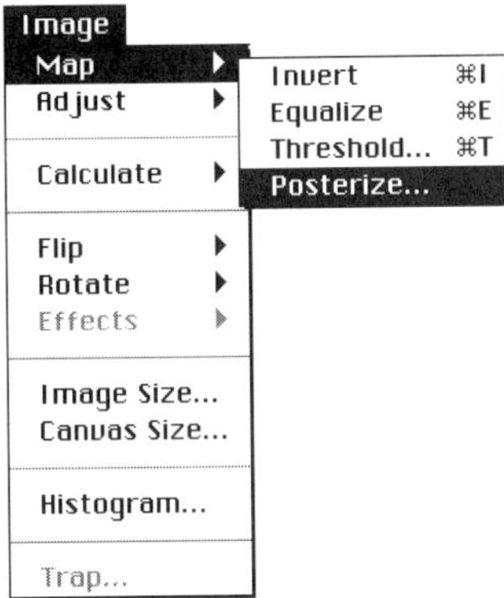

Figure 11. Choose **Posterize** from the **Map** pop-up menu under the **Image** menu.

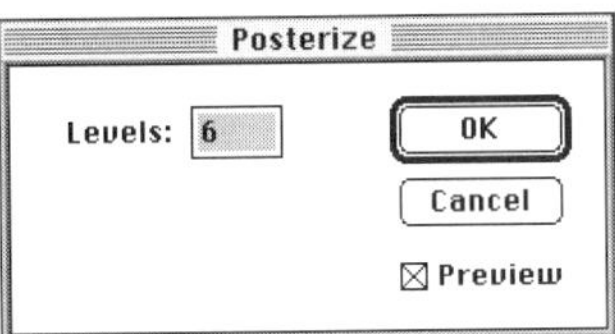

Figure 12. Enter a number between 2 and 255 in the **Levels** field in the **Posterize** dialog box.

Use the Posterize command to reduce the number of value levels in a picture.

To posterize a picture:

1. Choose Posterize from the Map pop-up menu under the Image menu **(Figure 11)**.
2. Enter a number between 2 and 255 in the Levels field. To produce a dramatic effect, enter a number below 15.
3. Click OK or press Return **(Figure 12-14)**.

✓ Tip

- If the number of shades is reduced using the Posterize command and the picture is saved, the original shade information will be permanently lost. Choose Undo from the Edit menu to undo the Posterize command.

Figure 13. The original picture.

Figure 14. After choosing the Posterize command.

To adjust a picture's brightness and contrast (method 1):

1. Choose Brightness/Contrast from the pop-up Adjust menu under the Image menu **(Figure 15)**.
   or
   Hold down ⌘ and press "B."
2. To lighten the picture, move the Brightness slider to the right **(Figure 16)**.
   or
   To darken the picture, move the Brightness slider to the left.
   or
   Enter a number between -100 and 100 in the Brightness field.
3. To increase the contrast, move the Contrast slider to the right.
   or
   To lessen the contrast, move the Contrast slider to the left. With the slider in the leftmost position, the picture will be solid gray.
   or
   Enter a number between -100 and 100 in the Contrast field.
4. Click OK or press Return **(Figures 17-19)**.

✔ Tip

- When you move a slider in any of the Adjust pop-up menu dialog boxes, note its position relative to the other sliders and how the picture changes.

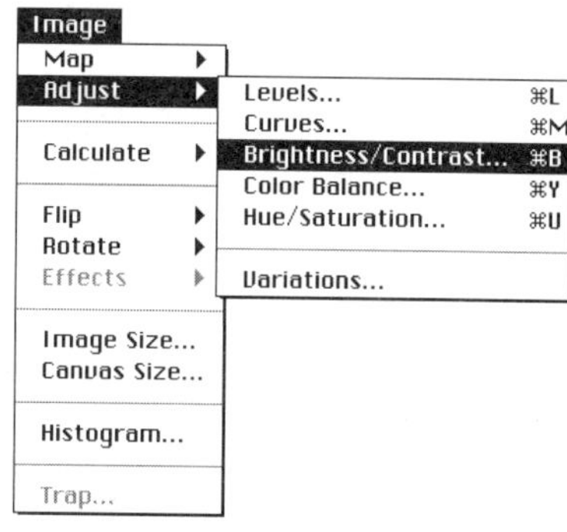

Figure 15. Choose **Brightness/Contrast** from the **Adjust** pop-up menu under the **Image** menu.

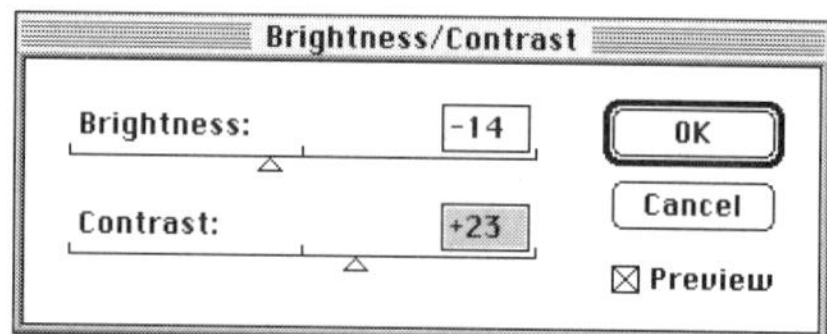

Figure 16. In the **Brigntness/Contrast** dialog box, move the sliders or enter numbers in the fields.

Figure 17. The original picture.

Figure 18. Brightness and contrast adjusted.

Figure 19. The Brightness slider moved right.

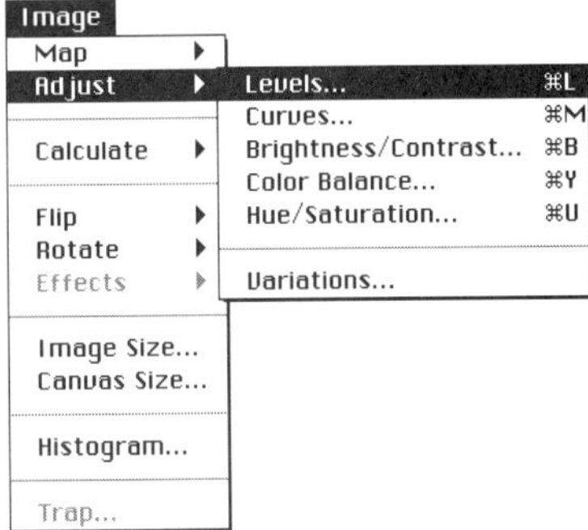

Figure 20. Choose **Levels** from the **Adjust** pop-up menu under the **Image** menu.

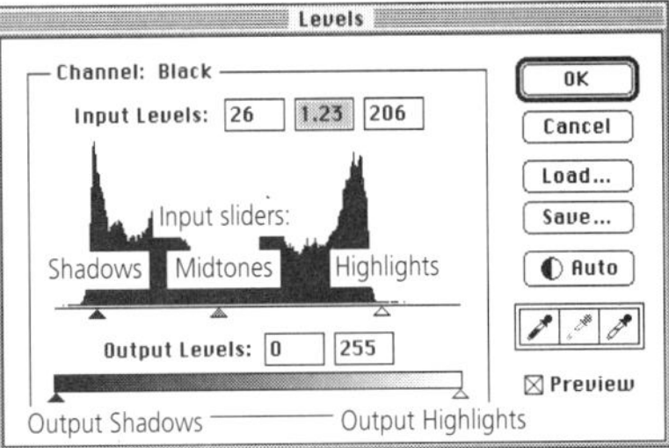

Figure 21. Move any of the Input or Output sliders in the **Levels** dialog box.

Figure 22. The original picture.

Figure 23. Picture after Levels adjustments.

Use the Levels dialog box to make fine adjustments to a picture's highlights, midtones, or shadows.

To adjust a picture's brightness and contrast (method 2):

1. Choose Levels from the pop-up Adjust menu under the Image menu **(Figure 20)**.
   or
   Hold down ⌘ and press "L."
2. To increase contrast, brighten the highlights by moving the Input Highlights slider to the left **(Figure 21)**.
   and/or
   To darken the shadows, move the Input Shadows slider to the right.
   and/or
   To lighten the midtones, move the Input Midtones slider to the left.
   and/or
   To darken the midtones, move the Input Midtones slider to the right.
3. To decrease contrast, move the Output Shadows slider to the right.
   and/or
   Move the Output Highlights slider to the left.
4. Click OK or press Return **(Figures 22-23)**.

✓ Tip

- To make a picture high contrast (black and white), move the Input Shadows and Highlights sliders very close together. Position them left of center to lighten the picture, right of center to darken the picture. You can use Threshold dialog box to produce the same effect.
  (See page 102)

To screen back a picture:

1. Choose Levels from the pop-up Adjust menu under the Image menu **(Figure 20)**.
   or
   Hold down ⌘ and press "L."
2. To reduce the contrast, move the Output Highlights slider slightly to the left **(Figure 24)**.
   and
   Move the Output Shadows slider to the right.
3. To lighten the midtones, move the Input Midtones slider to the left.
4. Click OK or press Return **(Figures 25-26)**.

✔ Tips

- To make a picture look like a film negative, reverse the position of the two Output sliders. The farther apart the sliders are, the more each pixel's brightness and contrast atrributes will be reversed. The Invert command produces a similar effect.
  (See page 100)
- To adjust the brightness or contrast in only a portion of a picture, select an area, then follow the steps above.

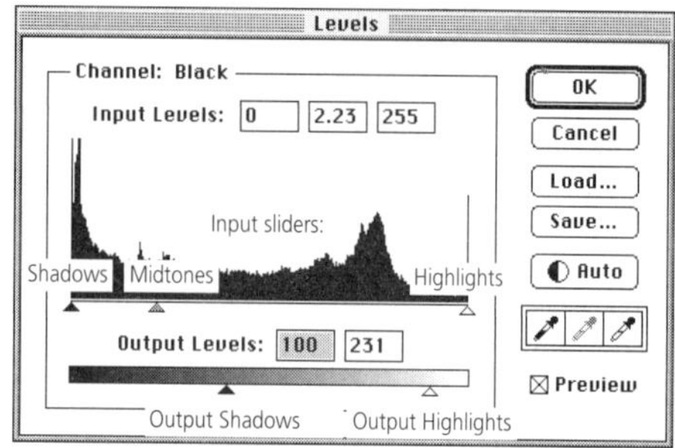

Figure 24. The **Levels** dialog box.

Figure 25. The original picture.

Figure 26. The picture screened back.

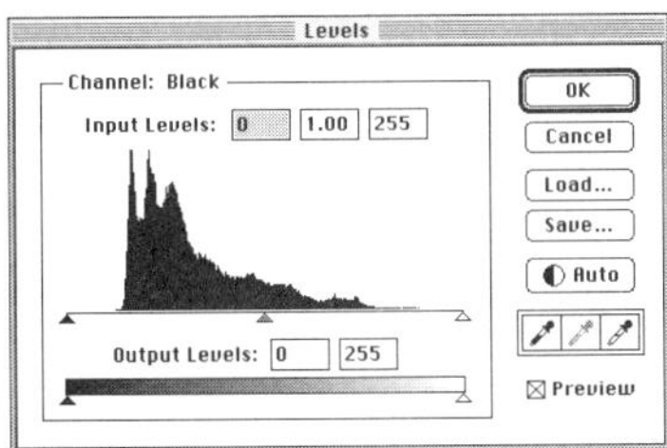

Figure 27. Click **Auto** in the **Levels** dialog box.

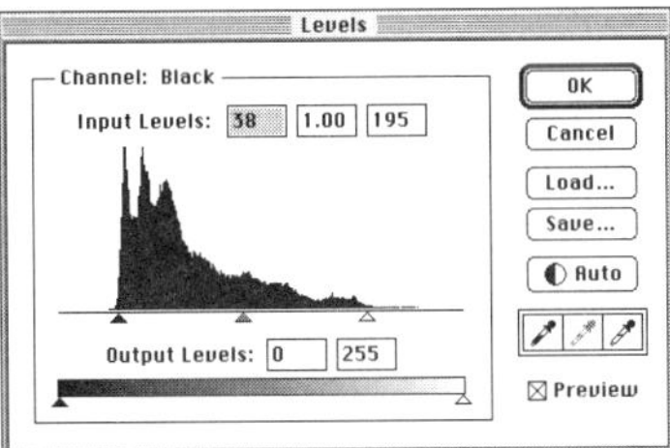

Figure 28. After clicking **Auto** in the **Levels** dialog box. Note the new position of the Input sliders.

To adjust brightness and contrast automatically:

1. Choose Levels from the Adjust pop-up menu under the Image menu **(Figure 20)**.
   or
   Hold ⌘ and press "L."
2. Click Auto **(Figures 27-28)**.
3. Click OK or press Return **(Figure 29-30)**.

Figure 29. The original picture.

Figure 30. The levels adjusted automatically.

Use the Dodge tool to lighten pixels, and the Burn tool to darken pixels. Brushes palette settings can be chosen separately for each tool.

Note: The Dodge/Burn tool can't be used on a picture in Bitmap or Indexed Color mode.

To lighten and darken using the Dodge/Burn tool:

1. Double-click the Dodge/Burn tool **(Figure 31)**.
2. From the Tool pop-up menu, choose Dodge or Burn **(Figure 32)**.
3. Click OK or press Return **(Figures 33-34)**.
4. If the Brushes palette is not displayed, choose Show Brushes from the Window menu to display it.
5. On the Brushes palette, click a hard-edged or soft-edged tip. A soft tip will produce the smoothest result.
   and
   Position the Exposure slider between 1% (low intensity) and 100% (high intensity). Try a low exposure first (20%-30%) so the tool won't bleach or darken areas too quickly.
   and
   Choose Shadows, Midtones, or Highlights from the pop-up menu to Dodge or Burn those pixels.
6. Stroke on any area of the picture, pausing to allow the screen to redraw. Each stroke over the same area will intensify the effect.

✔ Tips

- If you Dodge or Burn an area too much, choose Undo from the Edit menu or Revert from the File menu. Don't use the opposite tool to fix it — the effect will be uneven.
- Option click the Dodge/Burn tool to switch between the two tools. They will retain their separate Brushes palette settings.

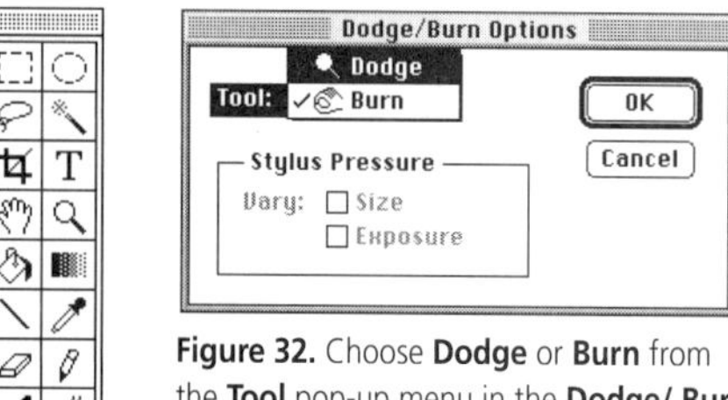

Figure 32. Choose **Dodge** or **Burn** from the **Tool** pop-up menu in the **Dodge/ Burn Options** dialog box.

Figure 31. Double-click the **Dodge/Burn** tool.

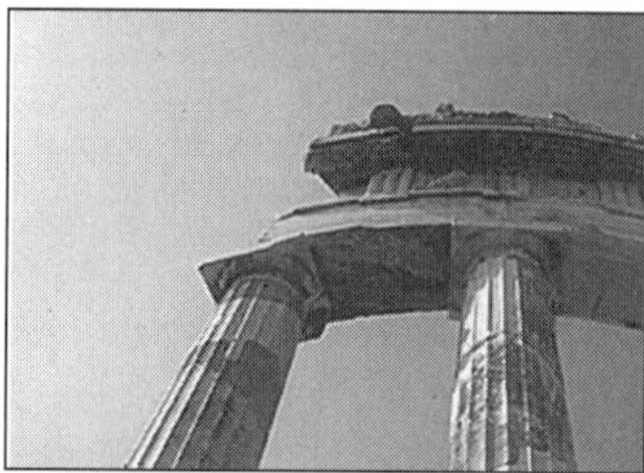

Figure 33. The original picture.

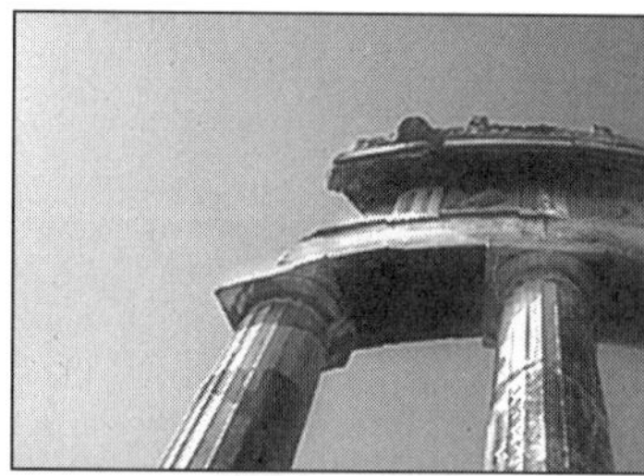

Figure 34. To produce this illustration, the Dodge tool was used with Highlights selected, and the Burn tool with Shadows and Midtones selected. Both tools were used with an Exposure setting of 30%.

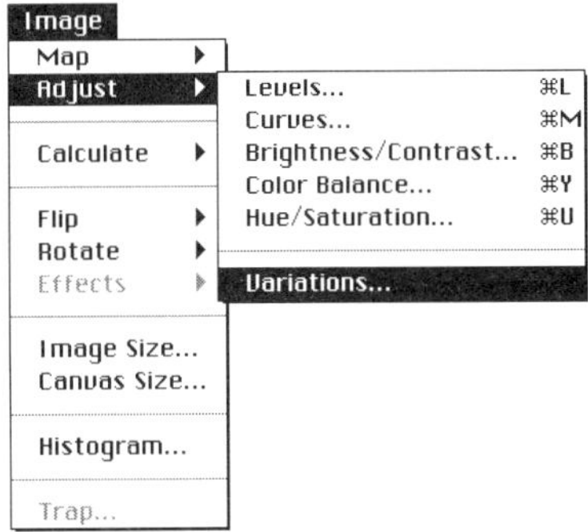

Figure 35. Choose **Variations** from the **Adjust** pop-up menu under the **Image** menu.

You can adjust lights and darks by clicking on thumbnails in the Variations dialog box.
(To adjust a color picture using the Variations dialog box, see pages 143-144)

To adjust lights and darks using thumbnail Variations:

1. Choose Variations from the Adjust pop-up menu under the Image menu **(Figure 35)**.
2. Position the Fine/Coarse slider right of center to make major adjustments or left of center to make minor adjustments. Each notch to the right doubles the adjustment per click. Each notch to the left halves the adjustment per click **(Figure 36)**.
3. Click the Lighter or Darker thumbnail in the Shadows, Midtones, or Highlights column.
4. *Optional:* Click the same thumbnail again to intensity the change, or click the opposite thumbnail to undo the modification.
5. Click OK or press Return **(Figures 37-38)**.

✔ Tips

- Click the Original thumbnail to undo changes made using the Variations dialog box.
- Use the Levels or Brightness/Contrast dialog box to make more precise adjustments on the full-screen image. *(See pages 104 and 105)*

Adjust using Variations

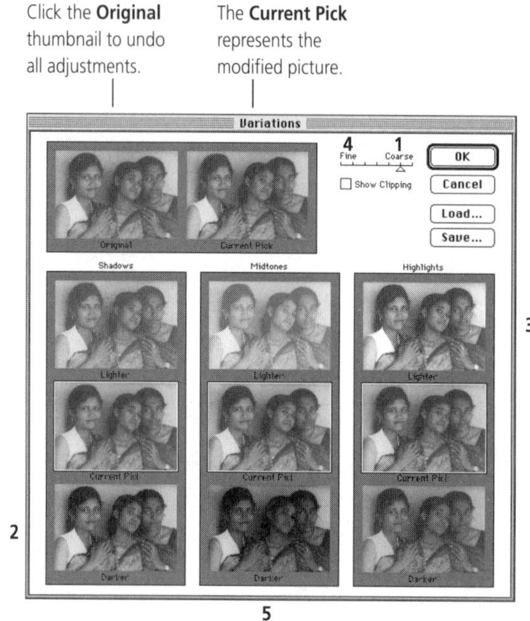

Figure 36. The **Variations** dialog box**.** The following steps were taken to produce the picture in Figure 38:

1 The Fine/Coarse slider was moved to the right 2 notches.
2 The Shadows-Darker box was clicked.
3 The Highlights-Lighter box was clicked.
4 The Fine/Coarse slider was moved to the left 4 notches.
5 The Midtones-Darker box was clicked.

Figure 37. The original picture.

Figure 38. After Variations adjustments.

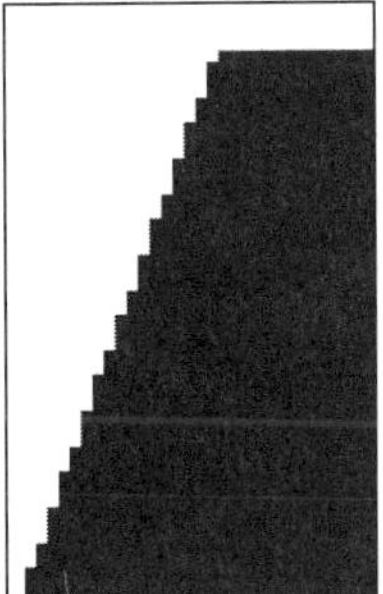
Figure 1. The side of a character with the Anti-aliased box unchecked in the Type Tool dialog box.

Figure 2. The Anti-aliased box checked in the Type Tool dialog box.

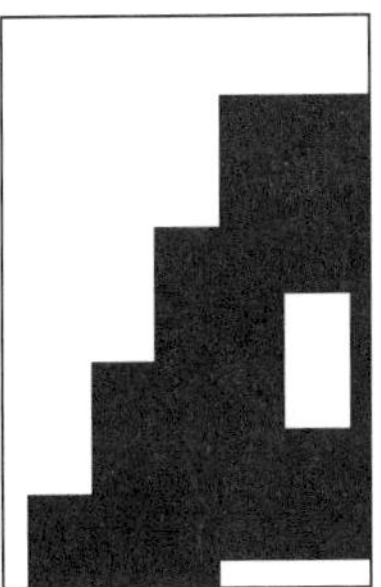
Figure 3. Adobe Type Manager turned off or not installed.

IN PHOTOSHOP, type is composed of pixels. Type first appears on a picture as a floating selection, which can be modified. Once deselected, the type replaces the underlying pixels, like any other selection.

This chapter covers how to create, move, deselect and delete a type selection, how to screen back type and screen back a picture behind type, how to fill type with imagery, and how to emphasize type with a drop shadow. Type can also be rotated, imported from Adobe Illustrator, filled with a blend, filled with a pattern, or modified by applying a filter. You'll learn these techniques in other chapters.

The resolution of type always matches the picture's resolution. To create the smoothest possible type for high-resolution output, set the picture's resolution to 200 dpi or higher. Unfortunately, increasing a file's resolution causes its file size to increase.

Check the Anti-aliased box in the Type Tool dialog box for smooth rendering **(Figures 1-2)**. Photoshop uses Adobe Type Manager when rendering Adobe PostScript fonts **(Figure 3)**. TrueType fonts can also be used with System 7 or later.

If you want to superimpose type over a picture for a particular design and are not creating a special Photoshop type effect, import your Photoshop picture into a page layout program or into an illustration program, like Adobe Illustrator, and layer PostScript type over it.

To create a type selection:

1. Click the Type tool **(Figure 4)**.
2. Click on the picture where you wish the type to appear.
3. In the Type Tool dialog box, type the desired characters in the text field. Press Return when you want to start a new line. Otherwise, all the type will appear in one line on the picture **(Figure 5)**.
4. Choose from the Font pop-up menu.
5. Choose Points or Pixels from the pop-up menu next to the Size field, then enter a number between 4 and 1000 in the Size field.

Steps 6 through 9 are optional.

6. If you enter more than one line of type, enter a number between 0 and 1000 in the Leading field (the space between lines of type).
7. Enter a number between -99.9 and 999.9 in the Spacing field (the space between characters).
8. Check a Style.
9. Click Left, Center, or Right Alignment.
10. Check the Anti-aliased box to smooth the type.
11. Click OK. The floating type selection will automatically fill with the Foreground color **(Figure 6)**.

Figure 4. Click the **Type** tool.

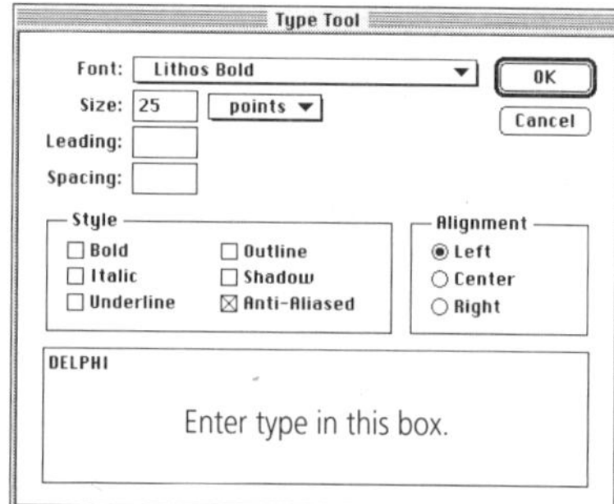

Figure 5. The **Type Tool** dialog box. It may take several seconds for this dialog box to appear.

Figure 6. Type appears as a floating selection.

✓ Tips

- **Type can only be modified while selected** (and cannot be reselected easily). If you unintentionally deselect, immediately choose Undo from the Edit menu. You can save type to an alpha channel.
- Don't double Style a font. For example, if you choose Garamond Italic from the Font menu, don't apply the Italic style to it.
- Don't use city-name fonts (Chicago, Geneva, Monaco, etc.) unless they are TrueType fonts.

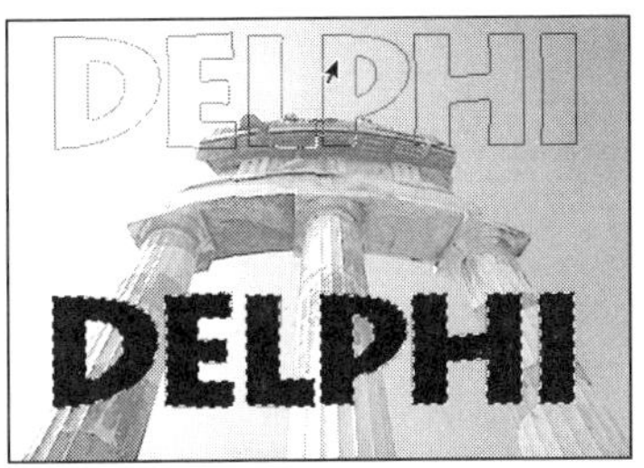

Figure 7. A floating type selection being moved.

To move a floating type selection:

Position the pointer over the type, then drag with the arrow pointer **(Figure 7)**.

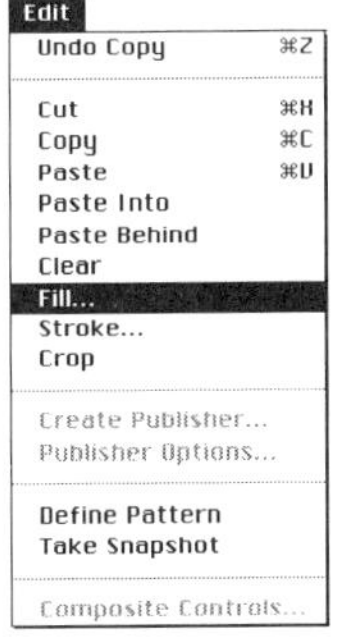

Figure 8. Choose **Fill** from the **Edit** menu.

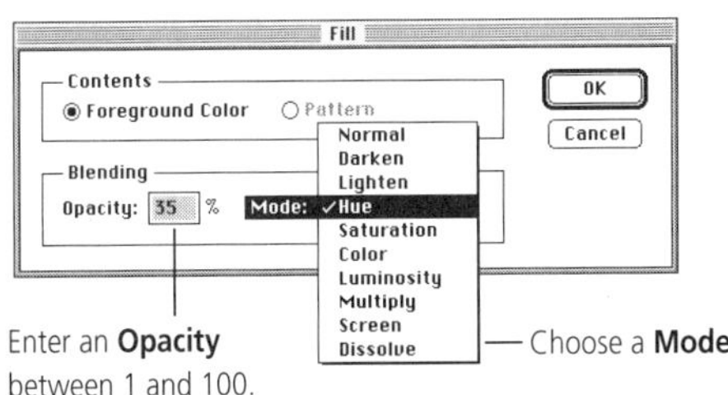

Enter an **Opacity** between 1 and 100.

Choose a **Mode**.

Figure 9. The **Fill** dialog box.

To recolor a type selection:

1. Choose a Foreground color.
   (See pages 130-132)
2. Choose Fill from the Edit menu **(Figure 8)**.
3. Enter a number between 1 and 100 in the Opacity field **(Figure 9)**.
4. Choose a mode from the Mode pop-up menu.
   (See page 147)
5. Click OK or press Return.

✓ Tip

- You can also choose a fill Opacity and mode for a type selection from the Brushes palette.

Type can be filled with a lighter screen of a picture.

To screen back a type selection:

1. If the Brushes palette is not displayed, choose Show Brushes from the Window menu.
2. On the Brushes palette, move the Opacity slider to 1% **(Figure 10)**.
3. Make sure the type is in the desired position, then choose Defloat from the Select Menu **(Figure 11)**. (The Defloat command will replace the underlying pixels with the type.)
4. Choose Levels from the Adjust pop-up menu under the Image menu **(Figure 12)**.
5. Move the Input Midtones slider to the left to lighten the midtones in the type. Pause to preview **(Figure 14)**.
6. Move the Output Shadows slider to the right to reduce the contrast in the type. Pause to preview.
7. Click OK or press Return **(Figure 13)**.

✔ **Tip**

- You can also use the Composite Controls dialog box, opened from the Edit menu, to make type translucent. *(See pages 179-180)*

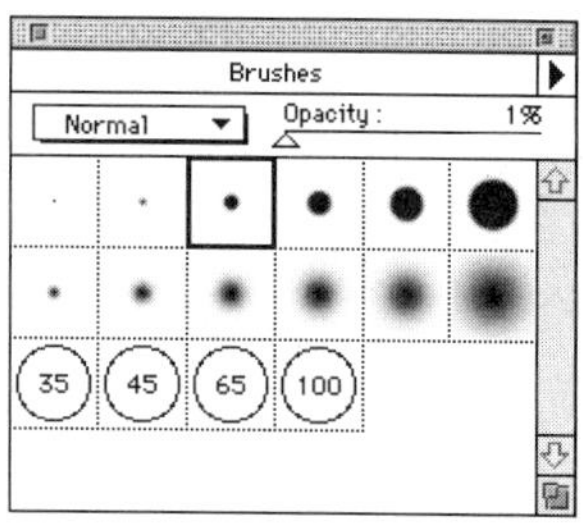

Figure 10. Move the **Opacity** slider to 1% on the Brushes palette.

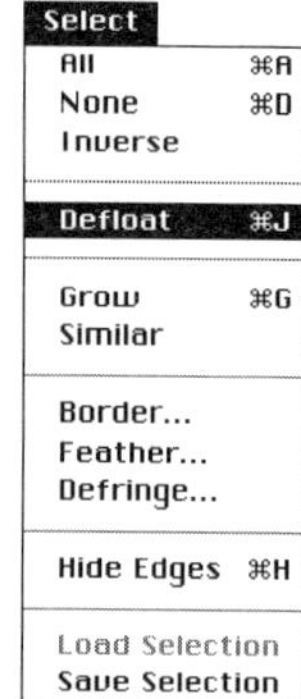

Figure 11. Choose **Defloat** from the **Select** menu.

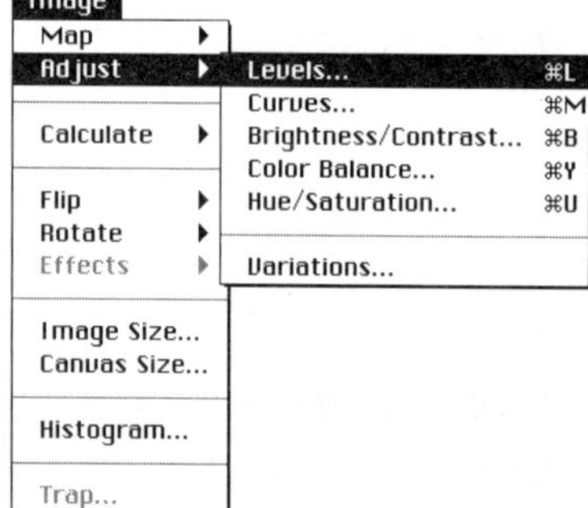

Figure 12. Choose **Levels** from the **Adjust** pop-up menu under the **Image** menu.

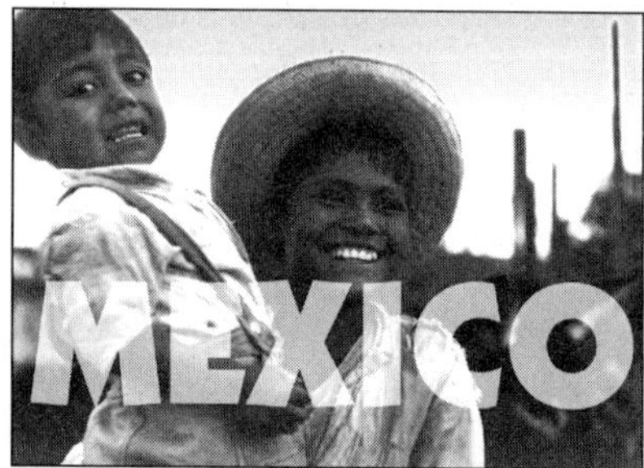

Figure 13. Screened back type.

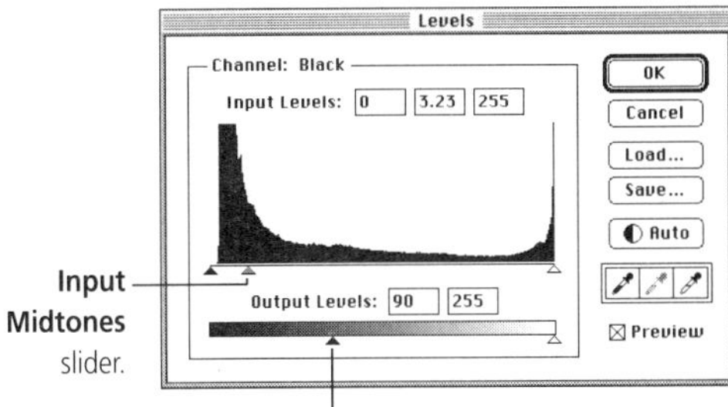

Figure 14. In the **Levels** dialog box, move the Input Midtones slider to the left, and the Output Shadows slider to the right.

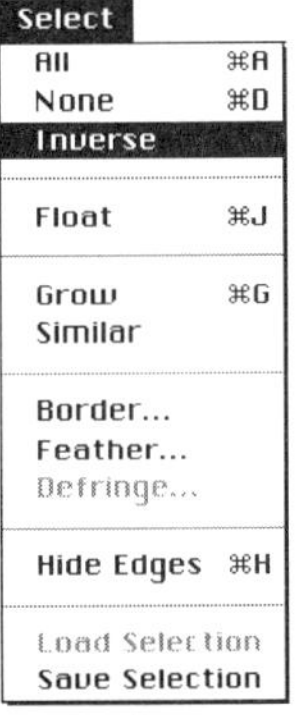

Figure 15. Choose **Inverse** from the **Select** menu.

To screen back a picture with type:

1. Follow the steps on page 112 to create a type selection, and reposition the type, if desired.
2. If the Brushes palette is not displayed, choose Show Brushes from the Window menu.
3. On the Brushes palette, move the Opacity slider to 1% **(Figure 10)**.
4. Choose Inverse from the Select menu to select the background of the picture **(Figure 15)**.
5. Choose Levels from the Adjust pop-up menu under the Image menu **(Figure 12)**.
6. Move the Input Midtones slider to the left to lighten the picture's midtones. Pause to preview **(Figure 14)**.
7. Move the Output Shadows slider to the right to reduce the picture's contrast. Pause to preview.
8. Click OK or press Return **(Figure 16)**.

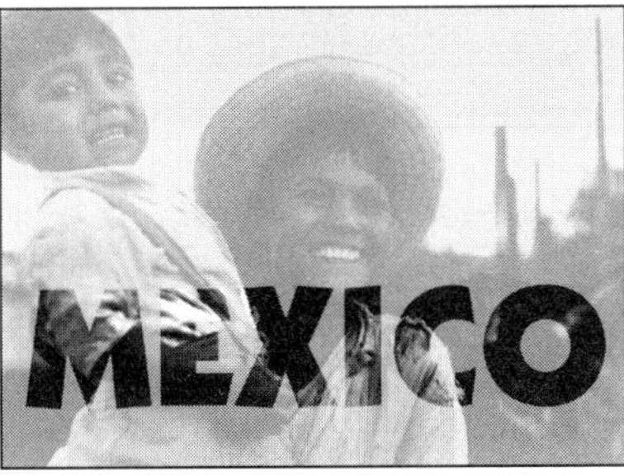

Figure 16. A screened back picture.

To fill type with an image:

1. Follow the steps on page 112 to create a type selection. Reposition the type, if desired.
2. Open another picture.
3. Choose All from the Select menu.
   or
   Select an area of the picture.
   (See pages 62-65)
4. Choose Copy from the Edit menu.
5. With the picture containing the type selection active, choose Paste Into from the Edit menu **(Figures 17-18)**. The pasted image will be selected; the type will no longer be selected.
6. *Optional:* Drag within the selection to reposition the image.
   (See options for modifying a pasted image on pages 179-181)

Other ways to modify a type selection:

- **Flip** it (see instructions on page 72).
- **Rotate** it (see instructions on page 73).
- Apply a **filter** to it (see instructions on pages 183-205).
  (And see "Apply the Wind filter to type" on page 190)
- Paste a **pattern** or **texture** into it (see instructions on pages 177 and 203) **(Figure 19)**.
- Fill it with a **blend** (see instructions on pages 159-162) **(Figure 20)**.

✔ Tips

- You can import an Adobe Illustrator file containing type. It will automatically be rendered as bitmapped pixels in the Photoshop picture's resolution. *(See pages 38-39)*
- Type will become distorted if you resize it using the Scale command (including type imported from Adobe Illustrator).

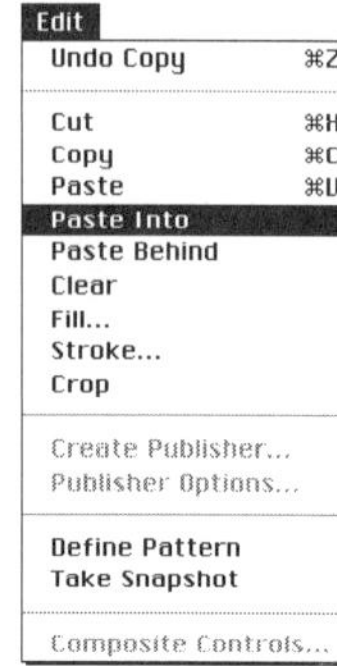

Figure 17. Choose **Copy,** then **Paste Into** from the **Edit** menu.

Figure 18. Type filled with a picture using the Paste Into command.

Figure 19. Type filled with a pattern.

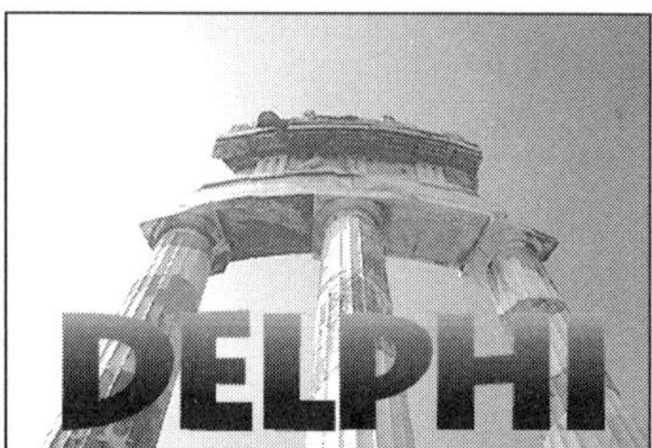

Figure 20. Type filled with a blend.

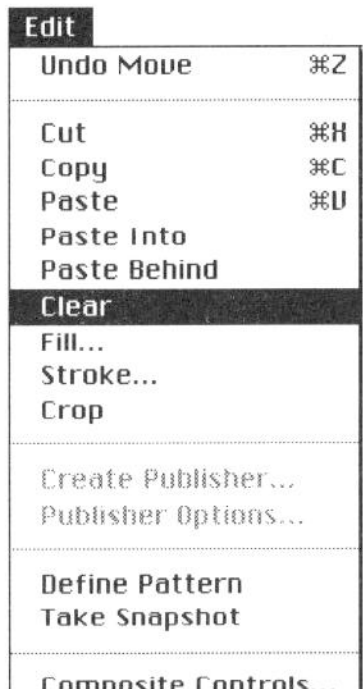

Figure 21. Choose **Clear** from the **Edit** menu.

To delete a type selection:

Choose Clear from the Edit menu **(Figure 21)**.
or
Press Delete.

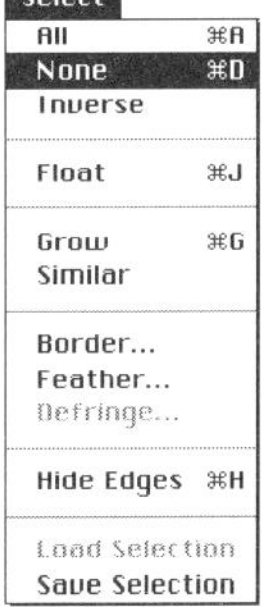

Figure 22. Choose **None** from the **Select** menu.

To deselect a type selection:

Click outside the selection. The type will replace the underlying pixels.
or
Choose None from the Select menu **(Figure 22)**.

Tip

- To replace the underlying pixels *and* create a copy of the floating selection, choose Defloat from the Select menu. To create a hard-edged shadow for the type, choose a Background color for the shadow, choose Defloat, then move the type selection slightly to the left and upward **(Figure 23)**.

Figure 23. Type with a shadow.

To produce a shadow under type, type is saved to an alpha channel. The channel is duplicated and the duplicate is moved slightly. Then the duplicate channel is loaded and a shadow color is applied to it. The original type channel is then loaded and colored. A shadow can also be created for a non-type selection. *(See "Masks" on page 81)*

To create shadow type:

1. Open a picture. A textured background will work well.
2. Click the Default Colors icon on the toolbox to reset the default Foreground and Background colors **(Figure 24)**.
3. Click the Type tool **(Figure 4)**.
4. Click on the picture.
5. In the Type Tool dialog box, type into the text field **(Figure 25)**.
   and
   Choose a Font.
   and
   Enter a number in the Size field.
   and
   Check the Anti-aliased box.
6. Click OK or press Return **(Figure 26)**.
7. *Optional:* Drag the type to a new position with the arrow pointer.
8. If the Brushes palette is not displayed, choose Show Brushes from the Window menu.
9. Move the Opacity slider to 1%.
10. Choose Save Selection from the Select menu **(Figures 27)**. A new selection name will appear on the Channels palette **(Figures 28)**.
11. Choose None from the Select menu.

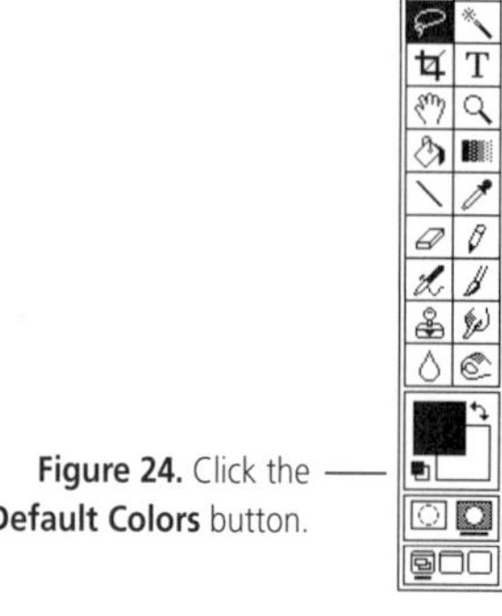

Figure 24. Click the **Default Colors** button.

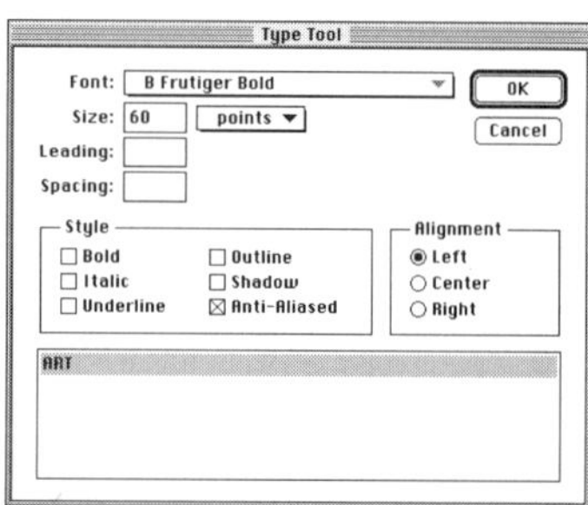

Figure 25. In the **Type Tool** dialog box, enter text, choose a **Font** and **Size**, and make sure the **Anti-aliased** box is checked.

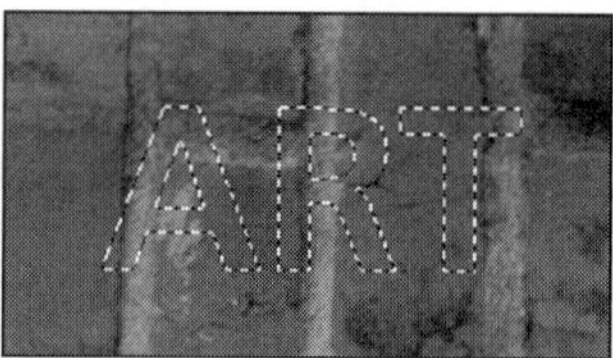

Figure 26. A floating type selection.

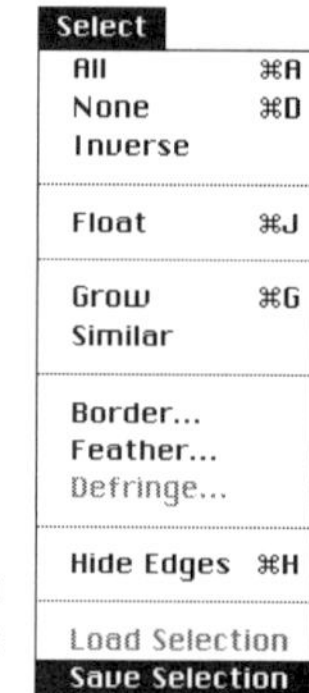

Figure 27. From the **Select** menu, choose **Save Selection**, then choose **None.**

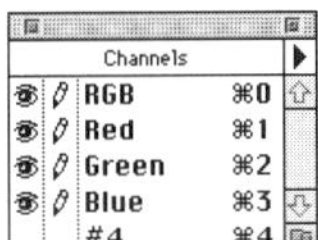

Figure 28. The new channel is listed on the **Channels** palette.

Figure 29. The new alpha channel.

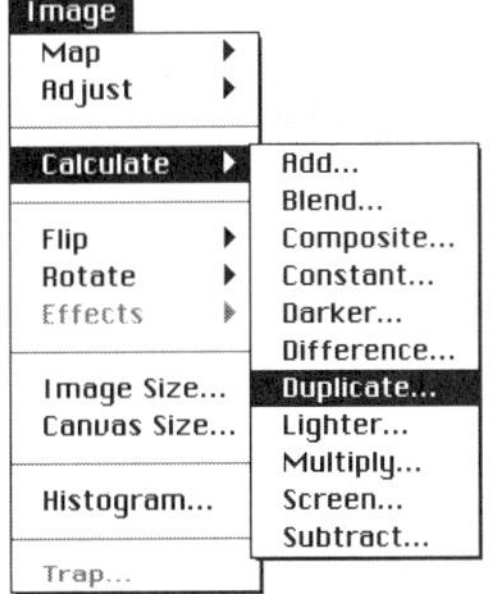

Figure 30. Choose **Duplicate** from the **Calculate** pop-up menu under the **Image** menu.

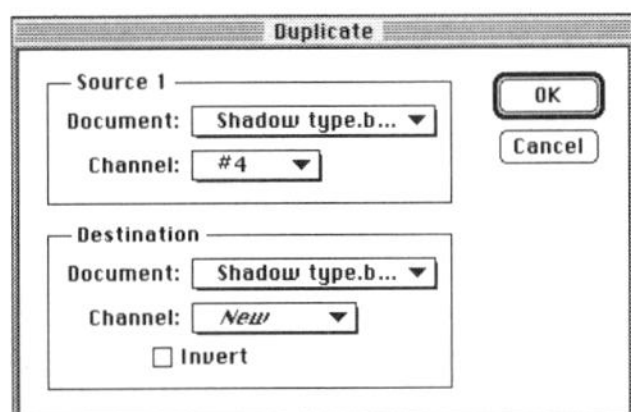

Figure 31. In the **Duplicate** dialog box, choose the current document as the **Source** and **Destination Document** and the newly created alpha channel as the **Source Channel.**

12. Choose Duplicate from the Calculate pop-up menu under the Image menu **(Figure 30)**.

13. In the Duplicate dialog box, make sure the Source and Destination pop-up boxes display the current Document name **(Figure 31)**.
and
Choose the newly created channel number as the Source Channel.
and
Choose New as the Destination Channel.

14. Click OK or press Return. A second alpha channel is created and will be the active channel **(Figure 32)**.

15. Choose Offset from the Other pop-up menu under the Filter menu **(Figure 33)**.

16. In the Offset dialog box, enter 15 in the Horizontal field **(Figure 34)**.
and
Enter 15 in the Vertical field.
and
Click Repeat Edge Pixels.

17. Click OK or press Return.

18. Choose Gaussian Blur from the Blur pop-up menu under the Filter menu **(Figure 35)**.

19. Enter 5 or 6 in the Radius field **(Figure 36)**.

20. Click OK or press Return **(Figure 37)**.

(Instructions continue on page 121)

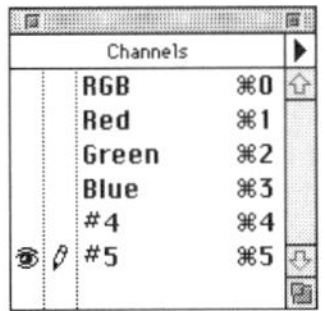

Figure 32. The newest channel is active.

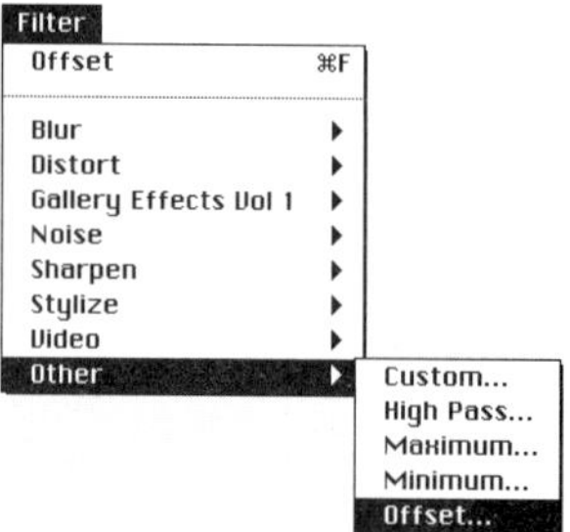

Figure 33. Choose **Offset** from the **Other** pop-up menu under the **Filter** menu.

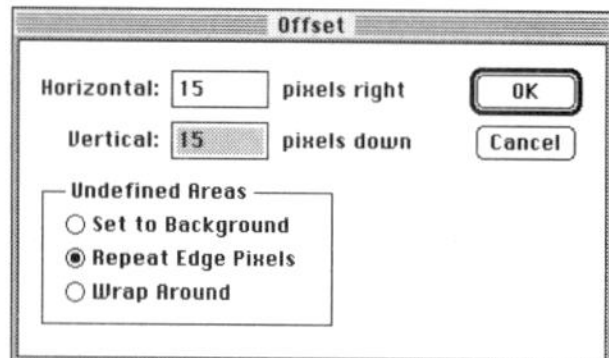

Figure 34. In the **Offset** dialog box, enter 15 in the **Horizontal** and **Vertical** fields and click **Repeat Edge Pixels**.

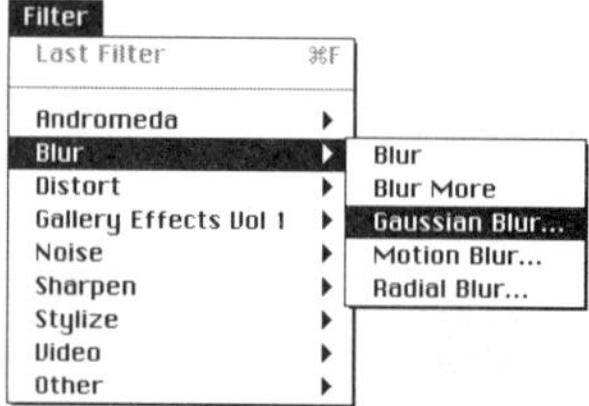

Figure 35. Choose **Gaussian Blur** from the **Blur** pop-up menu under the **Filter** menu.

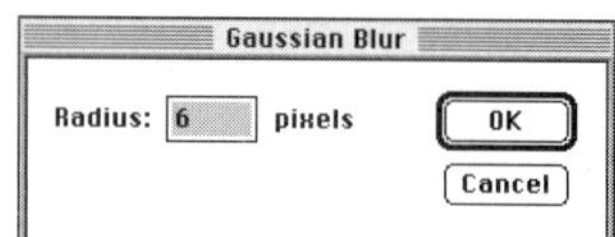

Figure 36. Enter 5 or 6 in the **Radius** field in the **Gaussian Blur** dialog box.

Figure 37. The second alpha channel.

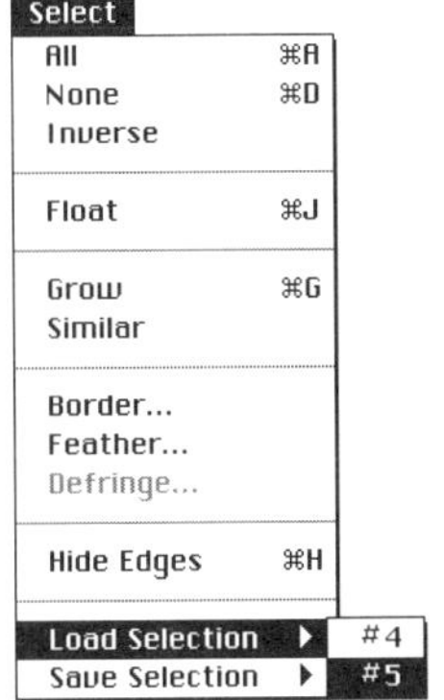

Figure 38. Choose the first alpha channel from the **Load Selection** pop-up menu under the **Select** menu.

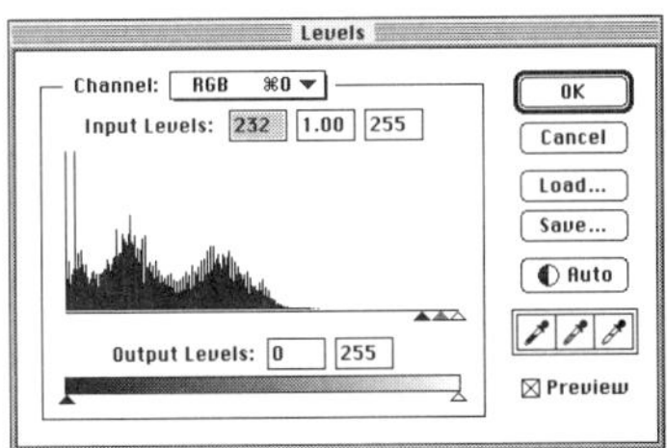

Figure 39. Move the black **Input** triangle to the far right in the **Levels** dialog box.

21. Click top channel on the Channels palette.
22. Choose the last channel from the Load Selection pop-up menu under the Select menu **(Figure 38)**.
23. With the shadow selection still active, choose Levels from the Adjust pop-up menu under the Image menu.
24. Move the black Input triangle to the far right to darken the selection **(Figure 39)**.
25. Click OK or press Return.
26. Choose the first alpha channel from the Load Selection pop-up menu under the Select menu **(Figure 38)**.
27. Choose a Foreground color.
    (See pages 130-132)
28. Choose Fill from the Edit menu.
29. Enter a number between 85 and 100 in the Opacity field.
    and
    Choose Normal from the Mode menu.
30. Click OK or press Return **(Figure 40)**. You did it!

Figure 40. The completed shadow type.

EDGES

Show Brushes.

The Brushes palette is used throughout this chapter. Choose Show Brushes from the Window menu to display it **(Figure 1)**.

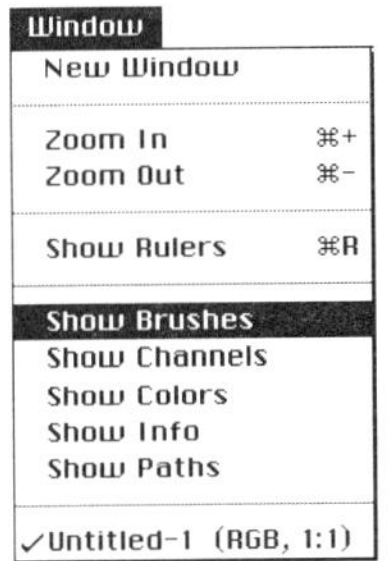

Figure 1. Choose **Show Brushes** from the **Window** menu.

THIS CHAPTER covers three of Photoshop's editing tools: Blur/Sharpen, Smudge, and Eraser **(Figure 2)**.

The **blur** function of the **Blur/Sharpen tool** decreases contrast between pixels. Use it to soften edges between shapes.

The **sharpen** function of the Sharpen/Blur tool increases contrast between pixels. Use it to delineate edges between shapes.

The **Smudge tool** smudges colors into each other, and can be used to create painterly effects. When used with the tool's Finger Painting option, the smudge starts with the Foreground color.

The **Eraser tool** replaces pixels with squares of the Background color.

Note: The Blur/Sharpen and Smudge tools cannot be used on a picture in Bitmap or Indexed Color mode.

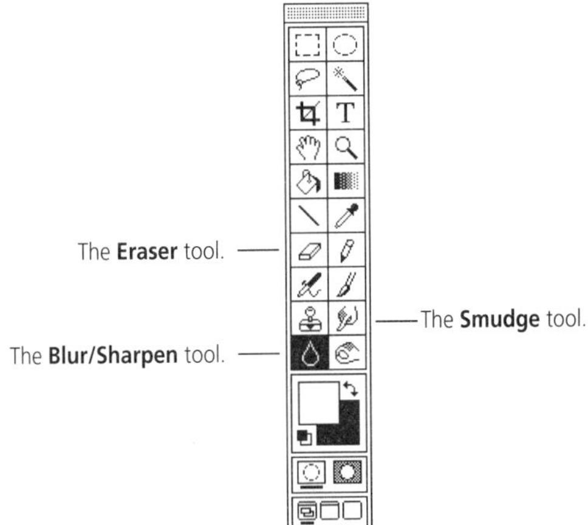

Figure 2.

To sharpen or blur edges:

1. Double-click the Blur/Sharpen tool **(Figure 3)**.
2. Choose Sharpen or Blur from the Tool pop-up menu **(Figure 4)**.
3. Click OK or press Return.
4. Click a hard-edged or soft-edged tip on the Brushes palette **(Figure 5)**.
5. Move the Pressure slider left or right to decrease or increase the effect. Try a setting of approximately 30% first.
6. Choose a mode from the pop-up menu on the left side of the palette **(Figure 6)**:

   Normal to sharpen or blur pixels of any shade or color.
   or
   Darken to sharpen or blur only pixels darker than the Foreground color.
   or
   Lighten to sharpen or blur only pixels lighter than the Foreground color.
   (For a full description of paint and fill modes, see page 147)
7. Drag across any area of the picture **(Figures 7-9)**. Each stroke on the same area will intensify the effect.

✓ Tips

- Hold down Option and click the Blur/Sharpen tool to switch between its Sharpen and Blur functions. Each function will retain its own Brushes palette settings.
- Hold down Option to switch between the Sharpen and Blur functions without clicking on the Toolbox. When the Sharpen or Blur function is accessed using this shortcut, the current Brushes palette settings apply.
- Use the Sharpen tool with a medium Pressure setting and stroke only once on an area to avoid creating a grainy texture.

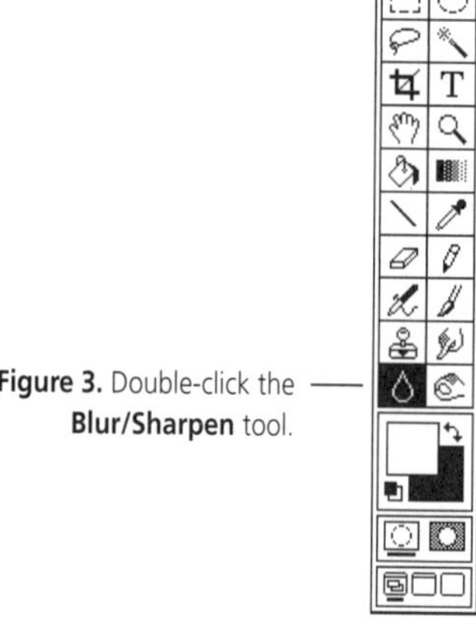

Figure 3. Double-click the **Blur/Sharpen** tool.

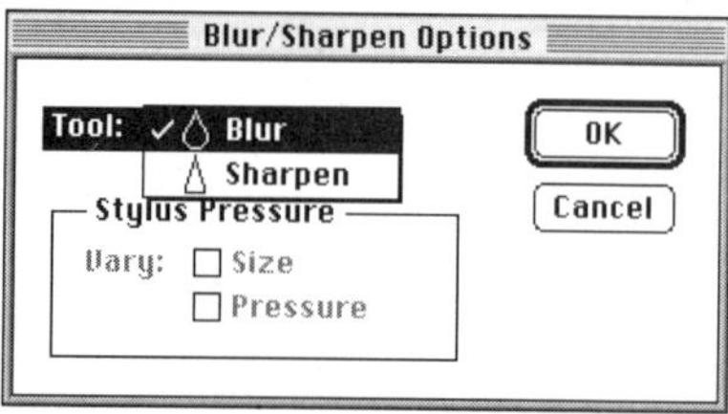

Figure 4. Choose **Blur** or **Sharpen** from the **Tool** pop-up menu in the **Blur/Sharpen Options** dialog box.

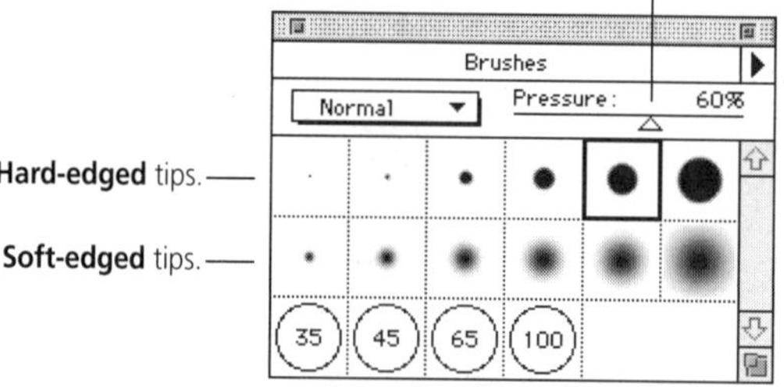

Figure 5. The **Brushes** palette.

Sharpen or Blur Edges

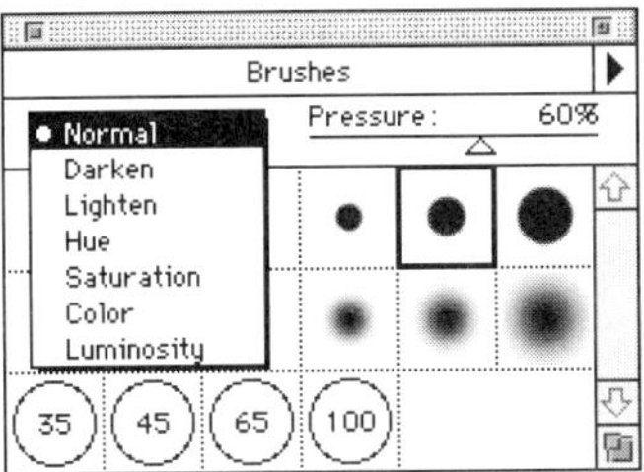

Figure 6. Choose a mode from the pop-up menu on the **Brushes** palette.

Figure 7. The original picture.

Figure 8. After using the Sharpen tool on the top of the vase (70% Pressure, Normal mode).

Figure 9. After using the Blur tool on the areas around the vase (80% Pressure, Normal mode).

To smudge edges:

1. Click the Smudge tool **(Figure 10)**.
2. Click a hard-edged or soft-edged tip on the Brushes palette **(Figure 11)**.
3. Move the Pressure slider left or right to decrease or increase the effect.
4. Choose a mode from the pop-up menu on the left side of the palette **(Figure 12)**:

   Normal to smudge all shades or colors.
   or
   Darken to push dark colors into lighter colors.
   or
   Lighten to push light colors into darker colors.
   or
   Saturation to push the starting color's intensity into other colors.
   or
   Color to push the starting color's tint into other colors.
   or
   Luminosity to push the starting color's light and dark values into other colors.
5. Drag across any area of the picture **(Figures 14-18)**.

✔ Tip

- To Smudge with the Foreground color, double-click the Smudge tool, then check the Finger Painting box in the Options dialog box **(Figure 13)**. To temporarily turn on the Finger Painting option, hold down option with the Smudge tool selected. The higher the Pressure percentage, the more the Foreground color will be applied.

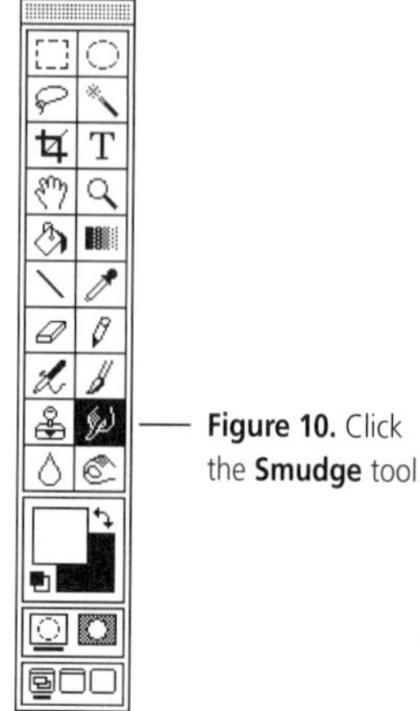

Figure 10. Click the **Smudge** tool.

Move the **Pressure** slider left or right.

Hard-edged tips.

Soft-edged tips.

Brushes

Normal

Pressure: 60%

35 45 65 100

Figure11. The **Brushes** palette.

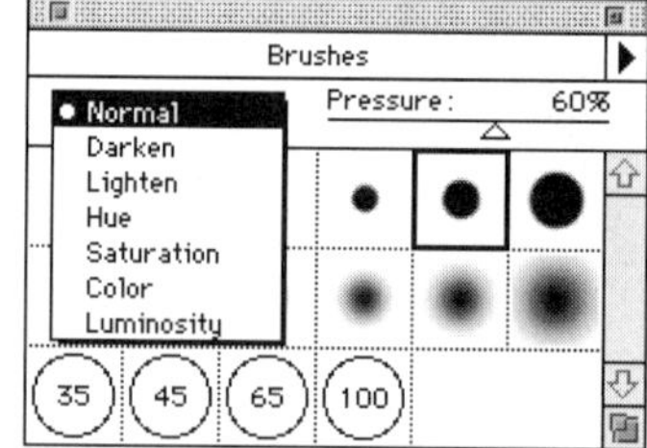

Figure 12. Choose a mode from the **Brushes** palette.

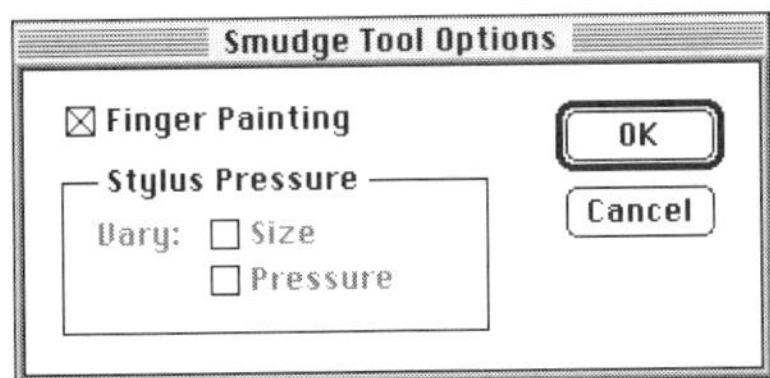

Figure 13. To smudge with the Foreground color, double-click the Smudge tool, then check the **Finger Painting** box in the **Smudge Tool Options** dialog box.

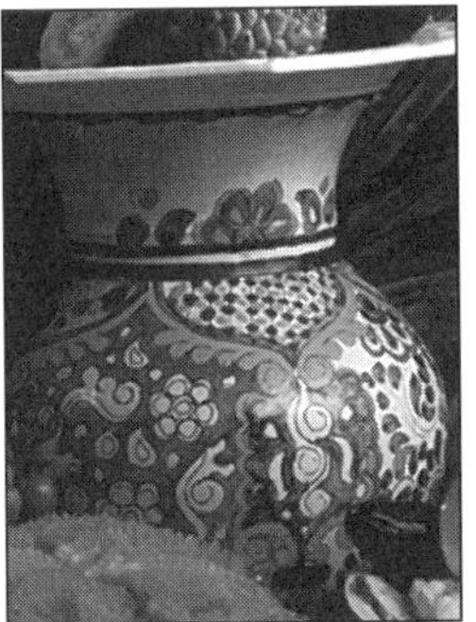

Figure 14. The original picture.

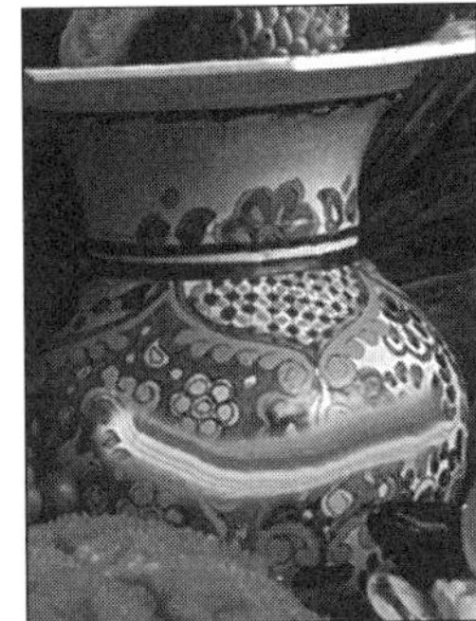

Figure 15. Smudge (Normal mode, 100% Pressure).

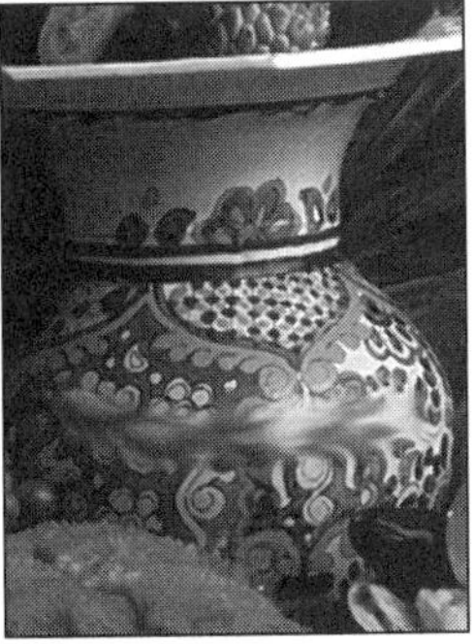

Figure 16. Smudge (Normal mode, 50% Pressure).

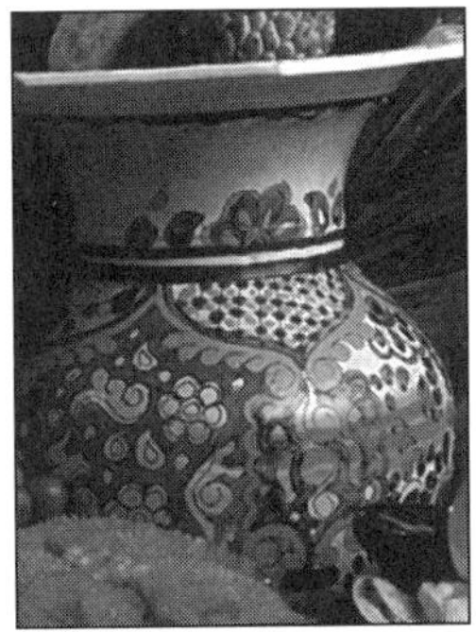

Figure 17. Smudge (Darken mode, 100% Pressure). Only the light side of the pot is modified.

Figure 18. Smudge (Lighten mode, 100% Pressure). Only the dark side of the pot is modified.

The Eraser tool replaces areas of a picture with large squares of the Background color. It can be used to silhouette a shape. The size of the Eraser tool tip cannot be changed, however, so it can only be used to erase large blocks. Use the Paintbrush tool with a small tip to erase small areas.

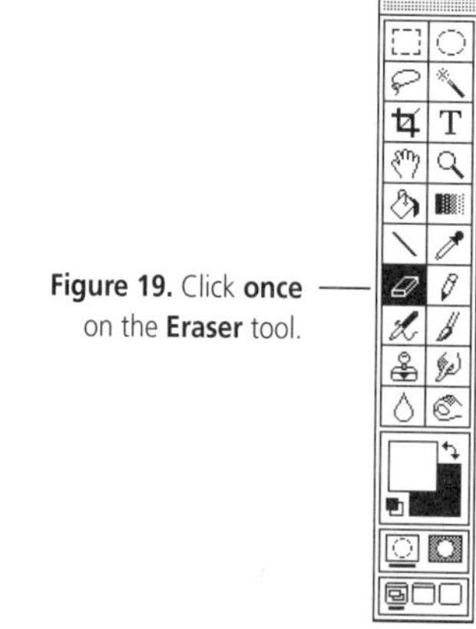

Figure 19. Click **once** on the **Eraser** tool.

WARNING! If you double-click the Eraser tool, a warning prompt will appear **(Figure 20)**. If you Click OK, **your entire picture will be erased**!

To erase part of a picture:

1. Click the Eraser tool **(Figure 19)**.
2. Choose a Background color.
   (See pages 130-132)
3. Click on or drag across any area of the picture **(Figure 21)**.

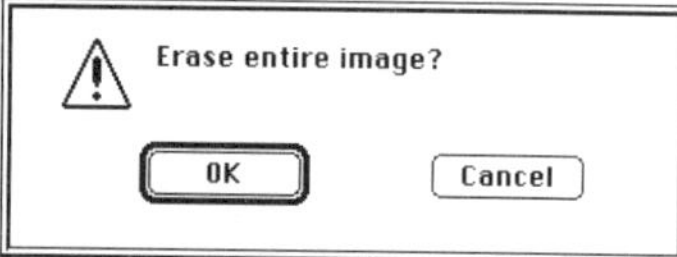

Figure 20. If you double-click the Eraser tool, this warning prompt will appear. Click **Cancel** to keep the picture.

✔ Tip

- To restore areas of the last saved version of a picture, click the Eraser tool, then hold down Option and drag. It may take a moment for the "magic eraser" to start working. It will not work if you changed the mode, dimensions or resolution of the picture since it was last saved.

  You can also use the Rubber Stamp tool with its From Saved Option and Brushes palette settings of your choice to restore areas of the last saved version.
  (See page 172)

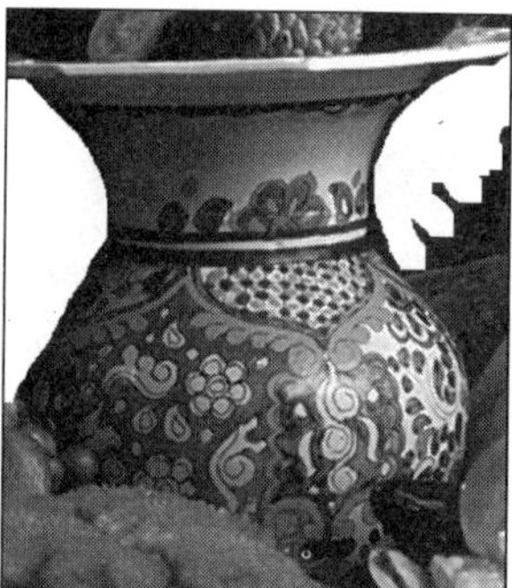

Figure 21. Part of the area around the vase is erased.

CHOOSE COLORS 12

Show Colors.

The Colors palette is used throughout this chapter. Choose Show Colors from the Window menu to display it.

IN THIS CHAPTER you will learn to choose and mix Foreground and Background colors and add, delete, save, append, and load Colors palette swatches.

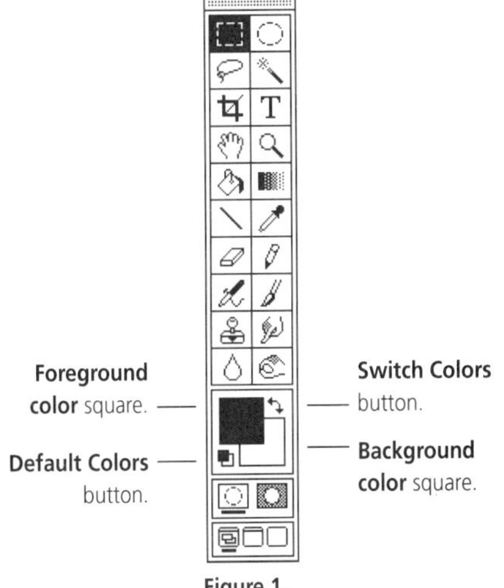

Figure 1.

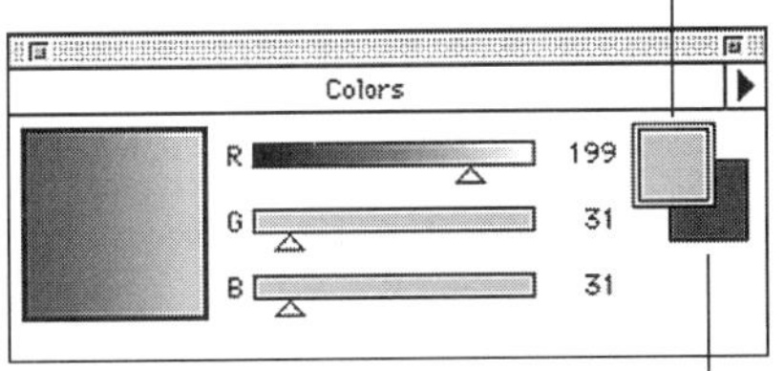

Figure 2. The **Colors** palette.

Foreground and Background colors:

When you use a fill command or painting tool or create type, the current Foreground color is applied.

When you use the Eraser tool, add a border to a picture using the Canvas Size dialog box, or move a selection, the current Background color is applied. If you move a copy of a selection, it becomes a floating selection. The underlying pixels do not change.

The Gradient tool produces blends with the Foreground and Background colors.

The Foreground and Background colors are displayed on the Toolbox and Colors palettes in the Foreground and Background color squares **(Figures 1-2)**. (When written with an uppercase "F" or "B," these terms refer to colors, not the foreground or background areas of an image.)

Switch the Foreground and Background colors by clicking the Switch Colors button on the Toolbox **(Figure 1)**.

Restore the Foreground color to black and the Background color to white by clicking the Default Colors button on the Toolbox.

Methods for choosing Foreground and Background colors are described on the next three pages.

To choose a custom Foreground or Background color using the Color Picker:

1. Click the Foreground or Background color square on the Toolbox **(Figure 1)**.
   or
   Click the Foreground or Background color square on the Colors palette if it is already active **(Figure 2)**.
   or
   Double-click the Foreground or Background color square on the Colors palette if it is not active **(Figure 2)**.
2. Move the slider up or down on the vertical bar to choose a hue, then click a variation of that hue in the large rectangle **(Figure 3)**.
   or
   To mix a process color, enter percentages from a matching guide in the C, M, Y, and K fields.
   or
   To choose a predefined color, click Custom in the Color Picker **(Figure 4)**. Choose a matching guide system from the Book pop-up menu, enter a number in the "Find #" field or click a swatch, then click OK **(Figure 5)**.
3. Click OK or press Return.

✓ Tips

- To use the Photoshop Color Picker, Photoshop must be chosen from the Color Picker pop-up menu in the General Preferences dialog box, opened from the File menu.
  (See page 222)
- You can enter numbers in the HSB, RGB, or LAB fields. RGB colors range from 0 (black) to 255 (pure R,G,or B).

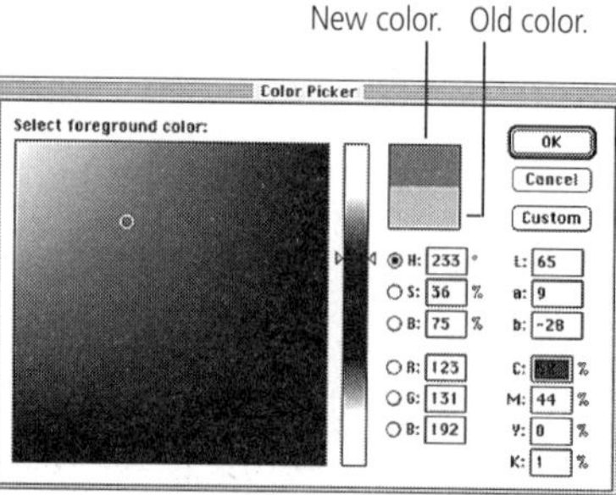

Figure 3. In the **Color Picker,** move the slider up or down on the spectrum bar, then click a color in the large rectangle, or enter numbers in the fields.

Figure 4. An **exclamation point** indicates there is no ink equivalent for the color you chose — it is **nonprintable**. Choose a different color or click the exclamation point to have Photoshop substitute the closest printable color (shown in the swatch below the exclamation point).

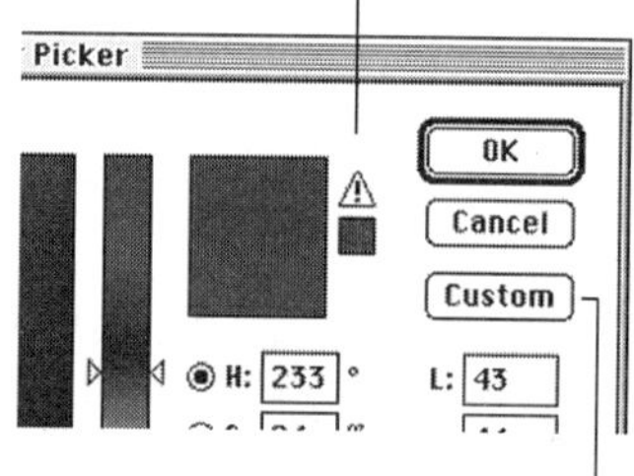

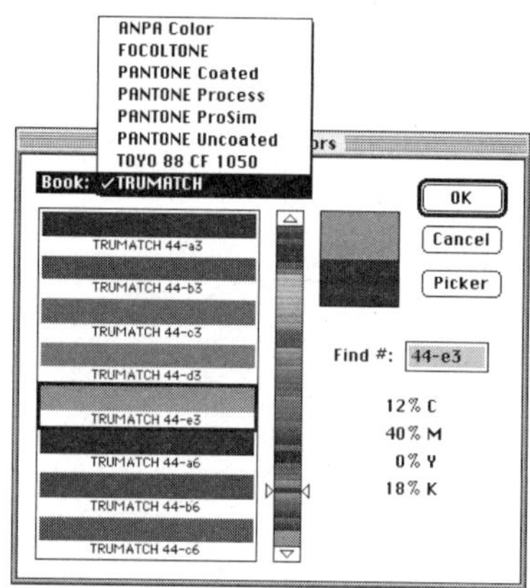

Figure 5. In the **Custom Colors** dialog box, choose a matching system from the **Book** pop-up menu, then click a swatch or enter a number in the **Find #** field. *(Follow instructions on page 134 to load a predefined swatch palette onto the Colors palette.)*

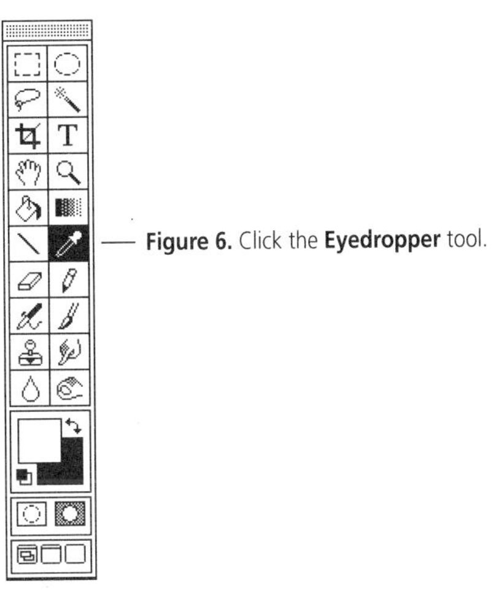
Figure 6. Click the **Eyedropper** tool.

To choose a Foreground or Background color from a picture:

1. Click the Foreground or Background color square if it is not already active.
2. Click the Eyedropper tool **(Figure 6)**.
3. Click on a color in the picture.

✓ **Tip**

- Hold down Option and click to choose a Background color when the Foreground color square is active, or to choose a Foreground color when the Background color square is active.

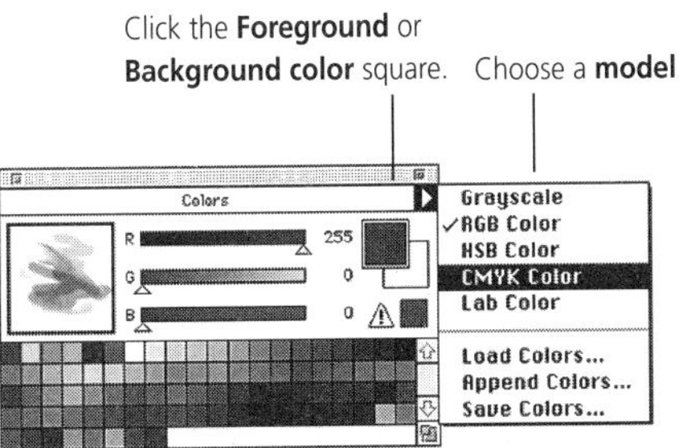

Figure 7. Click a swatch or move any of the sliders on the **Colors** palette.

To choose a Foreground or Background color from the Colors palette:

1. Click the Foreground or Background color square if it is not already active.
2. Choose a color model from the pop-up menu on the right side of the palette **(Figure 7)**.
3. Click a color swatch.
   or
   Move any of the sliders.
   (See Figure 4 on the previous page)

✓ **Tips**

- In RGB mode, white (the presence of all colors) is produced when all the sliders are in their rightmost positions. Black (the absence of all colors) is produced when all the sliders are in their leftmost positions. Gray is produced when all the sliders are vertically aligned in any other position.
- The model you choose for the Colors palette does not have to match the current picture mode. For example, you can choose the CMYK Color model from the Colors palette for a picture in RGB Color mode.

To mix a color "by hand":

1. Click a painting tool.
2. Choose a Foreground color.
   (See pages 130-132)
3. If the Brushes palette is not displayed, choose Show Brushes from the Window menu.
4. Choose Normal from the mode pop-up menu **(Figure 8)**.
5. Move the Opacity slider to below 80%.
6. Scribble on the scratch pad on the Colors palette **(Figure 9)**.
7. Choose a new Foreground color.
8. Scribble again on the scratch pad.
9. *Optional:* Click the Smudge tool, and drag across the scratch pad.
10. To choose the new color as the Foreground color, click the Eyedropper tool, then click on the color.
    or
    To choose the new color as the Background color, click the Eyedropper tool, then hold down Option and click on the color.

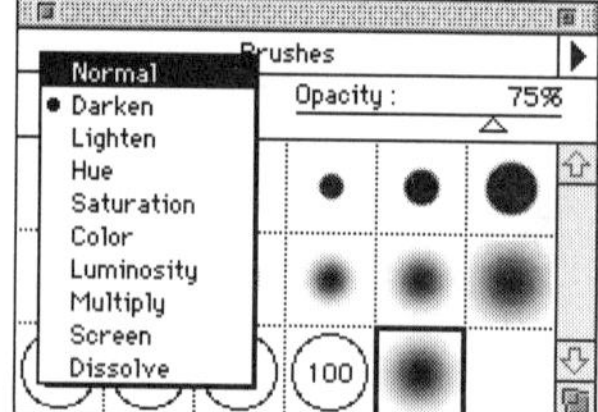

Figure 8. Choose **Normal** from the mode pop-up menu on the Brushes palette, and move the **Opacity** slider to below 80%.

Figure 9. Scribble on the scratch pad on the **Colors** palette.

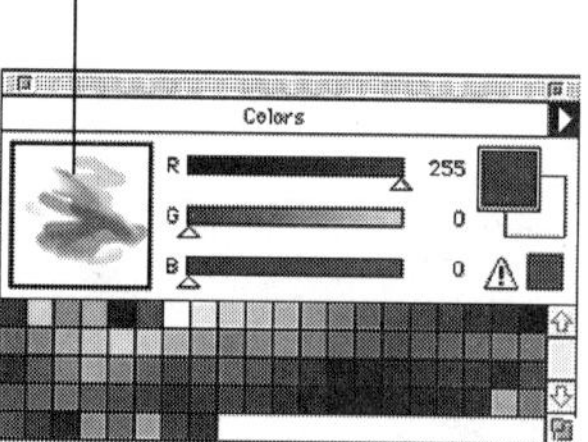

✔ Tips

- To clear the scratch pad, choose white as the Background color, click the Eraser tool, then drag across the pad.
- To clone an area of a picture onto the scratch pad, double-click the Rubber Stamp tool, choose Clone (Aligned) from the Options pop-up menu, choose an Opacity from the Brushes palette, Option-click on the picture, then drag across the scratch pad.
  (See page 168)
- To magnify the scratch pad, click on it with the Zoom tool.

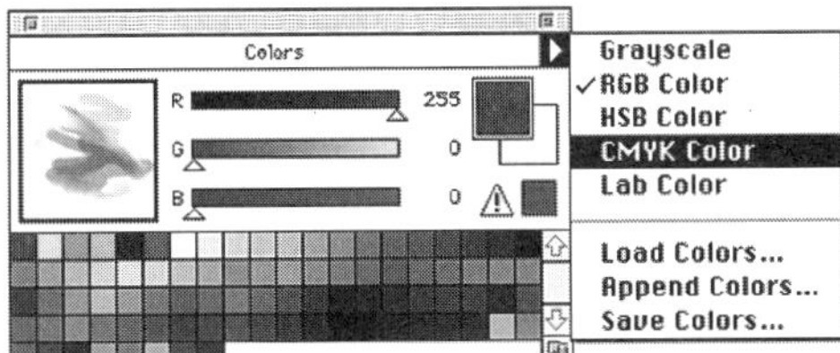

Figure 10. Choose a model from the pop-up menu, then mix a color.

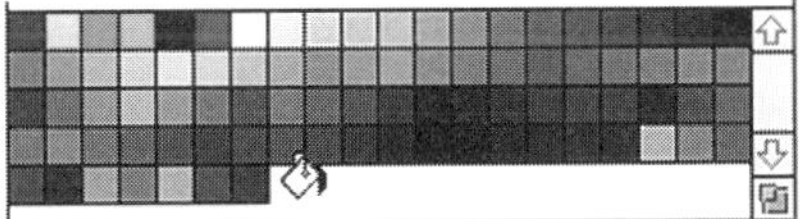

Figure 11. Click in the white area below the swatches.

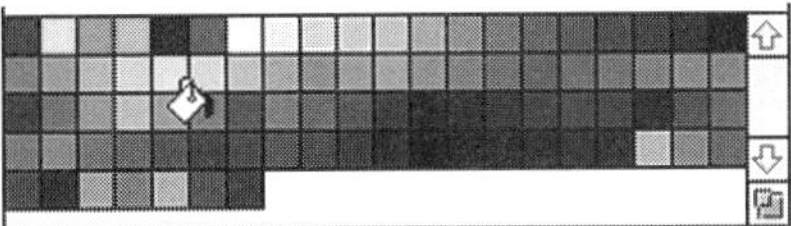

Figure 12. Click between two swatches to insert a color between them.

To add a color to the Colors palette:

1. Choose a model from the pop-up menu on the right side of the Colors palette **(Figure 10)**.
2. Mix a Foreground or Background color.
   (See pages 130-132)
3. Position the pointer below the swatches on the palette, and click with the bucket pointer icon **(Figure 11)**.
   The new color will appear next to the last swatch.

✓ Tips

- To replace an existing swatch with the new color, hold down Option and click on the color to be replaced.
- To insert the new color between two swatches, hold down Option and Shift and click on either swatch **(Figure 12)**.

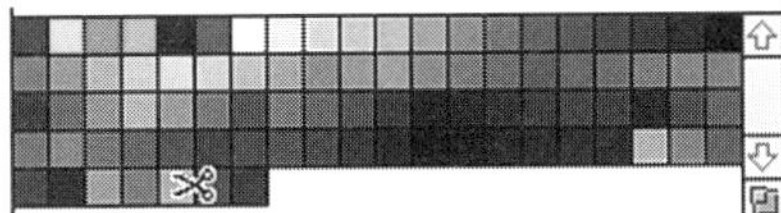

Figure 13. Hold down ⌘ and click on a swatch to delete it.

To delete a color from the Colors palette:

Hold down ⌘ and click on a swatch with the scissors pointer icon **(Figure 13)**.

Ten color swatch palettes are supplied with Photoshop, and can be loaded into any file. They include ANPA, Default, Focoltone, Pantone (Coated, Process, ProSim, and Uncoated), System, Toyo, and Trumatch.

To load a swatch palette:

1. Choose Load Colors from the pop-up menu on the right side of the Colors palette **(Figure 14)**.
2. Open the Color Palettes folder in the Photoshop application folder.
3. Double-click a palette **(Figure 15)**. The loaded swatches will appear on the Colors palette.
   or
   Highlight a palette and click Open.

✔ **Tip**

■ Load Default Colors to restore the default Photoshop palette.

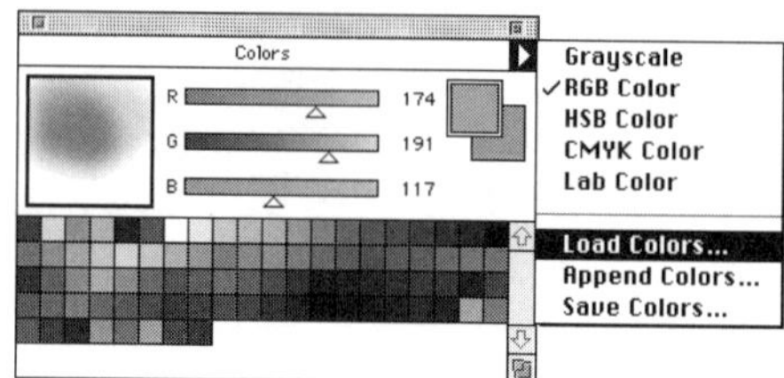

Figure 14. Choose **Load Colors** from the **Colors** palette.

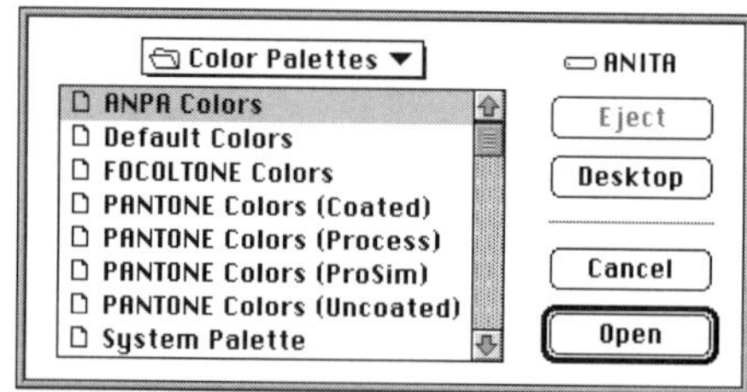

Figure 15. Double-click a palette in the **Color Palettes** folder.

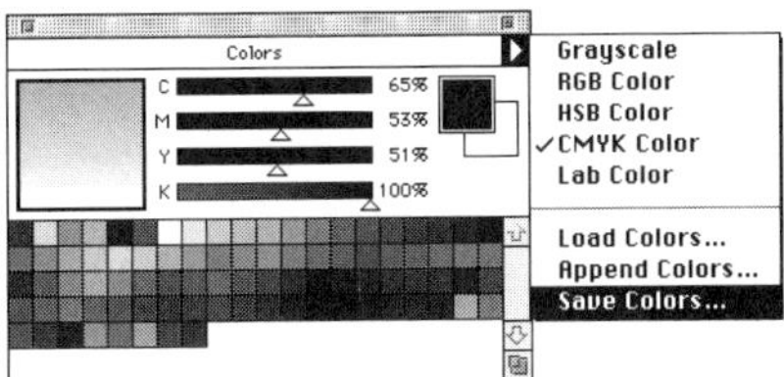

Figure 16. Choose **Save Colors** from the **Colors** palette.

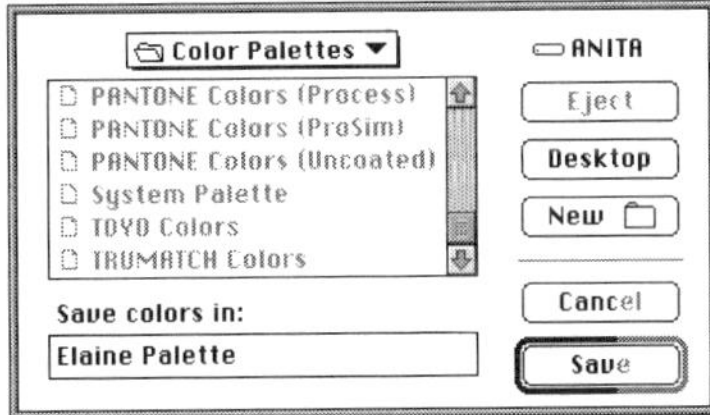

Figure 17. Enter a name in the **Save colors in** field, choose a location in which to save the palette, then click **Save**.

Swatches can be added to or deleted from any palette, and an edited palette can be saved.

To save an edited swatch palette:

1. Follow the instructions on page 133 to add or delete swatches from the Colors palette.
2. Choose Save Colors from the pop-up menu on the Colors palette **(Figure 16)**.
3. Enter a name for the edited palette in the "Save colors in" field **(Figure 17)**.
4. Choose a location in which to save the palette.
5. Click Save.

✔ **Tip**

■ Do not save over the Default palette, because you may want to reload it later. Instead, enter a new name for the edited version.

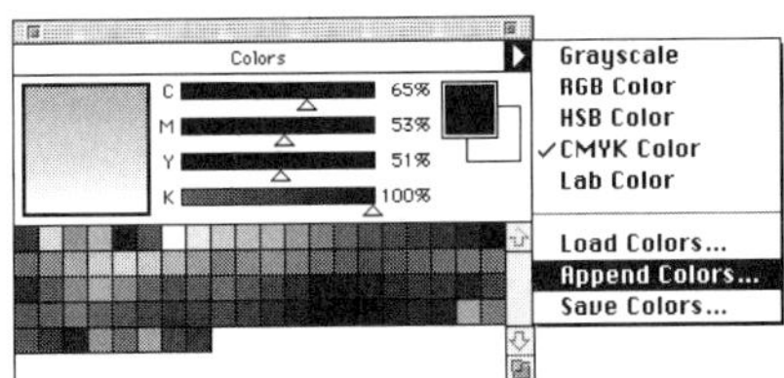

Figure 18. Choose **Append Colors** from the **Colors** palette.

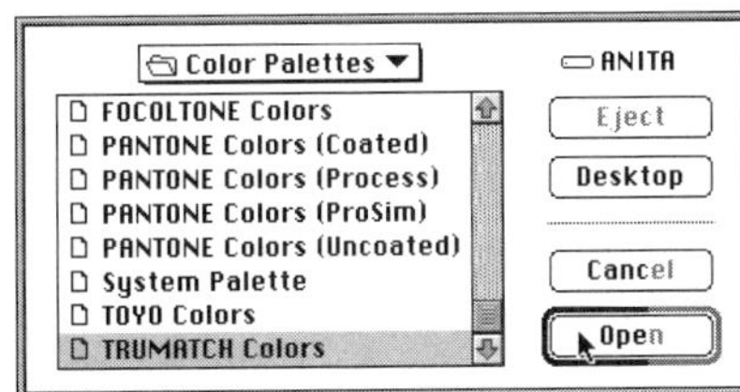

Figure 19. Open the Color Palettes or other folder, highlight a palette, then click **Open**.

A palette can be appended to another palette.

To append a swatch palette:

1. Choose Append Colors from the pop-up menu on the Colors palette **(Figure 18)**.
2. Open the Color Palettes or another palettes folder located in the Photoshop application folder **(Figure 19)**.
3. Double-click a palette.
   or
   Highlight a palette and click Open.
4. The appended swatches will appear below the existing swatches.

CHANGE COLOR

IN THIS CHAPTER you will learn to fill a selection with color, color the edge of a selection, tint a Grayscale picture or adjust a color picture using the Hue/Saturation and Color Balance dialog boxes, and adjust color using the Variations dialog box.

(See also "To create a duotone" on page 220)

Edit
Undo Copy ⌘Z
Cut ⌘X
Copy ⌘C
Paste ⌘V
Paste Into
Paste Behind
Clear
Fill...
Stroke...
Crop
Create Publisher...
Publisher Options...
Define Pattern
Take Snapshot
Composite Controls...

Figure 1. Choose **Fill** from the **Edit** menu.

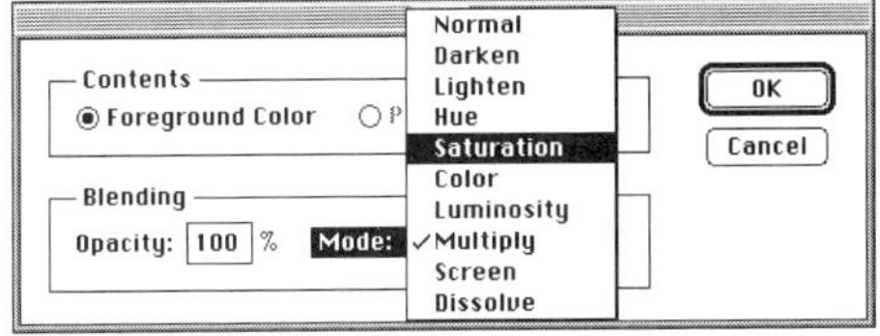

Figure 2. In the **Fill** dialog box, enter an **Opacity** and choose a **Mode**.

To fill a selection with color:

1. Select an area of a picture.
   (See pages 62-65)
2. Choose a Foreground color.
   (See pages 130-132)
3. Choose Fill from the Edit menu **(Figure 1)**.
4. Enter a number in the Opacity field **(Figure 2)**
5. Choose a mode from the Mode pop-up menu.
   (See page 147)
6. Click OK or press Return **(Gallery 13a)**.

✔ Tips

- If you don't like the new fill color, choose Undo from the Edit menu immediately so it won't blend with your next color or mode choice.
- Press Delete to fill a selection with the Background color, 100% opacity.
- Hold down Option and press Delete to fill a selection with the Foreground color, 100% opacity.
  (To create a Fill pattern from a picture, see page 203)

To color the edge of a selection:

1. Select an area of a picture **(Figure 3)**.
   (See pages 62-64)
2. Choose a Foreground color.
   (See pages 130-132)
3. Choose Stroke from the Edit menu **(Figure 4)**.
4. Enter a number between 1 and 16 in the Width field **(Figure 5)**.
5. Click Inside, Center, or Outside (the Location of the stroke on the selection edge).
6. Enter a number in the Opacity field.
7. Choose a mode from the Mode pop-up menu.
8. Click OK or press Return **(Gallery 13b)**.

Figure 3. Select an area (or areas) of a picture.

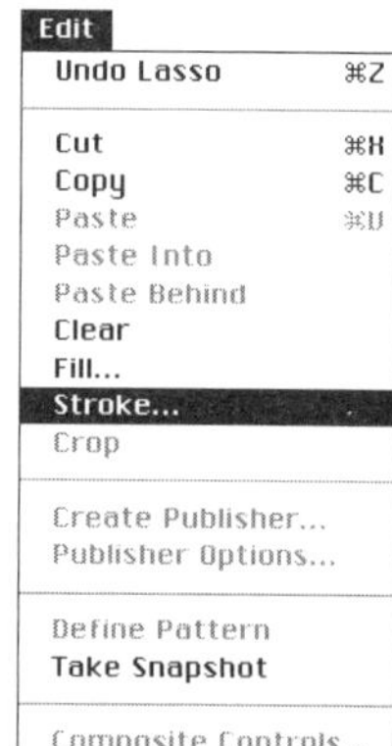

Figure 4. Choose **Stroke** from the **Edit** menu.

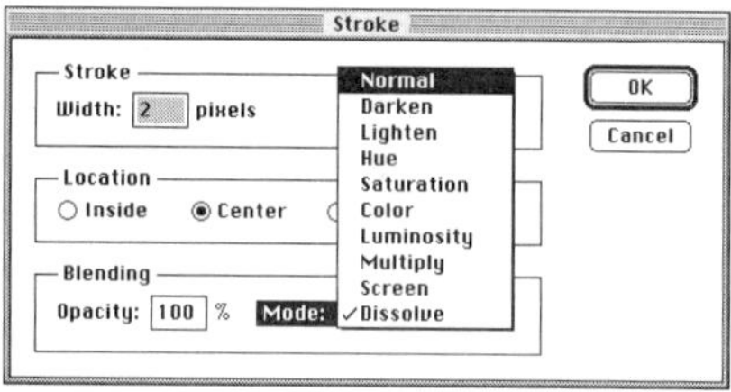

Figure 5. In the **Stroke** dialog box, enter a **Width** and **Opacity**, and choose a **Mode**.

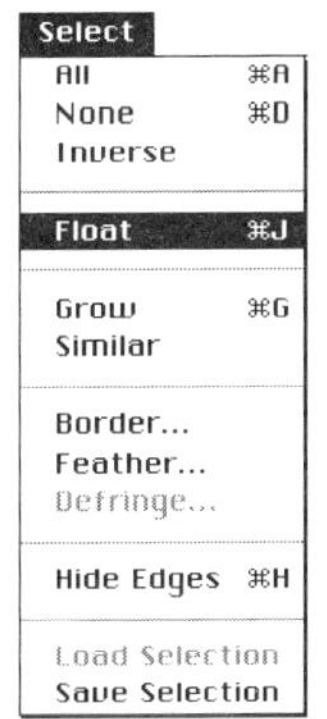

Figure 6. Choose **Float** from the **Select** menu.

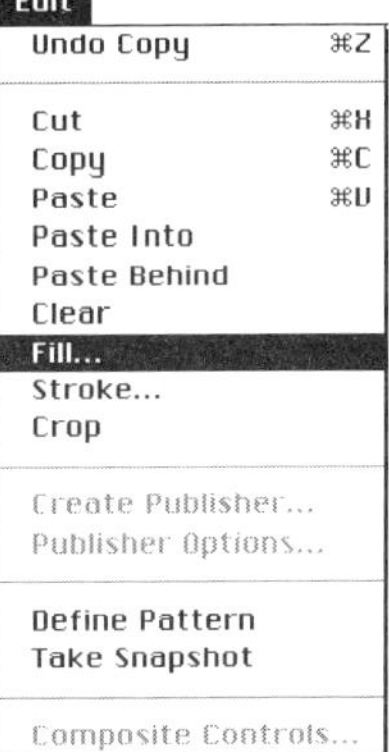

Figure 7. Choose **Fill** from the **Edit** menu.

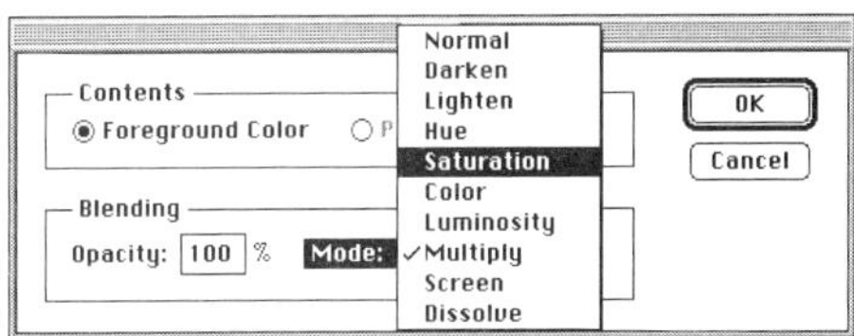

Figure 8. In the **Fill** dialog box, enter an **Opacity** and choose a **Mode**.

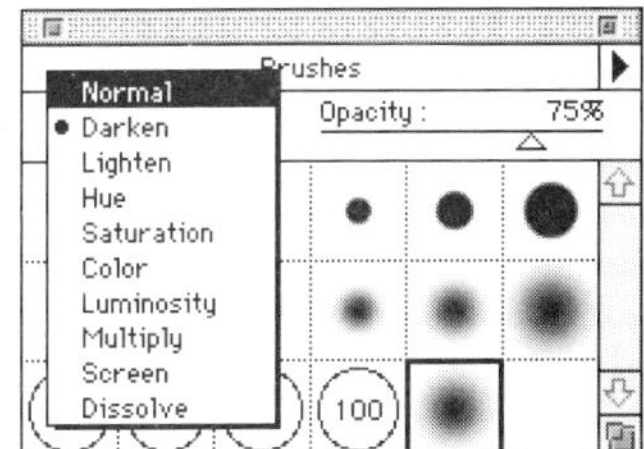

Figure 9. Choose a **mode** and **Opacity** from the **Brushes** palette.

To fill a selection and preview fill options:

1. Select an area of the picture. *(See pages 62-65)*
2. Choose Float from the Select menu **(Figure 6)**.
3. Choose a Foreground color. *(See pages 130-132)*
4. Choose Fill from the Edit menu **(Figure 7)**.
5. Enter 100 in the Opacity field **(Figure 8)**.
6. Choose Normal from the Mode pop-up menu.
7. Click OK or press Return.
8. If the Brushes palette is not displayed, choose Show Brushes from the Window menu.
9. Choose a mode from the pop-up menu on the left side of the palette **(Figure 9)**.
   and/or
   Move the Opacity slider.
10. Choose None from the Select menu **(Gallery 13e-h)**.
    or
    Click outside the selection with the Rectangular Marquee, Elliptical Marquee, or Lasso tool (not the Magic Wand tool).

✓ Tips

- Choose Clear from the Edit menu to remove the selection. The underlying pixels will not change.
- You can also use the Composite Controls dialog box, opened from the Edit menu, to modify a floating selection. *(See pages 179-181)*

To colorize a grayscale picture using Hue/Saturation:

1. Open a Grayscale picture **(Figure 10)**.
2. Choose RGB Color or CMYK Color from the Mode menu **(Figure 11)**.
3. Choose Hue/Saturation from the Adjust pop-up menu under the Image menu **(Figure 12)**.
4. Check the Colorize box. The picture will be tinted red **(Figure 13)**.
5. Move the Hue slider left or right to apply a different tint. Pause to preview.
6. Move the Saturation slider.
7. Move the Lightness slider.
8. Click OK or press Return **(Gallery 13c)**.

✓ Tips

- To restore the original dialog box settings, hold down Option and click Reset.
- You can also tint a Grayscale picture by converting it into a duotone. *(See page 220)*
- To colorize pure black, move the Lightness slider to the right. To colorize pure white, move the Lightness slider to the left **(Gallery 13c)**.

The Preview check box.

Dialog boxes opened from the Map and Adjust pop-up menus (Image menu) have a Preview box. Changes affect the entire screen with the Preview box unchecked. Changes preview only in the picture with the Preview box checked. CMYK color displays more acccurately with Preview on.

Figure 10. The original Grayscale picture.

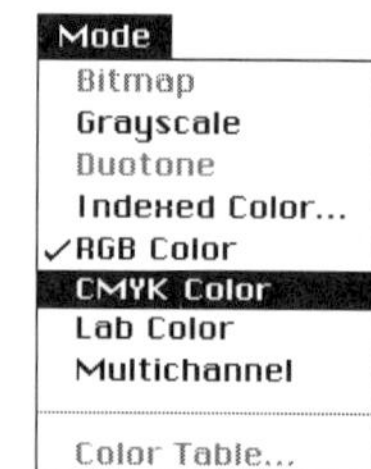

Figure 11. Choose **RGB** or **CMYK** from the **Mode** menu.

Hue/Saturation
Master, R, Y, G, C, B, M
Hue: -7
Saturation: 93
Lightness: +19
Sample:
OK
Cancel
Load...
Save...
☒ Colorize
☒ Preview

Move the **Hue, Saturation,** or **Lightness** sliders.

Check the **Colorize** box.

Figure 12. The **Hue/Saturation** dialog box.

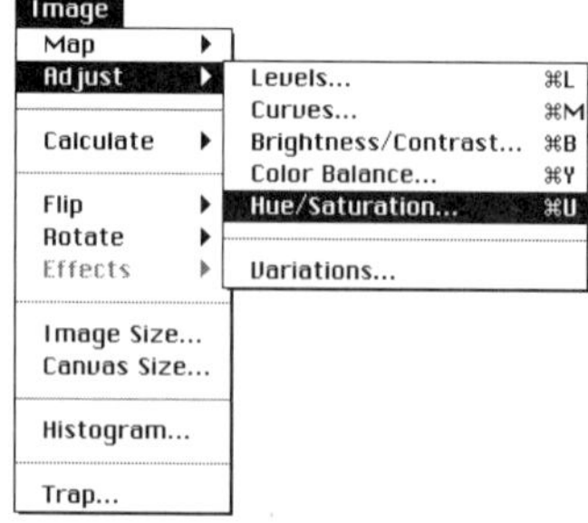

Figure 13. Choose **Hue/Saturation** from the **Adjust** pop-up menu under the **Image** menu.

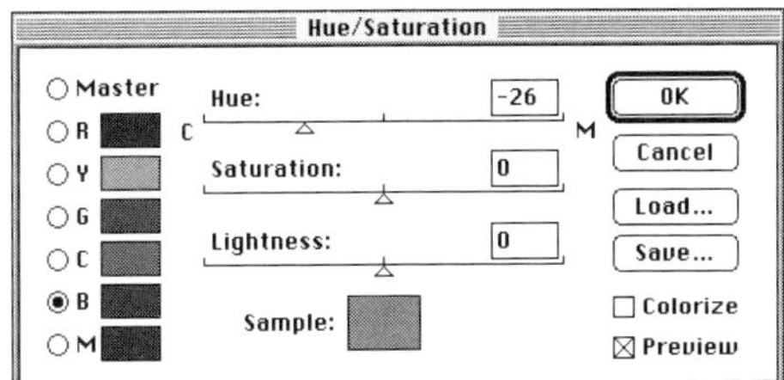

Figure 14. In the **Hue/Saturation** dialog box, click Master or a color button, then move the **Hue, Saturation,** or **Lightness** slider.

Color adjustments using the Hue/Saturation dialog box are easiest to make in a picture with clearly defined color areas.

To adjust a color picture using Hue/Saturation:

1. Choose Hue/Saturation from the Adjust pop-up menu under the Image menu **(Figure 14)**.
2. Click Master to adjust all colors.
   or
   Click a color button to adjust only that color.
3. Move the Hue slider left or right. If you clicked Master, the hues will change in the entire picture. If you clicked a color button, that hue will be redefined. Pause to preview.
4. Move the Saturation slider to the left to decrease saturation or to the right to increase saturation.
5. Move the Lightness slider to the left to add black or to the right to add white.
6. Click OK or press Return **(Gallery 13d)**.

✔ Tips

- To recolor only a portion of a picture, select an area of the picture, then proceed with the steps above. *(See page 62-65)*
- Use the Save and Load command buttons in the Levels, Hue/Saturation, and Variations dialog box to save color adjustment settings in a picture, then apply them to another picture.
- To restore the original dialog box settings, hold down Option and click Reset.

Use the Color Balance dialog box to apply a warm or cool cast to a picture's highlights, midtones, or shadows. Color adjustments are easiest to make in a picture with a good tonal range.

To colorize or color correct using Color Balance:

1. To colorize a Grayscale picture, choose a color mode from the Mode menu.
2. Choose Color Balance from the Adjust pop-up menu under the Image menu **(Figure 15)**.
3. Click Shadows, Midtones, or Highlights **(Figure 16)**.
4. Move any of the sliders toward a color name to add more of that color. Cool and warm colors are paired opposite each other. Pause to preview.
5. Repeat with any other button selected.
6. Click OK or press Return **(Figure 17** and **Gallery 13i** and **l)**.

✔ Tips

- Move sliders toward related colors to make a picture warmer or cooler. For example, move sliders toward Cyan and Blue to produce a cool cast.
- Use a Paintbrush with a light opacity to recolor small areas.
- With the Color Balance or any other Adjust dialog box open, the Info palette shows a color breakdown of the original and modified pixel under the cursor.

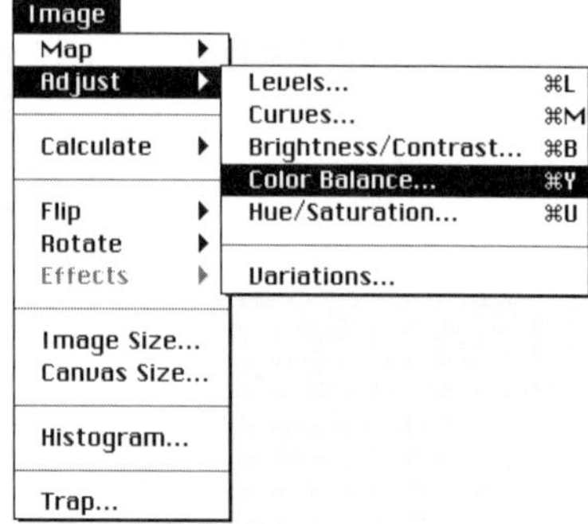

Figure 15. Choose **Color Balance** from the **Adjust** pop-up menu under the **Image** menu.

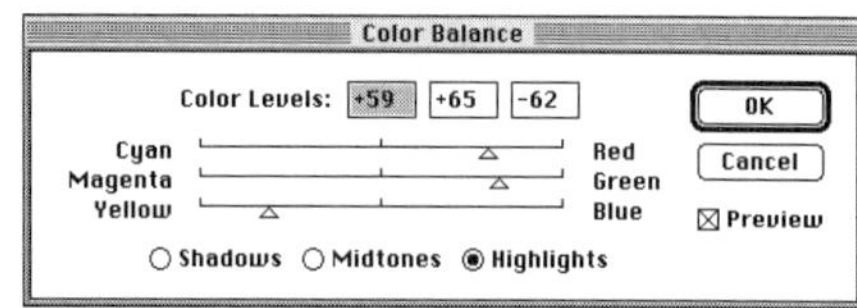

Figure 16. In the **Color Balance** dialog box, click **Shadows, Midtones,** or **Highlights,** then move any slider toward a color name.

Figure 17. A Grayscale picture.

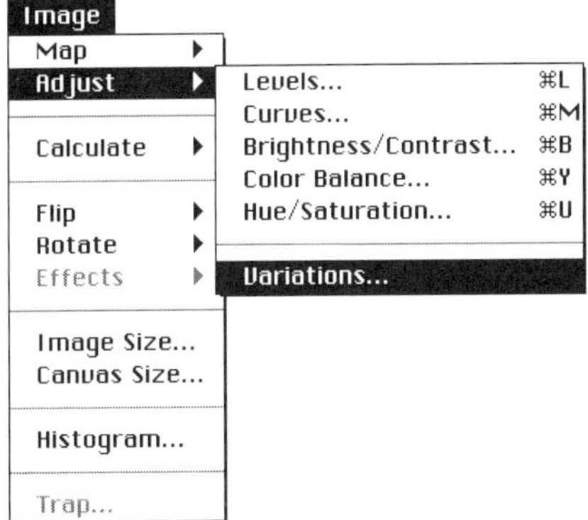

Figure 18. Choose **Variations** from the **Adjust** pop-up menu under the **Image** menu (the Variations plug-in module must be installed for Variations to be available).

Thumbnail previews in the Variations dialog box represent how a picture will look with various color adjustments. To make more precise adjustments with a full-screen preview, use the Color Balance dialog box.

To adjust color using thumbnail Variations:

1. Choose RGB Color or CMYK Color from the Mode menu.
2. Choose Variations from the Adjust pop-up menu under the Image menu **(Figure 18)**.
3. Click Shadows, Midtones, or Highlights to modify only those areas **(Figure 19)**.
   or
   Click Saturation to adjust the saturation of the entire picture.
4. Position the Fine/Coarse slider right of center to make major adjustments or left of center to make minor adjustments. Each notch to the right doubles the adjustment per click. Each notch to the left halves the adjustment per click.
5. Click any "More..." thumbnail to add more of that color to the picture. Pause to preview. The Current Pick thumbnail represents the modified picture.
6. *Optional:* Repeat steps 3 and 4.
7. Click OK or press Return **(Gallery 13j-k)**.

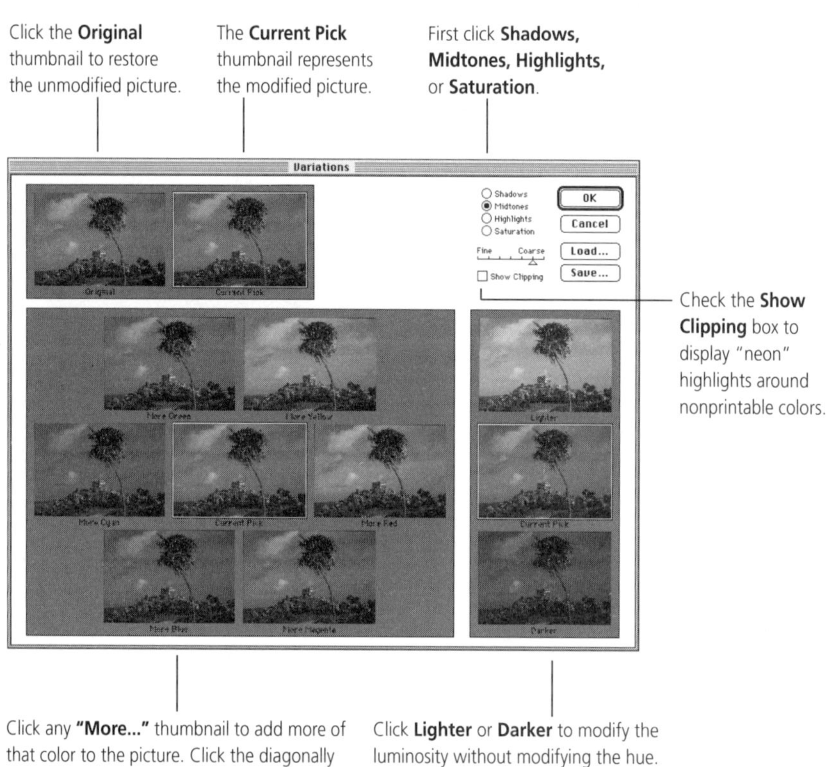

Figure 19. The **Variations** dialog box.

PAINT 14

Show Brushes.

The Brushes palette is used throughout this chapter. Choose Show Brushes from the Window menu to display it **(Figure 1)**.

IN THIS CHAPTER you will learn to use Photoshop's Line, Airbrush, Pencil and Paintbrush tools **(Figure 2)**. You can apply strokes to a scanned image or to a new document. You will learn to create custom brushes using the Brushes palette and each tool's Options box, to save and load brush palettes, and to create drop shadows. The Paint Bucket tool is also covered because it produces painterly effects.

Window
New Window
Zoom In ⌘+
Zoom Out ⌘−
Show Rulers ⌘R
Show Brushes
Show Channels
Show Colors
Show Info
Show Paths
✓Untitled-1 (RGB, 1:1)

Figure 1. Choose **Show Brushes** from the **Window** menu.

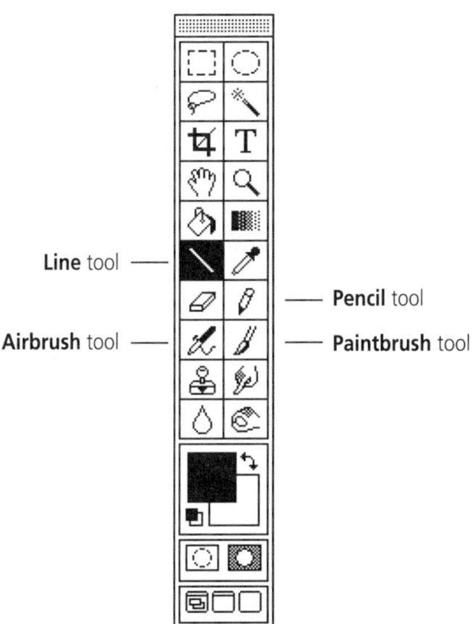

Figure 2. Painting tools covered in this chapter.

To use the Paintbrush or Airbrush tool:

1. Click the Paintbrush or Airbrush tool **(Figure 2)**.
2. Choose a Foreground color. *(See pages 130-132)*
3. Click a hard-edged tip in the first row of the Brushes palette or a soft-edged tip in the second row **(Figure 3)**.
4. For the Paintbrush tool, move the Opacity slider. At 100% opacity, the stroke will completely cover the underlying pixels.
   or
   For the Airbrush tool, move the Pressure slider.
5. Choose a mode from the mode pop-up menu. *(See "Paint and fill modes" on the next page)*
6. Drag across any area of the picture **(Gallery 14a-d)**. If you press and hold on an area with the Airbrush tool without dragging, the "paintdrop" will gradually widen and become more saturated.

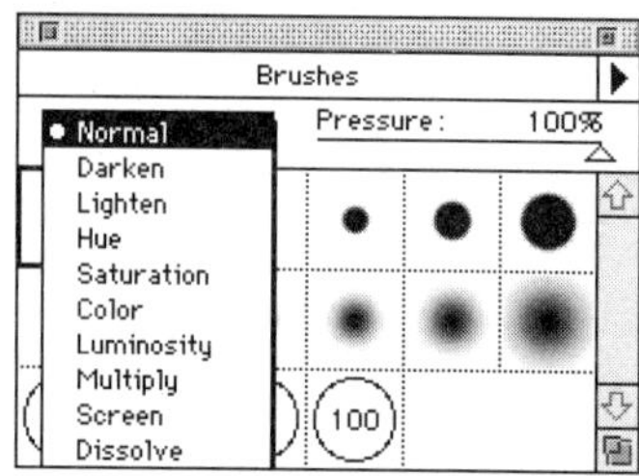

Figure 3. Click a tip, move the Pressure or Opacity slider, and choose a mode on the **Brushes** palette.

✔ Tips

- To undo the last stroke, choose Undo from the Edit menu immediately. Only the last stroke can be undone.
- To paint in a restricted area while protecting the rest of the picture, select the area before painting.
- To draw a straight stroke, click once to begin the stroke, then hold down Shift and click in a different location to complete the stroke.
- You can choose a Fade-out Distance for the Paintbrush or Airbrush tool. *(See page 148)*
- To choose a Foreground color from the picture with a painting tool selected, hold down Option and click on the picture.

The original picture.

13a. Three fill opacities and modes. Clockwise from lower left: untouched, 45% Normal, 90% Saturation, 50% Hue.

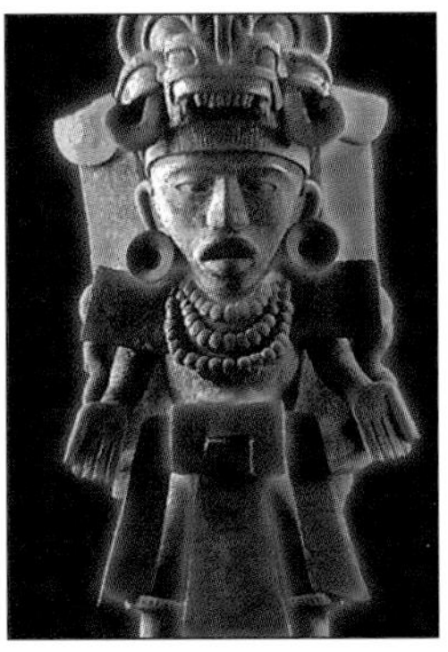

13b. A selection stroked using the Paintbrush tool with a soft-edged tip.

13b. A rectangular selection with the stroke command applied.

13c. A Grayscale picture colorized using Hue/Saturation. Clockwise from lower left: Hue -26, Lightness -20; Hue -142, Lightness +8; Hue 15, Lightness 0; Hue 113, Lightness 0. A Saturation of 50 was used for all sections.

13d. Parts of a Grayscale picture colorized using Threshold and Hue/Saturation.The Hue/Saturation Lightness slider was moved to add color to darks (on the left) and lights (on the right).

The original picture.

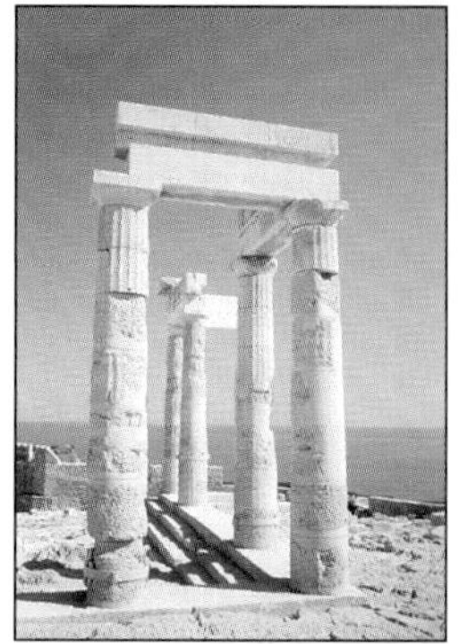

13e. Yellow fill — Normal mode, 60% Opacity.

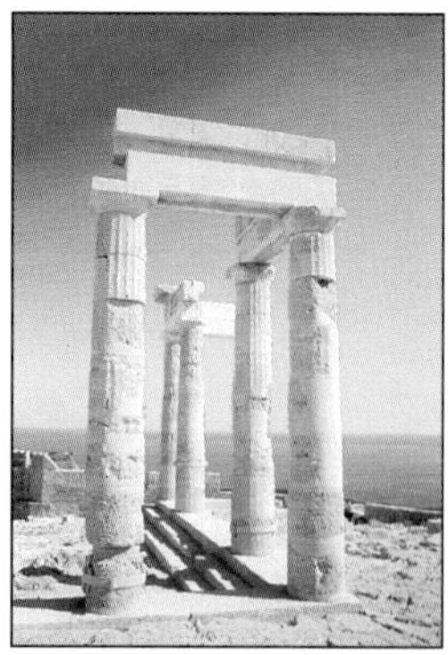

13f. Orange fill — Lighten mode, 90% Opacity.

13g. Purple fill — Multiply mode, Opacity 60%.

13h. Yellow fill — Dissolve mode, Opacity 50%.

13i. A Grayscale picture colorized using the Color Balance dialog box.

13j. The Variations dialog box is used for color adjustment.

The original picture.

13k. The picture adjusted using the Variations dialog box.

13l. The picture adjusted using the Color Balance dialog box. Use the Color Balance dialog box to see a full screen image when making color adjustments.

The original picture.

14a. The Paintbrush tool — Normal mode, 85% Opacity.

14b. The Paintbrush tool — Darken mode, 85% Opacity.

14c. The Paintbrush tool — Hue mode, 85% Opacity.

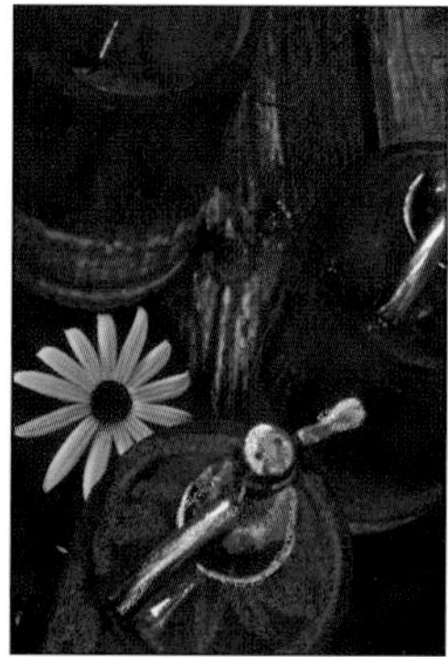

14d. The Paintbrush tool — Dissolve mode, 48% Opacity.

14e. The Paintbrush tool — Normal mode, Fade-out option.

14f. Custom brush tips used with various Foreground colors and modes.

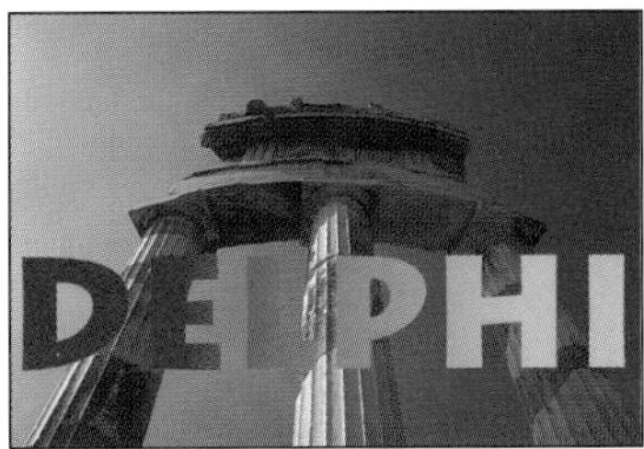

15a. Type filled with a linear blend.

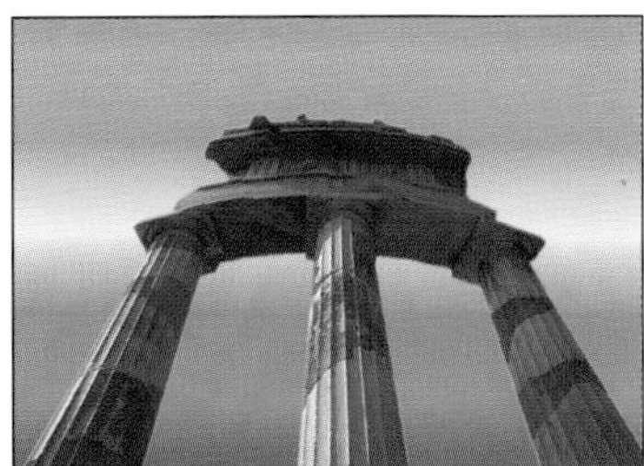

15b. A linear, counterclockwise spectrum blend.

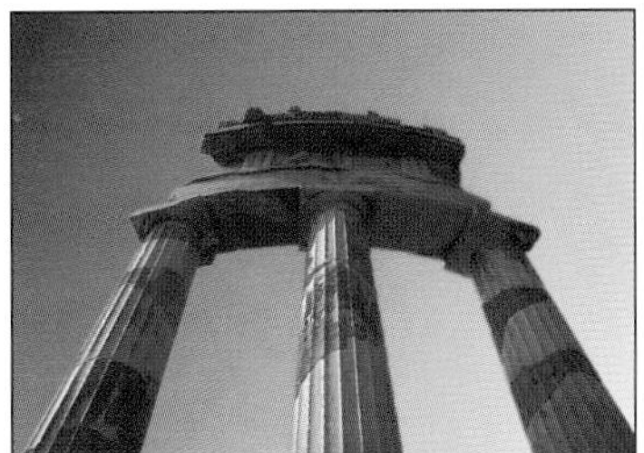

15c. A linear blend — red Foreground color, yellow Background color.

15d. A multicolor wash created with the Gradient tool. A low opacity blend was applied to the entire picture and a second light opacity blend was applied to the inner selection. The Rubber Stamp tool was used to restore some original colors.

16. This picture was converted from RGB mode to Grayscale mode, then back to RGB mode. The Rubber Stamp tool was then used with an Opacity of 50%, Color mode to restore some of the original color.

17a. The Trace Contour and Minimum filters.

17b. The Find Edges filter, without the Solarize filter step *(See 17c)*. The Rubber Stamp tool was used with a light opacity to restore color from the last saved version.

17c. The Find Edges filter, the Invert command, then the Solarize filter. The Rubber Stamp tool was used with a light opacity to restore color from the last saved version.

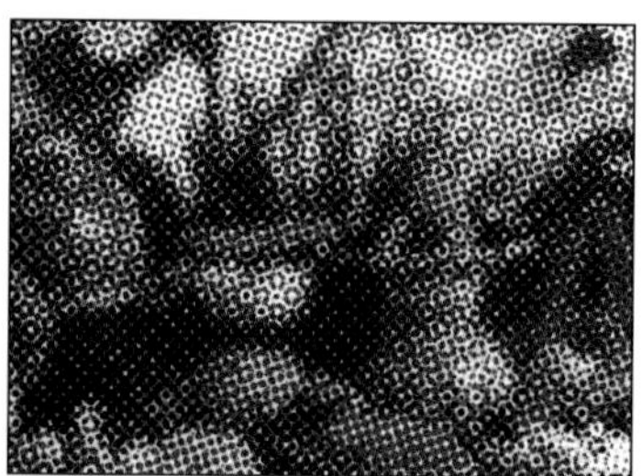

17d. The Color Halftone filter.

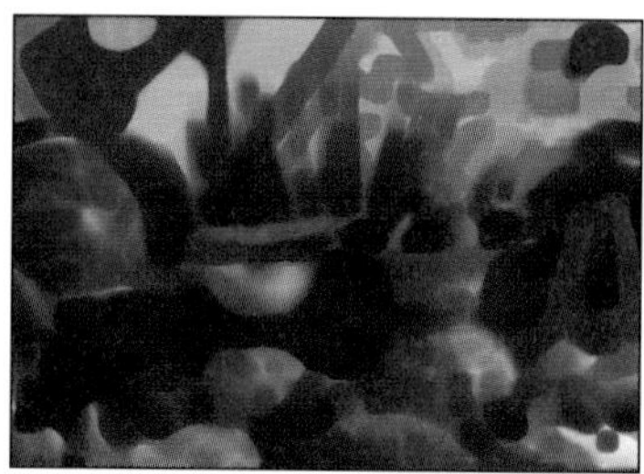

17e. A "watercolor."

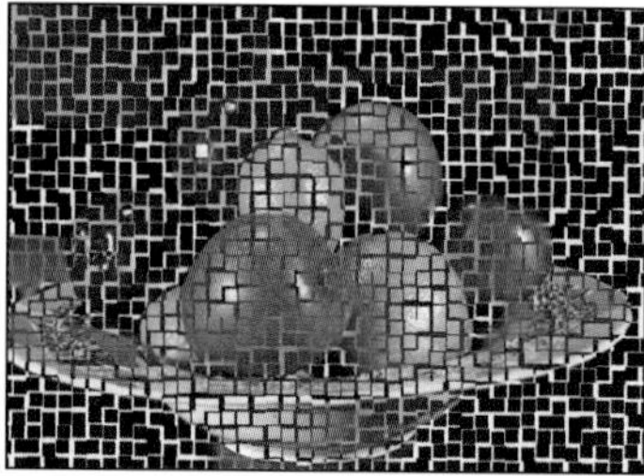

17f. The Tiles filter with the Inverse Image fill option.

17g. A woven texture.

18a. A picture converted to Indexed Color mode.

18b. A picture in Indexed Color mode with the Spectrum Color Table.

18c. Indexed color image pasted onto original image, then modified using Composite Controls — Normal mode, 50% Opacity.

18d. Indexed color image pasted onto original image, then modified using Composite Controls — Hue mode, 80% Opacity.

18e. Indexed color image pasted onto original image, then modified using Composite Controls — Normal mode, 90% Opacity, Underlying black slider moved to 30.

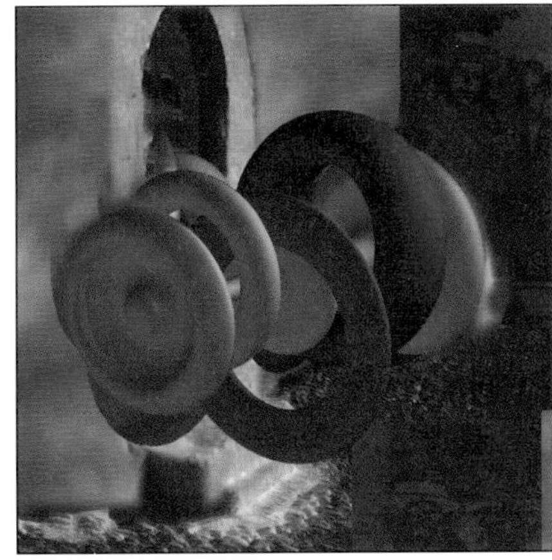

Memories. Peter Lourekas.
Created using Adobe Dimensions, Photoshop and scanned images.

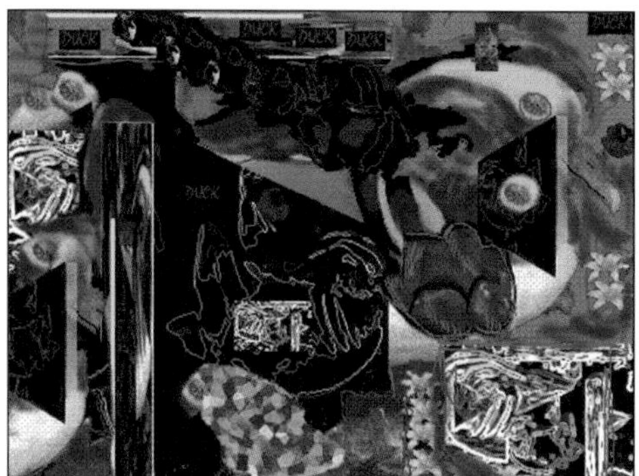

Duck Wuck Phil Allen

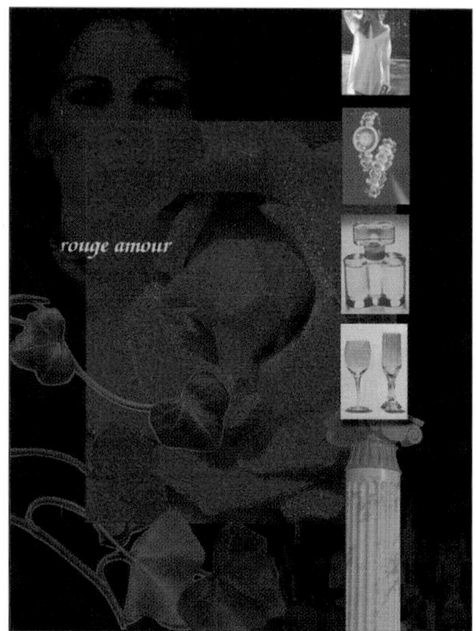

Leah Krivan

Raisa Grubshteyn

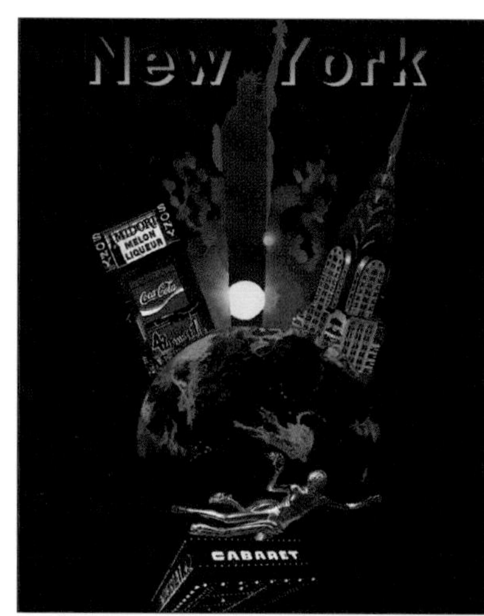

Jin Kim

Paint and fill modes

You can select from ten modes for a painting tool from the pop-up menu on the left side of the Brushes palette **(Figure 3)**: Normal, Darken, Lighten, Hue, Saturation, Color, Luminosity, Multiply, Screen, and Dissolve. You can choose from the same modes in the Composite Controls, Fill, and Fill Path dialog boxes. The mode you choose affects how underlying pixels are modified. Here are the effects they create.

NORMAL
Pixels of any color are modified.

DARKEN
Pixels lighter than the Foreground color are modified; pixels darker than the Foreground color are not. When using Darken, choose a Foreground shade or color that is just darker than the colors you wish to modify.

LIGHTEN
Pixels darker than the Foreground color are modified; pixels lighter than the Foreground color are not. When using Lighten, choose a Foreground shade or color that is just lighter than the colors you wish to modify.

HUE
The Foreground color hue is applied. Saturation and luminosity values are not modified.

SATURATION
Only saturation values are modified.

COLOR
The Foreground color's saturation and hue are applied. Luminosity (light and dark) values are not modified.

LUMINOSITY
Only luminosity values are modified.

MULTIPLY
Pixels become darker and more saturated.

SCREEN
Pixels become lighter and closer to the hue of the Foreground color.

DISSOLVE
Pixels are randomly replaced with the Foreground color, creating a chalky, dry brush texture. The higher the pressure or opacity, the more solid is the application of color.

You can specify how a stroke made with some tools ends — whether it stops abruptly or fades gently as it finishes.

To specify a fade-out distance:

1. Double-click the Pencil, Airbrush, or Paintbrush tool **(Figure 2)**.
2. Enter a number between 0 and 9999 in the Distance field **(Figure 4)**. The higher the number, the longer the stroke will be before it fades.
3. Click To Transparent to fade from the Foreground color to no color.
   or
   Click To Background to fade from the Foreground color to the Background color.
4. Click OK or press Return **(Gallery 14e)**.

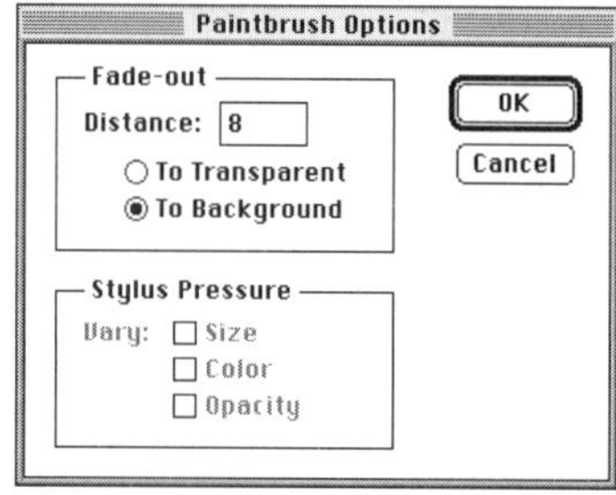

Figure 4. Double-click a tool, then enter a number in the **Distance** field in the tool **Options** dialog box.

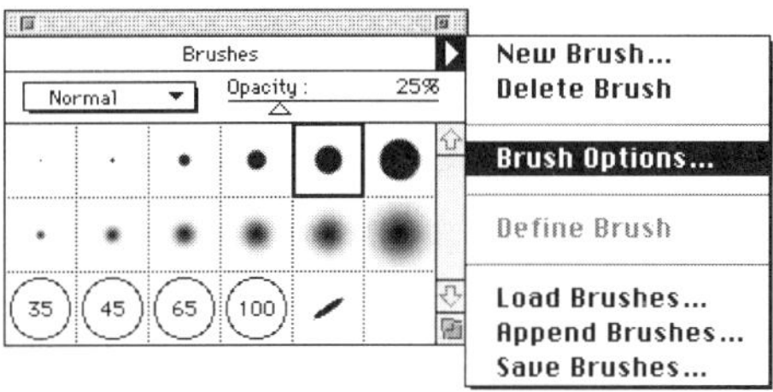

Figure 5. Double-click a brush tip on the **Brushes** palette, or choose **Brush Options**.

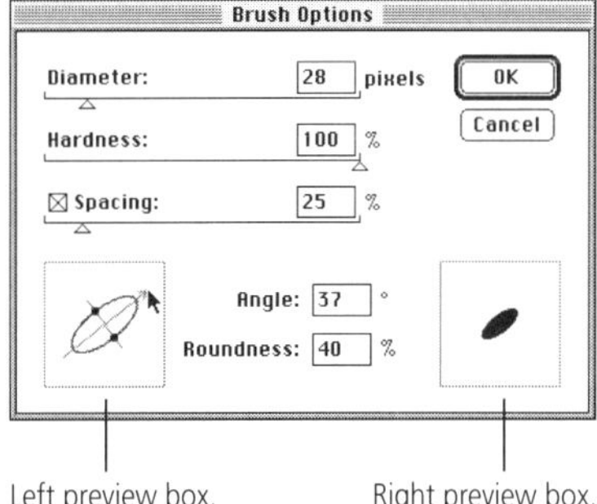

Figure 6. Choose **Diameter, Hardness, Spacing, Angle,** and **Roundness** values for a brush in the **Brush Options** dialog box.

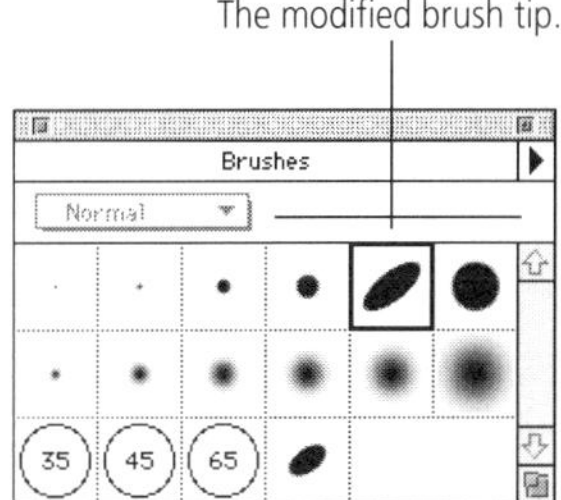

Figure 7.

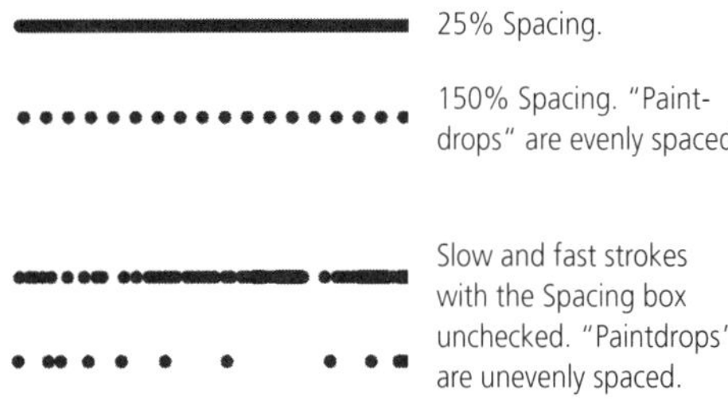

To modify a brush tip:

1. Double-click a brush tip on the Brushes palette **(Figure 5)**.
   or
   Choose Brush Options from the pop-up menu in the upper right corner of the palette.
2. Drag the Diameter slider **(Figure 6)**.
   or
   Enter a number between 1 and 999 in the Diameter field.
3. Drag the Hardness slider.
   or
   Enter a number between 0 and 100 in the Hardness field (the percentage of the diameter of the stroke that is opaque).
4. Drag the Spacing slider.
   or
   Enter a number between 0 and 999 in the Spacing field. The higher the number, the farther apart each "paint-drop" will be.
   or
   Uncheck the Spacing box to have the brush respond to mouse speed. The faster the mouse is dragged, the more "paintdrops" will skip.
5. Enter a number between 0 to 100 in the Roundness field. The higher the number, the rounder the tip.
   or
   Move either black dot up or down in the left preview box.
6. Enter a number between -180 and 180 in the Angle field.
   or
   Move the gray arrow in a circular direction in the left preview box.
7. Click OK or press Return **(Figure 7)**.

✔ Tip

- Only the Spacing percentage can be modified for the Assorted brushes and most of the Drop Shadow brushes.

To create a new brush tip:

1. Click on the white area in the lower right hand corner of the Brushes palette **(Figure 8)**.
   or
   Choose New Brush from the pop-up menu on the right side of the palette.
2. Follow steps 2-7 on the previous page to customize the tip. The new tip will appear after the last tip on the palette **(Figure 9)**.

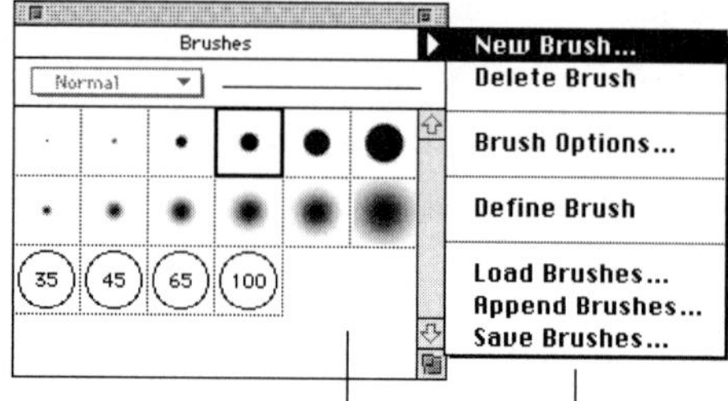

Figure 8. Click on the white area at the bottom of the **Brushes** palette, or choose **New Brush** from the pop-up menu.

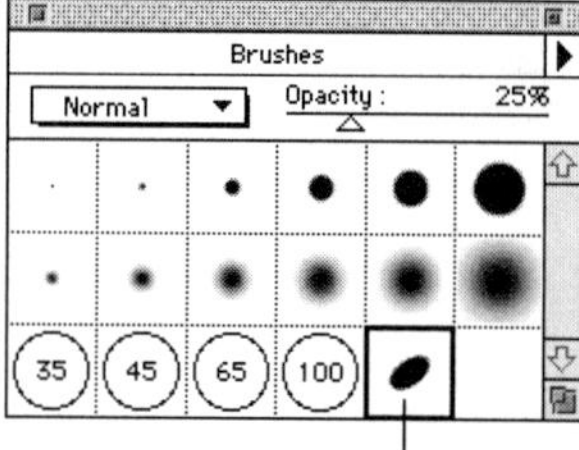

Figure 9. The new tip appears after the last tip.

To delete a brush tip:

1. Click a brush tip on the Brushes palette.
2. Choose Delete Brush from the pop-up menu on the right side of the palette **(Figure 10)**.

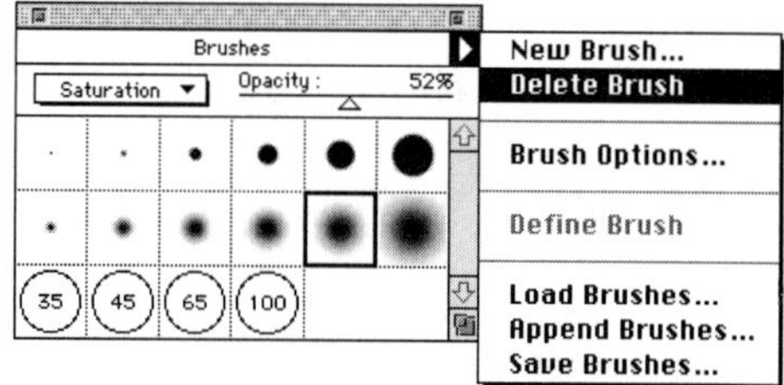

Figure 10. Click a tip, then choose **Delete Brush** from the pop-up menu on the right side of the palette.

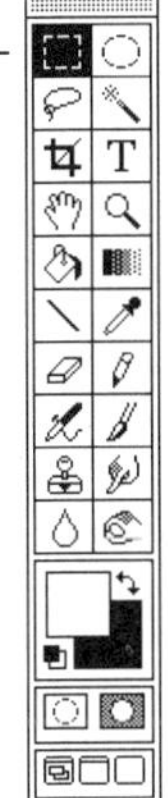

Figure 11. Click the **Rectangular Marquee** tool.

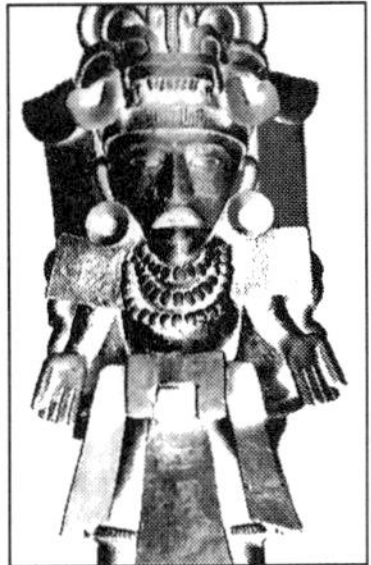

Figure 12. Select an area of a picture.

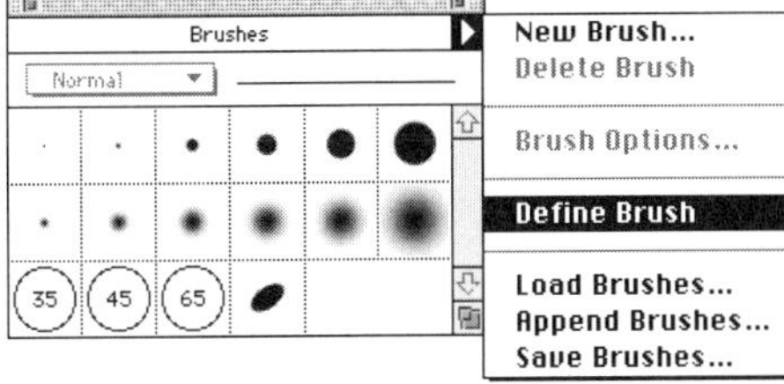

Figure 13. Choose **Define Brush** from the pop-up menu on the right side of the **Brushes** palette.

Monochromatic shades of the Foreground color are applied when you use a brush tip created from an area of a picture.

To create a brush tip from a picture:

1. Click the Rectangular Marquee tool **(Figure 11)**.
2. Select an area of a picture. The selection cannot exceed 1,000 by 1,000 pixels **(Figure 12)**.
3. Choose Define Brush from the pop-up menu on the right side of the Brushes palette. The new tip will appear after the last tip in the palette **(Figures 13-14** and **Gallery 14f)**.

✔ Tips

- Use the tip with the Paintbrush, Airbrush, or Pencil tool, and click (don't drag) on a white or monochromatic area.
- To smooth the edges of the stroke, double-click the custom brush tip, then check the Anti-aliased box. This option is not available for a large brush. You can also specify a Spacing value in the same dialog box. The higher the percentage, the greater the distance between "paintdrops."

Figure 14. A custom brush tip.

To save a Brushes palette:

1. Choose Save Brushes from the pop-up menu on the right side of the Brushes palette **(Figure 15)**.
2. Enter a name in the "Save brushes in" field **(Figure 16)**.
3. Choose a location in which to save the palette.
4. Click Save or press Return.

✓ Tip

- To keep the option to reload the original Default Brushes palette, don't save the palette under the name "Default Brushes."

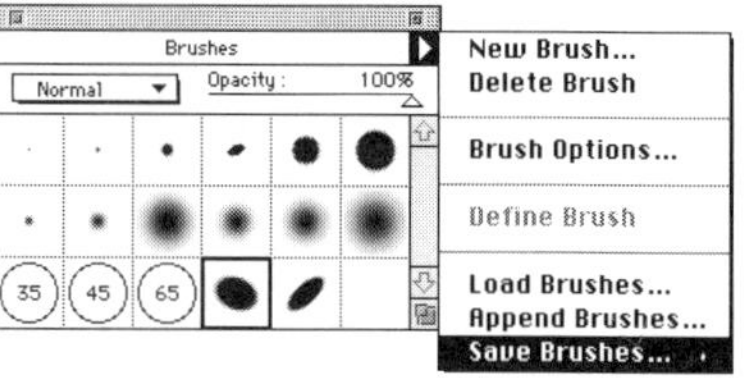

Figure 15. Choose **Save Brushes** from the pop-up menu on the right side of the **Brushes** palette.

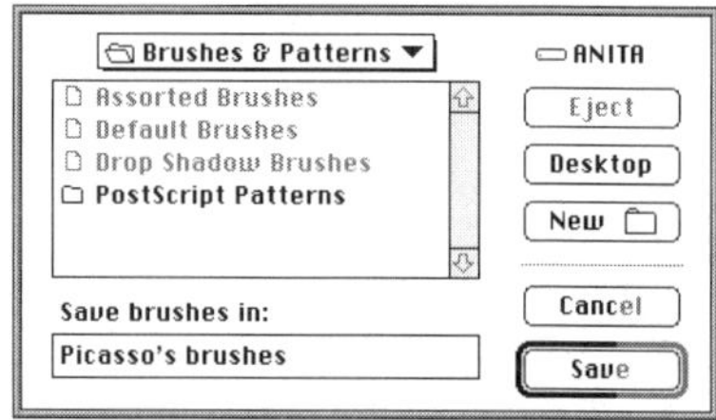

Figure 16. Enter a name in the **Save brushes in** field, choose a location in which to save it, then click **Save**.

To load a Brushes palette:

1. Choose Load Brushes from the pop-up menu on the right side of the Brushes palette **(Figure 17)**.
2. Double-click a palette name **(Figure 18)**.
   or
   Click a palette name, then click Open.

✓ Tip

- Two Brushes palettes are supplied with Photoshop in addition to the Default Brushes: Assorted Brushes, which are predefined shapes and symbols, and Drop Shadow Brushes, which are brush tips with soft edges you can use to make drop shadows. *(See page 156)*

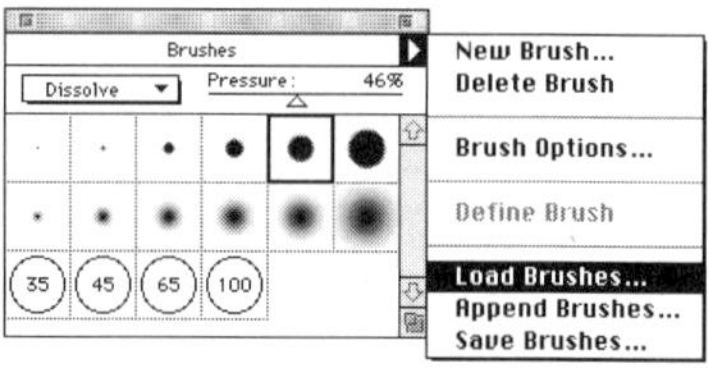

Figure 17. Choose **Load Brushes** from the **Brushes** palette.

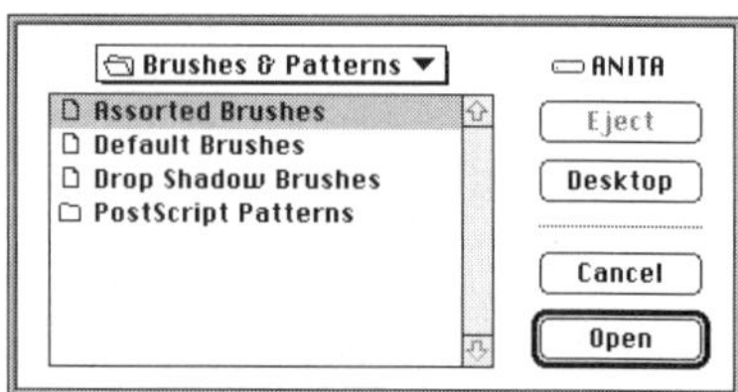

Figure 18. Highlight a palette, then click **Open**.

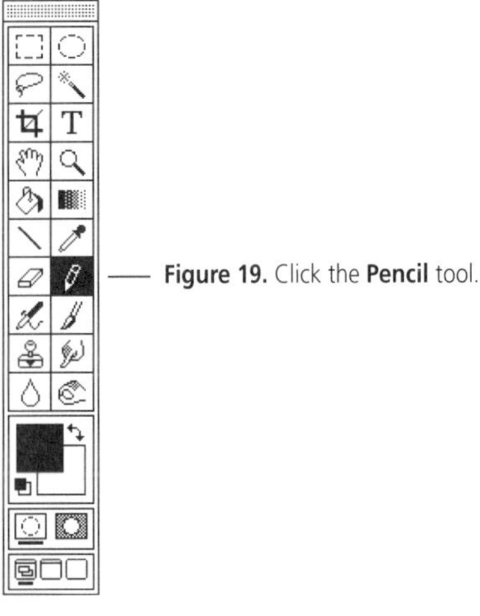

Figure 19. Click the **Pencil** tool.

You can use the Pencil, Airbrush, or Paintbrush tool to create a linear element, such as a squiggly or a calligraphic line. Use different Angle and Roundness values to create your own line shapes.

To draw a calligraphic line:

1. Click the Pencil, Airbrush, or Paintbrush tool **(Figure 19)**.
2. Choose a Foreground color. *(See pages 130-132)*
3. Double-click a hard-edged brush tip on the Brushes palette. (Only hard-edged tips are available for the Pencil tool).
4. Enter a number in the Diameter field.
5. Enter a number between 1 and 25 in the Spacing field.
6. Position the Hardness slider at 100%.
7. Enter 34 in the Angle field **(Figure 20)**.
8. Enter 20 in the Roundness field. Note the brush preview in the dialog box.
9. Click OK or press Return.
10. *Optional:* Drag the Opacity slider on the Brushes palette.
11. Draw shapes or letters **(Figure 21)**.

 **Tip**

- To make a stroke that fades as it finishes, double-click the Pencil, Airbrush, or Paintbrush tool, then enter a number in the Distance field.

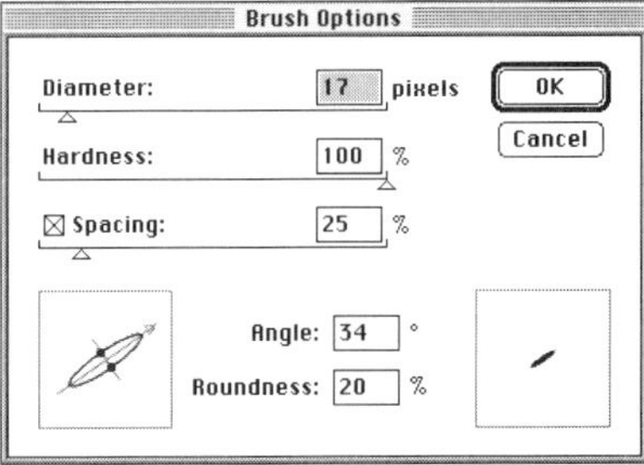

Figure 20. In the **Brush Options** dialog box, enter 34 in the **Angle** field and 20 in the **Roundness** field.

Figure 21. A calligraphic line added to a picture.

To draw a straight line:

1. Double-click the Line tool **(Figure 22)**.
2. Enter a number between 0 and 1000 in the Width field **(Figure 23)**.
3. Click OK or press Return.
4. Choose a Foreground color. *(See pages 130-132)*
5. Draw a line. The line will fill with the Foreground color when the mouse is released **(Figure 24a)**.

✔ Tips

- Hold down Shift while dragging to constrain the line to the nearest 45° angle.
- You can choose a mode and Opacity for the Line tool from the Brushes palette.
- You can also draw a straight line with any other painting tool. Click once to begin the stroke, then hold down Shift and click in a different location to complete the stroke **(Figure 24b)**.
- To create an arrow, click At Start and/or At End in the Line Tool Options dialog box, enter numbers in the Width, Length, and Concavity fields, then draw a line.

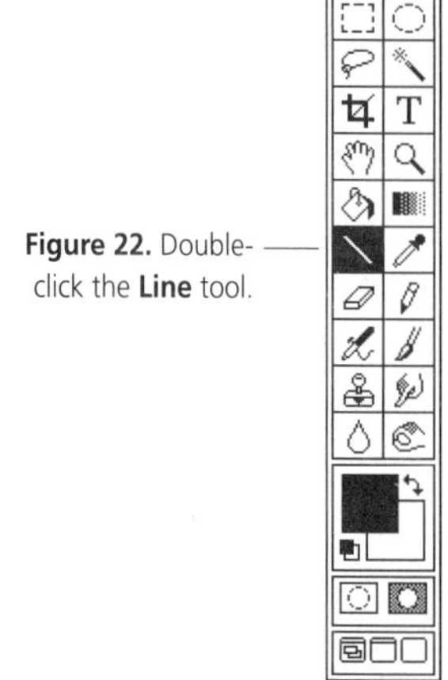

Figure 22. Double-click the **Line** tool.

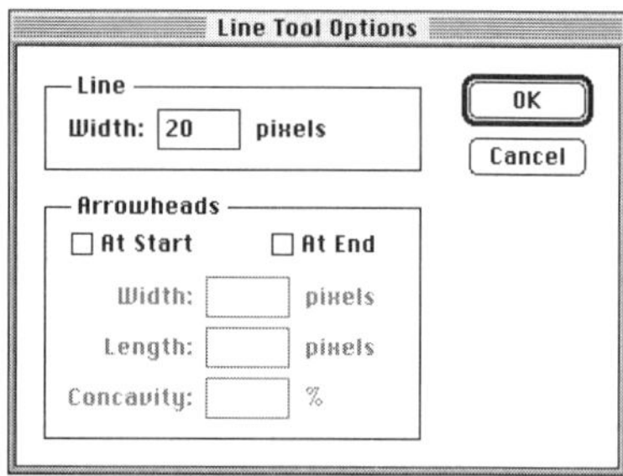

Figure 23. Enter a **Width** in the **Line Tool Options** dialog box.

Figure 24a. Straight lines added to a picture using the Line tool.

Figure 24b. A border added using the Pencil tool in Dissolve mode at 85% opacity.

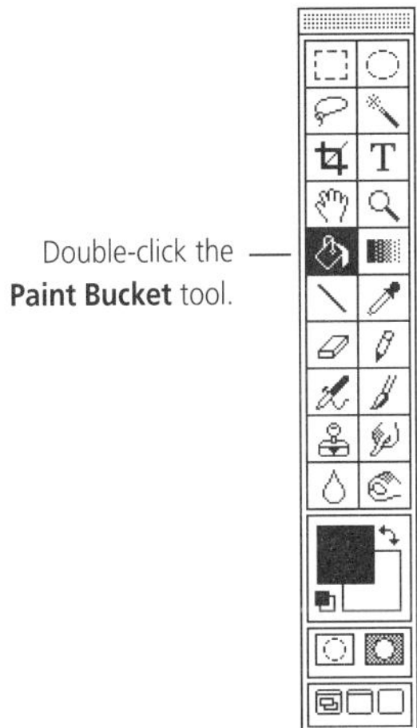

Figure 25.

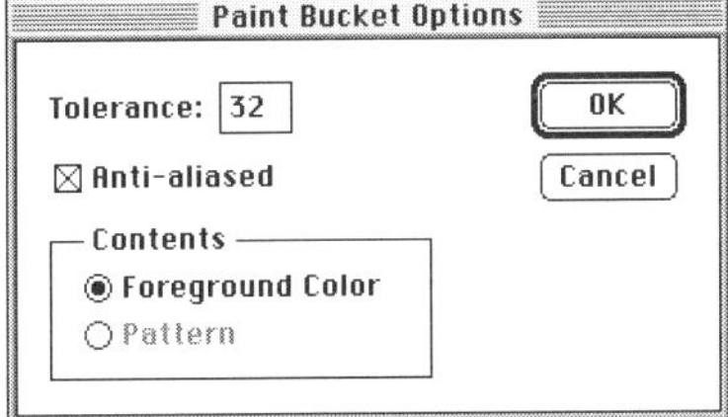

Figure 26. Enter a number in the **Tolerance** field in the **Paint Bucket Options** dialog box.

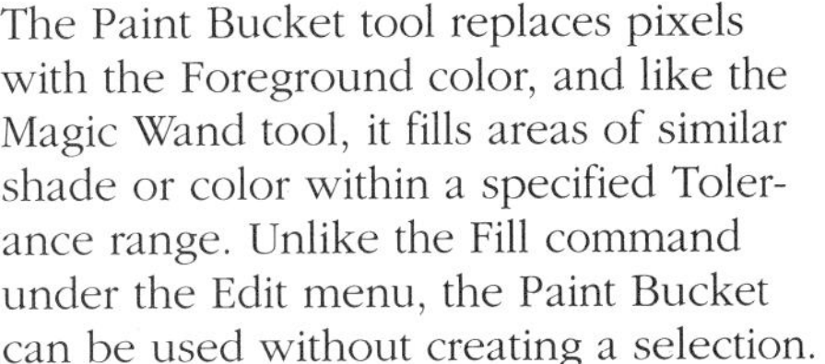
The Paint Bucket tool replaces pixels with the Foreground color, and like the Magic Wand tool, it fills areas of similar shade or color within a specified Tolerance range. Unlike the Fill command under the Edit menu, the Paint Bucket can be used without creating a selection.

To fill an area using the Paint Bucket tool:

1. Double-click the Paint Bucket tool **(Figure 25)**.
2. Enter a number between 0 and 255 in the Tolerance field **(Figure 26)**. The higher the Tolerance value, the wider the range of colors the Paint Bucket will fill. Try a low number first.
3. Make sure the Anti-aliased box is checked.
4. Click OK or press Return.
5. Choose a Foreground color. *(See pages 130-132)*
6. Choose a mode and Opacity from the Brushes palette. *(See page 147)*
7. Click on the picture **(Figures 27-28)**.

✔ Tip

■ To undo the fill, choose Undo from the Edit menu immediately.

Figure 27. The original picture.

Figure 28. After clicking with the Paint Bucket tool.

To create a drop shadow:

1. Open a picture with a white border.
   or
   Follow the instructions on page 43 to add a white border to a picture.
2. Click the Magic Wand tool **(Figure 29)**.
3. Click on the white border **(Figure 30)**.
4. Click the Paintbrush tool.
5. Click the Default colors button on the Toolbox.
6. Follow the instructions on page 152 to load the Drop Shadow Brushes.
7. Choose Grayscale from the pop-up menu on the right side of the Colors palette.
8. Position the "K" slider between 40% and 50%.
9. On the Brushes palette, click a large tip **(Figure 31)**.
   and
   Choose Normal mode.
   and
   Move the Opacity slider to 50%.
10. Position the pointer on the bottom edge of the image, then hold down Shift and drag slowly to the right until the pointer is slightly to the right of the image. Do not release the mouse or the Shift key! **(Figure 32)**
11. Keep Shift held down and drag upward along the right edge of the image. Release Shift when the pointer is just below the top of the image **(Figures 33-34)**.

✔ **Tips**

- To delete the Paintbrush stroke, press Delete or choose Undo from the Edit menu. The selected area will turn white.
- Don't create two separate brush strokes. The area where they overlap will be darker.

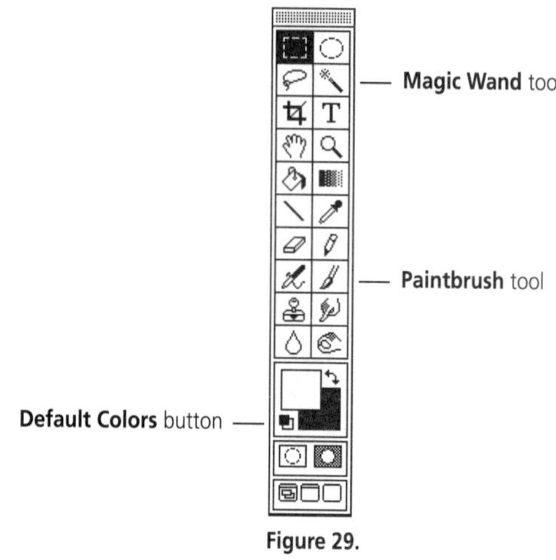

Figure 29.

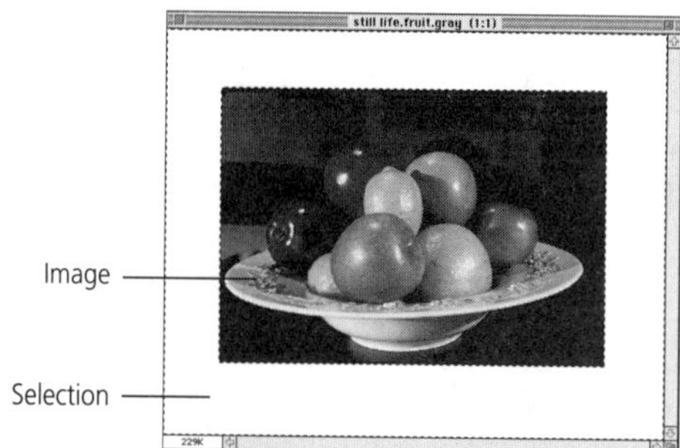

Figure 30. Click on the white border with the Magic Wand tool.

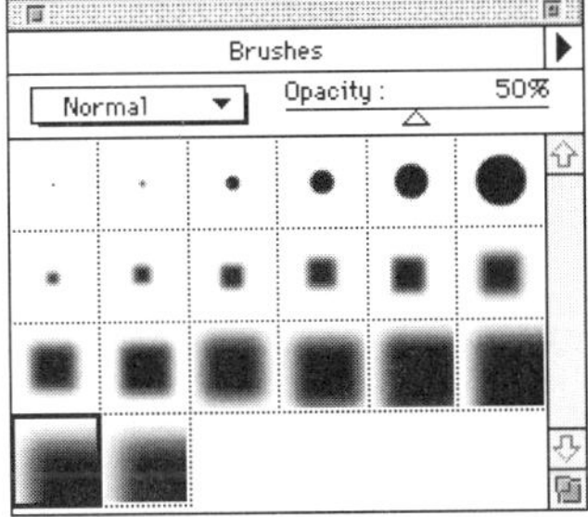

Figure 31. On the **Brushes** palette, click a large tip, choose **Normal** mode, and move the **Opacity** slider to 50%.

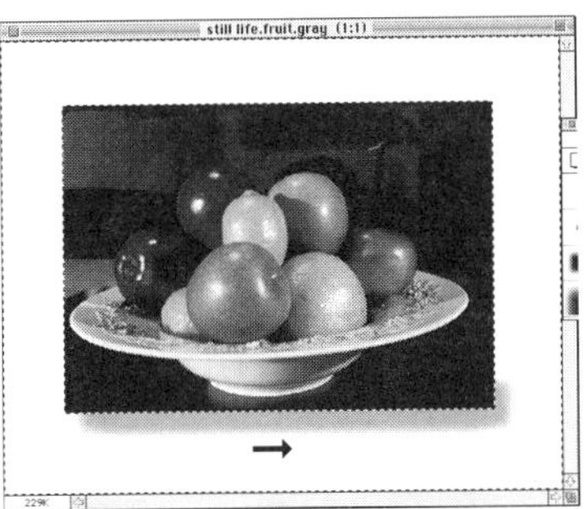

Figure 32. Hold down Shift, then drag to the right. Do not release Shift!

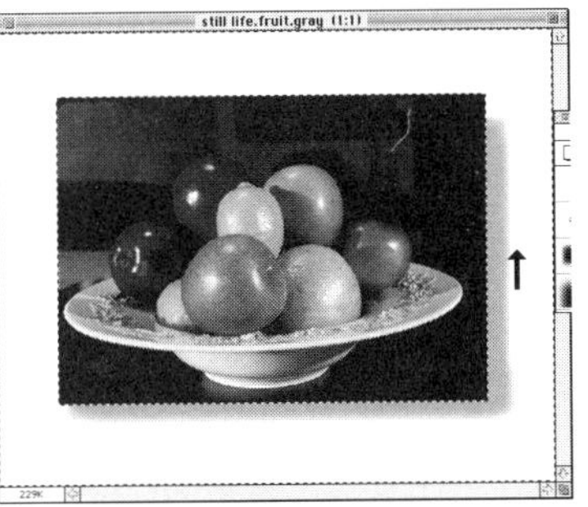

Figure 33. Drag upward to create the second part of the drop shadow, then release Shift.

Figure 34. The completed drop shadow.

BLENDS 15

Show Brushes, Show Colors.

The Brushes and Colors palettes are used throughout this chapter. Choose Show Brushes and Show Colors from the Window menu to display them **(Figure 1)**.

THE GRADIENT TOOL produces linear and radial blends using the Foreground color as the starting color and the Background color as the ending color. In this chapter you will learn to create linear and radial blends, fill type with a blend, fill the background of a picture with a blend, and layer multiple blends.

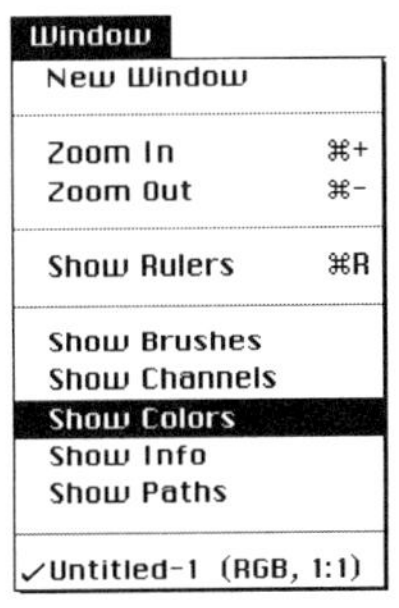

Figure 1. Choose **Show Colors** and **Show Brushes** from the **Window** menu.

Note: Try a linear blend first on a new document, or in a selection with a white background. To fill the background of a picture with a blend, follow the instructions on page 163.

Create a Linear Blend

To create a linear blend:

1. Choose a Foreground color (the starting color).
   (See pages 130-132)
2. Choose a Background color (the ending color).
3. Double-click the Gradient tool **(Figure 2)**.
4. Click Linear **(Figure 3)**.
5. Click OK or press Return.
6. From the Brushes palette, choose Normal from the mode pop-up menu **(Figure 4)**.
   and
   Move the Opacity slider.
7. Drag from one side of the document or selection to the other **(Figures 5a-b** and **6b)**.
   or
   To produce a diagonal blend, drag from corner to corner **(Figures 5c-d)**.

(See figures on the following two pages)

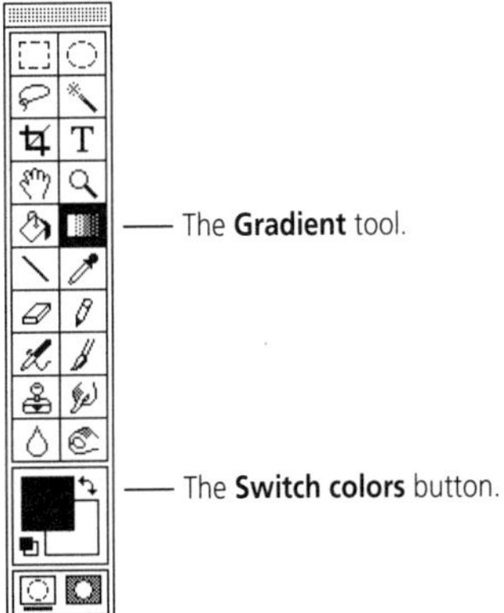

Figure 2.

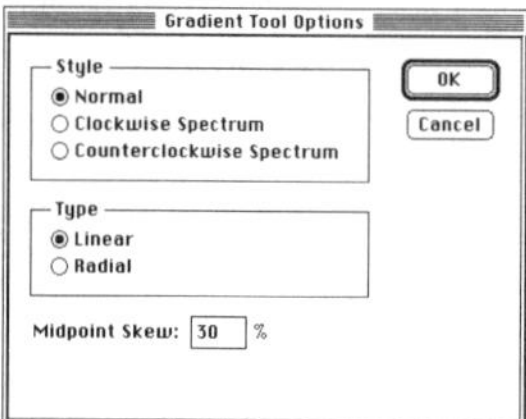

Figure 3. Click **Linear** in the **Gradient Tool Options** dialog box.

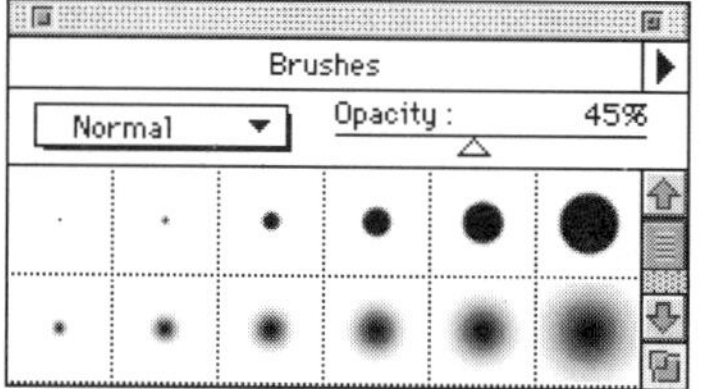

Figure 4. Choose **Normal mode** and move the **Opacity** slider on the **Brushes** palette.

In the illustrations below, the arrow shows where the mouse was dragged.

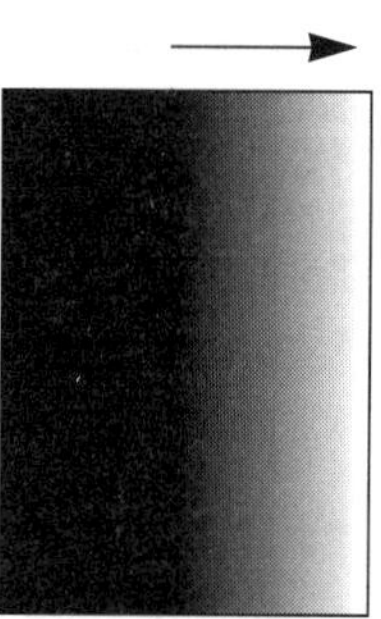

Figure 5a. The Gradient tool dragged from the middle to the right.

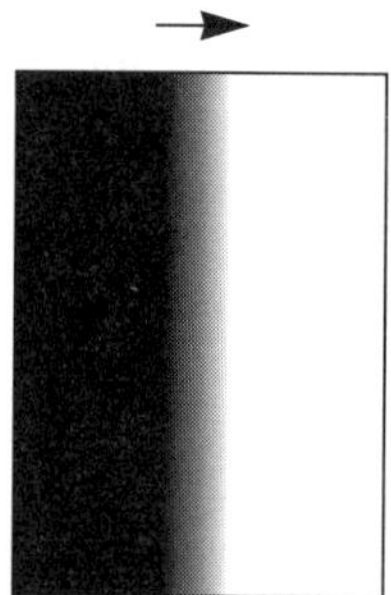

Figure 5b. The Gradient tool dragged a short distance in the middle with the same colors.

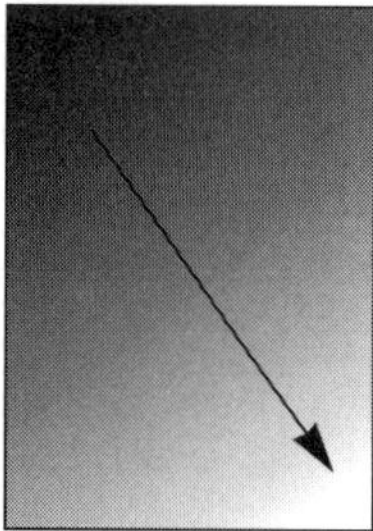

Figure 5c. The Gradient tool dragged from upper left to lower right.

Figure 5d. The Gradient tool dragged from lower right to upper left with the same colors.

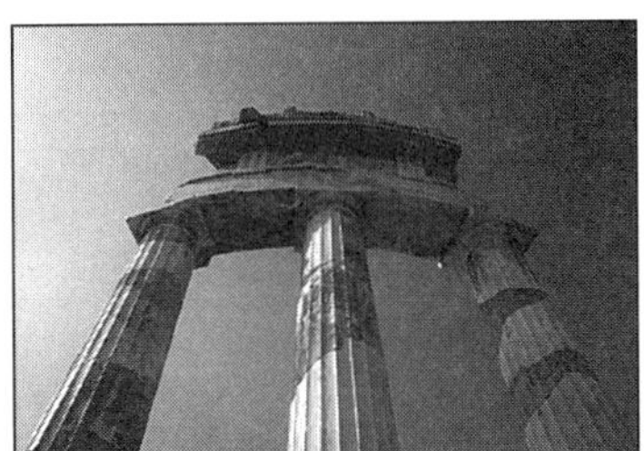

Figure 6a. The original picture.

Figure 6b. Type was created, and filled with a blend.

Blend Tips.

- To delete a blend, choose Undo from the Edit menu immediately.
- To reverse the order of colors, drag in the opposite direction. Or, click the Switch colors button on the toolbox before dragging **(Figure 2)**.
- The distance you drag defines the width of the transition area. Drag a long distance to produce a subtle transition; drag a short distance to produce an abrupt transition **(Figures 5a-b)**.
- To produce more of the Foreground color than the Background color, double-click the Gradient tool, then enter a number between 13 and 50 in the Midpoint Skew field. To produce more of the Background color than the Foreground color, enter a number between 50 and 87.
- Test the blend on the scratch pad on the Colors palette. Use the Eraser tool with white as the Background color to erase the scratch pad.
- To create a blend in type, create a type selection, follow the instructions on page 159, then drag across the type with the Gradient tool **(Figures 6a-b** and **Gallery 15a)**. To temporarily hide the selection marquee while keeping the type selected, choose Hide Edges from the Select menu. Choose Show Edges to restore the marquee.
- Follow the instructions on page 164 to layer translucent blends.
- To produce a "rainbow" in a blend, double-click the Gradient tool and click Clockwise Spectrum or Counterclockwise Spectrum **(Gallery 15b)**.

To create a radial blend:

1. Choose a Foreground color (the starting color).
   (See pages 130-132)
2. Choose a Background color (the ending color).
3. Double-click the Gradient tool **(Figure 2)**.
4. Click Radial **(Figure 7)**.
5. Click OK or press Return.
6. From the Brushes palette, choose Normal from the mode pop-up menu **(Figure 4)**.
   and
   Move the Opacity slider.
7. Press to establish a center point, then drag outward **(Figures 8-9)**.
   (See Tips on the previous page)

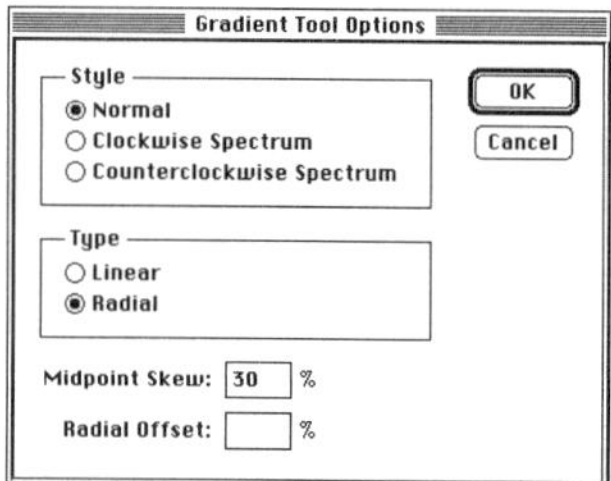

Figure 7. Click **Radial** in the **Gradient Tool Options** dialog box.

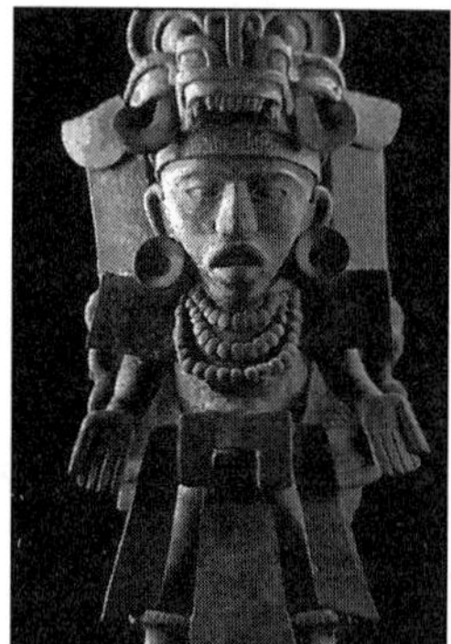

Figure 8. The original picture.

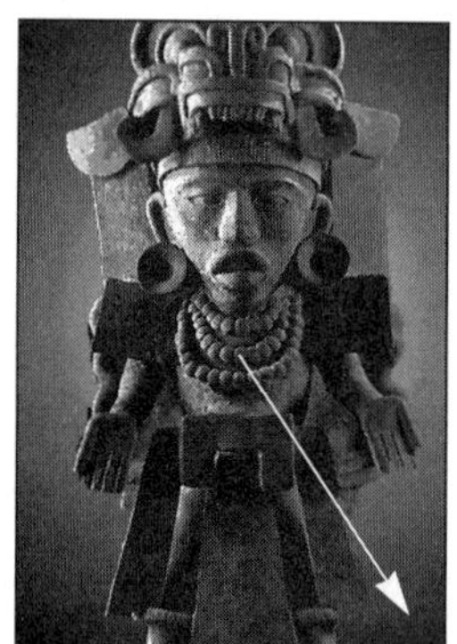

Figure 9. A radial blend in the background. The arrow shows where the mouse was dragged.

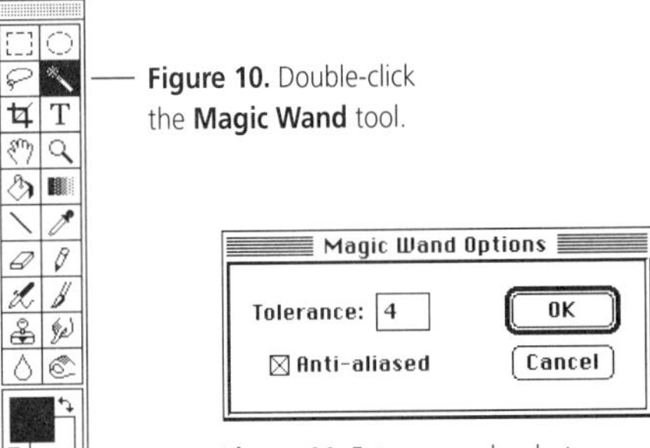

Figure 10. Double-click the **Magic Wand** tool.

Figure 11. Enter a number between 1 and 10 in the **Tolerance** field in the **Magic Wand Options** dialog box.

Figure 12. The original picture with the background selected.

Select
All ⌘A
None ⌘D
Inverse
Defloat ⌘J
Grow ⌘G
Similar
Border...
Feather...
Defringe...
Hide Edges ⌘H
Load Selection
Save Selection

Figure 13. Choose **Feather** from the **Select** menu.

Feather Selection
Feather Radius: 1 pixels
OK
Cancel

Figure 14. Enter 1 in the **Feather Radius** field in the **Feather Selection** dialog box.

To fill the background of a picture, first select it with the Magic Wand tool. The fewer colors or shades the background contains, the easier it will be to select.

Note: In the following instructions, the terms "foreground" and "background" refer to areas of the picture, not the Foreground and Background color squares.

To create a background blend:

1. Double-click the Magic Wand tool **(Figure 10)**.
2. Enter a number between 1 and 10 in the Tolerance field **(Figure 11)**. The fewer shades or colors in the background of the picture, the lower the Tolerance value needed. If the background contains only one color, enter 1.
   (See page 65)
3. Click OK or press Return.
4. Click on the background of the picture **(Figure 12)**. If the entire background does not select, use the Magic Wand tool again with Shift held down and a higher number in the Tolerance field, or choose Grow from the Select menu. Make sure the entire background is selected and no part of the foreground is selected.

Steps 5-7 are optional.

5. Choose Feather from the Select menu **(Figure 13)**.
6. Enter 1 in the Radius field **(Figure 14)**.
7. Click OK or press Return.
8. Follow steps 1-7 on page 159 **(Gallery 15c)**.

✓ Tip

- Use the Lasso tool with the Shift key to add to or subtract from the Magic Wand selection.

To create a soft, multicolor wash, apply a translucent blend, then apply a second blend over the first in another direction. Use the Gradient tool with a low opacity so the picture will be visible underneath.

To create a multicolor wash:

1. Open a picture.
2. Choose a warm-toned Foreground color from the Colors palette as the starting color.
   (See pages 130-132)
3. Choose a cool-toned Background color for the ending color.
4. Double-click the Gradient tool **(Figure 16)**.
5. Click Linear **(Figure 17)**.
6. Click OK or press Return.
7. From the Brushes palette, choose Normal from the mode pop-up menu **(Figure 15)**.
   and
   Position the Opacity slider between 40% and 50%.
8. Drag across the picture from left to right.
9. Repeat steps 4-7 above, but choose a different warm-toned Foreground color. Leave the Background color the same.
10. Drag across the picture from top to bottom **(Gallery 15d)**.

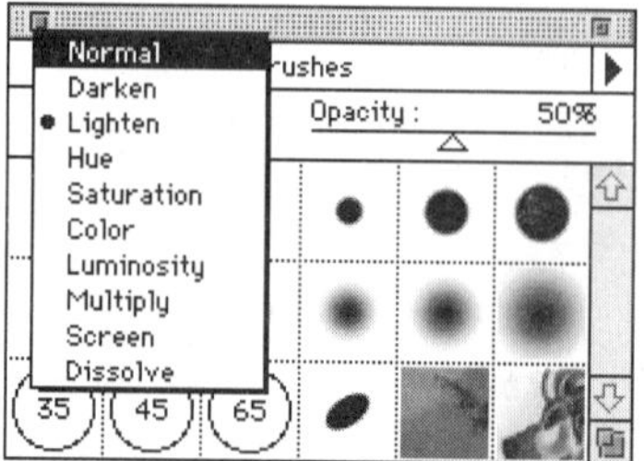

Figure 15. On the **Brushes** palette, choose **Normal** mode and an **Opacity** between 40% and 50%.

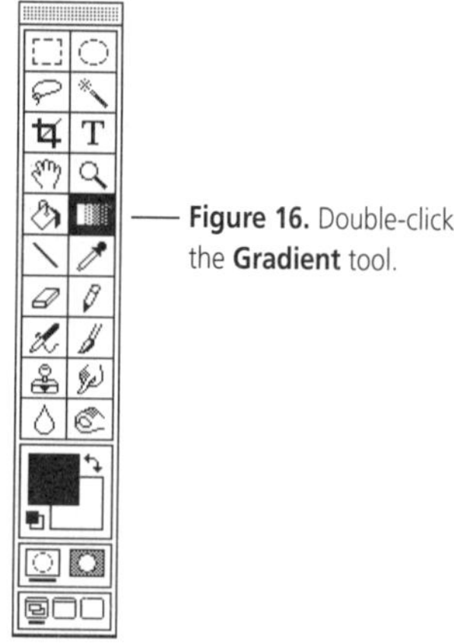

Figure 16. Double-click the **Gradient** tool.

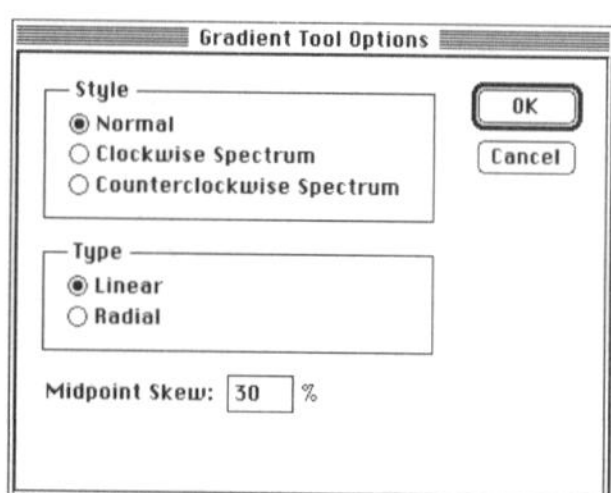

Figure 17. Click **Linear** in the **Gradient Tool Options** dialog box.

✔ **Tips**

- To restore a portion of the original picture, double-click the Rubber Stamp tool, choose From Saved from the Option pop-up menu, and click OK. Position the Opacity slider on the Brushes palette at about 50%, and click a soft, medium-sized tip. Then drag over any area of the picture you wish to restore. To restore some of the hue and saturation of the original pixels but not their light and dark values, choose Color from the Mode pop-up menu on the Brushes palette.
- To produce a soft-edged blend, first select an area of the picture. Choose Feather from the Select menu and enter 15 in the Feather Radius field. Drag over the selection with the Gradient tool **(Figure 18)**.

Figure 18. A soft edge blend in a feathered selection over another blend in the background.

Show Brushes.

The Brushes palette is used throughout this chapter. Choose Show Brushes from the Window menu to display it **(Figure 1)**.

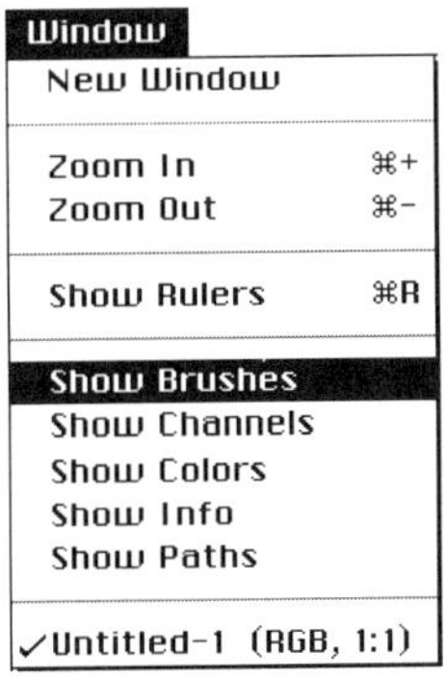

```
Window
New Window
-----------------
Zoom In        ⌘+
Zoom Out       ⌘-
-----------------
Show Rulers    ⌘R
-----------------
Show Brushes
Show Channels
Show Colors
Show Info
Show Paths
-----------------
✓Untitled-1 (RGB, 1:1)
```

Figure 1. Choose **Show Brushes** from the **Window** menu.

IN THIS CHAPTER you will learn to use the Rubber Stamp tool and the Clipboard commands (Cut, Copy and Paste) to copy images from one picture to another and to clone and rearrange imagery within a picture. You will also learn to use the Composite Controls dialog box to reveal underlying pixels under a pasted image.

By exploiting these electronic collage techniques, you can produce painterly, whimsical, poetic, or visionary pictures. For example, by superimposing translucent images, you can create a "double-exposure," like a Robert Rauchenberg painting. You can create your own variations by slightly altering any of the steps in this chapter. This is the time to be daring and experimental!

The Rubber Stamp tool:

Use the Rubber Stamp tool to clone areas of a picture. The default Rubber Stamp tool brush is 21 pixels in diameter. To retouch a small detail, choose a small brush tip. To duplicate larger areas, choose a medium- to large-sized tip.

To establish a source point for cloning, hold down the Option key and click on the picture. Then drag the mouse across another area. Two pointers will appear on the screen: a crosshair pointer over the source point and a Rubber Stamp pointer icon where you drag the mouse. Imagery from the source point will appear where the mouse is dragged, and replace the underlying pixels. Several variables control how uniformly pixels are copied.

To clone a shape within a picture:

1. Double-click the Rubber Stamp tool **(Figure 2)**.
2. Choose Clone (aligned) from the Option pop-up menu **(Figure 3)**.
3. Click OK or press Return.
4. On the Brushes palette, click a brush tip.
   and
   Move the Opacity slider.
5. Hold down Option and click on the area of the picture you wish to clone from.
6. Drag the mouse back and forth where you wish the clone to appear **(Figure 4)**.

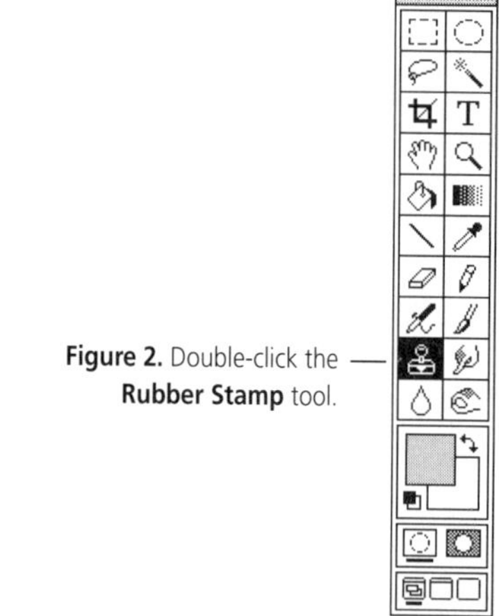

Figure 2. Double-click the **Rubber Stamp** tool.

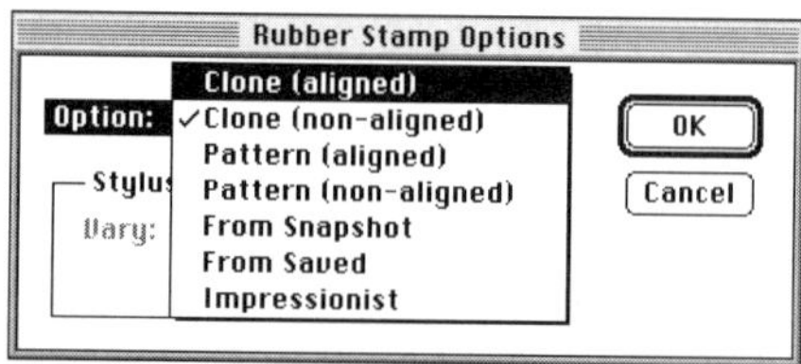

Figure 3. Choose **Clone (aligned)** from the **Option** pop-up menu in the **Rubber Stamp Options** dialog box.

✔ Tips

- Using the Rubber Stamp tool with the Clone (aligned) Option, you can clone the entire picture, as long as you don't change the source point. The distance between the source point pointer and Rubber Stamp pointer icon will remain constant, so you can release the mouse and drag in another area. To establish a new source point to clone from, hold down Option and click on a different area.
- Choose Clone (non-aligned) for the Rubber Stamp tool to create multiple clones from the same source point. The crosshair pointer will return to the same source point each time the mouse is released. You can create a pattern with Clone (non-aligned) chosen by cloning a picture element multiple times **(Figure 5)**.
- You can modify Brushes palette settings for the Rubber Stamp tool between strokes. To create a "double exposure," choose a low Opacity percentage so the underlying pixels partially show through the cloned pixels **(Figure 6)**.

Figure 4. Drag the mouse where you wish the clone to appear. To produce this illustration, Clone (aligned) was chosen for the Rubber Stamp tool.

Figure 5. Choose Clone (non-aligned) for the Rubber Stamp tool to create multiple clones from the same source point. *(See also "Create a pattern from a picture" on page 203)*

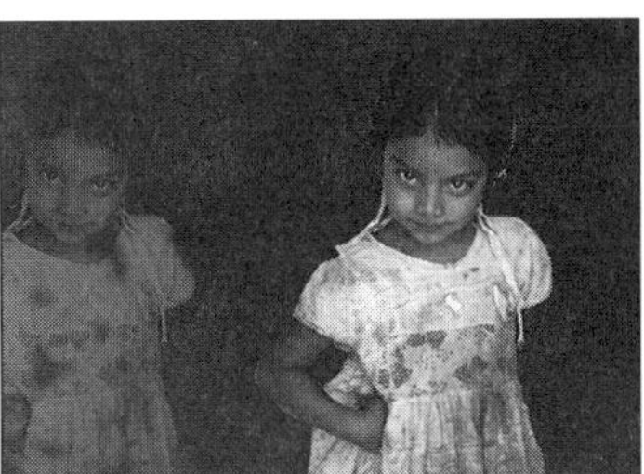

Figure 6. An Opacity of 45% was chosen for the Rubber Stamp tool to create this double exposure effect.

To clone a shape from picture to picture:

1. Open two pictures, and position the two windows side by side.
2. If both pictures are color, choose the same mode from the Mode menu for both pictures. You can also clone between a color picture and a Gray-scale picture.
3. Double-click the Rubber Stamp tool.
4. Choose Clone (aligned) from the Option pop-up menu to reproduce a continuous area from the source point **(Figure 7)**.
   or
   Choose Clone (Non-aligned) to produce multiple clones from the source point.
5. Click OK or press Return.
6. On the Brushes palette, click a brush tip.
   and
   Move the Opacity slider.
7. Click on the picture where the clone is to appear.
8. Hold down Option and click the Rubber Stamp tool on an area within the non-active picture that is to be cloned from.
9. Drag back and forth on the active picture to make the clone appear **(Figure 8)**.

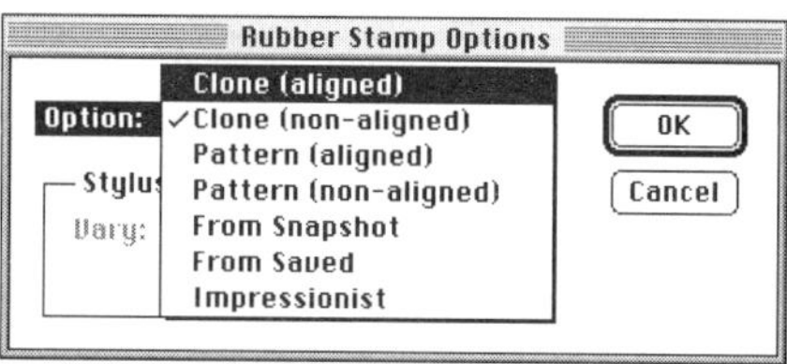

Figure 7. Choose **Clone (aligned)** from the **Option** pop-up menu in the **Rubber Stamp Options** dialog box.

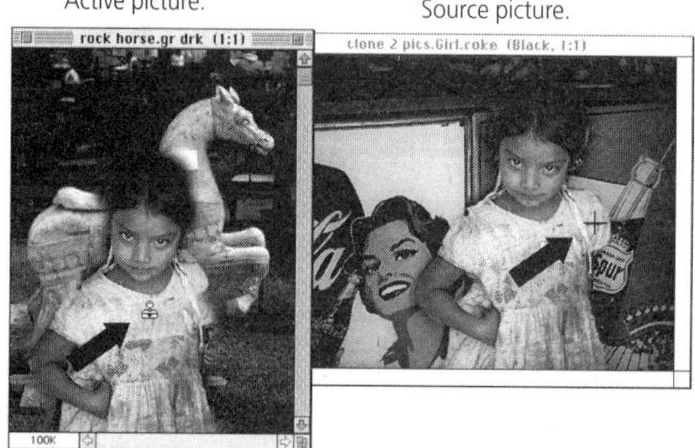

Figure 8. Option-click on the inactive picture to establish a source point. Drag back and forth in short strokes on the active picture to make the clone appear.

✓ Tips

- To create a brush stroke version of a picture, clone to a new document with a white or solid-colored background **(Figure 9)**.
- Any painting mode can be chosen for the Rubber Stamp tool. To test a mode, create a new document with a white background, make part of the background black, choose Clone (non-aligned) in the Rubber Stamp Options dialog box, choose a mode

Figure 9. To create this effect, a picture was cloned to a new document with a white background.

Figure 10. The image on the left was cloned with Luminosity mode chosen. The image on the right was cloned with Lighten mode chosen. 50% Opacity was used first, then 85% Opacity for the highlights.

from the Brushes palette, then clone to the new document **(Figure 10)**.

Choose Darken to clone onto a white background, choose Lighten to clone onto a black background, choose Luminosity to produce a gray-scale clone from a color picture, or choose Dissolve with an opacity of less than 100% to produce a grainy, chalky clone **(Figures 11-13)**.

Figure 11. The original picture.

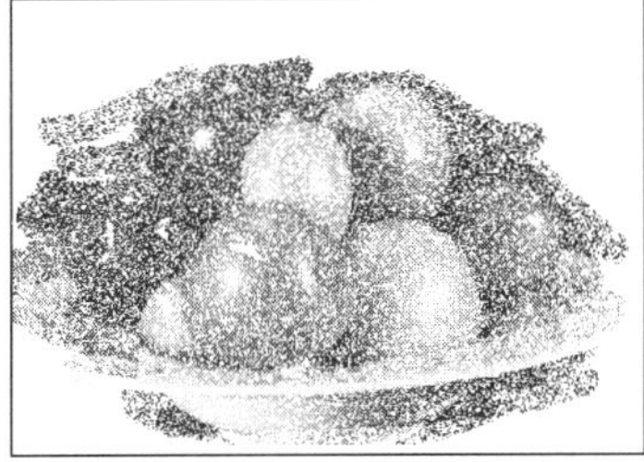

Figure 12. A clone of the same image created with Dissolve mode chosen for the Rubber Stamp tool.

Figure 13. The image on the left side was cloned on a light gray background using the Rubber Stamp tool with Darken mode chosen. The same picture was cloned on the right side on a dark gray background using the Rubber Stamp tool with Lighten mode chosen. The background colors prevented some shades from being cloned.

If you save a picture and then modify it, you can restore portions of the saved version to contrast with the modifications using the Rubber Stamp tool with its From Saved option. Remember to save your document at a stage you would like to restore.

Note: The From Saved option cannot be used if you cropped the picture, changed its mode, or changed its dimensions since it was saved.

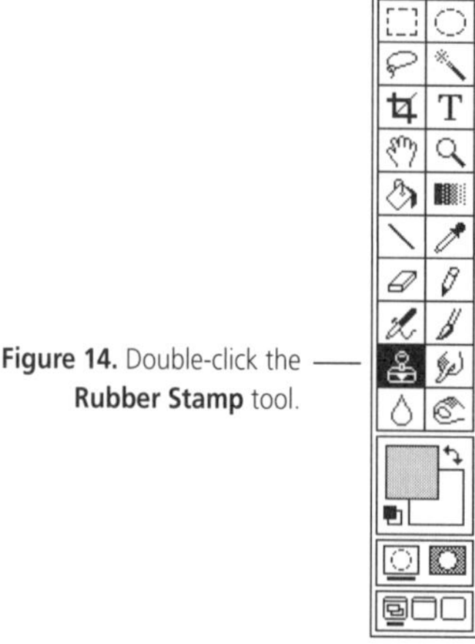

Figure 14. Double-click the **Rubber Stamp** tool.

To restore part of the last saved version of a picture:

1. Double-click the Rubber Stamp tool **(Figure 14)**.
2. Choose From Saved from the Option pop-up menu **(Figure 15)**.
3. Click OK or press Return.
4. On the Brushes palette, click a brush tip.
   and
   Move the Opacity slider.
   and
   Choose a mode.
5. Drag across any area of the picture **(Figure 16)**.

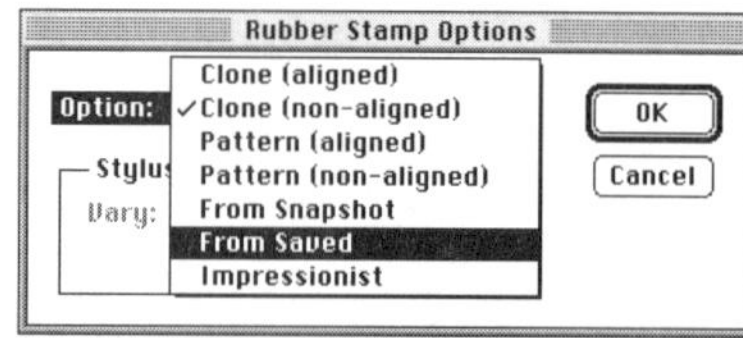

Figure 15. Choose **From Saved** from the **Option** pop-up menu in the **Rubber Stamp Options** dialog box.

✔ Tips

- To undo the last stroke, choose Undo from the Edit menu immediately.
- Choose a low Opacity to restore a light impression of the saved picture. Each subsequent stroke over the same area will restore it more.
- Choose the Impressionist Option to produce a soft rendition of the last saved version.

Figure 16. Part of a picture is restored. The Rubber Stamp tool was used with 100% Opacity on the left side and 40% Opacity on the right side.

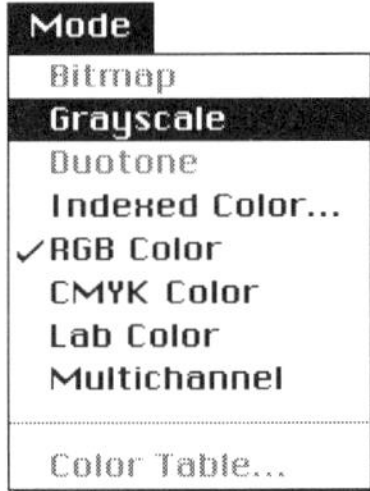

Figure 17. Choose **Grayscale** from the **Mode** menu.

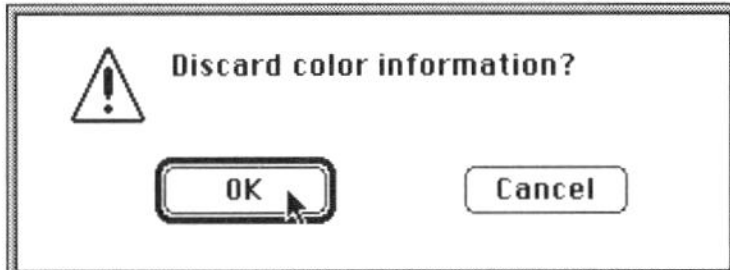

Figure 18. Click OK when this prompt appears.

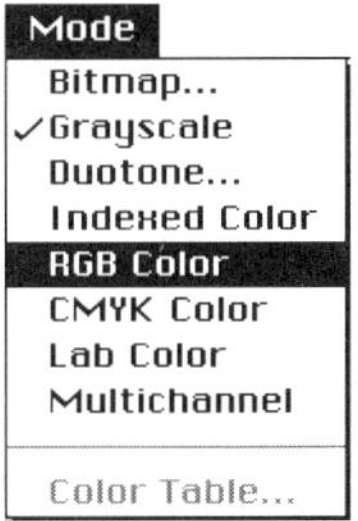

Figure 19. Choose **RGB Color** from the **Mode** menu.

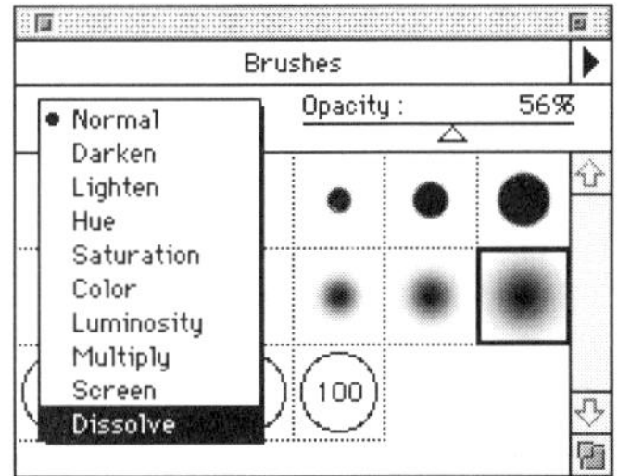

Figure 20. From the **Brushes** palette, choose a **mode** and **opacity**.

To convert an RGB picture to Grayscale and selectively restore its color:

1. Choose Grayscale from the Mode menu **(Figure 17)**.
2. Click OK in the Discard Color dialog box **(Figure 18)**.
3. Choose RGB Color from the Mode menu **(Figure 19)**.
4. Double-click the Rubber Stamp tool **(Figure 14)**.
5. Choose From Saved from the Option pop-up menu **(Figure 15)**.
6. Click OK or press Return.
7. From the Brushes palette, choose a mode **(Figure 20)**.
   and
   Move the Opacity slider.
8. Drag across any area of the picture **(Gallery 16)**.

✓ Tip

- Try any of the following mode/opacity combinations:

  Dissolve with a 40%-50% Opacity to restore color with a chalky texture.

  Multiply with a 100% Opacity to darken and intensify the color in the restored areas.

  Color at 100% Opacity to restore only the hues from the last saved version of the picture while retaining the light and dark values and any modifications made while the picture was in Grayscale mode.

The Clipboard:

You can use the Cut and Copy commands to save a selection to a temporary storage area called the Clipboard. You then can use any of the Paste commands (Paste, Paste Into, or Paste Behind) to paste the Clipboard contents in the same picture or in another picture. Cut, Copy, Paste Into and Paste Behind are available only when an area of a picture is selected.

When a Paste command is chosen, the Clipboard contents appear in a floating selection. A floating selection can be repositioned and modified without affecting underlying pixels.

To remove a floating selection, choose Cut or Clear from the Edit menu. The underlying pixels will not be modified. The Clear command does not change the Clipboard contents.

Once deselected, a selection becomes part of the picture, replacing underlying pixels. If you Cut or Clear a non-floating selection, the selection is removed from the picture and the exposed area fills with the Background color.

The Clipboard can contain only one selection at a time, which is replaced each time Cut or Copy is chosen. The same Clipboard contents can be pasted an unlimited number of times. The Clipboard will empty when you quit Photoshop, and if you switch to another application unless Export Clipboard is checked in the General Preferences dialog box (opened from the File menu). *(See page 222)*

While a large selection is on the Clipboard, the available memory for processing is reduced. To increase the available memory, Cut or Copy a smaller selection when you are finished using the Clipboard.

Clipboard Tips

- Before using the Clipboard commands, compare the dimensions of the image to be Cut or Copied with the dimensions of the picture onto which it will be pasted (the "destination picture"). If the image on the Clipboard is larger than the destination picture (or the selection on the destination picture), the Clipboard image will be cropped when pasted.
- Follow the instructions on page 178 to paste into a smaller picture.
- The size of an image may also change when pasted, because it is rendered in the resolution of the destination picture. If the resolution of the destination picture is higher than that of the image you are pasting, the Clipboard image will become smaller when pasted. Conversely, if the resolution of the destination picture is lower than the resolution of the Clipboard image, the Clipboard image will be enlarged when pasted.
- A pasted image, like any other image, may become blurry if you enlarge it using the Scale command.
- The dimensions in the New dialog box conform automatically to the dimensions of the current contents of the Clipboard.

To copy and paste a selection:

1. Select an area of a picture **(Figure 21)**.
   (See pages 62-65)
2. *Optional:* Feather the selection.
   (See page 76)
3. Choose Copy from the Edit menu **(Figure 22)**.
4. Choose None from the Select menu **(Figure 23)**.
5. Click on the same picture or on another picture.
6. Choose Paste from the Edit menu. The Clipboard contents will appear as a floating selection **(Figure 24)**.
7. *Optional:* Defringe the selection.
   (See page 78)

Steps 8 and 9 are optional.

8. To subtract from the selection, click the Lasso tool, then hold down ⌘ and drag around the area you wish to subtract.
9. Drag the selection to a new location, or use Composite Controls (see pages 179-181) or any other feature to modify the selection.
10. Choose None from the Select menu **(Figure 23)**.
    or
    Hold down ⌘ and press "D."

✔ **Tip**

■ If you choose Cut instead of Copy for Step 3, the selection will be cut from the picture and the exposed area will fill with the Background color.

Figure 21. Select an area of a picture.

Edit
Undo Copy ⌘Z
Cut ⌘X
Copy ⌘C
Paste ⌘V
Paste Into
Paste Behind
Clear
Fill...
Stroke...
Crop
Create Publisher...
Publisher Options...
Define Pattern
Take Snapshot
Composite Controls...

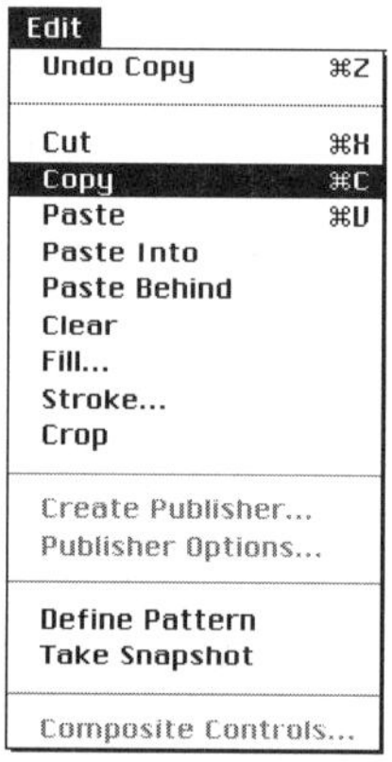

Figure 22. Choose **Copy** from the **Edit** menu.

Select
All ⌘A
None ⌘D
Inverse
Float ⌘J
Grow ⌘G
Similar
Border...
Feather...
Defringe...
Hide Edges ⌘H
Load Selection
Save Selection

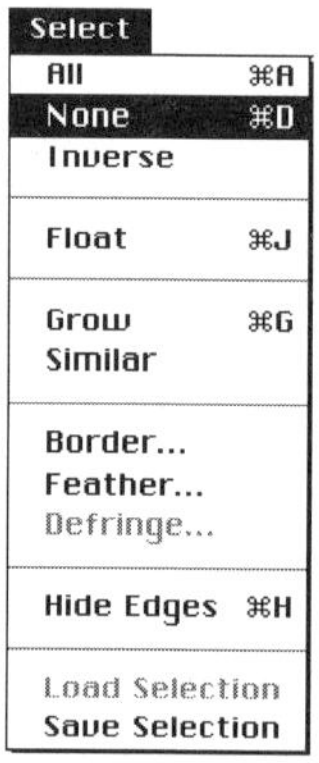

Figure 23. Choose **None** from the **Select** menu.

Figure 24. The pasted image appears as a floating selection.

Figure 25. Select an area of a picture.

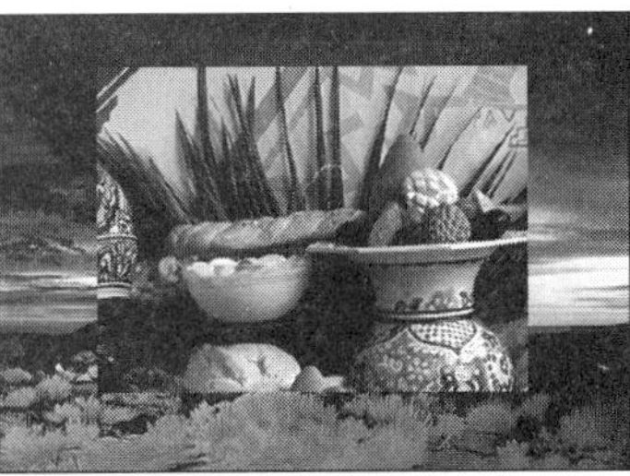

Figure 26. A landscape image was copied to the Clipboard, then pasted behind a selection.

In addition to the Paste command, two other commands can be used to paste from the Clipboard: Paste Into and Paste Behind. They are available only when an area of a picture is selected.

Choose Paste Into to paste the Clipboard contents within the boundary of a selection. The active marquee will then surround the Clipboard image. The pasted image can be repositioned within the boundary of the previous selection or otherwise modified.

Choose Paste Behind to paste the Clipboard contents behind a selection.

To paste into or paste behind a selection:

1. Select an area of a picture **(Figure 25)**.
   (See pages 62-66)
2. *Optional:* Feather the selection.
   (See page 76)
3. Choose Copy from the Edit menu **(Figure 22)**.
4. In the same picture or in another picture, select an area (or areas) into which or behind which the Clipboard image will be pasted.
5. Choose Paste Into or Paste Behind from the Edit menu **(Figure 22)**.

Steps 6 and 7 are optional.

6. To subtract from the selection, click the Lasso tool, then hold down ⌘ and drag around the area you wish to subtract.
7. Drag the selection to a new location, or use Composite Controls (instructions on pages 179-181) or any other feature to modify the selection.
8. Choose None from the Select menu **(Figure 26)**.

Note: Read page 175 before proceeding with the following instructions.

To paste into a smaller picture:

1. Click on the destination picture, then hold down Option and press and hold on the Image Size bar in the lower left corner of the document window. Jot down the picture's dimensions.
2. Create a selection on another (larger) picture.
   (See pages 62-66)
3. Choose Copy from the Edit menu **(Figure 27)**.
4. Choose New from the File menu.
5. From the Mode pop-menu, choose the mode of the picture from which the selection was copied. The Width and Height will automatically conform to the dimensions of the Clipboard image.
6. Click OK or press Return.
7. Choose Paste from the Edit menu.
8. Choose Image Size from the Image menu.
9. Enter smaller numbers than the dimensions of the destination picture (Step 1, above) in the Width and Height fields **(Figure 28)**. Make sure the File Size box is unchecked so the resolution doesn't change.
   (See page 40)
10. Click OK or press Return.
11. If you deselected the pasted image, Choose All from the Select menu **(Figure 29)**.
12. Choose Copy from the Edit menu.
13. Click in the destination picture.
14. Follow steps 6-10 on page 176 or steps 4-8 on page 177.

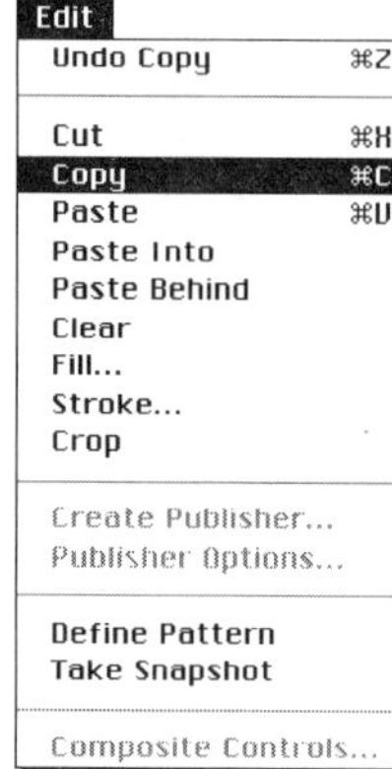

Figure 27. The **Edit** menu.

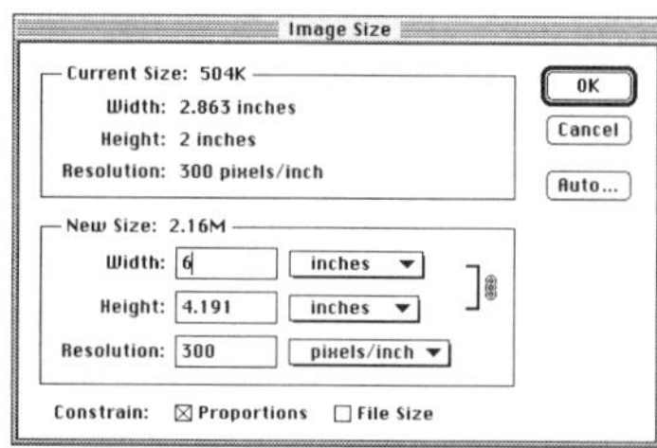

Figure 28. Enter smaller numbers in the **Width** and **Height** fields in the **Image Size** dialog box. Make sure the File Size box is unchecked.

Figure 29. Choose **All** from the **Select** menu.

Paste into a Smaller Picture

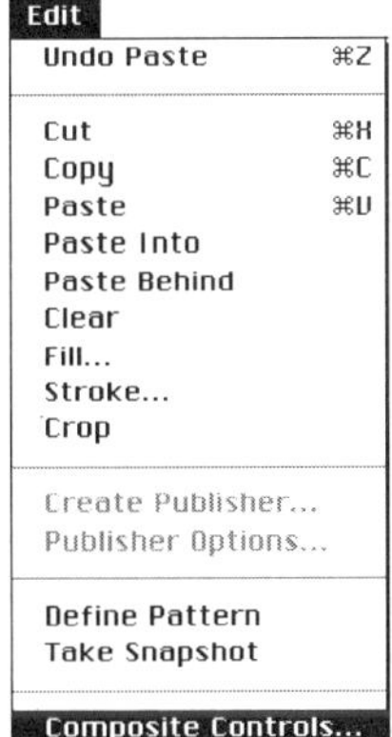

Figure 30. Choose **Composite Controls** from the **Edit** menu.

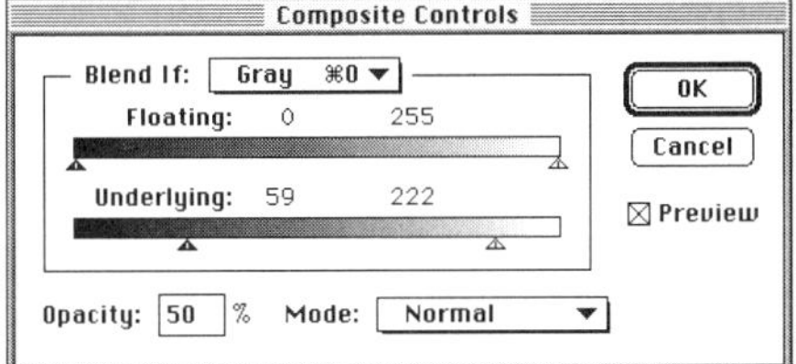

Figure 31. Enter a number below 100 in the **Opacity** field In the **Composite Controls** dialog box.

You can modify the opacity of a floating selection using the Composite Controls dialog box. If you choose a low opacity, underlying pixels will partially show through the pasted image. Ways to create a floating selection: create type *(see page 112)*, move a copy of a selection *(see page 71)*, create a selection, then choose Float from the Select menu, or copy and paste a selection *(steps 1-9 on page 176 or steps 1-7 on page 177)*.

To modify the opacity of a floating selection:

1. Choose Composite Controls from the Edit menu **(Figure 30)**.
2. Enter a number below 100 in the Opacity field **(Figure 31)**. Make sure the Preview box is checked, and pause to preview.
3. Click OK or press Return **(Figures 32a-b)**.

 **Tip**

- The Composite Controls dialog box will open if you hold down Option while choosing a paste command.

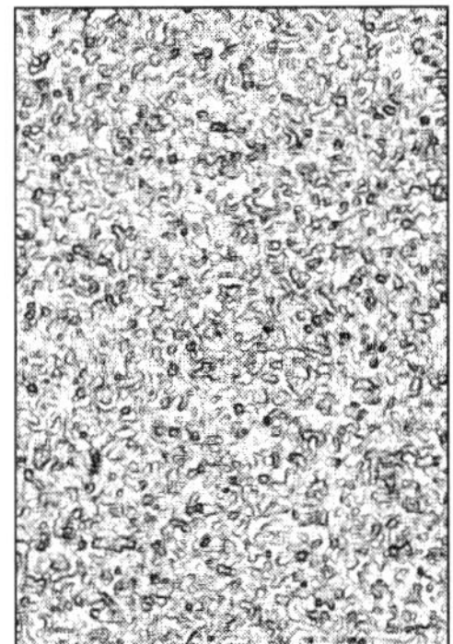

Figure 32a. This pattern was selected, then pasted in the "Lindos" picture on the right.

Figure 32b. An Opacity of 40% was chosen for the pasted pattern.

By moving the Underlying sliders in the Composite Controls dialog box, you can selectively restore underlying pixels.

To restore pixels under a floating selection:

1. Follow steps 1-9 on page 176 or steps 1-7 on page 177 to copy and paste a selection.
2. Choose Composite Controls from the Edit menu **(Figure 33)**.
3. Make sure the Preview box is checked, then move the Underlying black slider to the right to restore shadow areas from the underlying picture **(Figure 34)**.
   or
   Move the white slider to the left to restore highlights from the underlying picture.
4. Click OK or press Return **(Figures 35)**.

✔ Tips

- To eliminate the white background in the floating image, move the white Floating slider to about 250.
- To define a range for an individual channel, choose from the Blend If pop-up menu before moving the sliders.

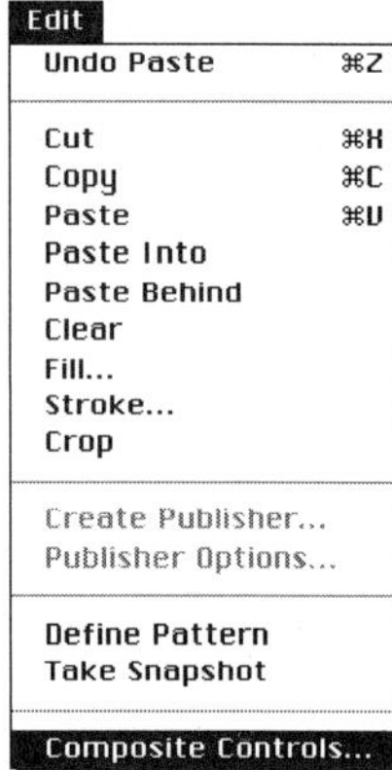

Figure 33. Choose **Composite Controls** from the **Edit** menu.

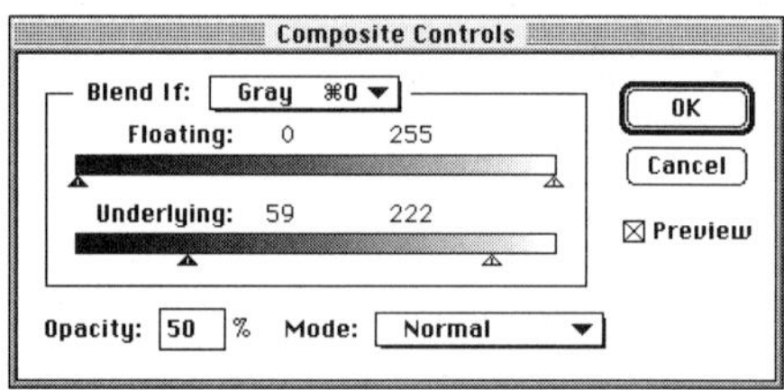

Figure 34. Move the black and/or white **Underlying** sliders in the **Composite Controls** dialog box.

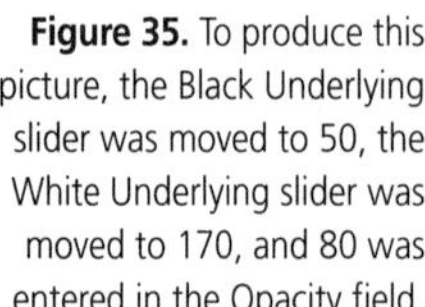

Figure 35. To produce this picture, the Black Underlying slider was moved to 50, the White Underlying slider was moved to 170, and 80 was entered in the Opacity field.

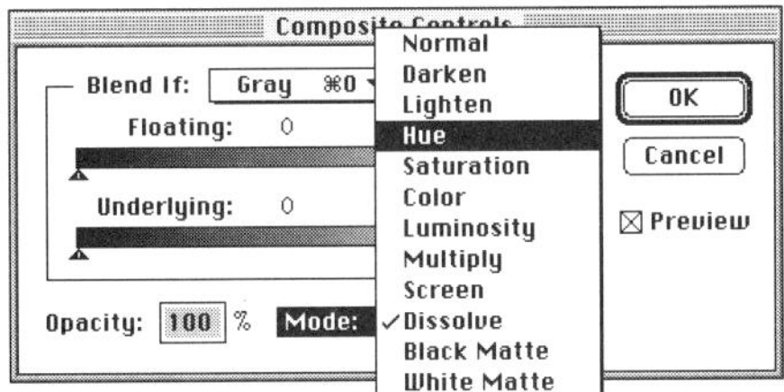

Figure 36. Choose from the **Mode** pop-up menu in the **Composite Controls** dialog box.

To choose a mode for a floating selection:

1. Follow steps 1-9 on page 176 and steps 1-7 on page 177 to copy and paste a selection.
2. Choose Composite Controls from the Edit menu **(Figure 33)**.
3. Choose from the Mode pop-up menu. Make sure the Preview box is checked, and pause to preview **(Figure 36)**.
4. *Optional:* Modify the number in the Opacity field.
5. Click OK or press Return **(Figures 37-38)**.

✓ Tip

- The effect of a painting mode will depend on the color and luminosity of the pasted image. For a dramatic change, choose Luminosity mode.

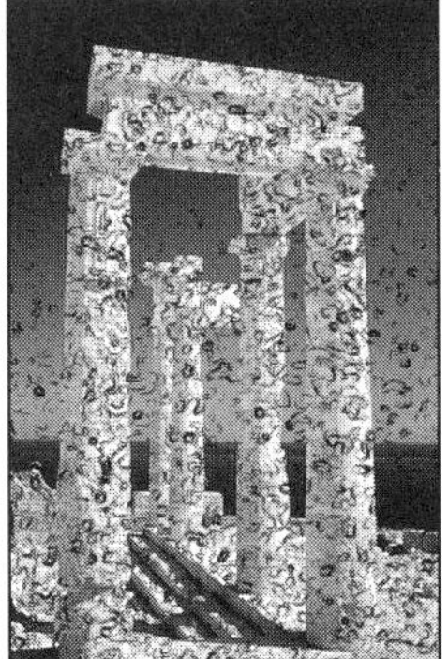

Figure 37. Darken mode was chosen for the pasted image at 100% opacity.

Figure 38. Lighten mode was chosen for the pasted image at 100% opacity.

FILTERS

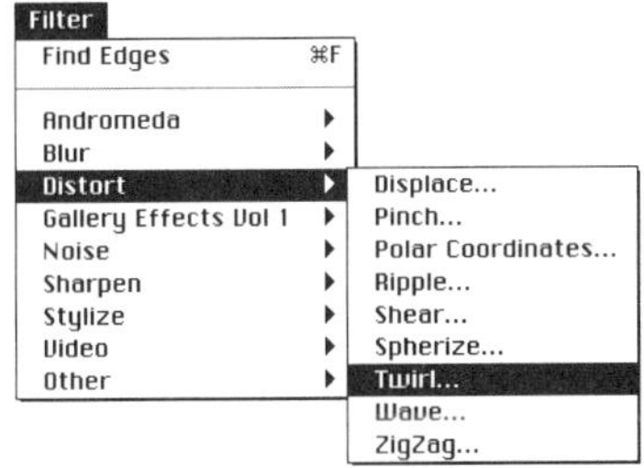

Figure 1. Filters are grouped into pop-up menu categories under the **Filter** menu. Choose the top entry to reapply the last filter applied. *(See page 236 for a list of shortcuts for applying filters)*

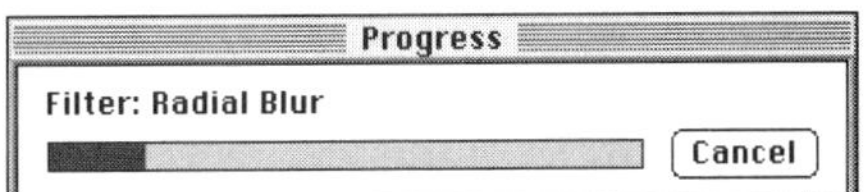

Figure 2. A Progress dialog box appears while some filters are processing.

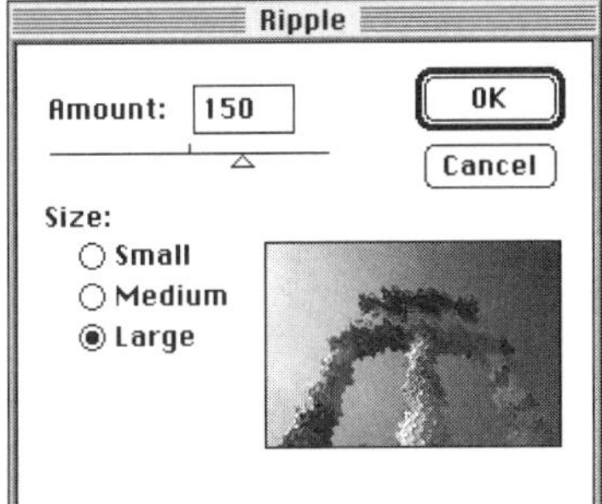

Figure 3. To use sliders and a preview box in some Distort filter dialog boxes, hold down Option and choose Displace from the About Plug-in pop-up menu under the Apple menu. In the About dialog box, check the "Show preview & sliders" box. (Thanks to Deke McClelland and MacWorld for this tip.)

THIS CHAPTER covers some of Photoshop's many filters. Filters are grouped into eight pop-up menu categories under the Filter menu **(Figure 1)**. Any third-party filter added to the program will have its own pop-up menu. *(See the Photoshop User Guide for information about installing third-party filters)*

You can use some filters, such as Blur, Blur More, Sharpen, and Sharpen More, for retouching. You can use the "arty" filters, such as Color Halftone, Find Edges, Emboss, Mosaic, Tiles, Trace Contour, and Wind, to stylize an image. You can completely transform a picture into curves, twists, and spiral patterns by applying a "wild & wavy" filter, like Ripple, Zigzag, or Twirl. Later in this chapter we'll show you how to create patterns and textures you can use in a Photoshop picture or in a document in another application.

Filters can be applied to a whole picture or just to a selection. Some filters are applied in one step by selecting them from a pop-up menu. Other filters are applied via dialog boxes in which one or more variables are specified. Highlight the top entry under the Filter menu to reapply the last filter chosen using the same variables. Choose the filter from its pop-up menu to modify its variables. A filter cannot be applied to a picture in Bitmap or Indexed Color mode.

Use the instructions in this chapter as a foundation to create your own formulas. Choose different variables in a filter dialog box, or apply more than one filter to the same picture. The stronger the amount you specify for a filter, the more abstract your image will become.

Like the Blur tool, the Blur filter subtly blends colors. Use the Blur tool to blend small areas, and apply the Blur filter to evenly blur an entire picture or a selected area.
(See page 124)

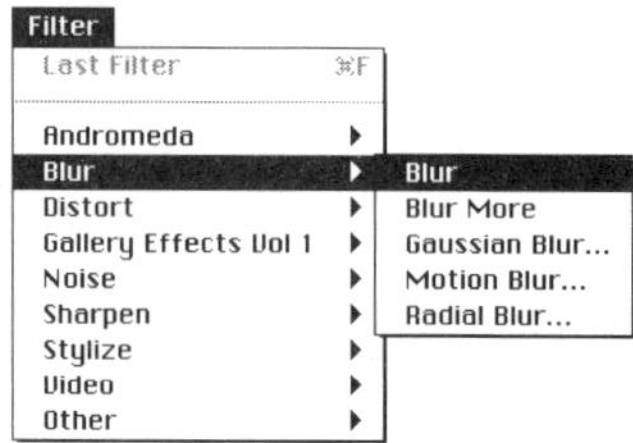

Figure 4. Choose **Blur** from the **Blur** pop-up menu under the **Filter** menu.

To apply the Blur filter:

1. Choose Blur from the Blur pop-up menu under the Filter menu **(Figures 4-6)**.
2. *Optional:* Choose Blur again to magnify the effect.
   or
   Choose Blur More to produce an effect about four times stronger.

Figure 5. The original picture.

Figure 6. The Blur filter applied.

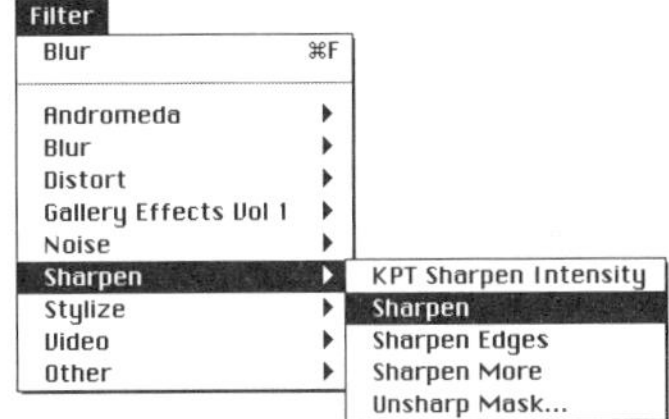

Figure 7. Choose **Sharpen** from the **Sharpen** pop-up menu under the **Filter** menu.

Like the Sharpen tool, the Sharpen filter increases contrast between pixels. Use the sharpen tool to sharpen small details. Apply the Sharpen filter to a picture or a selected area that was blurry before it was scanned or became blurry as a result of scanning to improve overall contrast.
(See also page 124)

To apply the Sharpen filter:

1. Choose Sharpen from the Sharpen pop-up menu under the Filter menu **(Figures 7-9)**.
2. *Optional:* Choose Sharpen again to magnify the effect.
   or
   Choose Sharpen More to produce an effect about four times stronger. Be careful not to over sharpen.

Figure 8. The original picture.

Figure 9. The Sharpen filter applied.

Apply the Find Edges filter to transform a continuous tone picture into a line art drawing. The lines are stroked with complementary colors to those in the original picture and the background turns white.

A method for applying the Find Edges filter:

1. Choose Find Edges from the Stylize pop-up menu under the Filter menu **(Figure 10)**.
2. *Optional:* Choose Hue/Saturation from the Adjust pop-up menu under the Image menu, move the Saturation slider all the way to the left to remove the picture's color **(Figure 11)**, then click OK or press Return.
3. Choose Solarize from the Stylize pop-up menu under the Filter menu. The picture's highlights will darken; the midtones and shadows will remain the same.
4. Double-click the Rubber Stamp tool.
5. Choose From Saved from the Option pop-up menu **(Figure 12)**.
6. Click OK or press Return.
7. If the Brushes palette is not displayed, choose Show Brushes from the Window menu.
8. Move the Opacity slider to 50%.
   and
   Choose a mode.
9. Drag over any area to restore that area's original color or shade **(Figure 13** and **Gallery 17b)**.

✔ Tips

- To produce colored lines on a dark background, choose Find Edges, then choose Invert from the Map pop-up menu under the Image menu **(Gallery 17c)**.
- Apply the Solarize filter by itself to create the illusion of a partial film negative.

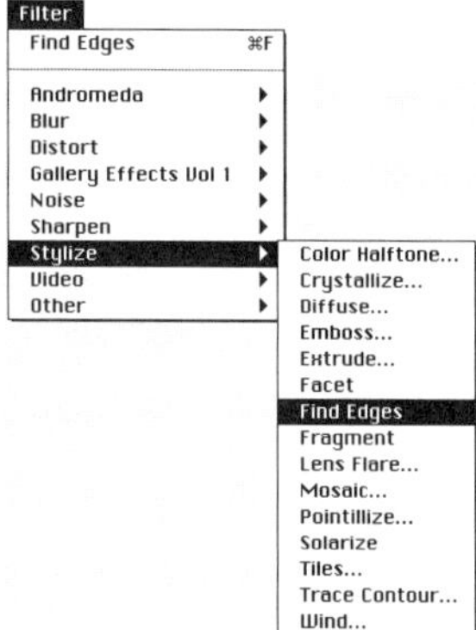

Figure 10. Choose **Find Edges** from the **Stylize** pop-up menu under the **Filter** menu.

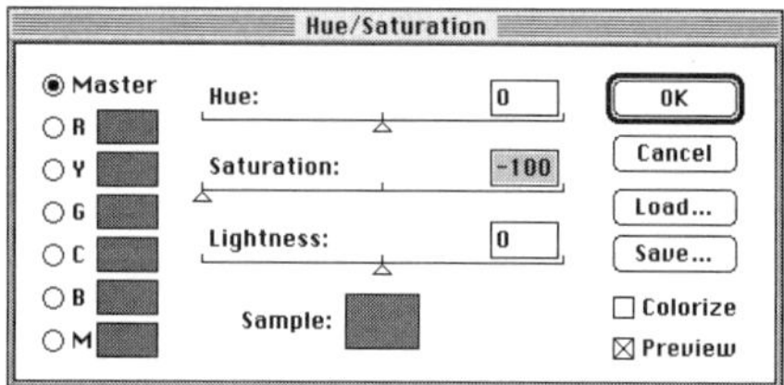

Figure 11. Move the **Saturation** slider all the way to the left in the **Hue/Saturation** dialog box.

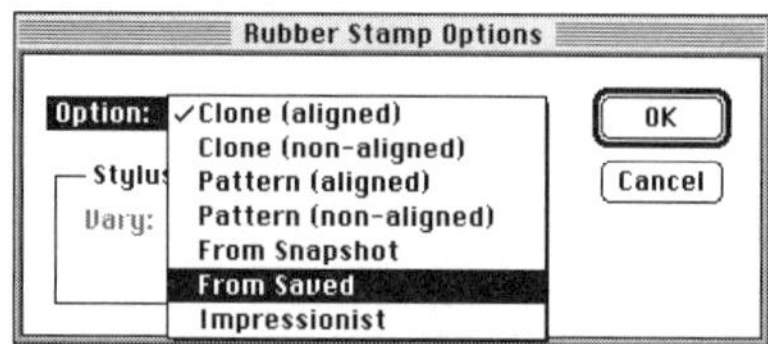

Figure 12. Choose **From Saved** from the **Option** pop-up menu in the **Rubber Stamp Options** dialog box.

Figure 13. Drag across any area to restore that area's original colors or shades.

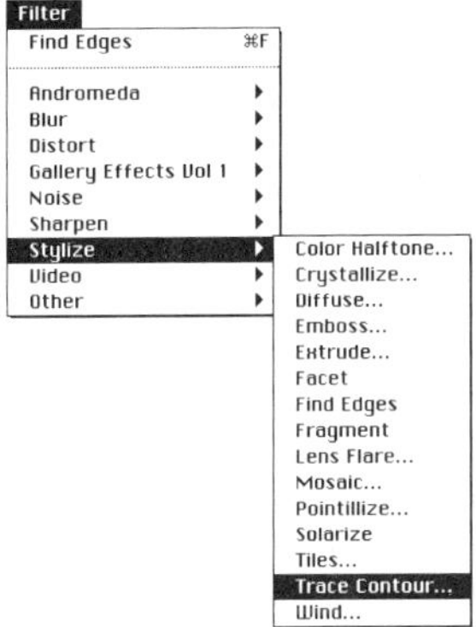

Figure 14. Choose **Trace Contour** from the **Stylize** pop-up menu under the **Filter** menu.

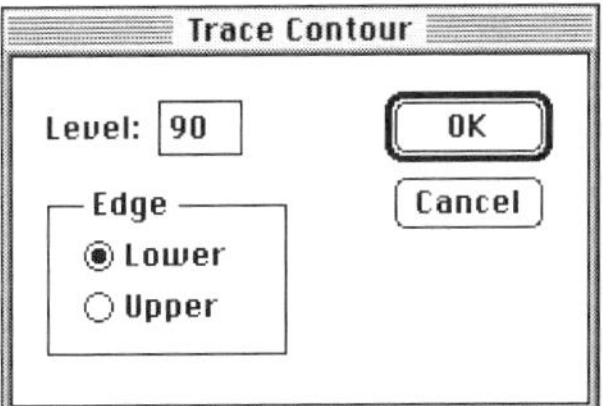

Figure 15. Enter a number in the **Level** field in the **Trace Contour** dialog box.

Figure 16. The Trace Contour filter with a Level value of 50 was applied to produce this picture.

The Trace Contour filter transforms a continuous tone picture into a contour drawing on a white background. The lines are colored with the channel colors of the current picture mode. Apply the Trace Contour filter to a picture with many shapes and colors.

To apply the Trace Contour filter:

1. Choose Trace Contour from the Stylize pop-up menu under the Filter menu **(Figure 14)**.
2. Enter a number between 0 and 255 in the Level field. The lower the number, the more lines will be created **(Figure 15)**.
3. Click OK or press Return **(Figure 16)**.
4. *Optional:* To make the picture look like a magic marker drawing, choose Minimum from the Other pop-up menu under the Filter menu, enter 1 or 2 in the Radius field, then click OK **(Gallery 17a)**.

✔ Tips

- The Edge options do not noticeably vary the filter's effects.
- To recolor the lines on a dark background, after step 3 or 4, choose Invert from the Map pop-up menu under the Image menu. To thicken the lines on a dark background, choose Maximum from the Other pop-up menu under the Filter menu.

The Emboss filter removes most of the color from a picture and makes it look as if it is stamped onto porous paper or carved into stone, like a bas-relief.

To apply the Emboss filter:

1. If the picture is low contrast, choose Levels from the Adjust pop-up menu under the Image menu, move the black Input slider to the right and the white Input slider to the left to increase the contrast, then click OK.
2. Choose Emboss from the Stylize pop-up menu under the Filter menu **(Figure 17)**.
3. Enter a number in the Angle field, or move the dial in the circle **(Figure 18)**.
4. Enter a number between 1 and 10 in the Height field. Try 3 first.
5. Enter a number between 1 and 500 in the Amount field. The lower the number, the more color will be removed from the picture.
6. Click OK or press Return **(Figure 19)**.

✔ Tip

- To change the midtone color after applying the Emboss filter, choose Hue/Saturation from the Adjust pop-up menu under the Image menu, check the Colorize box, then move the Hue, Saturation, or Lightness sliders.

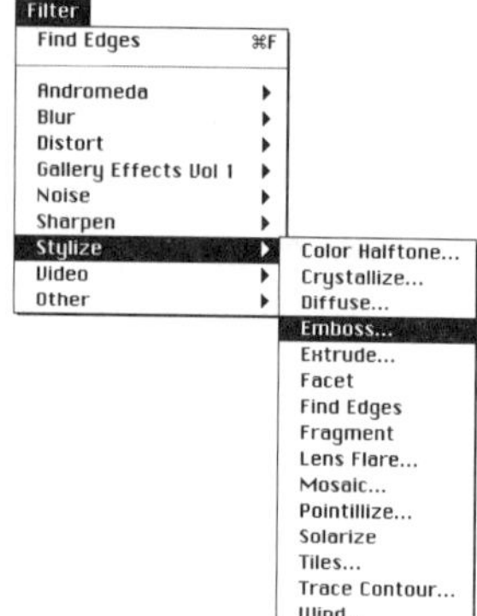

Figure 17. Choose **Emboss** from the **Stylize** pop-up menu under the **Filter** menu.

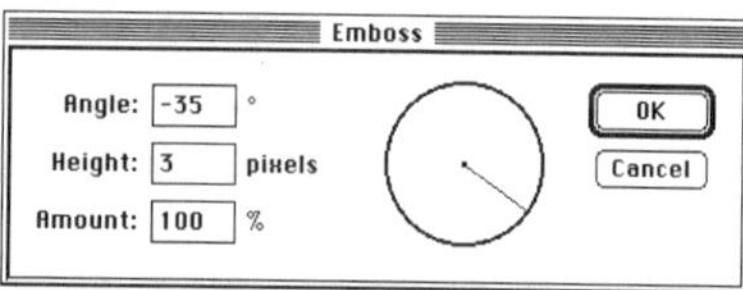

Figure 18. Where the dial is positioned in this illustration, highlights will appear on the left and shadows will appear on the right.

Figure 19. To produce this picture, the Emboss filter was applied with an Angle of -35, Height of 3, and Amount of 100.

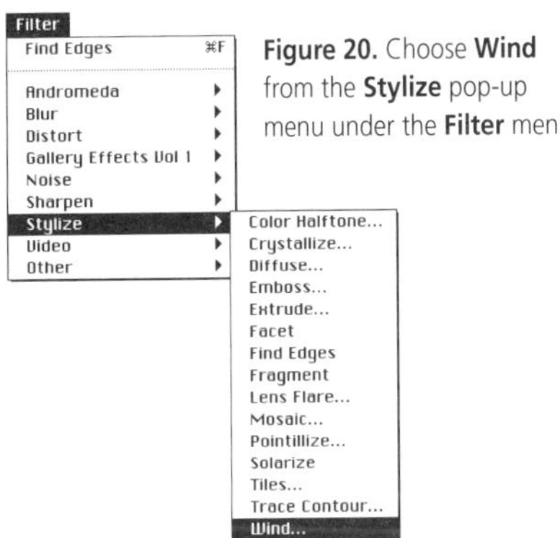

Figure 20. Choose **Wind** from the **Stylize** pop-up menu under the **Filter** menu.

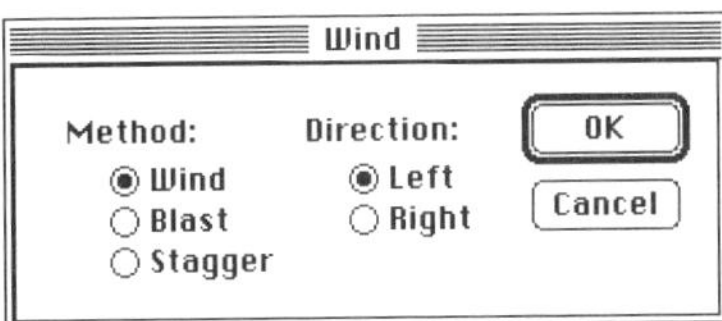

Figure 21. In the **Wind** dialog box, click **Wind, Blast,** or **Stagger**, and click **Left** or **Right**.

The Wind filter produces an illusion of wind blowing across an image.

To apply the Wind filter:

1. Choose Wind from the Stylize pop-up menu under the Filter menu **(Figure 20)**.
2. Click Wind to produce a light breeze **(Figure 21)**.
   or
   Click Blast to produce a hurricane force wind. Blast will slightly diminish a picture's saturation.
   or
   Click Stagger to create an Impressionistic effect with the picture's original colors.
3. Click Left or Right (the Wind direction).
4. Click OK or press Return **(Figures 22-24)**.

Figure 22. The Wind filter was applied to this picture with the Wind Method and Left Direction chosen (a "Nor'easter").

Figure 23. The Wind filter was applied to this picture with the Blast Method and Left Direction chosen.

Figure 24. The Wind filter was applied to this picture with the Stagger Method and Left Direction chosen.

Use the following instructions as a starting point. You can experiment with other Brushes palette Opacity settings, other Hue/Saturation box settings, and other filters, such as Emboss, Facet, and Pointillize. Choose Undo from the Edit menu to undo a filter.

To apply the Wind filter to type:

1. Create type. Choose a bold font in a large size relative to the picture. *(See page 112)*
2. If the Brushes palette is not displayed, choose Show Brushes from the Window menu.
3. Move the Opacity slider to the left.
4. Choose Defloat from the Select menu.
5. If your picture is in a color mode, choose Hue/Saturation from the Adjust pop-up menu under the Image menu, then move the Saturation slider to the right **(Figures 25-26)**.
6. Click OK or press Return.
7. Choose Wind from the Stylize pop-up menu under the Filter menu **(Figure 27)**.
8. Click a Method and Direction **(Figure 28)**.
9. Click OK or press Return.
10. *Optional:* Follow steps 7-9 again, but click the opposite Direction button.
11. Choose None from the Select menu **(Figure 29)**.

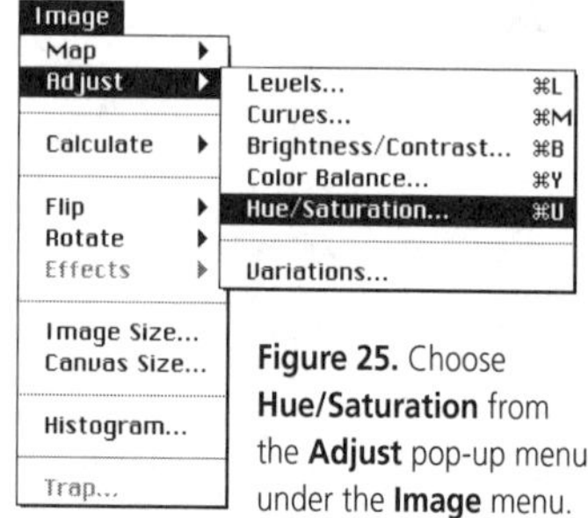

Figure 25. Choose **Hue/Saturation** from the **Adjust** pop-up menu under the **Image** menu.

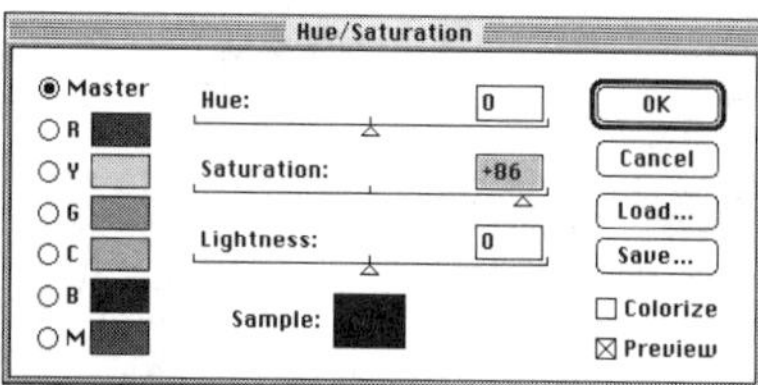

Figure 26. Move the **Saturation** slider to the right in the **Hue/Saturation** dialog box.

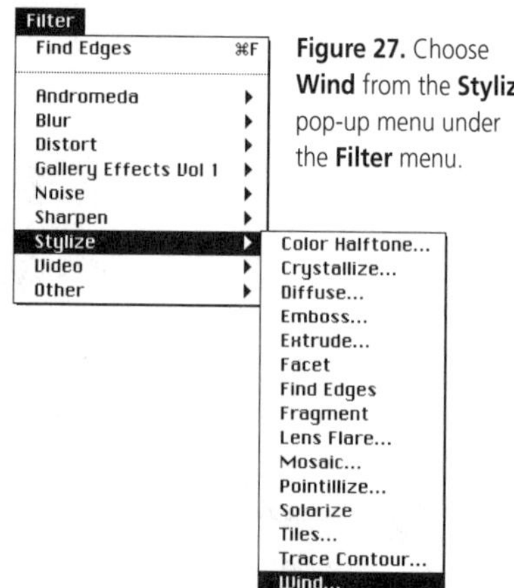

Figure 27. Choose **Wind** from the **Stylize** pop-up menu under the **Filter** menu.

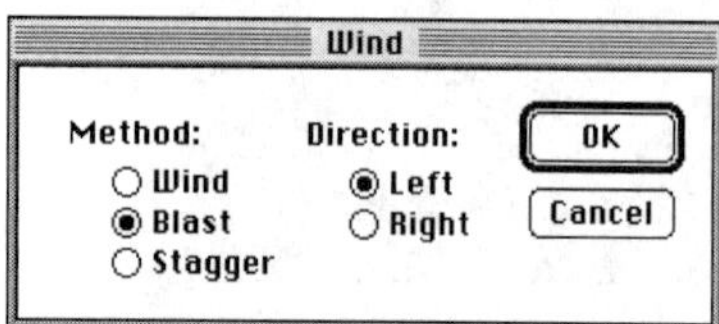

Figure 28. Click **Blast** or **Stagger** and click a **Direction** in the **Wind** dialog box.

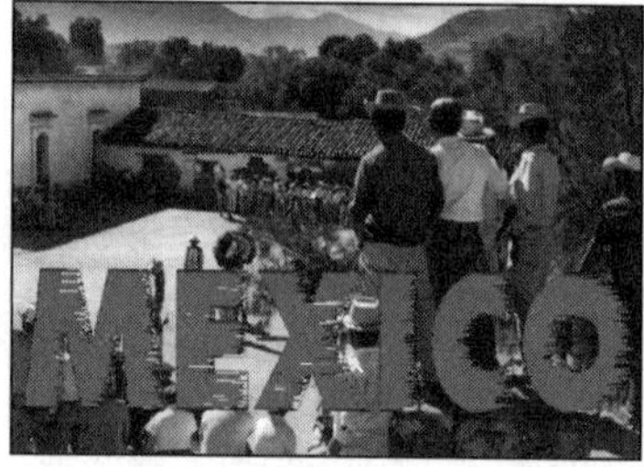

Figure 29. The Wind filter applied to type.

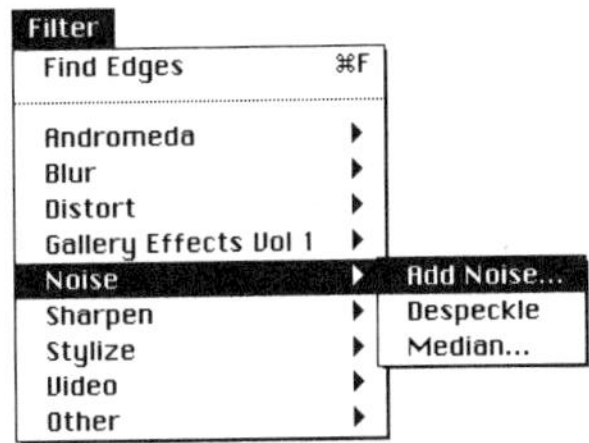

Figure 30. Choose **Add Noise** from the **Noise** pop-up menu under the **Filter** menu.

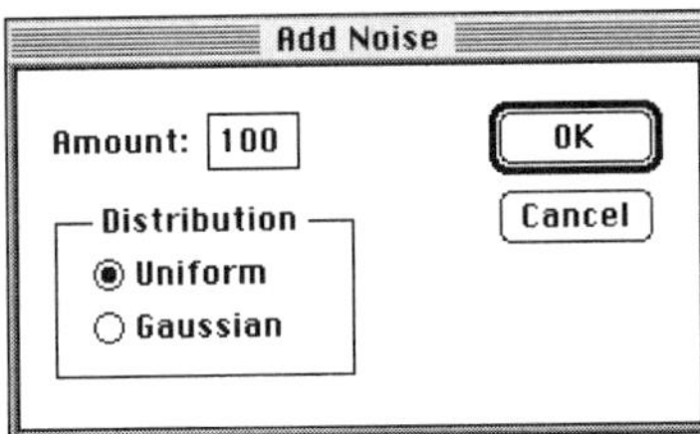

Figure 31. In the **Add Noise** dialog box, enter a number in the **Amount** field, and click **Uniform** or **Gaussian**.

Figure 32. The Add Noise filter was applied to this picture with an Amount of 60 and Gaussian Distribution.

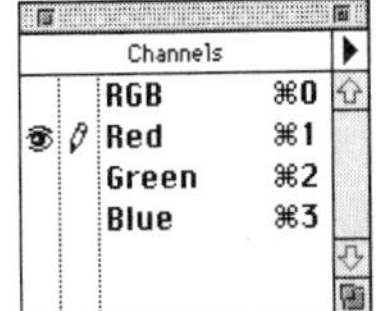

Figure 33. Click a channel name on the **Channels** palette.

The Add Noise filter randomly recolors pixels. Apply it to a new document with a solid white background to create a speckled, grainy pattern. You can then use the pattern as an element in another Photoshop picture or in a document in another application. Apply the Add Noise filter to an existing picture to create a grainy, high-speed film effect.

(To paste a pattern behind an image, see page 177. To save a pattern to use in another application, see pages 48-49. The Add Noise filter is also discussed on page 201)

To apply the Add Noise filter:

1. Choose Add Noise from the Noise pop-up menu under the Filter menu **(Figure 30)**.
2. Enter a number between 1 and 999 (the intensity of the filter) in the Amount field **(Figure 31)**.
3. Click Uniform or Gaussian.
4. Click OK or press Return **(Figure 32)**.

✔ Tip

- To create a subtler effect, add pixels of a single color by applying the Add Noise filter to only one of a picture's channels. Click a channel color name on the Channels palette **(Figure 33)**, apply the Add Noise filter following the steps above, then click the top channel on the palette to display the composite picture.

Note: For drama, apply the Ripple, Zigzag, or Twirl filter to a picture with a wide, white border. Follow the instructions on page 195 to create a "wrinkled" edge using the Ripple filter.

The Ripple filter will make an image look as if it is reflected on water.

To apply the Ripple filter:

1. Choose Ripple from the Distort pop-up menu under the Filter menu **(Figure 34)**.
2. Enter a number between -999 and 999 in the Amount field **(Figure 35)**. The further the number is from 0, the more distortion will be produced.
3. Click Small, Medium or Large. Large produces the most distortion.
4. Click OK or press Return **(Figures 36-38)**.

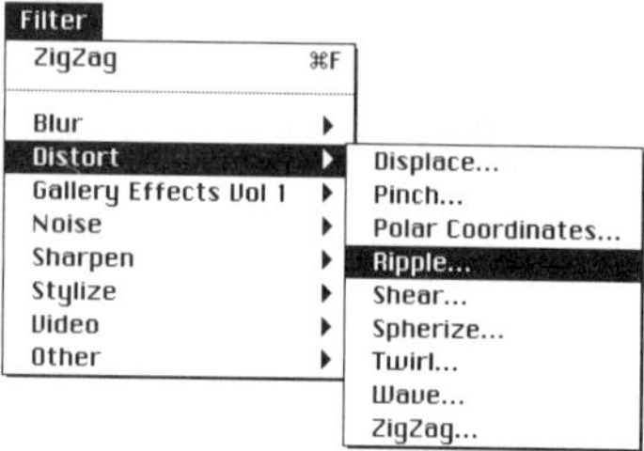

Figure 34. Choose **Ripple** from the **Distort** pop-up menu under the **Filter** menu.

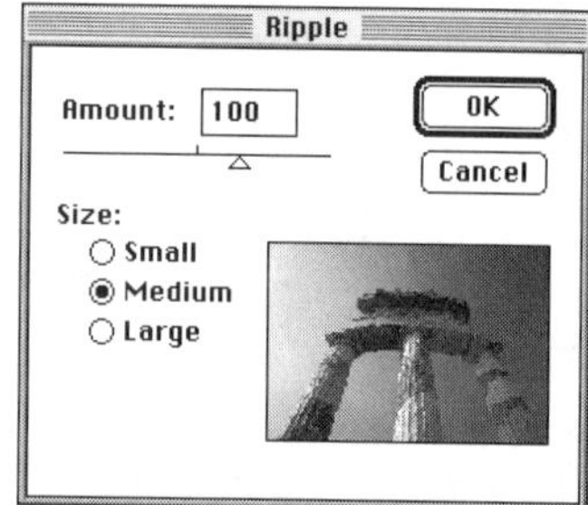

Figure 35. In the **Ripple** dialog box, enter a number in the **Amount** field, and click **Small, Medium,** or **Large**.
(Instructions for accessing the slider and preview options are on page 183)

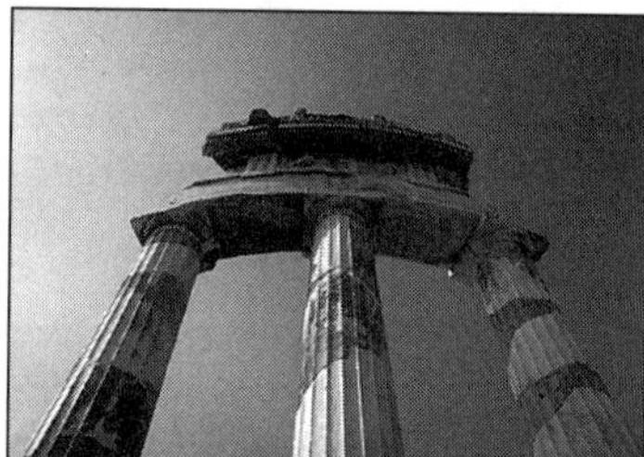

Figure 36. The original picture.

Figure 37. The Ripple filter — Amount 150, Large.

Figure 38. The Ripple filter — Amount 100, Medium.

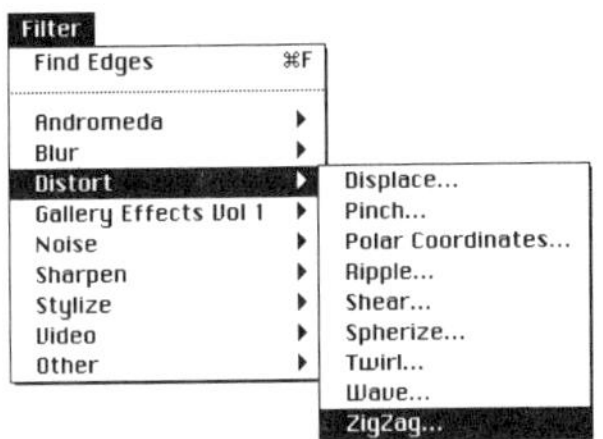

Figure 39. Choose **ZigZag** from the **Distort** pop-up menu under the **Filter** menu.

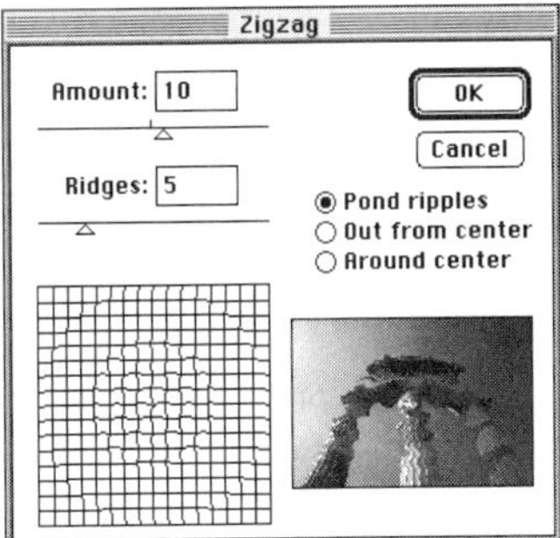

Figure 40. In the **Zigzag** dialog box, enter an **Amount**, a number of **Ridges**, and click **Pond ripples, Out from center,** or **Around center.**
(Instructions for accessing the slider and preview options are on page 183)

The Zigzag filter produces an illusion of patterns on the surface of water, as if a stone was thrown into it or a canoe passed by. The distortion is greatest in the center of the picture or selection.

To apply the Zigzag filter:

1. Choose Zigzag from the Distort pop-up menu under the Filter menu **(Figure 39)**.
2. Enter a number between 100 and -100 in the Amount field **(Figure 40)**. The further the number is from 0, the more distortion will be produced.
3. Enter a number between 1 and 20 in the Ridges field (the number of zigzags or rings).
4. Click Pond Ripples to distort pixels diagonally.
   or
   Click Out from Center to produce patterns radiating from the picture's center.
   or
   Click Around Center to produce zigzags around the picture's center.
5. Click OK or press Return **(Figures 41-42)**.

Figure 41. The Zigzag filter applied to a picture with an Amount of -100, 5 Ridges, and Pond ripples chosen.

Figure 42. The Zigzag filter applied to a picture with an Amount of 10, 5 Ridges, and Pond ripples chosen.

The Twirl filter spirals the middle of a picture around its center.

To apply the Twirl filter:

1. Choose Twirl from the Distort pop-up menu under the Filter menu **(Figure 43)**.
2. Enter a number between -999 and 999 in the Angle field **(Figure 44)**. The further the number is from 0, the more distortion will be produced.
3. Click OK or press Return **(Figures 45-46)**.

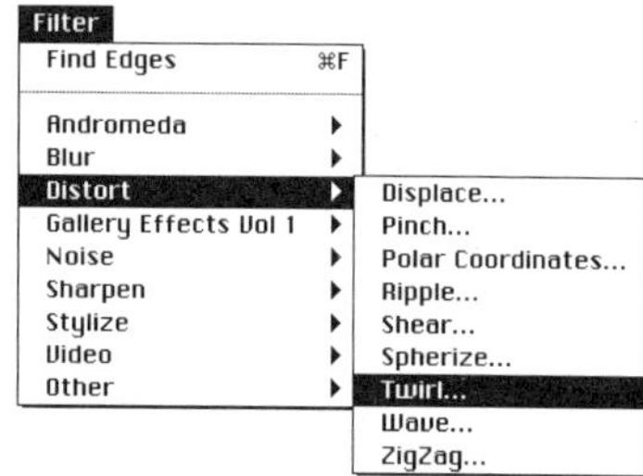

Figure 43. Choose **Twirl** from the **Distort** pop-up menu under the **Filter** menu.

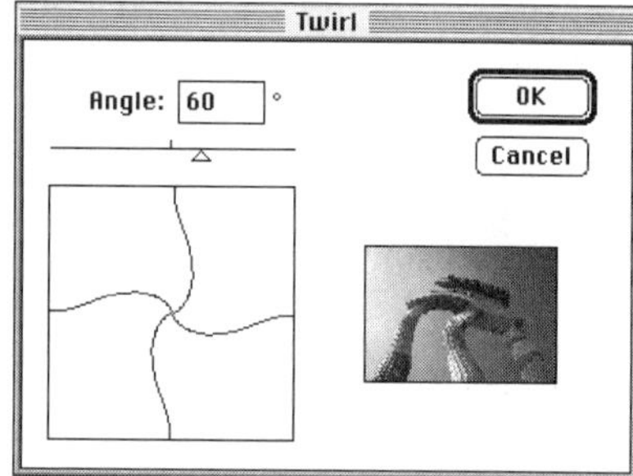

Figure 44. Enter a number in the **Angle** field in the **Twirl** dialog box.
(Instructions for accessing the slider and preview options are on page 183)

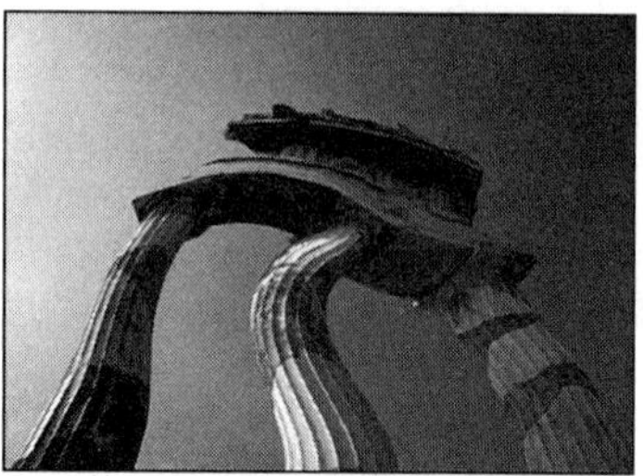

Figure 45. The Twirl filter applied at a 60° Angle.

Figure 46. The Twirl filter applied at a 180° Angle.

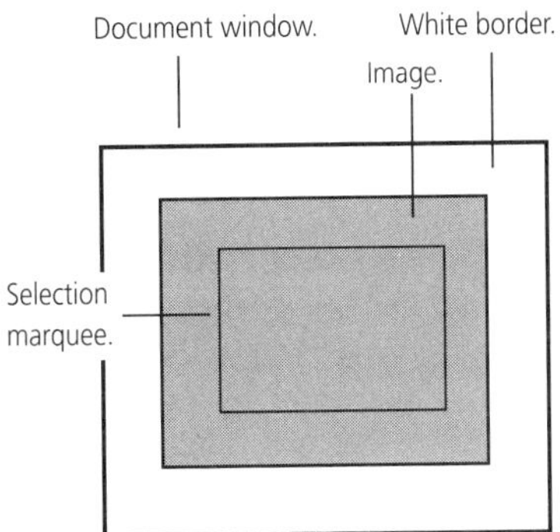

Figure 47. A selection before choosing the Inverse command.

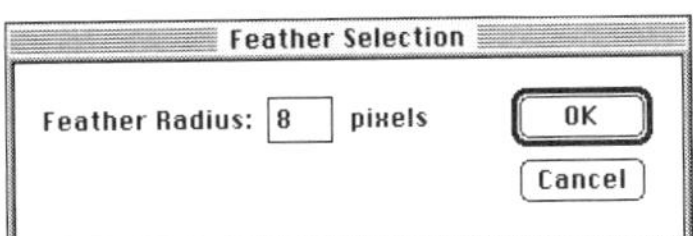

Figure 48. Enter 8 in the **Feather Radius** field in the **Feather Selection** dialog box.

Apply the Ripple, Twirl, or Zigzag filter to a picture with a white border to produce a "warped paper" texture.

To create a "wrinkled" edge:

1. Follow the steps on page 43 to create a white border around a picture.
2. Click the Rectangular Marquee tool.
3. Drag a rectangle across about three quarters of the picture **(Figure 47)**.
4. Choose Feather from the Select menu.
5. Enter 8 in the Feather Radius field **(Figure 48)**.
6. Click OK.
7. Choose Inverse from the Select menu. The border will become the active selection.
8. Follow the steps on page 192, 193, or 194 **(Figures 49-51)**.

Figure 49. A "wrinkled edge" produced using the Ripple filter — Amount 100, Medium.

Figure 50. A "wrinkled edge" produced using the Twirl filter — Angle -300.

Figure 51. A "wrinkled edge" produced using the Zigzag filter — Amount 40, Ridges 8, Around center.

The Color Halftone filter transforms a picture into enlarged "halftone screen" dots. You can specify the size of the dots.

Note: Despite its name, the Color Halftone filter can be applied to a picture in Grayscale mode.

To apply the Color Halftone filter:

1. Choose Color Halftone from the Stylize pop-up menu under the Filter menu **(Figure 52)**.
2. Enter a number between 4 and 8 in the Radius field **(Figure 53)**. The higher the Radius value, the larger the dots. The minimum is 4, the maxiumum is 127.
3. *Optional:* To produce a different "rosette" pattern, modify the numbers in the Screen Angle fields.
4. Click OK or press Return **(Figure 54** and **Gallery 17d)**.

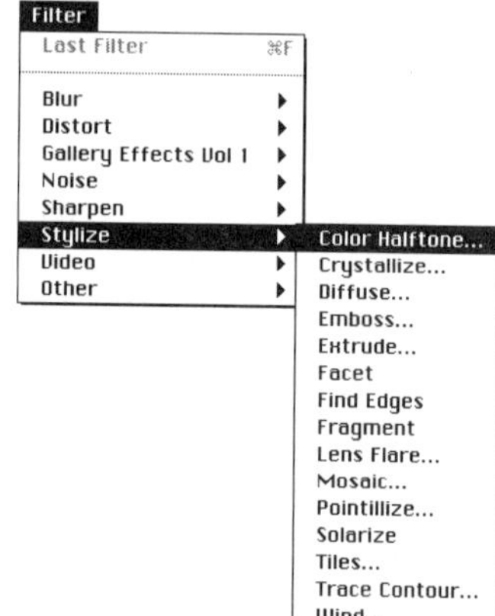

Figure 52. Choose **Color Halftone** from the **Stylize** pop-up menu under the **Filter** menu.

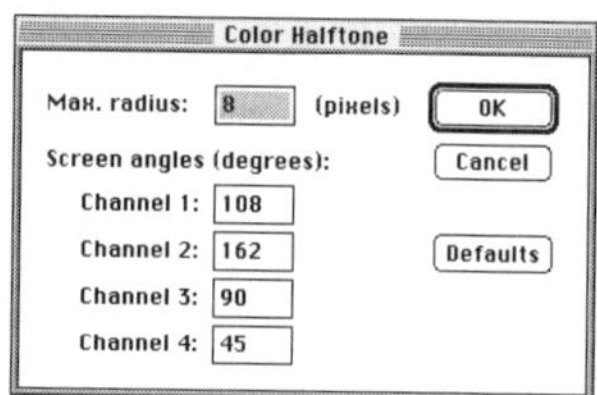

Figure 53. Enter a number in the **Radius** field in the **Color Halftone** dialog box.

Figure 54. The original picture.

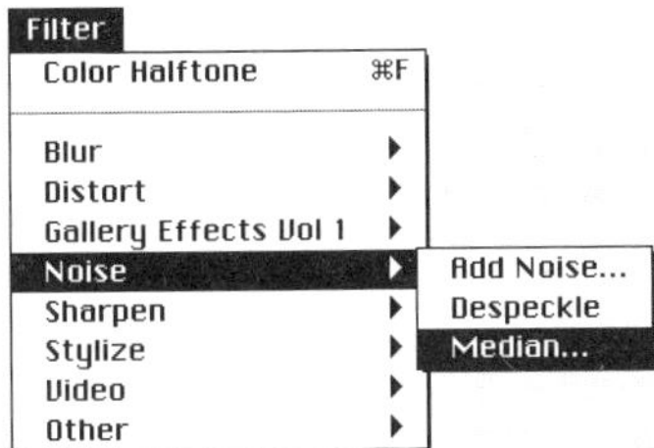

Figure 55. Choose **Median** from the **Noise** menu.

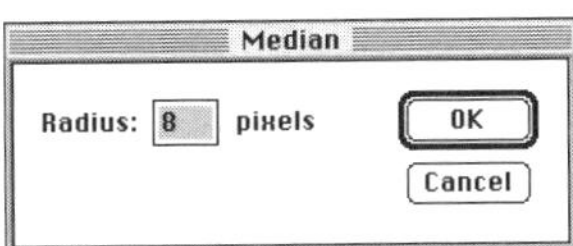

Figure 56. Enter a number between 3 and 8 in the **Radius** field in the **Median** dialog box.

Figure 57. The Median filter applied with a Radius value of 8.

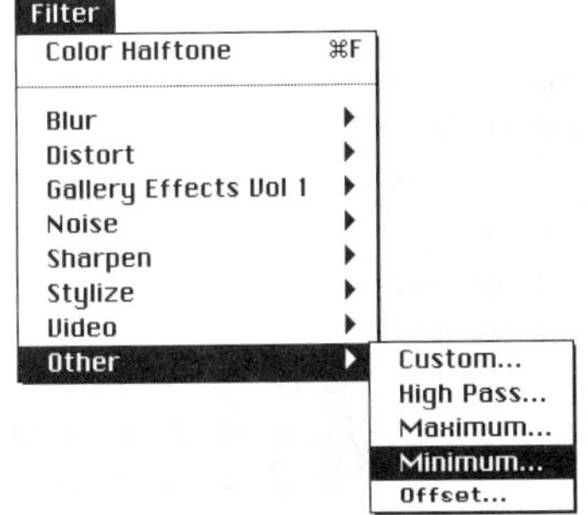

Figure 58. Choose **Minimum** from the **Other** pop-up menu under the **Filter** menu.

Apply the Median Noise and Minimum filters to a picture to transform it into a "watercolor."

To create a "watercolor":

1. Choose Median from the Noise pop-up menu under the Filter menu **(Figure 55)**.
2. Enter a number between 3 and 8 in the Radius field **(Figure 56)**. 1 is the minimum; 16 is the maximum.
3. Click OK or press Return. **(Figure 57)**
4. Choose Minimum from the Other pop-up menu under the Filter menu **(Figure 58)**.
5. Enter 3 or 4 in the Radius field. 1 is the minimum; 16 is the maximum **(Figure 59)**.
6. Click OK or press Return **(Gallery 17e)**.

✔ Tip

■ The Minimum filter applied by itself will darken and blur a picture.

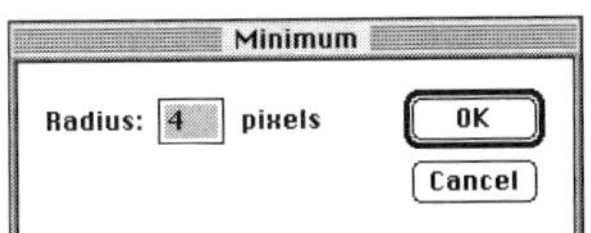

Figure 59. Enter 3 or 4 in the **Radius** field in the **Minimum** dialog box.

Apply the Tiles filter to transform a picture into unevenly spaced tiles. You can specify the "grout" color to appear between the tiles.

Apply the Tiles filter:

1. Choose Tiles from the Stylize pop-up menu under the Filter menu **(Figure 60)**.
2. Enter the Number of Tiles to appear across the narrowest dimension of the picture **(Figure 61)**. The fewer the tiles, the larger each tile will be. The minimum is 1, the maximum is 99.
3. Enter a number in the Maximum Offset field (the maximum distance between tiles as a percentage of tile size). The minumum is 1, the maximum is 90.
4. Click an option to fill the background area ("grout") between the tiles: Background Color, Foreground Color, Inverse Image, or Unaltered Image.
5. Click OK or press Return **(Figures 62-63** and **Gallery 17f)**.

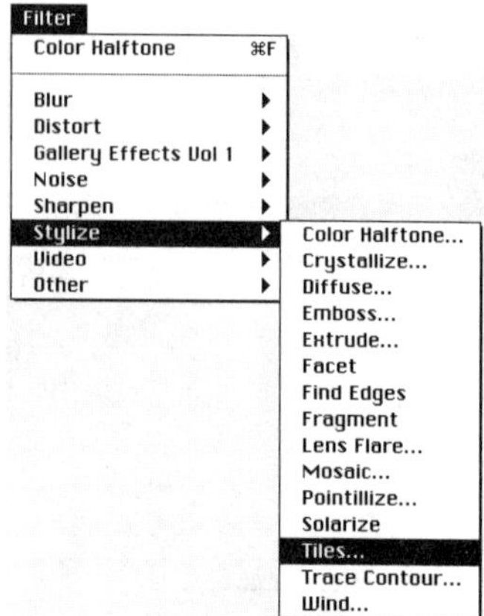

Figure 60. Choose **Tiles** from the **Stylize** pop-up menu under the **Filter** menu.

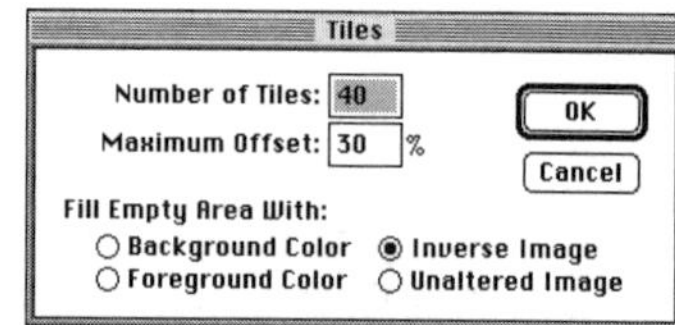

Figure 61. In the **Tiles** dialog box, enter a **Number of Tiles**, a **Maximum Offset**, and click a "grout" color.

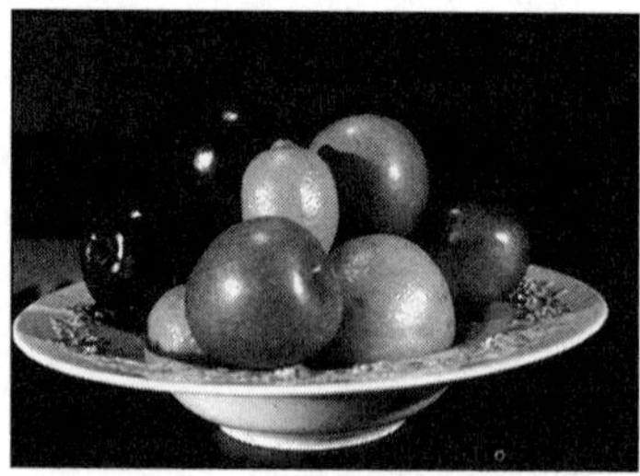

Figure 62. The original picture.

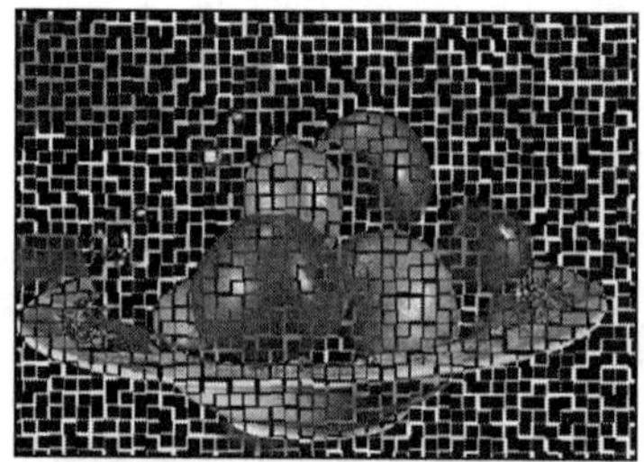

Figure 63. To produce this illustration, 30 was entered in the Number of Tiles field and Inverse Image was clicked. The picture is 2 inches wide.

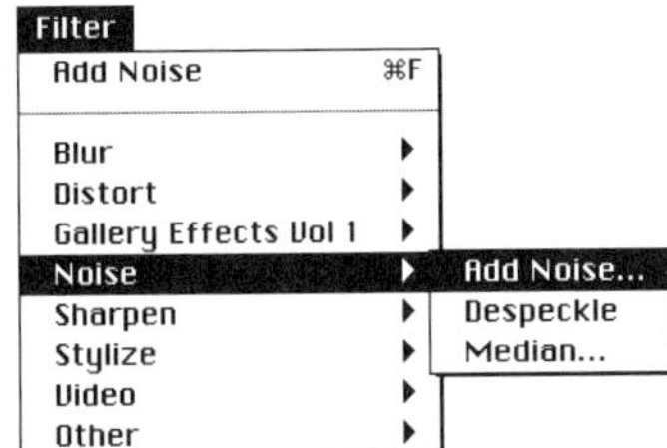

Figure 64. Choose **Add Noise** from the **Noise** pop-up menu under the **Filter** menu.

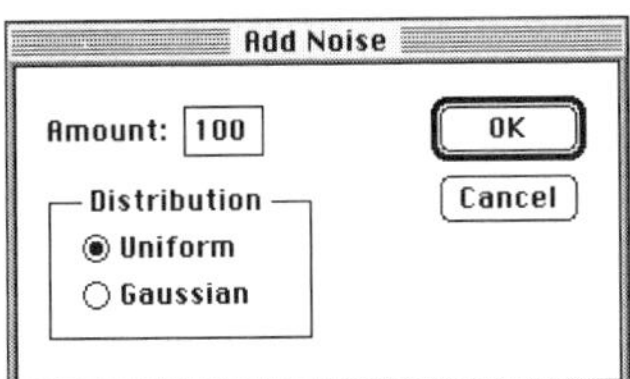

Figure 65. In the **Add Noise** dialog box, enter a number between 1 and 999 in the **Amount** field and click **Uniform** or **Gaussian**.

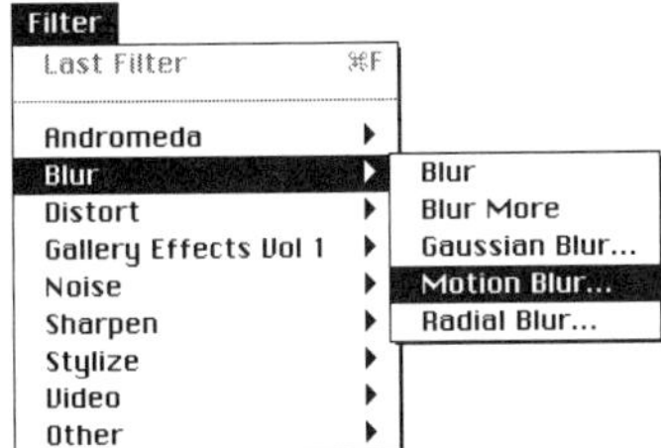

Figure 66. Choose **Motion Blur** from the **Blur** pop-up menu under the **Filter** menu.

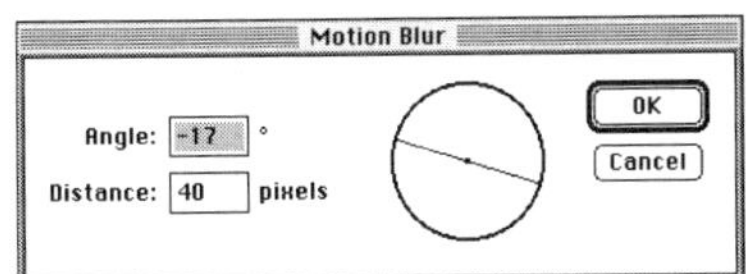

Figure 67. In the **Motion Blur** dialog box, enter -17 in the **Angle** field and 40 in the **Distance** field.

A variety of textures can be created using the Add Noise filter as the starting point. Earlier in this chapter the Add Noise filter was applied to an image. On this and the next page, it is applied to a blank picture.

To create a woven texture:

1. Create a New document.
   (See page 35)
2. Choose Add Noise from the Noise pop-up menu under the Filter menu **(Figure 64)**.
3. Enter a number between 1 and 999 (the amount of noise) in the Amount field **(Figure 65)**.
4. Click Uniform or Gaussian.
5. Click OK or press Return.
6. Choose Motion Blur from the Blur pop-up menu under the Filter menu **(Figure 66)**.
7. Enter -17 in the Angle field **(Figure 67)**.
8. Enter 40 in the Distance field.
9. Click OK or press Return.

Follow steps 10-12 for a color picture.

10. Choose Hue/Saturation from the Adjust pop-up menu under the Image menu **(Figure 68)**.
11. In the Hue/Saturation dialog box, check the Colorize box **(Figure 69)**.
    and
    Move the Hue, Saturation, or Lightness sliders.
12. Click OK or press Return **(Figure 70** and **Gallery 17g)**.
13. *Optional:* To add a wave to the texture, choose Twirl from the Distort pop-up menu under the Filter menu, enter 72 in the Amount field, then click OK **(Figures 71-72)**.

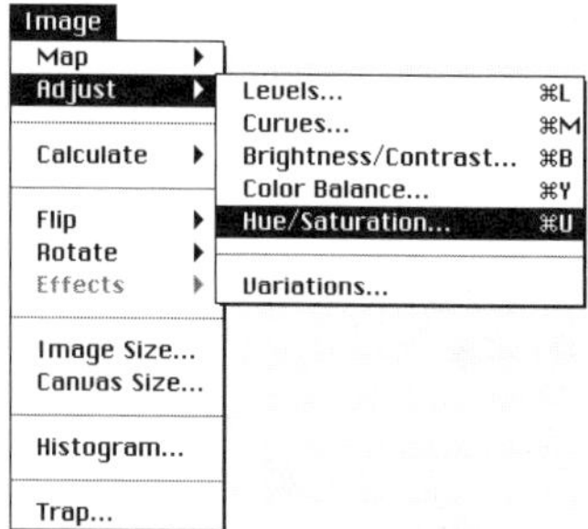

Figure 68. Choose **Hue/Saturation** from the **Adjust** pop-up menu under the **Image** menu.

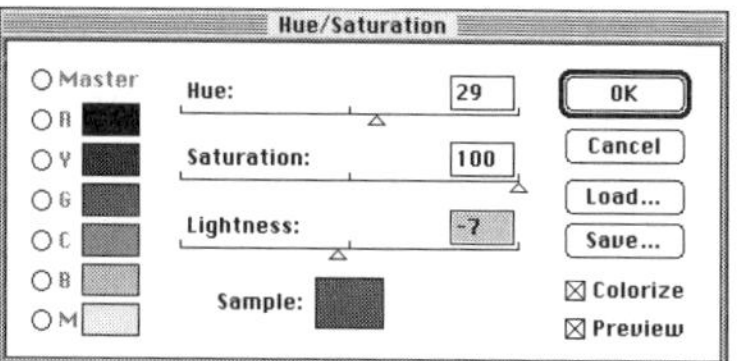

Figure 69. In the **Hue/Saturation** dialog box, check the **Colorize** box, then move the **Hue** and **Lightness** sliders.

Figure 70. A woven texture.

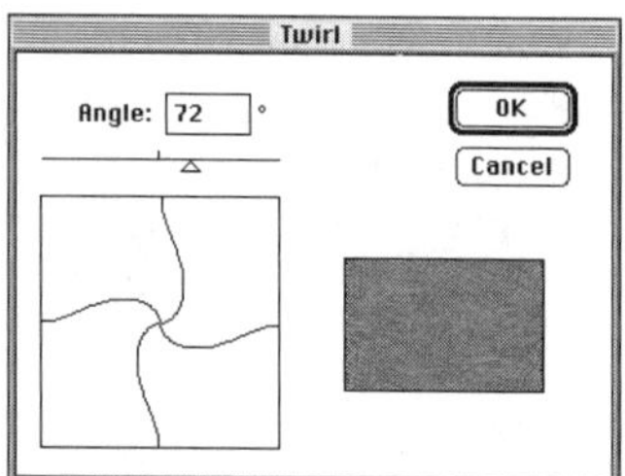

Figure 71. Enter 72 in the **Angle** field in the **Twirl** dialog box.

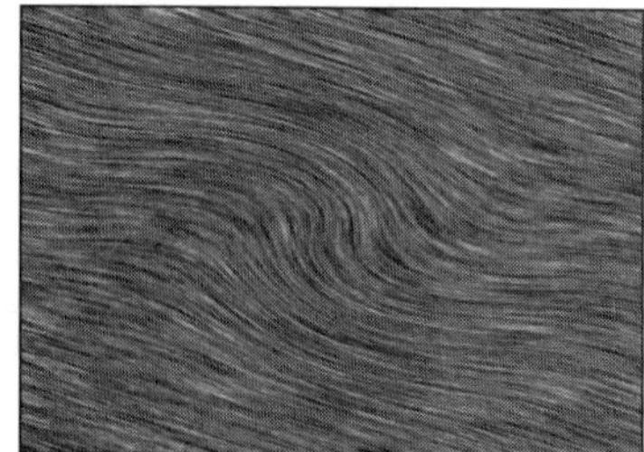

Figure 72. A woven texture with the Twirl filter applied.

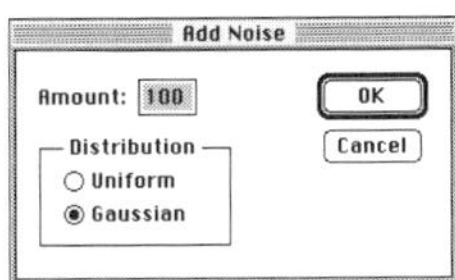

Figure 73. Enter a number in the **Amount** field in the **Add Noise** dialog box.

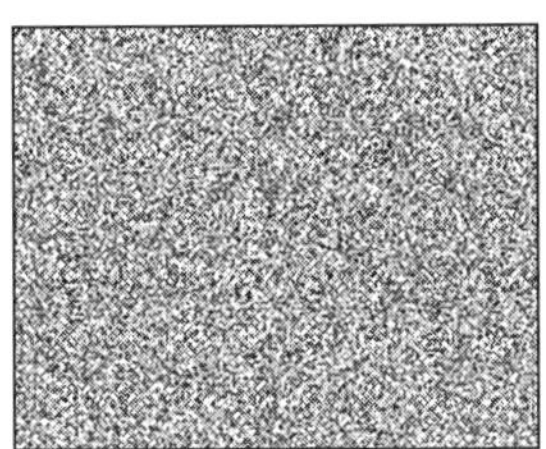

Figure 74. A new document with the Add Noise filter applied.

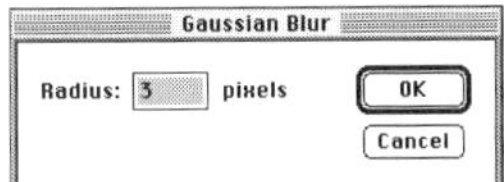

Figure 75. Enter 3 in the **Radius** field in the **Gaussian Blur** dialog box.

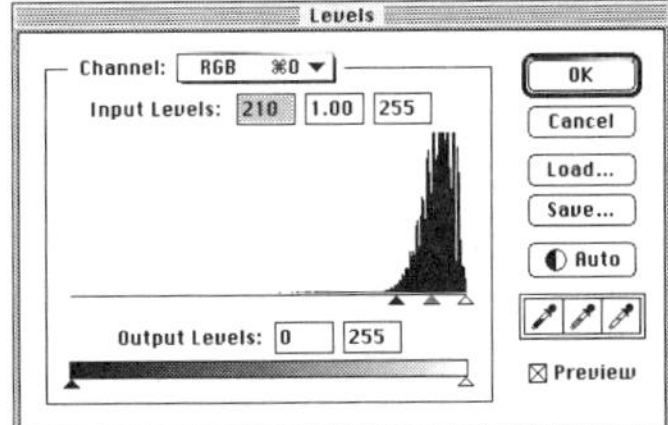

Figure 76. Move the black Input slider to the right in the **Levels** dialog box.

To create a spaghetti texture:

1. Create a New document. *(See page 35)*
2. Choose Add Noise from the Noise pop-up menu under the Filter menu.
3. Enter a number between 400 and 700 in the Amount field **(Figure 73)**.
4. Click Gaussian.
5. Click OK or press Return **(Figure 74)**.
6. Choose Gaussian Blur from the Blur pop-up menu under the Filter menu.
7. Enter 3 in the Radius field **(Figure 75)**.
8. Click OK or press Return
9. Choose Find Edges from the Stylize pop-up menu under the Filter menu.
10. Choose Levels from the Adjust pop-up menu under the Image menu.
11. Move the black Input slider to the right **(Figure 76)**. Pause to preview.
12. Click OK or press Return **(Figure 77)**.
13. *Optional:* Choose Sharpen from the Sharpen pop-up menu under the Filter menu.

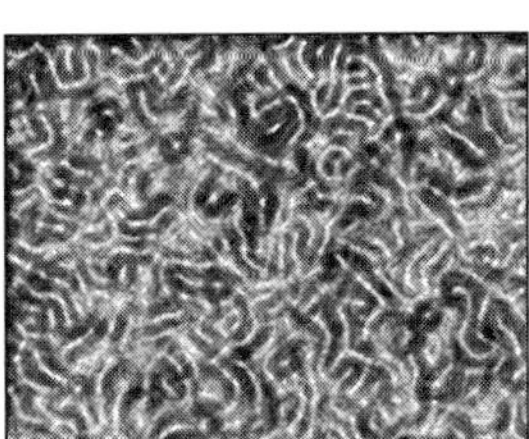

Figure 77. Spaghetti.

In the following instructions, the Mosaic filter is applied to multiple selections to break a picture into pixel blocks that gradually enlarge from left to right.

To apply the Mosaic filter:

1. Open a picture.
2. Click the Rectangular Marquee tool.
3. Drag a rectangle across about a quarter of the picture **(Figure 78)**.
4. Choose Mosaic from the Stylize pop-up menu under the Filter menu **(Figure 79)**.
5. Enter 4 in the Cell Size field **(Figure 80)**.
6. Click OK or press Return.
7. With the selection still active, hold down ⌘ and Option and drag the marquee to the right **(Figure 78)**.
8. Repeat steps 4-7 three more times, entering 8, then 16, then 32 in the Cell Size field.
9. Choose None from the Select menu **(Figure 81)**.
   or
   Hold down ⌘ and press "D."

✔ Tips

- To create larger pixel blocks, enter higher numbers — like 6, 12, 24, and 34 — in the Cell Size field.
- To open the dialog box of the last filter applied, hold down ⌘ and Option and press "F."

Figure 78. Select an area with the Rectangular Marquee tool. After applying the Mosaic filter, move the marquee to the right.

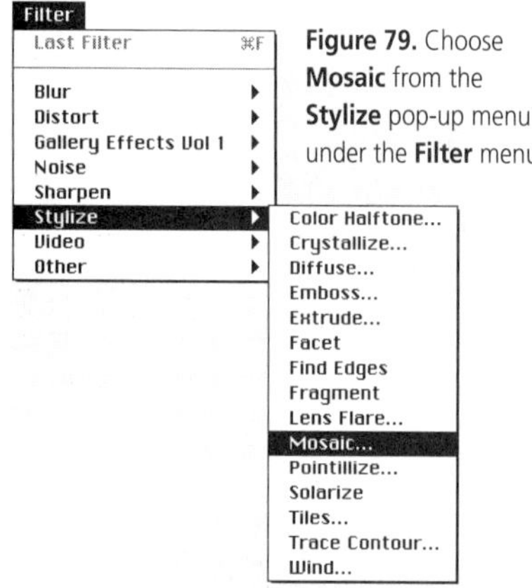

Figure 79. Choose **Mosaic** from the **Stylize** pop-up menu under the **Filter** menu.

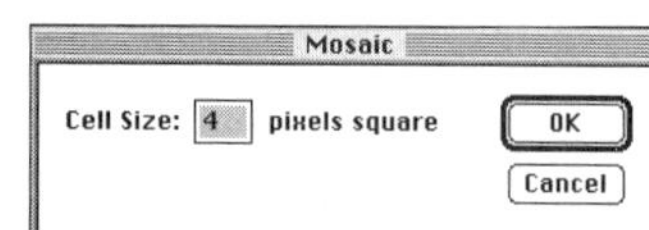

Figure 80. Enter a number in the **Cell Size** field in the **Mosaic** dialog box. Enter progressively higher numbers when repeating steps 4 and 5.

Figure 81. The Mosaic filter applied to a picture.

Mosaic Filter

Figure 82. Select an area of a picture.

Figure 83. Choose **Define Pattern** from the **Edit** menu.

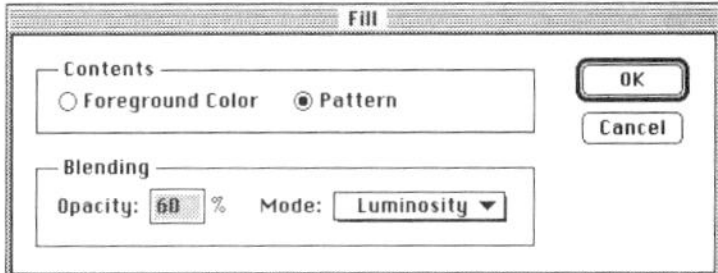

Figure 84. In the **Fill** dialog box, click **Pattern**, enter an **Opacity** value, and choose from the **Mode** pop-up menu.

Figure 85. A pattern created using a shape as a Fill.

Follow the instructions on this page to create a pattern from a selected area of a picture and use the pattern as a Fill. Then follow the instructions on the next page to enhance the pattern using filters.

To create a pattern from a picture:

1. Open a picture.
2. Click the Rectangular Marquee tool.
3. Create a rectangular selection to become the fill pattern **(Figure 82)**.
4. Choose Define Pattern from the Edit menu **(Figure 83)**.
5. Create a New document in the same picture mode as the picture from which the pattern was created, and choose All from the Select menu. *(See page 35)*
   or
   Select an area of a picture.
6. Choose Fill from the Edit menu.
7. In the Fill dialog box, click Pattern **(Figure 84)**.
   and
   Enter a number in the Opacity field.
   and
   Choose a mode from the Mode pop-up menu.
8. Click OK **(Figure 85)**.

   Note: To texturize the pattern, follow the instructions on the next page. Do not deselect.

✔ Tip

- To fill an area with a pattern using strokes, follow the steps above to define a pattern. Double-click the Rubber Stamp tool and choose Pattern (aligned) or Pattern (non-aligned) from the Option pop-up menu. Then drag back and forth across a picture. You can choose a tip, mode, and opacity for the Rubber Stamp tool from the Brushes palette.

To texturize a pattern:

1. Follow the instructions on the previous page, and don't deselect.
2. Choose Find Edges from the Stylize pop-up menu under the Filter menu **(Figure 86)**.
3. Choose a light Foreground color. *(See pages 130-132)*
4. Choose Fill from the Edit menu.
5. In the Fill dialog box, click Foreground Color **(Figure 87)**.
   and
   Enter 60 in the Opacity field.
   and
   Choose Color from the Mode pop-up menu.
6. Click OK or press Return.
7. Choose None from the Select menu.

Steps 8-13 are optional.

8. Click the Magic Wand tool.
9. Click on a light area of the picture.
10. Choose Similar from the Select menu.
11. Choose Fill from the Edit menu.
12. In the Fill dialog box, click Foreground **(Figure 88)**.
    and
    Enter 40 in the Opacity field.
    and
    Select Normal from the Mode pop-up menu.
13. Click OK or press Return **(Figure 89)**.

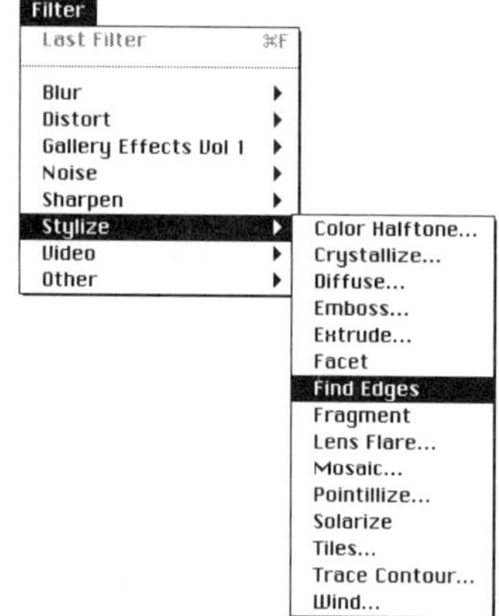

Figure 86. Choose **Find Edges** from the **Stylize** pop-up menu under the **Filter** menu.

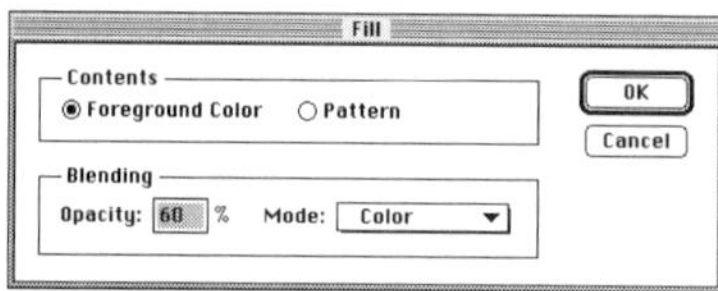

Figure 87. In the **Fill** dialog box, click **Foreground**, enter 60 in the **Opacity** field, and choose **Color** from the **Mode** pop-up menu.

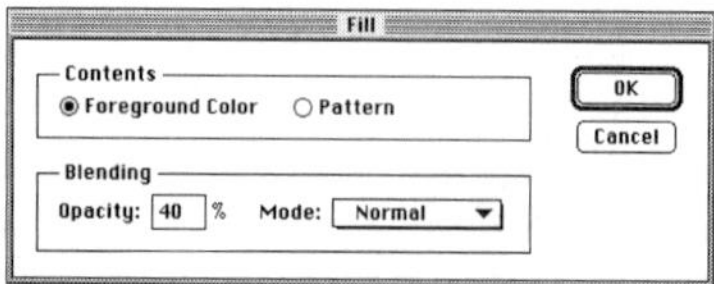

Figure 88. In the **Fill** dialog box, click **Foreground**, enter 40 in the **Opacity** field, and choose **Normal** from the **Mode** pop-up menu.

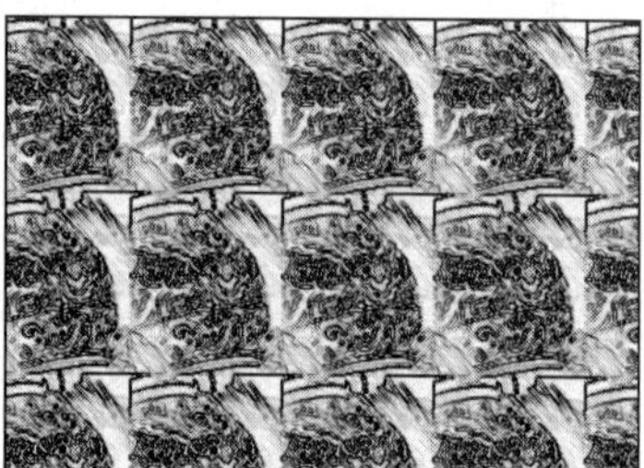

Figure 89. A texturized pattern.

Figure 90. Select an object in a picture.

Select
All ⌘A
None ⌘D
Inverse
Defloat ⌘J
Grow ⌘G
Similar
Border...
Feather...
Defringe...
Hide Edges ⌘H
Load Selection
Save Selection

Figure 91. Choose **Feather** from the **Select** menu.

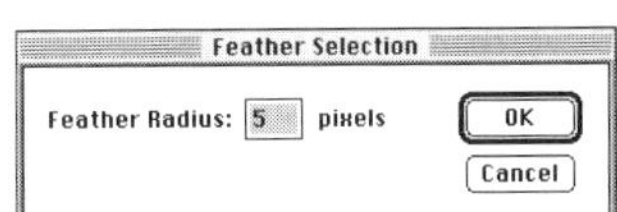

Figure 92. Enter 5 in the **Feather Radius** field in the **Feather Selection** dialog box.

To create an illusion of motion, select an object in a picture to remain "stationary," then apply the Motion Blur filter to the rest of the picture.

To apply the Motion Blur filter:

1. Select an object in a picture that is to remain "stationary" **(Figure 90)**. *(See pages 62-65)*
2. Choose Feather from the Select menu **(Figure 91)**.
3. Enter 5 in the Feather Radius field **(Figure 92)**.
4. Click OK or press Return.
5. Choose Copy from the Edit menu.
6. Choose None from the Select menu.
7. Choose Motion Blur from the Blur pop-up menu under the Filter menu.
8. Enter a number between -360 and 360 in the Angle field **(Figure 93)**. We entered -17 to produce Figure 95.
   or
   Drag the axis line.
9. Enter a number between 1 and 999 in the Distance field (the amount of blur). We entered 250 to produce Figure 95.
10. Click OK or press Return.
11. Choose Paste from the Edit menu.
12. Drag the floating selection to a new position.

Steps 13-15 are optional.

13. Choose Composite controls from the Edit menu.
14. Enter a number between 40 and 70 in the Opacity field. Pause to let the screen preview **(Figure 94)**.
15. Click OK or press Return **(Figure 95)**.

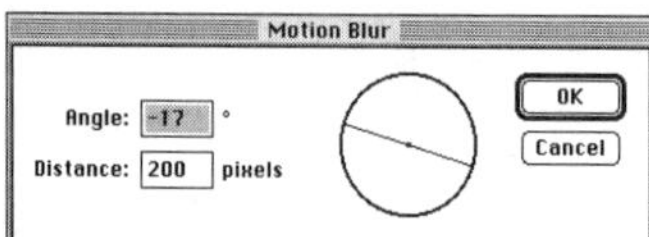

Figure 93. In the **Motion Blur** dialog box, enter numbers in the **Angle** and **Distance** fields.

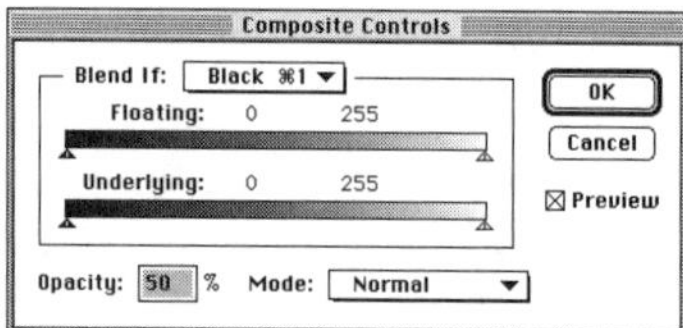

Figure 94. Enter a number betwen 40 and 70 in the **Opacity** field In the **Composite Controls** dialog box**.**

Figure 95. The completed **Motion Blur**.

Figure 96. The Groucho filter, one of many third-party filters.

Figure 97. The Zapatista filter, by Oroz Co.

INDEXED COLOR

Mode
Bitmap
Grayscale
Duotone
Indexed Color...
✓RGB Color
CMYK Color
Lab Color
Multichannel
Color Table...

Figure 1. Choose **Indexed Color** from the **Mode** menu.

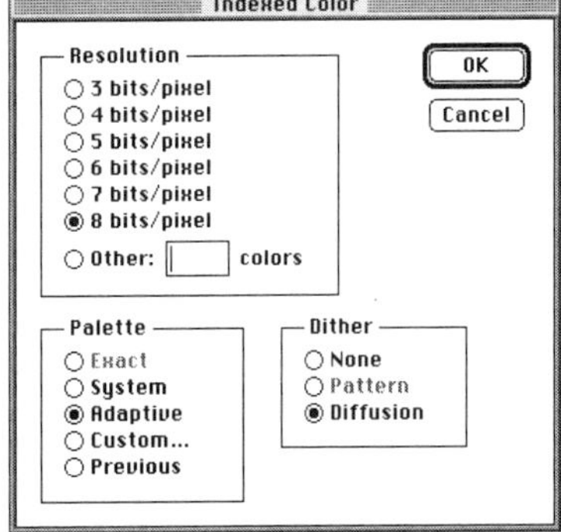

Figure 2. Click **Resolution, Palette,** and **Dither** options in the **Indexed Color** dialog box.

SOME MULTIMEDIA and video programs and some computer systems will not import a Photoshop picture containing more than 256 colors. By converting a picture to Indexed Color mode, the number of colors in its color table can be reduced. This chapter covers conversion to Indexed Color mode as well as some "arty" effects that can be produced by editing the color table of an Indexed Color picture.

To convert a picture to Indexed Color mode:

1. If the picture is not in RGB mode, choose RGB Color from the Mode menu.
2. Choose Indexed Color from the Mode menu **(Figure 1)**.
3. Click a Resolution to specify the number of colors in the table **(Figure 2)**. If you click 4 bits/pixel, the table will contain 16 colors. If you click 8 bits/pixel, the table will contain 256 colors. The fewer bits/pixel, the more dithered the picture will be.
4. Click a Palette. If the RGB Color picture contains 256 or fewer colors, you can click Exact.
   or
   Click Adaptive for the best color substitution.
   or
   Click System if you are exporting the file to an application that only accepts the Macintosh default palette.
5. Click None, Pattern, or Diffusion Dither. Diffusion may produce the closest color substitution.
6. Click OK or press Return **(Gallery 18a)**.

To edit an Indexed Color table:

1. Choose Color Table from the Mode menu **(Figure 3)**. The Color Table will display all the picture's colors.
2. Click on a color to be replaced **(Figure 4)**.
   or
   Drag across a series of colors.
3. Move the slider up or down on the vertical bar to choose a hue, then click a variation of that hue in the large rectangle **(Figure 5)**.
4. Click OK to exit the Color Picker.
5. Click OK or press Return.

✔ Tip

- In Indexed color mode, the Pencil, Airbrush, and Paintbrush tools produce only opaque strokes. For those tools, leave the Opacity slider on the Brushes palette at 100%. Dissolve is the only tool mode that will produce a different stroke.

Mode
Bitmap
Grayscale
Duotone
✓Indexed Color
RGB Color
CMYK Color
Lab Color
Multichannel
Color Table...

Figure 3. Choose **Color Table** from the **Mode** menu.

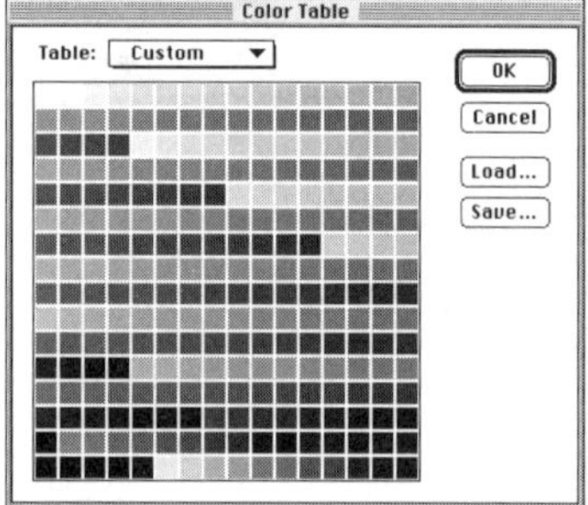

Figure 4. Click a color in the **Color Table** dialog box, or drag across a series of colors.

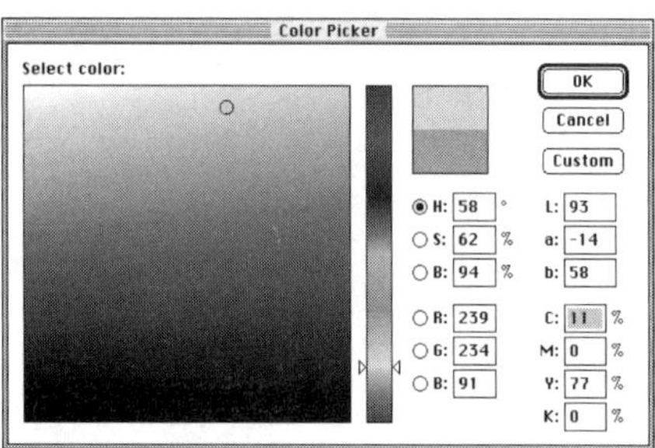

Figure 5. Choose a replacement color in the **Color Picker**.

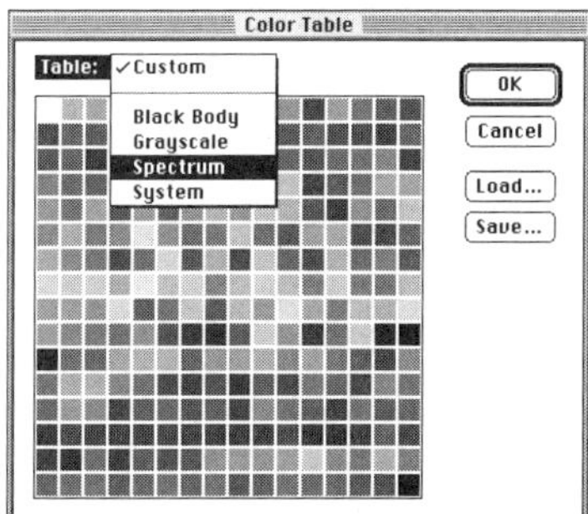

Figure 6a. Choose **Spectrum** from the **Table** pop-up menu in the **Color Table.**

Choose the Spectrum Color Table to produce a rainbow effect.

To choose the Spectrum table:

1. Choose Color Table from the Mode menu **(Figure 3)**.
2. Choose Spectrum from the Table pop-up menu **(Figures 6a-b** and **Gallery 18b)**.
3. Click OK or press Return.

✓ **Tip**

- You can convert a Grayscale picture directly to Indexed Color mode, then modify its Color Table.

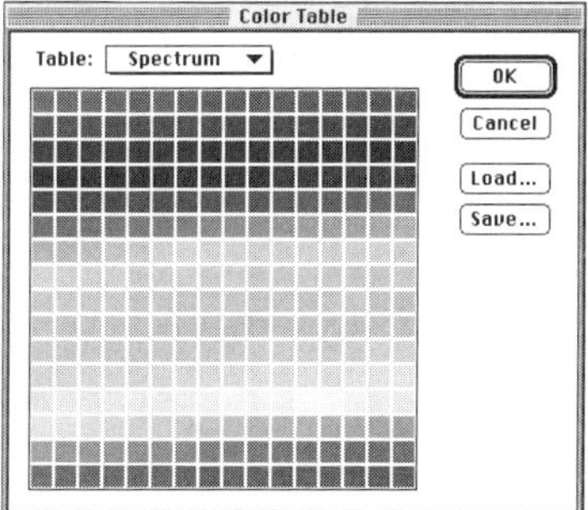

Figure 6b. The **Spectrum Color Table**.

For the best results, choose a warm "First color" and a cool "Last color," or vice versa, for steps 3 and 5 below.

To reduce an Indexed Color table to two colors and the shades between them:

1. Choose Color Table from the Mode menu **(Figure 3)**.
2. Drag across the Color Table from the first swatch in the upper left corner to the last swatch in the lower right corner.
3. Choose a "First color" from the Color Picker: move the slider up or down on the vertical bar to choose a hue, then click a variation of that hue in the large rectangle **(Figure 7)**.
4. Click OK.
5. Choose a "Last color" from the Color Picker.
6. Click OK to exit the Color Picker.
7. Click OK or press Return.

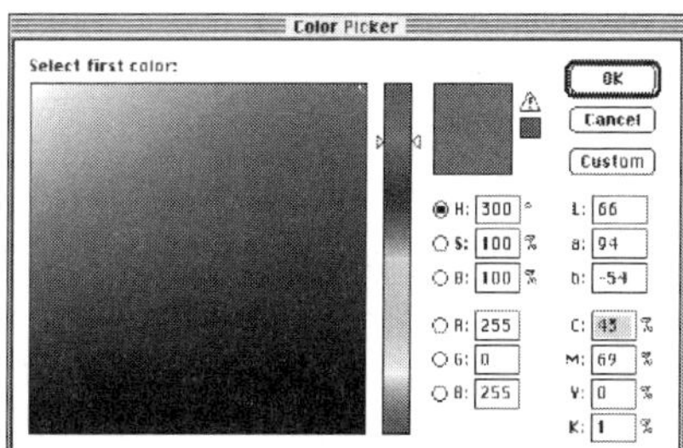

Figure 7. Choose a first and last color from the **Color Picker**.

Edit an Indexed Color Table

You can create a painterly effect by generating an Indexed Color picture from an RGB Color picture, then pasting the Index Color picture back into the RGB Color picture.

To recolor an RGB picture:

1. If the picture is not in RGB mode, choose RGB Color from the Mode menu.
2. Follow the steps on page 207 to convert the picture to Indexed Color mode.
3. Choose Color Table from the Mode menu **(Figure 3)**.
4. In the Color Table box, choose Spectrum from the Table pop-up menu **(Figure 8)**.
5. Click OK or press Return.
6. Choose All from the Select menu.
7. Choose Copy from the Edit menu.
8. Choose Revert from the File menu.
9. Click Revert to restore the picture to RGB Color mode **(Figure 9)**.
10. Choose Paste from the Edit menu to paste the Indexed color picture. Do not deselect.
11. Choose Composite Controls from the Edit menu **(Figure 10)**.
12. Choose from the Mode pop-up menu **(Figure 11)**. Lighten and Luminosity produce interesting results.

Steps 13 and 14 are optional.

13. Modify the number in the Opacity field.
14. Move the black Underlying slider to the right to restore shadows of the original picture.
    and/or
    Move the white Underlying slider to the left to restore highlights of the original picture.
15. Click OK or press Return **(Gallery 18c-e)**.

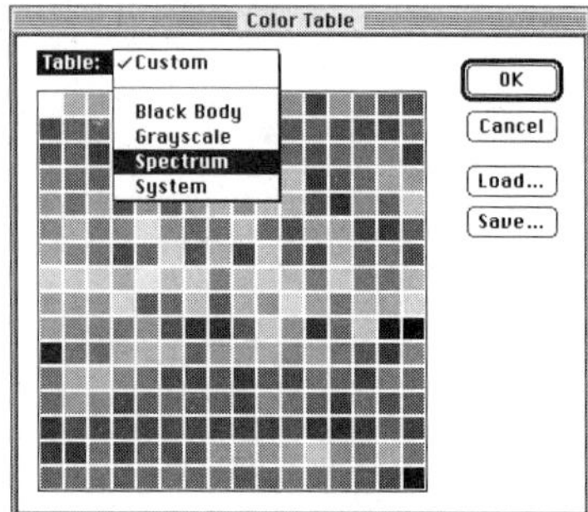

Figure 8. Choose **Spectrum** from the **Table** pop-up menu in the **Color Table** dialog box.

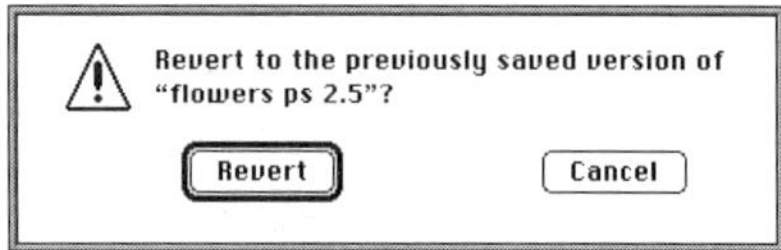

Figure 9. Click **Revert** to restore the picture to RGB mode.

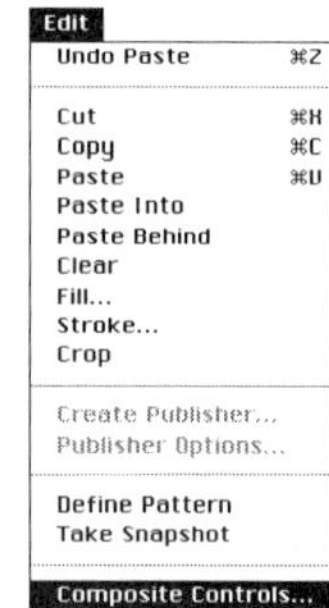

Figure 10. Choose **Composite Controls** from the **Edit** menu.

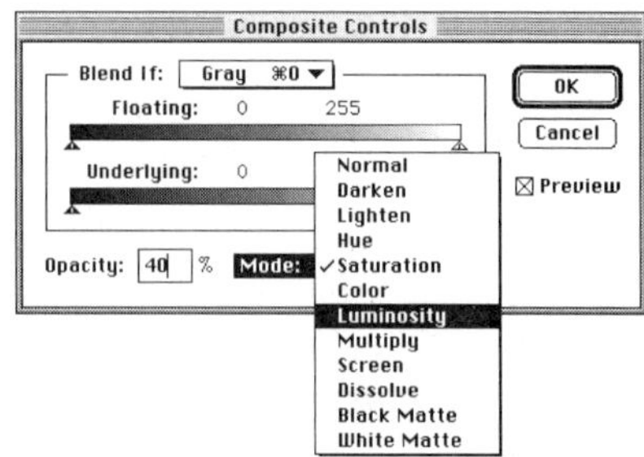

Figure 11. Choose a **Mode** in the **Composite Controls** dialog box.

Recolor an RGB Picture

PRINTING 19

Resolution of output devices.

Hewlett Packard LaserJet	300 *or* 600 dpi
Apple LaserWriter	300 *or* 600 dpi
IRIS SmartJet	300 dpi
3M Rainbow	300 dpi
QMS Colorscript	300 dpi
Canon Color Laser/Fiery	400 dpi
Linotronic imagesetter	1,200–3,386 dpi

A PICTURE can be printed from Photoshop to a laser printer, to a color printer (thermal wax, dye sublimation, etc.), or to an imagesetter. A Photoshop picture can also be imported into and printed from another application, such as QuarkXPress.

Printer settings are chosen in the Print dialog box and Page Setup dialog box, opened from the File menu. The following pages contain output tips, information about file compression, instructions for outputting to various types of printers, and instructions for creating duotones. Figure 13 on page 218 identifies Page Setup dialog box options.

Press and hold on the Image Size bar in the lower left corner of the document window to display a thumbnail preview of the image in relationship to the paper size and other specifications chosen in the Page Setup dialog box **(Figure 1)**.

Note: Many terms used in this chapter are defined in *Appendix A: Glossary,* including *CMYK, Color separation, DCS, DPI, Dye sublimation, EPS, Film negative, Halftone screen, Imagesetter, Ink jet, JPEG compression, Lab, LPI, Moirés, PostScript, Process color, Registration marks, Resolution, Screen angles, Screen frequency, Thermal wax,* and *TIFF.*

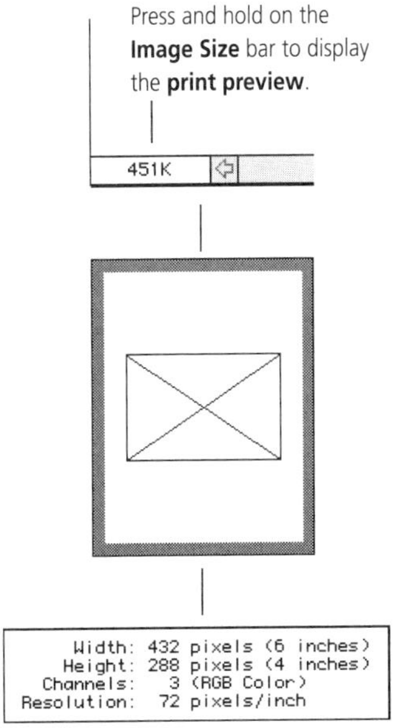

Press and hold on the **Image Size** bar to display the **print preview**.

451K

```
     Width: 432 pixels (6 inches)
    Height: 288 pixels (4 inches)
  Channels:   3 (RGB Color)
Resolution:  72 pixels/inch
```

Figure 1. Hold down **Option** and press and hold on the Image Size bar to display **file information**.

Output tips

Before outputting your file at a service bureau, ask your print shop or publisher if they have any specifications for the paper or film output you give them. If the picture contains a scan, make sure it was scanned at the appropriate resolution for the output device. Also ask what halftone screen frequency (lpi) the print shop will use and output your file at that frequency.

You might also ask your service bureau if you should save your file with special settings for a particular printer, such as in a particular picture mode or resolution. Let the service bureau calculate the halftone screen angle settings.

(See pages 23-24 and page 41)

(See also "Potential Gray Levels at various output resolutions and screen frequencies" on page 34)

File compression

To reduce the storage size of a picture, use a compression program, such as DiskDoubler or StuffIt. Compression using this kind of software is non-lossy, which means no information is lost during the compression process.

If you do not have compression software, choose Save As from the File menu, choose TIFF from the File Format pop-up menu, and in the TIFF Options dialog box, check the LZW Compression box. If you wish to save any alpha channels as part of the file, check the Save Alpha Channels box. LZW compression is also non-lossy. Some applications will not import an LZW TIFF; other applications will import an LZW TIFF only if it doesn't contain an alpha channel.

The authors do not recommend saving pictures in the JPEG file format or using the Compress EPS/JPEG command for pictures that will be printed. JPEG compression is lossy. More information is lost each time the Compress EPS/JPEG command is applied. The loss of data may not be noticeable on screen, but very noticeable on high resolution output.

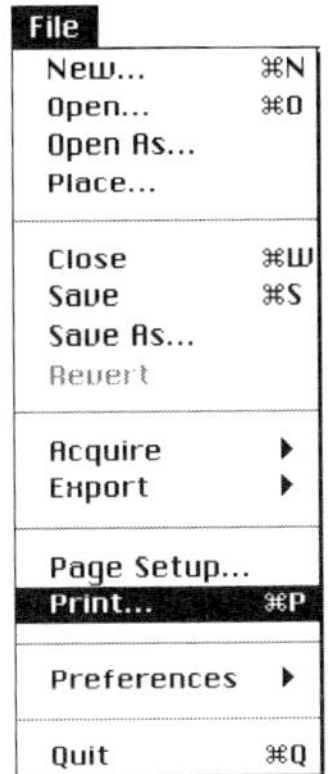

Figure 2. Choose **Print** from the **File** menu.

To print to a black-and-white laserwriter:

1. Choose Print from the File menu **(Figure 2)**.
   or
   Hold down ⌘ and press "P".
2. Click Color/Grayscale **(Figure 3)**.
3. Click Printer.
4. If the picture is in CMYK Color mode, make sure the Print Separations box is unchecked to print a composite image.
5. Click Binary.
6. Click Print or press Return.

✓ Tips

- If your picture does not print and you have a print spooler, try printing with ASCII Encoding selected. ASCII printing takes longer.
- To print only a portion of a picture, click the Rectangular Marquee tool, select an area, check the Print Selected Area box in the Print dialog box, then click Print.

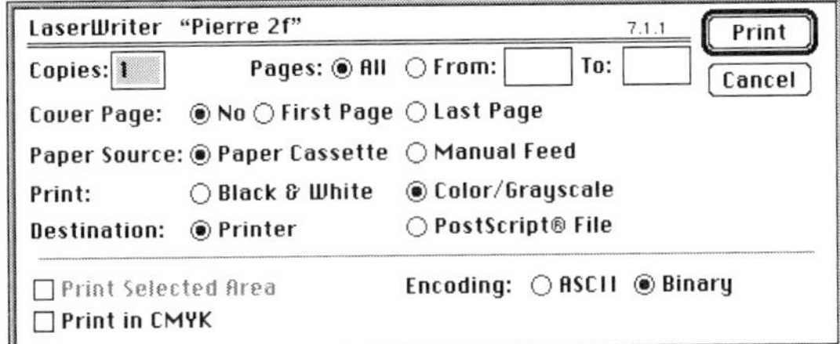

Figure 3. In the **Print** dialog box, click **Color/Grayscale**, leave the **Print In CMYK** (or **Print Separations box**) unchecked to print a composite picture, and click **Binary**. This illustration shows the Print dialog box for a picture in RGB mode.

To print to an Apple LaserWriter IIf or IIg with Photograde:

1. Choose Page Setup from the File menu **(Figure 4)**.
2. Click Screens **(Figure 5)**.
3. Click Use Printer's Default Screens, then click OK **(Figure 6)**.
4. Click OK or press Return.
5. Choose Print from the File menu **(Figure 2)**.
   or
   Hold down ⌘ and press "P".
6. Click Color/Grayscale.
7. Click Printer.
8. Make sure the Print in CMYK box is unchecked.
9. Click Print or press Return.

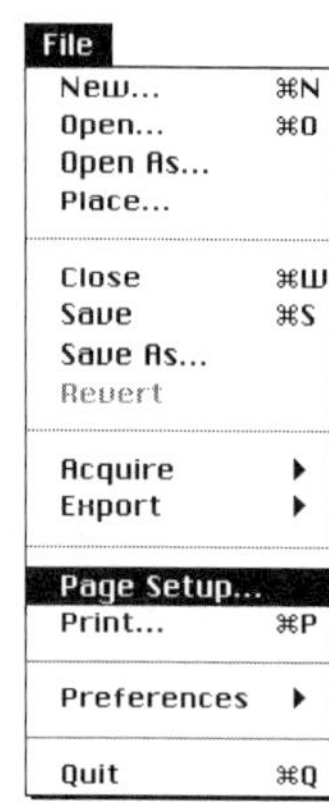

Figure 4. Choose **Page Setup** from the **File** menu.

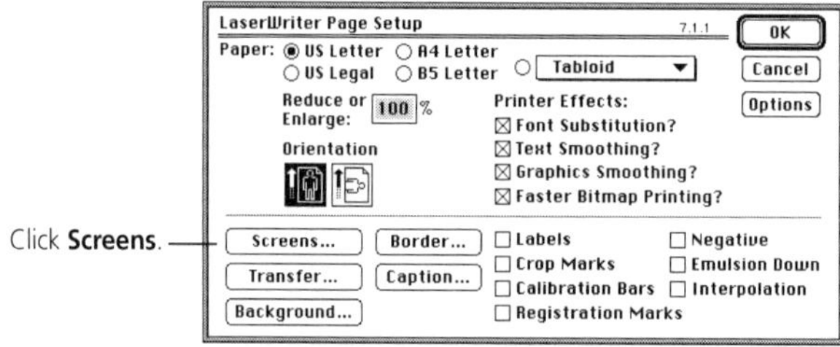

Figure 5. Click **Screens** in the **Page Setup** dialog box.

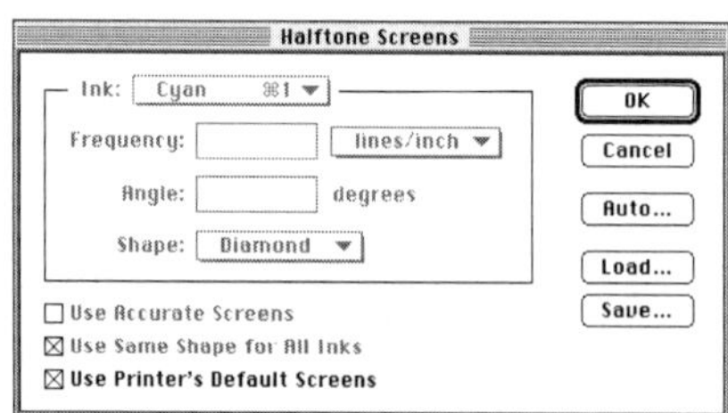

Figure 6. Check the **Use Printer's Default Screens** box in the **Halftone Screens** dialog box.

Print to a LaserWriter IIf or IIg

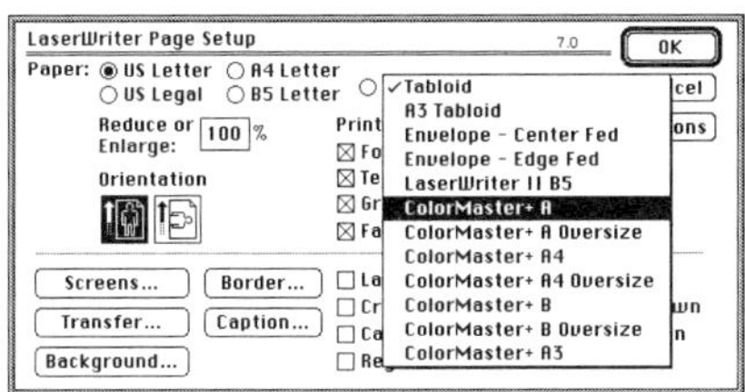

Figure 7. Choose the correct color printer option from the pop-up menu in the **Page Setup** dialog box.

LaserWriter "Pierre 2f" 7.1.1 Print
Copies: 1 Pages: ◉ All ○ From: To: Cancel
Cover Page: ◉ No ○ First Page ○ Last Page
Paper Source: ◉ Paper Cassette ○ Manual Feed
Print: ○ Black & White ◉ Color/Grayscale
Destination: ◉ Printer ○ PostScript® File
☐ Print Selected Area Encoding: ○ ASCII ◉ Binary
☐ Print Separations

Figure 8. In the **Print** dialog box, click **Color/Grayscale** and click **Binary**. This illustrations shows the Print dialog box for a CMYK file.

For each ink color you can enter a **Frequency** and **Angle** value and choose a **Shape**.

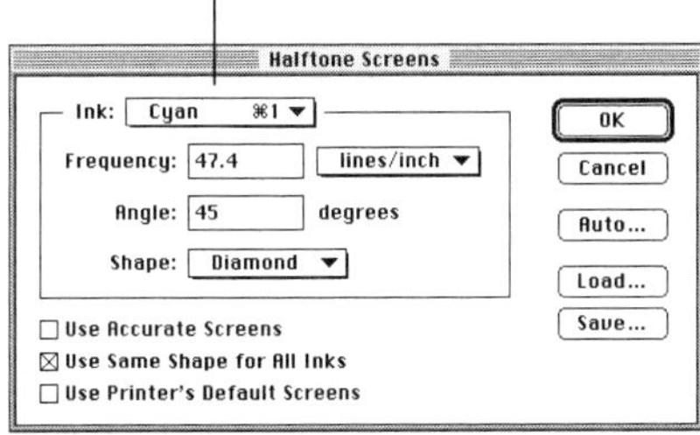

Figure 9. For thermal wax printing, in the **Halftone Screens** dialog box, enter 45 in the **Angle** field for each **Ink** color.

To print to a PostScript color printer:

1. To print to a PostScript Level 1 printer, choose CMYK Color from the Mode menu. CMYK color will be simulated on the screen **(Figure 10)**.
   or
   To print to a PostScript Level 2 printer, choose Lab Color from the Mode menu.
2. Choose Page Setup from the File menu.
3. Choose the correct color printer option from the pop-up menu **(Figure 7)**.
4. Click OK or press Return.
5. Choose Print from the File menu (or hold down ⌘ and press "P").
6. Click Color/Grayscale **(Figure 8)**.
7. Click Binary.
8. Click Print or press Return.

✔ Tips

- To optimize printing on some 300 dpi thermal wax printers, before printing choose Page Setup, click Screens, and uncheck the Use Printer's Default Screens box. In the Halftone Screens dialog box, choose a color from the Ink pop-up menu, then enter 45 in the Angle field. Follow the same procedure for the remaining ink colors **(Figure 9)**. Do not use these angle settings for any other kind of printer. For a PostScript Level 1 printer, check the Use Same Shape for All Inks box. For a PostScript Level 2 printer, check the Use Accurate Screens box, and do not change the ink angles.
- If the printout is too dark, lighten the picture using the Levels dialog box, opened from the Adjust pop-up menu under the Image menu. Move the gray Input slider a little to the left and the black Output slider a little to the right.

To prepare a file for an IRIS printer, a dye sublimation printer or an imagesetter:

1. To print on a PostScript Level 1 printer, choose CMYK Color from the Mode menu **(Figure 10)**.
   or
   To print on a PostScript Level 2 printer, choose Page Setup from the File menu **(Figure 11)**, click Screens, and check the Use Accurate Screens box. Ask your service bureau whether the file should be in CMYK Color or Lab Color mode.
2. Choose Save As from the File menu.
3. Choose EPS from the File Format pop-up menu.
4. Click 8-bit Macintosh **(Figure 12)**.
5. Click Binary.
6. Make sure Desktop Color Separation is Off.
7. Click OK or press Return.

✔ **Tips**

- Ask your service bureau to recommend a picture resolution for the color printer or imagesetter you plan to use.
  (See also "Resolution" on page 31)
- To superimpose type over a picture, import the Photoshop picture into a document in an illustration or page layout program, add the type, and output the file from that program. Your service bureau will need the original Photoshop file to output the file.
- If your picture is wider than it is tall, ask your service bureau if it will print more quickly if you rotate it first using Photoshop's Rotate command.
  (See "Orientation" information on page 218)

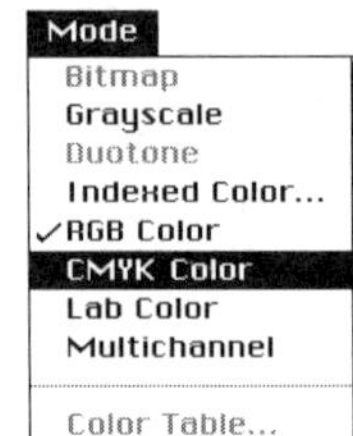

Figure 10. Choose **CMYK** from the **Mode** menu.

Figure 11. Choose **Page Setup** from the **File** menu.

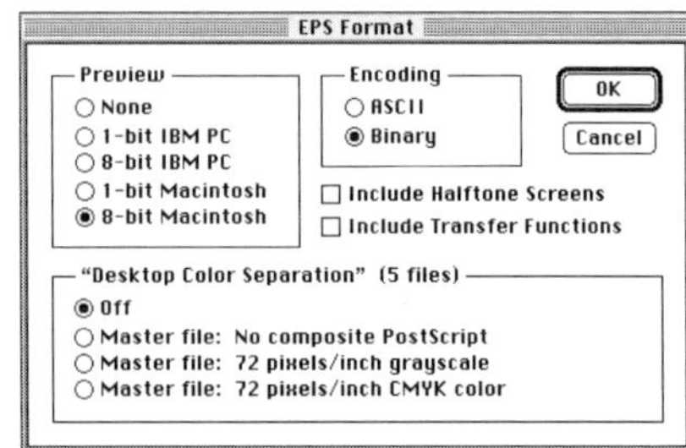

Figure 12. In the **EPS Format** dialog box, click **8-bit Macintosh Preview**, **Binary Encoding**, and **Desktop Color Separation Off**.

To print via QuarkXPress

To color separate a Photoshop picture from QuarkXPress, first convert it to CMYK Color mode. Ask your prepress service bureau whether to save it in the TIFF or EPS file format. For example, to color separate a picture on a Scitex–Dolev imagesetter, save it as an EPS with the Desktop Color Separation (DCS) option Off. Instructions for saving a file as an EPS are on page 48. Instructions for saving a file as a TIFF are on page 49.

Leave the Include Halftone Screens and Include Transfer Functions boxes unchecked. Your prepress service bureau will choose the proper settings.

Printing technology is developing rapidly. Your service bureau is in the best position to recommend appropriate file formats for color separation on its printers.

To output to a film recorder

Color transparencies, also called chromes, are widely used as a source for pictures in the publishing industry. A Photoshop file can be output to a film recorder to produce a chrome. Though the output settings for each film recorder may vary, to output to any film recorder, the height and width dimensions of the picture file must conform to the pixel count the film recorder requires for each line it images. If the picture originates as a scan, the pixel count should be taken into consideration when setting the scan's resolution, dimensions, and file storage size.

For example, let's say you need to produce a 4 x 5-inch chrome on a Solitaire film recorder. Your service bureau advises you that to output on the Solitaire, the 5-inch side of your picture should measure 2000 pixels and the file storage size should be at least 10 megabytes. (Other film recorders may require higher resolutions.) Choose New from the File menu, enter 2000 for the Width (in pixels) and 4 inches for the Height, enter a Resolution value to produce an Image Size of at least 10MB, and choose RGB Color Mode. Click OK to produce the picture entirely within Photoshop, or note the resolution and dimensions, and ask your service bureau to match those values when it scans your picture.

If the picture is smaller than 4 x 5 inches and you would like a colored background around it, click Background in the Page Setup dialog box, then choose the color your service bureau recommends.

A picture will print faster with **Portrait Orientation** (left) than with **Landscape Orientation** (right). If your picture is wider than it is tall, choose Rotate 90° CW from the Image menu. Then you can print it with the **Portrait** Orientation.

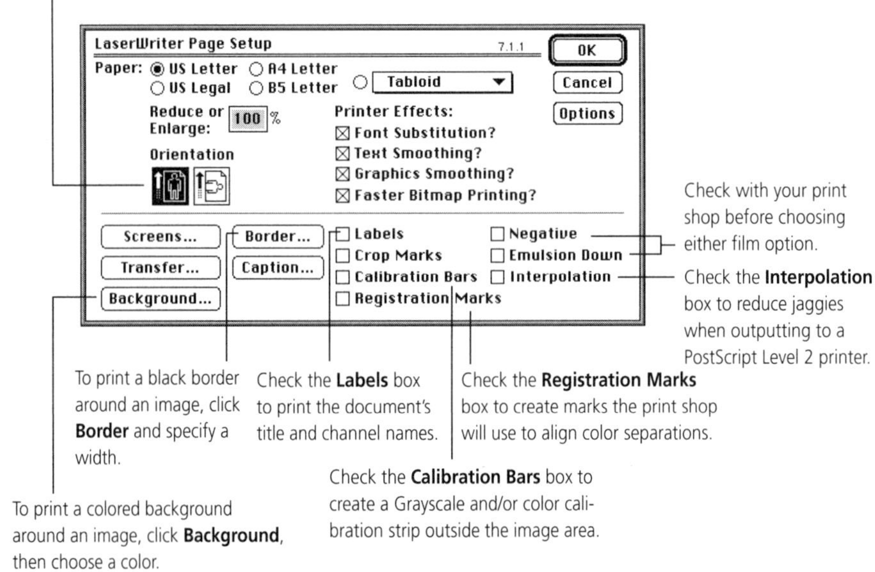

Check with your print shop before choosing either film option.

Check the **Interpolation** box to reduce jaggies when outputting to a PostScript Level 2 printer.

To print a black border around an image, click **Border** and specify a width.

Check the **Labels** box to print the document's title and channel names.

Check the **Registration Marks** box to create marks the print shop will use to align color separations.

Check the **Calibration Bars** box to create a Grayscale and/or color calibration strip outside the image area.

To print a colored background around an image, click **Background**, then choose a color.

Figure 13. The **Page Setup** dialog box.

Figure 14. A printout showing Page Setup options.

About 50 shades of an ink color can be printed from one plate. Printers sometimes print a grayscale picture using two or more plates instead of one to extend the tonal range. The additional plate can be a gray or color tint. You can convert a picture to Duotone mode in Photoshop to create a duotone (two plates), tritone (three plates), or quadtone (four plates).

Note: Printing a duotone is complex. For example, the proper order of inks must be selected in the Duotone options dialog box and then on the press. Ask your print shop for advice. A duotone effect cannot be "proofed" on a PostScript color printer.

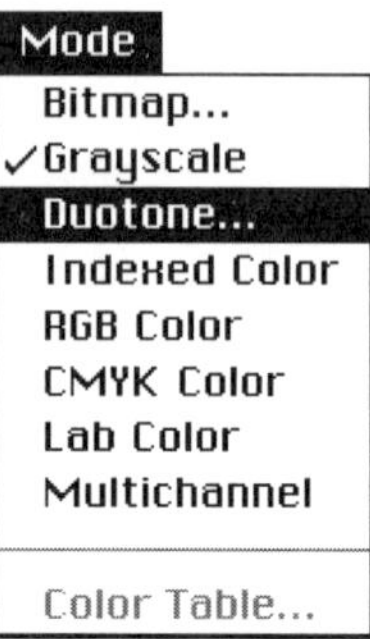

Figure 15. Choose **Duotone** from the **Mode** menu.

To create a duotone:

1. Choose Grayscale from the Mode menu.
2. Choose Duotone from the Mode menu **(Figure 15)**.
3. Choose Duotone from the Type pop-up menu **(Figure 16)**.
4. Click the Ink 2 color square.
5. If necessary, click Custom, choose from the Book pop-up menu, then enter a number in the Find # field or click a swatch.
   or
   If necessary, click Picker, then enter C,M,Y, and K percentages.
6. Click OK or press Return.
7. For a process color, enter a name next to the color square.
8. Click the Ink 2 curve.
9. Drag the curve in the Duotone Curve dialog box **(Figure 17)**.
10. Click OK or press Return.
11. Click the Ink 1 curve, then repeat steps 9 and 10.

✔ **Tip**

■ The Photoshop Tutorial folder contains sample dutone, tritone, and quadtone curves. Click Load in the Duotone Options box to access them.

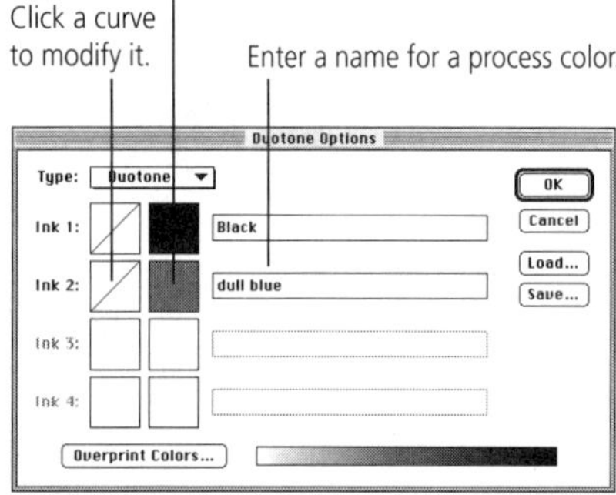

Figure 16. In the **Duotone Options** dialog box, choose **Duotone** from the **Type** pop-up menu, then click the **Ink 2** color square.

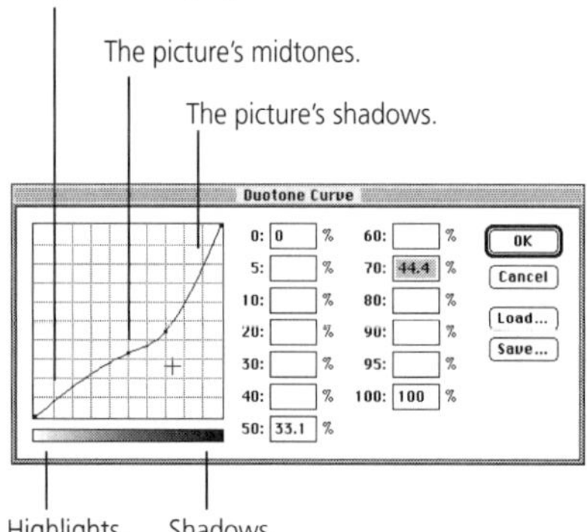

Figure 17. With this curve shape in the **Duotone Curve** dialog box, Ink 2 will tint the picture's midtones. **Make the Ink 1 curve different from the Ink 2 curve.**

DEFAULTS 20

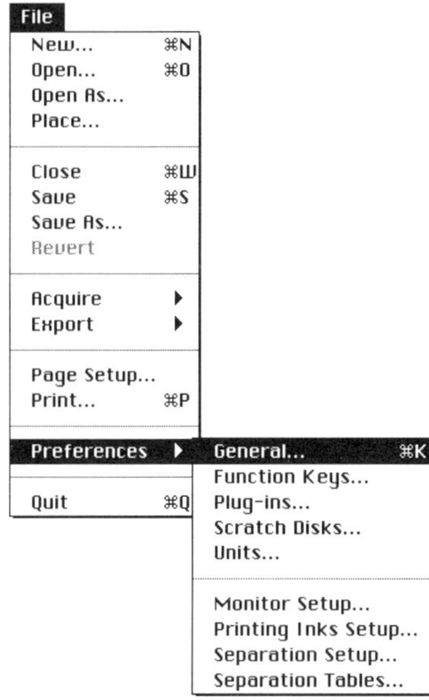

Figure 1. The **Preferences** pop-up menu under the **File** menu.

DEFAULTS are settings that are chosen to apply generally, such as which ruler units are used, or if channels display in color. Default dialog boxes are opened from the Preferences pop-up menu under the File menu **(Figure 1)**.

Choose basic defaults in the **General Preferences** dialog box, such as whether file icons will contain a thumbnail preview of the picture, or whether Pantone color names are displayed in their full or abbreviated form.

Assign commands to Function keys F1 through F15 in the **Function Keys** dialog box.
(Default Function key commands are listed in Appendix B)

Choose a hard disk to be used as Photoshop's extra work area in the **Scratch Disks** dialog box.

Choose ruler units in the **Units** dialog box.

Choose your monitor type and ambient lighting conditions in the **Monitor Setup** dialog box to optimize display and RGB-to-CMYK conversion.

Adjust your monitor in the **Gamma** dialog box, opened from the Control Panels folder.

Note: Don't move the program's internal **Plug-ins** module out of the Photoshop folder unless you have a specific reason for doing so. Moving it could inhibit access to the Acquire, Export and File Format commands. Don't confuse the Plug-ins module with third-party Plug-ins.

Key to the General Preferences dialog box.

1 Choose the Photoshop **Color Picker** to access the program's own Color Picker.

2 Choose an **Interpolation** option for reinterpretation of a picture as a result of resampling, scaling, etc. Bicubic is slowest, but the highest quality. Nearest Neighbor is the fastest, but the poorest quality.

3 Choose whether **CMYK Composites** for the RGB screen version of a CMYK file will be rendered Faster, but simpler, or Smoother and more refined.

4 Check **Color Channels in Color** to display individual RGB and CMYK channels in color. Otherwise, they will display grayscale.

5 Check **Use System Palette** to have the Apple System Palette be used rather than the document's own colors.

6 Check **Use Diffusion Dither** to smooth colors on an 8-bit monitor.

7 Uncheck **Video LUT Animation** to disable the interactive screen preview if you are using a video card that is causing conflicts between Photoshop and your monitor.

8 Check **Anti-alias Postscript** to optimize the rendering of EPS graphics in Photoshop.

9 Check **Export Clipboard** to have the current Clipboard contents stay on the Clipboard upon quitting Photoshop.

10 Check **Short PANTONE Names** if your picture contains Pantone colors and you are exporting it to another application.

11 With **Restore Windows** checked, windows and palettes that are open when you quit Photoshop will open the next time it is launched. With Restore Windows unchecked, only the Toolbox and Brushes palette will open.

12 Check **Save Preview Icons** to display a thumbnail of a picture in its file icon on the desktop.

13 Check **Beep When Done** for a beep to sound after any command, for which a progress bar displays, is completed.

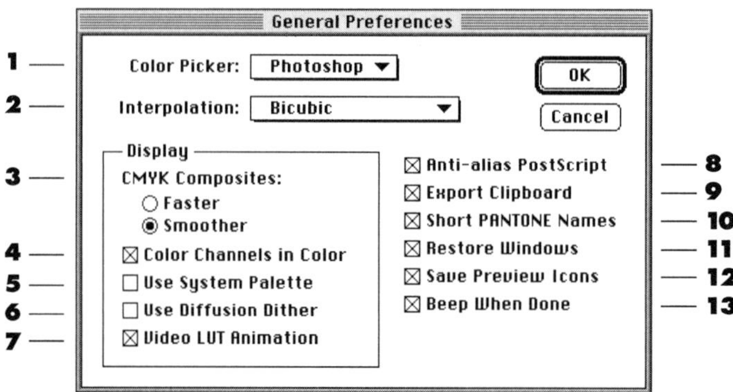

Figure 2. The **General Preferences** dialog box.

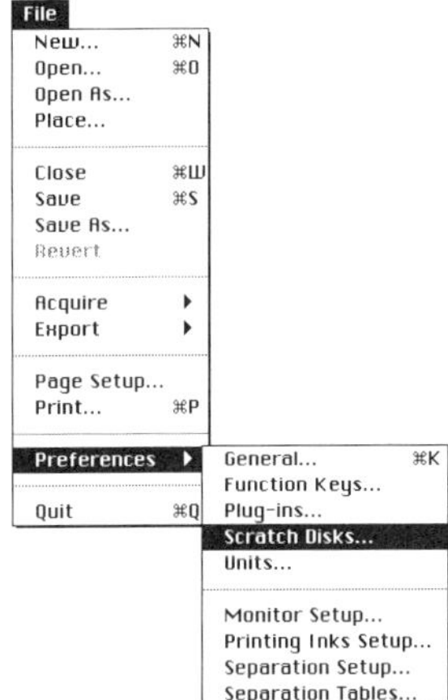

Figure 3. Choose **Scratch Disks** from the **Preferences** pop-up menu under the **File** menu.

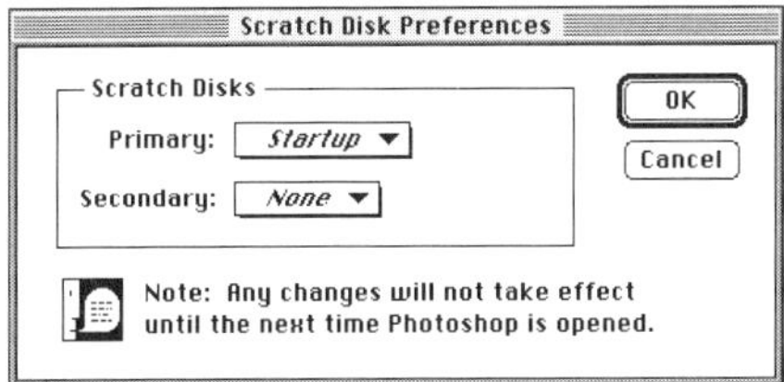

Figure 4. Choose a **Primary** and **Secondary** scratch disk in the **Scratch Disk Preferences** dialog box.

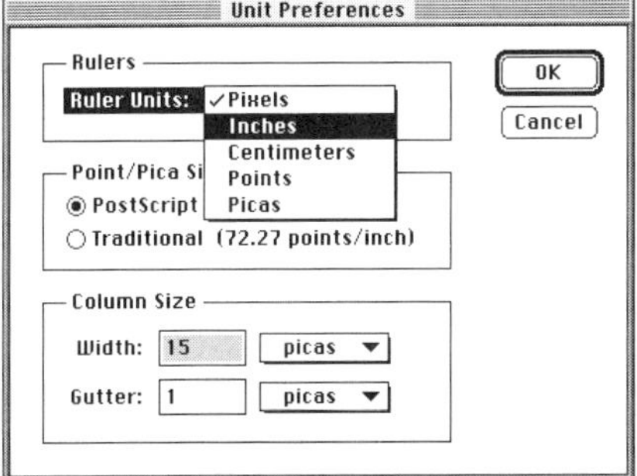

Figure 5. Choose a unit of measure from the **Ruler Units** pop-up menu in the **Unit Preferences** dialog box.

The Primary and Secondary scratch disks are used when available RAM is insufficient for processing or storage.

To choose scratch disks:

1. Choose Scratch Disks from the Preferences pop-up menu under the File menu **(Figure 3)**.
2. Choose an available hard drive from the Primary pop-up menu. Startup is the Default **(Figure 4)**. If you only have one hard drive, you will only be able to choose a primary Scratch Disk.
3. *Optional:* Choose an alternate hard drive from the Secondary pop-up menu to be used as extra work space when necessary.
4. Click OK or press Return.
5. For the changes take effect, choose Quit from the File menu, then launch Photoshop again.

✓ Tip

■ If you choose a removable cartridge as a Scratch Disk, do not remove the cartridge while Photoshop is running or the program may crash.

Choose Show Rulers from the Window menu to display rulers on the top and left sides of the document window. The position of the pointer will be indicated by a mark on each ruler.

To choose ruler units:

1. Choose Units from the Preferences pop-up menu under the File menu **(Figure 3)**.
2. Choose a unit of measure from the Ruler Units pop-up menu **(Figure 5)**.
3. Click OK or press Return.

✓ Tip

■ If you change the ruler units, the Info palette units will also change, and vice versa.

Follow the instructions on this page and the next page to adjust your monitor for Photoshop. These are the first steps in monitor-to-output calibration. See the Photoshop User Guide for information about calibrating your system.

Note: After choosing monitor specs and making your desktop gray (instructions on the next page), adjust the brightness and contrast knobs on your monitor and do not change them (put tape on them, if necessary). Then follow instructions on the next page to adjust the Gamma.

To choose Monitor Setup options:

1. Choose Monitor Setup from the Preferences pop-up menu under the File menu **(Figure 6)**.
2. Choose your monitor name from the Monitor pop-up menu. If it is not listed, consult the documentation supplied with your monitor to find the closest equivalent **(Figure 7)**.
3. Choose the manufacturer of your CRT from the Phosphors pop-up menu. This information should also be supplied with your monitor.
4. Choose Low, Medium, or High from the Ambient Light pop-up menu.
5. Click OK or press Return.

✔ Tips

- Leave the Gamma at 1.80 and the White Point at 6500°K, unless you have a specific reason to change it.
- The Monitors Setup affects color substitution when a picture is converted from RGB to CMYK mode.
- Try to keep the light in your computer room consistent while you are working.

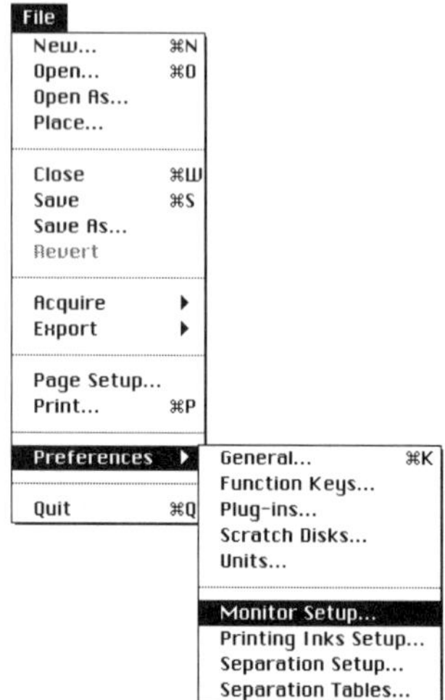

Figure 6. Choose **Monitor Setup** from the **Preferences** pop-up menu under the **File** menu.

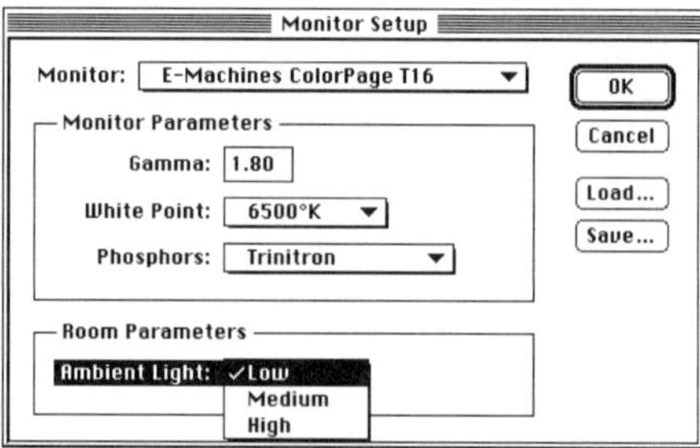

Figure 7. In the **Monitor Setup** dialog box, choose your monitor type from the **Monitor** pop-up menu, and choose **Low, Medium,** or **High** from the **Ambient Light** pop-up menu.

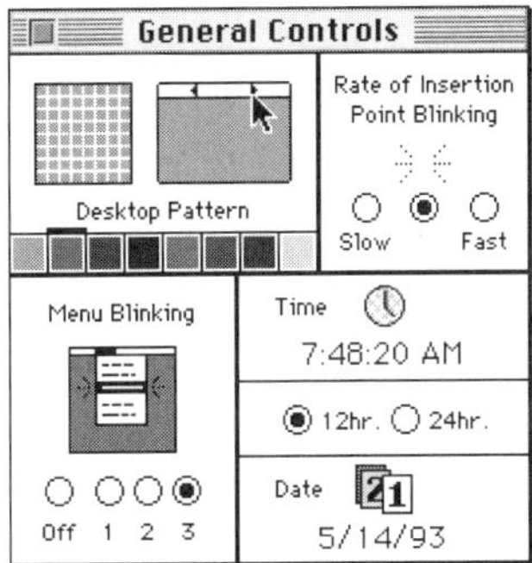

Figure 8. Choose a gray Desktop pattern in the **General Controls** dialog box.

Use the Gamma Control Panel to make your monitor grays as neutral as possible, and the color on your monitor slightly more accurate. If your desktop is already gray, proceed directly to "To adjust the Gamma."

To make the Desktop gray:

1. Choose Control Panels from the Apple menu.
2. Double-click General Controls in the Control Panels folder.
3. Click the left or right triangle to locate the gray Desktop pattern **(Figure 8)**.
4. Click the gray pattern.
5. Click the General Controls close box. *(Adjust the brightness and contrast knobs on your monitor. See "Note" on page 224)*

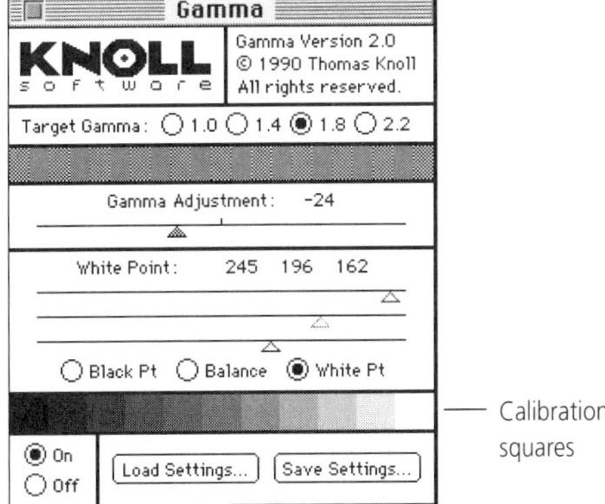

Figure 9. The **Gamma** dialog box.

To adjust the Gamma:

1. Choose Control Panels from the Apple menu.
2. Double-click Gamma.
3. Click 1.8 Target Gamma **(Figure 9)**.
4. Hold up a white piece of paper next to the monitor. The warm or cool cast of the paper will affect the Gamma settings you choose.
5. Click the White Pt button, then move the White Point sliders until the rightmost square on the calibration bar matches the paper.
6. Click the Black Pt button, then move the Black Pt sliders until the dark calibration squares look neutral.
7. Click the Balance button, then move the Balance sliders until the gray calibration squares look neutral.
8. Move the Gamma Adjustment slider to blend the light and dark bars.
9. Readjust any of the sliders, if needed.
10. *Optional:* Click Save Settings, then rename and save the Gamma settings.
11. Click the Gamma close box.

Appendix A: Glossary

Alpha channel

A special 8-bit grayscale channel used for saving a selection.

Anti-alias

The blending of pixel colors along the perimeters of hard-edged shapes, including type, to smoooth undesirable stair-stepped edges, or "jaggies."

ASCII

(American Standard Code for Information Interchange) A standard editable format for encoding data.

Background color

The color applied when the Eraser tool is used or when selected (non-floating) pixels are moved or deleted.

Bezier curve

A curved line segment drawn using the Pen tool. It consists of anchor points with direction lines with which the curve can be reshaped. Bezier curves can also be created using illustration software.

Binary

In Photoshop, a method for encoding data. Binary encoding is more compact than ASCII encoding.

Bit

(Binary digit) The smallest unit of information on a computer. Eight bits equal one byte. (see *Byte*)

Bit depth

The number of bits used to store a pixel's color information on a computer screen.

Bitmap

The display of a picture on a computer screen via the geometric mapping of a single layer of pixels on a rectangular grid. In Photoshop, Bitmap is also a one-channel mode consisting of black and white pixels.

Blend (see *Gradient*)

Brightness (see *Lightness*)

Burn

To bleach (lighten) an area of a picture.

Byte

The basic unit of storage memory. One byte is equal to eight bits.

Canvas size

The size of a picture, including a border, if any, around the image.

CD-ROM drive

A special digital drive for reading CD-ROM disks. One CD disk can store at least 650 megabytes of information. At this writing, most CD-ROM drives are read-only, and are used as a source for stock photographs, fonts, software, games, clip art, etc.

Channel

A color "overlay" which contains the pixel information for that color. A grayscale picture has one channel, an RGB picture has three channels, and a CMYK picture has four channels.

Clipboard

An area of memory used to temporarily store a selection. The Clipboard is accessed via the Cut, Copy, and Paste commands.

Clipping

In Photoshop, the automatic desaturation of colors that are too pure to print properly.

Clone

To duplicate all or part of a picture using the Rubber Stamp tool.

CMYK

(Cyan, Magenta, Yellow, and Black) The four colors of ink used in process printing. Cyan, Magenta, and Yellow are the three subtractive primaries. When combined in their purest forms, they theoretically produce black. Actually, they produce a dark muddy color. CMYK colors are simulated on a computer screen using additive colors. To color separate a picture from Photoshop, it must be in CMYK Color mode.

Color correction

The adjustment of color in a picture to match original artwork or a photograph. Color correction is usually done in CMYK Color mode to prepare for process printing.

Color separation

The production of a separate sheet of film for each color of ink that will be used to print a document. Four plates are used in process color separation, one each for Cyan, Magenta, Yellow, and Black.

Color table

The color palette of up to 256 colors of a picture in Indexed Color mode. Sometimes referred to as a color palette.

Continuous-tone image

A picture, such as a photograph, in which there are smooth transitions between gray shades or colors.

Contrast

The degree of difference between lights and darks in a picture. A high contrast picture is comprised of only the lightest and darkest pixels.

Crop

To cut away part of a picture.

Crop marks

Short, fine lines placed around the edges of a page to designate where the paper is to be trimmed by a print shop.

DCS

(Desktop Color Separation) A file format in which a color picture is broken down into five PostScript files: Cyan, Magenta, Yellow and Black for high resolution printing, and an optional low resolution PICT file for previewing and laser printing.

Defloat

To replace underlying pixels with the contents of a floating selection. A selection remains active when it is defloated.

Defringe

A technique used for softening the edge of a selection inward from the marquee a specified number of pixels.

Digitize

To translate flat art or a transparency into computer-readable numbers using a scanning device and scanning software.

Dimensions

The width and height of a picture.

Disk

A carrying medium for processing, reading, and storing electronic files, such as a hard drive, floppy disk, or CD-ROM disk.

Dither

The mixing of adjacent pixels to simulate additional colors when available colors are limited, such as on an 8-bit monitor.

Dodge

To darken an area of a picture. Also, a so-so car model.

Dot gain

The undesirable spreading and enlarging of ink dots on paper.

DPI

(Dots Per Inch) A unit used to measure the resolution of a printer. DPI is sometimes used to describe the input resolution of a scanner, but ppi, or "sampling rate" is a more accurate term.

Duotone

A grayscale picture printed using two plates for added tonal depth. A tritone is printed using three plates. A quadtone is printed using four plates.

Dye sublimation

A continuous-tone printing process in which a solid printing medium is converted into a gas before it reaches the paper. Each printing color can vary in intensity.

8-bit monitor

A monitor in which each pixel stores eight bits of information and represents one of only 256 available colors. Dithering is used to create the illusion of additional colors.

EPS

(Encapsulated PostScript) A picture file format containing PostScript code and, in the case of Photoshop, an optional PICT image for screen display. EPS is a commonly used format for moving files from one application to another and for imagesetting and color separating.

Equalize

To balance a picture's lights and darks.

Feather

To fade the edge of a selection a specified number of pixels (the Feather Radius).

Fill

To fill a selection with a shade, color, pattern, or blend.

Film negative

A film rendition of a picture in which dark and light areas are reversed.

Floating selection

An area of a picture that is surrounded by a marquee and can be moved or modified without affecting underlying pixels. The Paste and Float commands create floating selections. Newly created type also appears as a floating selection.

Font

A typeface in a distinctive style, such as Futura Bold Italic.

Foreground color

The color applied when a painting tool is used, type is created, or a Fill command is executed.

Gigabyte

(G, Gb) A unit of memory equal to 1,024 megabytes. (see *Megabyte*)

Gradient fill

In Photoshop, a graduated blend between the Foreground and Background colors produced by the Gradient tool.

Grayscale

A picture containing black, white, and up to 256 shades of gray, but no color. In Photoshop, Grayscale is a one-channel mode.

Halftone screen

A pattern of tiny dots used for printing a picture to simulate smooth tones. (see *Screen frequency*)

Highlights

The lightest areas of a picture.

Histogram

A graph showing the distribution of a picture's color and/or luminosity values.

HSB

See *Hue, Saturation,* and *Brightness.*

Hue

The wavelength of light of a pure color that gives a color its name, such as red or blue, independent of its saturation or brightness.

Imagesetter

A high-resolution printer (usually 1,270 or 2,540 dpi) used to generate paper or film output from computer files.

Indexed color

In Photoshop, a color mode in which there is only one channel and a color table containing up to 256 colors. All the colors of an Indexed color picture are displayed in its Colors palette.

Ink jet

A color printer in which four colors of ink are forced through small holes to produce dots.

Interpolation

The recoloring of pixels as a result of changing a picture's dimensions or resolution. Interpolation may cause a picture to look blurry when printed. You can choose an interpolation method in Photoshop.

Inverse

To switch the selected and non-selected areas of a picture.

Invert

To reverse a picture's light and dark values and/or colors.

Jaggies

Undesirable stair-stepped edges of computer rendered images. (see *Anti-alias*)

JPEG compression

(Joint Photographic Experts Group) A compression feature in Photoshop that can be used to reduce the storage size of a file. Some information is lost during JPEG Compression.

Kern

To adjust the horizontal spacing between a pair of characters.

Kilobyte

(K, Kb) A unit of memory equal to 1,024 bytes. (see *Byte*)

Lab

A mode in which colors are related to the CIE color reference system. In Photoshop, a picture in Lab Color mode is composed of three channels, one for lightness, one for green-to-magenta colors, and one blue-to-yellow colors.

Leading

The space between lines of type, measured from baseline to baseline. In Photoshop, leading can be measured in points or pixels.

Lightness

(Brightness) The lightness of a color independent of its hue and saturation.

Linear fill

A straight gradation from edge to edge. (See *Radial fill*)

LPI

(Lines Per Inch, halftone frequency, screen frequency) The unit used to measure the frequency of rows of dots on a halftone screen.

Luminosity

The distribution of a picture's light and dark values.

Marquee

The moving border that defines a selection.

Mask

A device used to protect an area of a picture from modification.

Megabyte

(M, MB) A unit of memory equal to 1,024 kilobytes. (see *Kilobyte*)

Midtones

The shades in a picture midway between the highlights and shadows.

Mode

A method for specifying how color information is to be interpreted. A picture can be converted to a different mode using the Mode menu; a mode can be chosen for a painting or editing tool via palette pop-up menus. Grayscale, RGB Color, CMYK Color, and Lab Color are commonly used picture modes.

Moirés

Undesirable patterns caused by the use of improper halftone screen angles or when the pattern in an image conflicts with proper halftone patterns.

Noise

In Photoshop, filters that randomly recolor pixels to create a texture or make an image look grainy.

Object-oriented

(also known as vector) A software method used for describing and processing computer files. Object-oriented graphics and PostScript type are defined by mathematics and geometry. Bitmapped graphics are defined by pixels on a rectangular grid. Photoshop pictures are bitmapped, not objected-oriented.

Opacity

The density of a color or shade, ranging from transparent to opaque. In Photoshop, the opacity for a painting or editing tool is specified by using the Brushes palette.

Palette

A floating window used to specify options for a tool or feature. Also, a collection of color swatches displayed on the Colors palette.

Path

A shape composed of straight and/or curved segments joined by anchor points. Paths are created with the Pen tool and modified via the Paths palette.

PICT

A Macintosh file format used to display and save pictures. Save a Photoshop picture as a PICT file to open it in a video or animation program. PICT files should not be color separated.

Pixels

(Picture elements) The individual dots used to display a picture on a computer screen.

PPI

(Pixels per inch) A unit used to measure of the resolution of a scan or a picture in Photoshop.

Plug-in module

Third-party software placed in the Photoshop Plug-ins folder so it is accessible from a Photoshop menu. Or, a plug-in module that comes with Photoshop that is used to facilitate the Acquire, Export, and file format conversion operations. There is no icon for the plug-in module in the Finder.

Point

A unit of measure used to describe type size (measured from ascender to descender), leading (measured from baseline to baseline), and line width.

Polygon

A closed shape composed of three or more straight sides.

Posterize

Produce a special effect in a picture by reducing the number of shades of gray or color to the darkest shade, the lightest shade, and a few shades in between.

PostScript

The page description language created and licensed by Adobe Systems Incorporated for displaying and printing fonts and pictures.

Process color

Ink printed from four separate plates, one each for Cyan (C), Magenta (M), Yellow (Y), and Black (K), which in combination produce a wide range of colors.

Quick Mask

In Photoshop, a screen mode in which a translucent colored mask covers selected or unselected areas of a picture. Painting tools can be used to modify a Quick Mask.

Radial fill

A gradation radiating from the center of the blend area outward.

RAM

(Random Access Memory) The system memory of a computer used for running an application, processing information, and temporary storage.

Rasterize

The conversion of an object-oriented picture into a bitmapped picture, such as when an Adobe Illustrator graphic is placed into Photoshop. All computer files are rasterized when printed.

Registration marks

Crosshair marks placed around the edge of a page that are used to align printing plates.

Resample

Modify a picture's resolution. Lowering a picture's resolution is called resampling down. Increasing a picture's resolution is called resampling up. Both cause interpolation. (see *Interpolation*)

Resolution

The fineness of detail of a digitized image (measured in pixels per inch), a monitor (measured in pixels per inch — usually 72 ppi), a printer (measured in dots per inch), or halftone screen (measured in lines per inch).

RGB

Color produced by transmitted light. When pure Red, Green, and Blue light (the additive primaries) are combined, as on a computer monitor, white is produced. In Photoshop, RGB Color is a three-channel picture mode.

Saturation

The purity of a color. The more gray a color contains, the lower its saturation.

Scan

To digitize a slide, photograph or other artwork using a scanner and scanning software so it can be displayed, edited, and output from a computer.

Scratch disk

(also known as virtual memory) Hard drive storage space designated as work space for processing operations and for temporarily storing part of an image and a backup version of the image when there is insufficient RAM for these functions.

Screen angles

Angles used for positioning halftone screens when producing film to minimize undesirable dot patterns (moirés).

Screen frequency

(also known as screen ruling) The resolution (density of dots) on a halftone screen, measured in lines per inch. (See *lpi*)

Selection

An area of a picture that is isolated so it can be modified while rest of the picture is protected. A moving marquee denotes the boundary of a selection, and can be moved independently of its contents. A selection can contain underlying pixels or temporarily float above underlying pixels.

Shadows

The darkest areas of a picture.

Sharpness

The degree of fineness of detail of an image, of a computer monitor, and of printer output.

Size

The number of storage units a file occupies, measured in kilobytes, megabytes, or gigabytes.

Spacing

The space between brush marks created with painting and editing tools. Also, the horizontal space between letters, specified in the Type Tool dialog box.

Spot color

A mixed ink color used in printing. A separate plate is used to print each spot color. Pantone is a commonly used spot color matching system.
(See Process color)

Thermal wax

A color printing process in which a sequence of three or four ink sheets are used to place colored dots on special paper.

TIFF

(Tagged Image File Format) A file format used for saving bitmapped images, such as scans. TIFF pictures can be color separated.

Tolerance

The range of pixels within which a tool operates. For example, the range of shades or colors the Magic Wand tool selects and the Paint Bucket tool fills.

Trap

The overlapping of adjacent colors to prevent undesirable gaps from occuring as a result of the misalignment of printing plates or paper.

24-bit monitor

A monitor with a video card in which each pixel can store up to 24 bits of information. The card contains three color tables for displaying an RGB picture, one each for Red, Green, and Blue, and each contains 256 colors. Together they can produce 16.7 million colors. On a 24-bit monitor, smooth blends can be displayed, so dithering is not necessary.

Underlying pixels

The pixels comprising the unmodified picture, on top of which a selection or placed image can float.

Virtual memory (See *Scratch Disk*)

Zoom

To enlarge or reduce a picture's display size.

Appendix B: **Keyboard Shortcuts**

Key

(click icon)	Click
(double-click icon)	Double-click
(drag icon)	Press and drag

File menu

New...	⌘ N
Open...	⌘ O
Close...	⌘ W
Save	⌘ S
Print...	⌘ P
Quit	⌘ Q

Edit menu

Undo	⌘ Z, or F1

The Clipboard

Cut	⌘ X, or F2
Copy	⌘ C, or F3
Paste	⌘ V, or F4

Mode menu

RGB Channels

RGB	⌘ 0
Red	⌘ 1
Green	⌘ 2
Blue	⌘ 3

CMYK Channels

CMYK	⌘ 0
Cyan	⌘ 1
Magenta	⌘ 2
Yellow	⌘ 3
Black	⌘ 4

Image menu

Map commands

Invert	⌘ I
Equalize	⌘ E
Threshold...	⌘ T

Note: The Function key commands listed here (F1, F2, etc.) are default settings. To assign alternative commands, use the Function Keys dialog box that opens from the Preferences pop-up menu under the File menu.

Adjust commands

Levels...	⌘ L
Curves	⌘ M
Brightness/Contrast...	⌘ B
Color Balance...	⌘ Y
Hue/Saturation...	⌘ U

Filter menu

Reapply last filter chosen	⌘ F
Last Filter dialog box	⌘ Option F
Cancel a filter while a Progress dialog box is displayed	⌘ . (period)

Select menu

All	⌘ A
None	⌘ D
Float/Defloat	⌘ J
Grow	⌘ G
Show/Hide Edges	⌘ H

Window menu

Zoom In	⌘ +
Zoom Out	⌘ -
Show/Hide Rulers	⌘ R
Hide/Show Brushes	F5
Show/Hide Channels	F6
Show/Hide Colors	F7
Show/Hide Info	F8
Show/Hide Paths	F9

Display sizes

Enlarge display size	⌘ Space bar *(works with some dialog boxes open)*
Reduce display size	Option Space bar *(works with some dialog boxes open)*
Magnify selected area	with Zoom tool
1:1 view	Zoom tool on Toolbox
Fit picture in document window	Hand tool on Toolbox

Toolbox

Show/Hide Toolbox and palettes	Tab
Open Tool options dialog box	any tool other than Type, Hand, Zoom or Eraser

Palettes

Shrink palette to a bar	palette name

With any painting or editing tool selected

Temporary arrow cursor	⌘

Temporary crosshair pointer with any painting or editing tool selected	Caps Lock
Opacity percentage (Brushes palette)	Keypad key 0=100%, 1=10%, 2=20%, etc.

Hand tool

Temporary Hand tool with any other tool selected	Space bar

Eyedropper tool

Select color for the non-highlighted color square	Option
Temporary Eyedropper tool with Paint Bucket, Gradient, Line, Pencil, Airbrush, or Paintbrush, tool selected	Option

Eraser tool

Magic eraser: Paints with last saved version	Option
Constrain eraser to 90° angle	Shift
Erase entire picture	Eraser tool

Line tool

Constrain to 45° or 90° angle	Shift

Pencil, Airbrush, Rubber Stamp, Smudge tool

Constrain to 90° angle	Shift

Pen Tool

Add anchor point with Selection pointer highlighted	⌘ Option line segment
Delete anchor point with Selection pointer highlighted	⌘ Option anchor point
Constrain straight line segment or anchor point to 45° angle	Shift or Shift
Erase path being drawn	Delete Delete
Delete last created anchor point	Delete
Temporary Selection pointer with any Pen tool selected	⌘
Temporary Corner tool with the Selection pointer or any Pen tool selected	⌘ Control

Sharpen/Blur tool

Switch between Sharpen and Blur	Option or Option Sharpen/Blur tool on Toolbox

Smudge tool

Temporary Finger Painting tool	Option ····↖

Selections

Add to a selection	Shift ····↖
Subtract from a selection	⌘ ····↖
Move a copy of a selection	Option ····↖ selection
Move selection marquee	⌘ Option ····↖ selection
Move selection in 1-pixel increments	Arrow keys
Connect separate selections	⌘ Shift ····↖
Maintain proportions of Scale command marquee	Shift ····↖ corner box
Fill selection with Foreground color	Option Delete
Switch Masked Areas/Selected Areas	Option ↖ Quick Mask icon on Toolbox

Rectangular Marquee and Elliptical Marquee tools

Draw selection from center	Option ····↖
Square or circle	Shift ····↖

Magic Wand tool

Add to a selection	Shift ↖
Subtract from a selection	⌘ ↖

Lasso tool

Create straight side in a selection	Option ↖
Create curved side in a selection	····↖ or Option ····↖

Dialog boxes

Restore original settings	Hold down Option, click Reset
Delete to the right of the cursor	del
Highlight next field	Tab
Highlight previous field	Shift Tab

Colors palette

Delete a color	⌘ ↖
Replace color with new color	Option ↖ color to be replaced
Insert new color between two colors	Option Shift ↖

Print preview box

Picture information	Option hold down on Image Size bar

Index

M

N

O

P

T

Send us your comments, compliments, corrections...
NEW YORK, NY 102
PM
7 OCT
199
Elaine Weinmann & Peter Lourekas
c/o Peachpit Press
2414 Sixth Street
Berkeley, CA 94710

More from Peachpit Press. . .

Art of Darkness (with disk)
Erfert Fenton

This book is the perfect companion to AFTER DARK, the world's most popular screen saver and one of the top-selling utility programs of all time. It explains how to install, operate, and customize the program, as well as how to create modules for new screen savers. Included are nine new AFTER DARK modules created exclusively for this book. *(128 pages)*

Canvas 3.0: The Book
Deke McClelland

This book takes you on a fact-filled tour of Canvas 3.0. It includes essential information about using the program with System 7, creating dynamic illustrations and text effects, and much more. *(384 pages)*

Desktop Publisher's Survival Kit
David Blatner

Here is a book that provides insights into desktop publishing on the Macintosh: troubleshooting print jobs, working with color, scanning, and selecting fonts. A disk containing 12 top desktop publishing utilities, 400K of clip art, and two fonts is included in this package. *(176 pages)*

Illustrator Illuminated
Clay Andres

This book is for people who want to know more about Adobe Illustrator than the manuals can tell them. *Illustrator Illuminated* uses full-color graphics to show how professional artists use Illustrator's tools to create a variety of styles and effects. Each chapter shows the creation of a specific illustration from concept through completion. Additionally, it covers using Illustrator in conjunction with Adobe Streamline and Photoshop. *(200 pages)*

The Little Mac Book, 3rd Edition
Robin Williams

Praised by scores of magazines and user group newsletters, this concise, beautifully written book covers the basics of Macintosh operation. It provides useful reference information, including charts of typefaces, special characters, and keyboard shortcuts. Totally updated for System 7. *(336 pages)*

The Little Mac Word Book
Helmut Kobler

Here's a fast way to learn Word 5.0 basics. This book provides concise and clear information about formatting text; using Word with Apple's new System 7 operating system; taking advantage of Word's writing tools; setting up complex tables, and much more! *(240 pages)*

The Little QuicKeys Book
Steve Roth and Don Sellers

This handy guide to CE Software's QuicKeys 2.0 explores the QuicKeys Keysets and the different libraries QuicKeys creates for each application; shows how to link together functions and extensions; and provides an abundance of useful macros. *(288 pages)*

The Macintosh Bible, 4th Edition
Arthur Naiman, Nancy E. Dunn, Susan McAllister, John Kadyk, and a cast of thousands

It's more than just a book—it's a phenomenon. Even Apple's own customer support staff uses it. Now the Fourth Edition is here, and its 1,248 pages are crammed with tips, tricks, and shortcuts to get the most out of your Mac. And to make sure the book doesn't get out-of-date, three 30-page updates are included in the price (we mail them to you free of charge). Every Mac owner should have one. *(1,248 pages)*

The Macintosh Bible Software Disks

Dave Mark

This three-disk companion to *The Macintosh Bible, 4th Edition* offers Mac users an introduction to the very best public-domain software and shareware that exists for the Mac (more than 2 megabytes!). The disks include useful utilities, modem software, sounds, games, and fonts.

The Macintosh Bible "What Do I Do Now?" Book, 2nd Edition

Charles Rubin

Completely updated through System 7, this bestseller covers just about every sort of basic problem a Mac user can encounter. The book shows the error message exactly as it appears on screen, explains the problem (or problems) that can produce the message, and discusses what to do. This book is geared for beginners and experienced users alike. *(352 pages)*

The Mac is not a typewriter

Robin Williams

This best-selling, elegant guide to typesetting on the Mac has received rave reviews for its clearly presented information, friendly tone, and easy access. Twenty quick and easy chapters cover what you need to know to make your documents look clean and professional. *(72 pages)*

The Photoshop WOW! Book

Linnea Dayton and Jack Davis

This heavily illustrated, four-color book will delight Photoshop users of all levels. Step-by-step instructions introduce beginners to Photoshop's tools and effects while seasoned users learn advanced techniques. The book comes with a disk that contains five filters from the acclaimed Kai's Power Tools (by HSC Software) among other goodies. *(200 pages)*

The QuarkXPress Book, 3rd Edition

David Blatner

This best-selling guide to the world's most powerful desktop publishing program is required reading for any serious XPress user. It explains how to import and modify graphics and provides tips for printing, using XTensions and other applications to customize the user interface. Totally updated for release 3.2. *(736 pages)*

QuarkXPress 3.1: Visual QuickStart Guide (Mac Edition)

Elaine Weinmann

Winner of the 1992 Benjamin Franklin Award, this book is a terrific way to get introduced to QuarkXPress in just a couple of hours. Lots of illustrations and screen shots make each feature of the program absolutely clear. *(200 pages)*

Real World FreeHand 3

Olav Martin Kvern

The ultimate insider's guide to FreeHand, this authoritative and entertaining book first lays out the basics and then concentrates on advanced techniques. *(528 pages)*

Silicon Mirage

Steve Aukstakalnis and David Blatner

Virtual reality is the amazing new technology of "pretend worlds," where individuals can completely immerse themselves in computer-generated environments. *Silicon Mirage* provides an easily understandable explanation of the "virtual senses" already possible, the strikingly broad array of fields where virtual reality is having an impact, and the breathtaking horizons yet to be discovered. *(300 pages)*

Zen and the Art of Resource Editing (with disk)

Derrick Schneider et al.

This book introduces the beginner to ResEdit 2.1, one of the most useful tools ever designed for the Macintosh. It covers ResEdit from a nonprogrammer's point of view, and shows how to customize the Finder, menus, keyboard map and icons. The book contains a disk with the lastest version of ResEdit and 1400K of sample resources. *(240 pages)*

Order Form

To order, call:

(800) 283-9444 or (510) 548-4393 (M-F) • (510) 548-5991 fax

#	Title	Price	Total
	Art of Darkness (with disk)	19.95	
	Canvas 3.0: The Book	21.95	
	Desktop Publisher's Survival Kit (with disk)	22.95	
	Illustrator Illuminated	24.95	
	The Little Mac Book, 3rd Edition	16.00	
	The Little Mac Word Book	15.95	
	The Little QuicKeys Book	18.95	
	The Macintosh Bible, 4th Edition	32.00	
	The Macintosh Bible Software Disks, 4th Edition	25.00	
	The Macintosh Bible "What Do I Do Now?" Book	15.00	
	The Macintosh Font Book, 2nd Edition	23.95	
	The Mac is not a typewriter	9.95	
	Photoshop 2.5: Visual QuickStart Guide (Mac Edition)	18.00	
	The Photoshop WOW! Book (available Summer 1993)	35.00	
	The QuarkXPress Book, 3rd Edition (Macintosh)	28.00	
	QuarkXPress 3.1: Visual QuickStart Guide (Mac Edition)	14.95	
	Real World FreeHand	27.95	
	Silicon Mirage	15.00	
	Zen and the Art of Resource Editing, 3rd Edition	24.95	

SHIPPING:	First Item	Each Additional
UPS Ground	$4	$1
UPS Blue	$7	$2
Canada	$6	$4
Overseas	$14	$14

Subtotal		
8.25% Tax (CA only)		
Shipping		
TOTAL		

Name

Company

Address

City State Zip

Phone Fax

❑ Check enclosed ❑ Visa ❑ MasterCard

Company purchase order #

Credit card # Expiration Date

Peachpit Press, Inc. • 2414 Sixth Street • Berkeley, CA • 94710

Your satisfaction is guaranteed or your money will be cheerfully refunded!